White-Collar Crime

T0295853

White-Collar Crime: An Opportunity Perspective analyzes white-collar crime using the opportunity perspective, which assumes that all crimes depend on offenders recognizing an opportunity to commit an offense. The authors explicate the processes and situational conditions that facilitate opportunities for white-collar crimes and the likelihood of being victimized by white-collar crime. In addition, they offer potential policy solutions that will mitigate this persistent and widespread social problem while being realistic and balanced in their treatment of the difficulties of control. With this fourth edition, Benson and Simpson have enlisted the aid of two young white-collar crime scholars, Jay P. Kennedy and Melissa Rorie, who bring new areas of expertise to the book that enhance its analytical depth and coverage of both white-collar crime and the opportunity perspective. New up-to-date case studies are included along with examinations of recent investigations into white-collar crime and its control. These timely updates reaffirm that this rigorous yet accessible book will remain a core resource for undergraduate and early graduate courses on white-collar crime.

Michael L. Benson is Professor Emeritus and Senior Research Associate in the School of Criminal Justice at the University of Cincinnati. He has published extensively on white-collar and corporate crime in leading journals, including *Criminology*, *Justice Quarterly*, *Journal of Research in Crime and Delinquency*, *American Sociological Review*, *American Journal of Sociology*, and *Social Problems*. He is a Fellow of the American Society of Criminology and a former President of its Division of White-Collar and Corporate Crime. In 2017, he was awarded the Division's Gilbert Geis Lifetime Achievement Award. He received the Outstanding Scholarship Award from the Society for the Study of Social Problems Division on Crime and Delinquency for his book, *Combating Corporate Crime: Local Prosecutors at Work*. In 2016, he co-edited *The Oxford Handbook on White-Collar Crime* with Shanna R. Van Slyke and Francis T. Cullen. A recent publication is "Race, Ethnicity, and Social Change: The Democratization of Middle-Class Crime", with Ben Feldmeyer, Shaun Gabbidon, and Hei Lam Chio, *Criminology*, 2021, 59:10–41. His research has been funded by the National Institute of Justice, the Centers for Disease Control, and private research foundations.

Sally S. Simpson is Distinguished University Professor Emerita of Criminology and Criminal Justice at the University of Maryland, College Park and past Director of the Center for the Study of Business Ethics, Regulation and Crime (C-BERC). Her areas of expertise include white-collar/corporate crime, criminological theory, and gender, crime, and justice. Simpson is Past President (2020) of the American Society of Criminology (ASC) and Vice-Chair of the Committee on Law and Justice, National Academy of Sciences, Engineering, Medicine. She is an ASC Fellow and 2018 recipient of the ASC Edwin H. Sutherland Award. Recent publications include "Perceptions of White-Collar Crime Seriousness: Unpacking and Translating Attitudes into Policy Preferences", in *JRCD*, Sally S. Simpson, Miranda A. Galvin, Thomas A. Loughran, and Mark A. Cohen (https://doi.org/10.1177/00224278221092094, 2022) and "Unpacking the Criminogenic Aspects of Stress over the Life Course: The Joint Effects of Proximal Strain and Childhood Abuse on Violence and Substance Use in a High-Risk Sample of Women", in *JRCD*, Lee Slocum, Jennifer Medel, Elaine Doherty, and Sally S. Simpson (https://doi.org/10.1177/00224278211068188, 2022).

Melissa Rorie received her Ph.D. in Criminology and Criminal Justice from the University of Maryland, College Park in 2013. She taught in the Department of Criminal Justice at the University of Las Vegas from 2013 to 2022. She is currently a Senior Research Manager at the OMNI Institute, a non-profit social science consultancy organization.

Jay P. Kennedy received his Ph.D. from the University of Cincinnati School of Criminal Justice in 2014. He taught at Michigan State University in the School of Criminal Justice and was Assistant Director of Research at the Center for Anti-Counterfeiting and Product Protection. He is currently Global Lead for Amazon's Customer Trust External Relations Anti-Counterfeiting team.

Criminology and Justice Studies

Series Editor: Shaun L. Gabbidon, Penn State Harrisburg

Criminology and Justice Studies publishes books for undergraduate and graduate courses that model the best scholarship and innovative thinking in the criminology and criminal justice field today, but in a style that connects this scholarship to a wide audience of students, researchers, and possibly the general public.

Criminological Perspectives on Race and Crime, 4th Edition
Shaun L. Gabbidon

Shopping While Black
Consumer Racial Profiling in America
Shaun L. Gabbidon and George E. Higgins

Race, Ethnicity, Crime, and Justice
An International Dilemma
Akwasi Owusu-Bempah and Shaun L. Gabbidon

She Took Justice
The Black Woman, Law, and Power – 1619 to 1969
Gloria J. Browne-Marshall

Human Trafficking
Interdisciplinary Perspectives, 3rd Edition
Edited by Mary C. Burke

Violence in the Heights
The Torn Social Fabric of Inner-city Neighborhoods
Eileen M. Ahlin

White-Collar Crime
An Opportunity Perspective, 4th Edition
*Michael L. Benson and Sally S. Simpson,
with Melissa Rorie and Jay P. Kennedy*

For more information about this series, please visit: https://www.routledge.com/Criminology-and-Justice-Studies/book-series/CRIMJUSTSTUDIES

White-Collar Crime

An Opportunity Perspective

Fourth Edition

Michael L. Benson and Sally S. Simpson
with Melissa Rorie and Jay P. Kennedy

Routledge
Taylor & Francis Group

NEW YORK AND LONDON

Designed cover image: Getty

Fourth edition published 2024
by Routledge
605 Third Avenue, New York, NY 10158

and by Routledge
4 Park Square, Milton Park, Abingdon, Oxon, OX14 4RN

Routledge is an imprint of the Taylor & Francis Group, an informa business

© 2024 Michael L. Benson, Sally S. Simpson, Melissa Rorie, and Jay P. Kennedy

First edition published by Routledge 2009
Third edition published by Routledge 2018

Library of Congress Cataloging-in-Publication Data
Names: Benson, Michael L., author. | Simpson, Sally S., author. |
Rorie, Melissa L., 1981- author. | Kennedy, Jay P., other. |
Title: White-collar crime : an opportunity perspective / Michael L. Benson
and Sally S. Simpson, with Melissa Rorie and Jay P. Kennedy.
Other titles: Understanding white-collar crime.
Description: Fourth Edition. | New York, NY : Routledge, 2024. |
Series: Criminology and justice studies | Revised edition of White-collar crime,
2018. | Includes bibliographical references and index. |
Identifiers: LCCN 2023033765 (print) | LCCN 2023033766 (ebook) |
ISBN 9781032007199 (hardcover) | ISBN 9780367774899 (paperback) |
ISBN 9781003175322 (ebook)
Subjects: LCSH: White collar crimes.
Classification: LCC HV6768 .B465 2024 (print) | LCC HV6768 (ebook) |
DDC 364.16/8--dc23/eng/20231002
LC record available at https://lccn.loc.gov/2023033765
LC ebook record available at https://lccn.loc.gov/2023033766

ISBN: 978-1-032-00719-9 (hbk)
ISBN: 978-0-367-77489-9 (pbk)
ISBN: 978-1-003-17532-2 (ebk)

DOI: 10.4324/9781003175322

Typeset in Sabon
by KnowledgeWorks Global Ltd.

Access the Support Material: www.routledge.com/9781032007199

For all past, current, and future students of white-collar crime.

Mike and Sally

Contents

Preface to the Fourth Edition   *xi*
Acknowledgments   *xiii*

PART I
White-Collar Crime: Introduction and Overview   **1**

1 What Is White-Collar Crime?   3

2 Who Is the White-Collar Offender?   15

PART II
Criminological Theory and the Opportunity Perspective   **37**

3 Explaining White-Collar Crime: Traditional and Modern
   Criminological Theories   39

4 Explaining White-Collar Crime: Individual Traits and
   Psychological Approaches   60

5 Explaining White-Collar Crime: The Opportunity
   Perspective   71

PART III
Applying the Opportunity Perspective to
White-Collar Crime   **87**

6 Financial Crimes in Health Care, Mortgages, Securities,
   Markets, and Crises   89

7 Corporate Violence: Environmental, Workplace, and
   Manufacturing Offenses   115

PART IV
**The Symbolic Construction and Social Distribution
of Opportunities**   **135**

8 The Symbolic Construction of Opportunity: Neutralization,
   Moral Disengagement, and Normalization of Deviance   137

9 The Social Distribution of Opportunity: Class, Gender, and Race   155

PART V
Control, Prevention, and the Future of White-Collar Crime   **173**

10 Legal Controls: The Criminal Justice, Regulatory, and
    Civil Justice Systems   175

11 Opportunities and Situational Prevention of White-Collar
    Crime: Using Legal and Extralegal Controls   188

12 Opportunities and the Future of White-Collar Crime   200

References   *208*
Index   *234*

Preface to the Fourth Edition

Most people recognize that they could be victims of crime and try to take reasonable precautions against that happening. They lock doors, install alarm systems, avoid dangerous neighborhoods, and keep their belongings close by when they are out. These simple precautionary measures work primarily because they make it hard for offenders to get close to us or our property. They probably do help reduce the chances that we will be the victims of certain types of crime, such as burglary, robbery, assault, and larceny.

Unfortunately, these measures are unlikely to have any effectiveness against the types of crimes and criminals discussed in this book—white-collar crimes. White-collar crimes are committed in ways that are difficult, indeed often impossible, to prevent by simply blocking the offender's access to his or her target. White-collar offenders use techniques and take advantage of opportunities that are unavailable to ordinary street crime offenders. Compared with ordinary street crimes, white-collar crimes pose significantly different risks and threats to individuals, government, and society in general.

This book is designed to help readers better understand how white-collar crimes work. We take what we call an "opportunity perspective." We assume that crime depends on the offender having an opportunity to commit an offense and that different types of crimes have different opportunity structures. This approach differs from how people typically think and talk about the causes of crime. Public discourse on crime often focuses on offenders and on the question of why they do it. The question of motivation is, of course, an important one, and we address it in this book. However, as we will show, the seemingly simple idea of opportunity is actually quite complex and has important implications for our understanding of the causes of white-collar crime as well its control.

This fourth edition of *White-Collar Crime: An Opportunity Perspective* builds upon the first three editions. It includes analyses of significant offenses that have come to light in the last few years, updated data on individual and organizational offenders, and discussions of the most recent theoretical and empirical investigations into white-collar crime and white-collar crime control. As with earlier editions, we show how the opportunity perspective can help us better understand crimes in relation to business even as the types of crime change and evolve over time. We have also tried to show how thinking about white-collar crimes from the perspective of opportunity theory can help suggest better ways to prevent and control these crimes, because control mechanisms must evolve in response to the ever-changing nature of white-collar crime.

Here is a brief summary of the major substantive changes in this edition.

Part I deals with the perennially controversial issues of how best to define white-collar crime and whom to count as a white-collar offender. Most of the changes in Part I occur in Chapter 2, where we have added new data on contemporary white-collar offenders and presented the latest data on organizational offenders from the United States Sentencing Commission.

In Part II, Chapter 3 discusses how traditional criminological theories apply to white-collar crime. In this chapter, we have added sections on race-based approaches to the understanding of white-collar crime. Chapter 4 is devoted to new research on the role of individual traits and psychological factors in white-collar crime, including an expanded discussion of psychopathy. Chapter 5 addresses the distinguishing characteristics of white-collar offenses and explicates the role of deception as the master modus operandi of white-collar offenders.

Part III presents our analyses of a number of different types of white-collar crime. Because of the ongoing interest in the cost of health care, we address how the Affordable Care Act changed the way that the federal government approached health care fraud. Chapter 6 also dives into bid rigging in the murky world of the London Interbank Offered Rate, which is also known as the Libor scandal. New material on disaster fraud with a specific focus on the COVID-19 pandemic has been added. Chapter 7 includes material on the growing international problem of environmental pollution in E-waste and harmful crimes in the pharmaceutical industry involving compounding pharmacies.

Part IV has remained largely the same as in earlier editions, except that a discussion of moral disengagement in organizations has been added to Chapter 8. In Chapter 9, new data on the "glass ceiling" in organizations has been added, and cross-national data on white-collar offenders in the Netherlands is presented. These additions suggest that the population of white-collar offenders—at least those caught and prosecuted in two Western societies—are quite similar. It remains to be seen if this observation is confirmed in other places across the world.

Part V includes a discussion of responsive regulation and the assorted implications of the U.S. Department of Justice's increased use of deferred prosecution and non-prosecution agreements in cases involving serious wrongdoing by large corporations. Woven throughout the discussion are the results of a recent meta-analysis on corporate deterrence. This material appears in Chapter 10. In Chapter 11, the use of data analytics by the Securities and Exchange Commission (SEC) and the Center for Medicaid Services is presented as an innovative example of the situational approach to white-collar crime prevention.

Ancillary teaching materials, including PowerPoint lectures and test banks are available at www.routledge.com/9781032007199.

Acknowledgments

Both Sally and I would like to thank Melissa Rorie and Jay P. Kennedy for joining us on the fourth edition of this book. They added fresh perspectives and much of the new material that is included in this edition. We hope that they will continue to be involved in future editions. We would also like to thank Ziyue Gu for her efforts in revising and updating the ancillary teaching materials for this edition. Thanks as well to Wim Huisman who was kind enough to provide us with helpful suggestions for revision. Finally, I would like to thank Shelley and Christopher for putting up with me all the times when I was distracted and lost in my own thoughts thinking about this work. Writing is gratifying, but it is much more fun and comforting to be with you two.

Mike

Mike and I have known one another since 1989 when we were both fortunate enough to be invited to The Edwin Sutherland Conference on White-Collar Crime: Fifty Years of Research and Beyond sponsored by The National Institute of Justice and Indiana University (hosted by IU faculty member Kip Schlegel). At that time, as new Assistant Professors, we sat together and talked about our ongoing research agendas, plans for future studies, and how to approach the phenomenon of white-collar crime. We developed a long-standing friendship, offered professional advice to one another, shared ideas and served as a sounding board over a glass or two of wine at the American Society of Criminology Meetings. I know/knew his doctoral students and he knows/knew mine. That friendship and mutual respect culminated in this book. I have learned a great deal from Mike over the years and am proud to call him my good friend.

I dedicate this edition of our book to Stas and Gabrys. Thank you for your unending, enthusiastic, and loving support over the years as I disappeared into my office for weeks (months? years?) at a time. Scholarly work is both challenging and gratifying, but family is everything.

Sally

Part I

White-Collar Crime

Introduction and Overview

Every republic runs its greatest risk not so much from discontented soldiers as from discontented multi-millionaires.

(The Nation, 1845)

On December 27, 1939, in the city of Philadelphia, Pennsylvania, a 56-year-old sociologist by the name of Edwin H. Sutherland gave a talk that fundamentally changed the study of crime. Professor Sutherland was addressing the annual meeting of the American Sociological Association, and his talk was entitled "The White-Collar Criminal" (Sutherland, 1940). In his address, the professor took aim at what he regarded as a fatal flaw in the criminological theory of his day, namely, the failure to recognize and take seriously the "monstrous amount of lawbreaking by persons in positions of power" (Geis and Goff, 1983, p. ix). He called this lawbreaking *white-collar crime*. Prior to Sutherland's address, lawbreaking by persons in positions of power had been largely ignored by academic criminologists, who instead focused almost exclusively on the ordinary street crimes committed by the poor and disadvantaged. In the 80-plus years since his address, the concept of white-collar crime, though much criticized and debated, has become an established part of both criminological thinking and public concern. Academics, politicians, and ordinary citizens now recognize that wrongdoing by the rich and powerful poses significant risks to everyone.

Part I of this book explicates the concept of white-collar crime and the debates that surround it. We begin by tracing the historical evolution of the concept and then introduce two different ways of defining it, called *offender based* and *offense based*. Next, we review what is known about the demographic, social, and psychological characteristics of the people who commit these types of crimes. Although Sutherland wanted to draw attention to lawbreaking by persons in positions of power, you will see that many of the people who commit what can only be called white-collar crimes are relatively powerless, at least when compared with the privileged scoundrels that populate the nightly news. Nevertheless, even though many white-collar criminals are not wealthy or powerful, they are also not like ordinary street criminals. Rather, they are drawn from a distinctly different segment of the American population—the middle class. Their crimes pose distinctly difficult problems for law enforcement and social control, as well as very real threats to social stability.

DOI: 10.4324/9781003175322-1

Chapter 1

What Is White-Collar Crime?

White-collar crime is not a legal category. Rather, it is a term coined by the sociologist Edwin Sutherland that has migrated out of the realms of science and academia to become part of public discourse. Nowadays stories about white-collar crime are often in the news. If you were to ask the proverbial man or woman on the street, you would surely find that most everyone has heard of white-collar crime. However, if you pressed them to explain just what white-collar crime is, the answers you would receive would not be very informative. Most people would probably say something about men in suits who steal money and don't go to prison and let it go at that. Yet, the problem of white-collar crime is enormously complex. It raises difficult social, legal, and scientific issues that have important implications for society and for the field of criminology. This book is designed to help you better understand the complexities of white-collar crime so that you can think critically and analytically about this important social problem. However, for those who are looking for a more compelling reason to keep reading, we hope that what you learn in these pages will also help you avoid being victimized by white-collar offenders.

Unfortunately, avoiding such offenders is not easy. White-collar criminals lurk in every industry and profession. For example, whenever you engage in a business transaction with any sort of professional, there is the potential for what we will call a "white-collar victimization". We use the term *professional* here in a very loose sense to include anyone who offers to provide a specialized service for a fee. Besides the traditional professions such as law, medicine, and accounting, our definition includes blue-collar and other service "professionals", such as home remodelers, auto mechanics, plumbers, electricians, and real estate agents. Typically, when you hire any sort of professional to do something for you, it is because the professional knows more about it than you do, or can do it better than you can, or simply has more time than you do. In other words, you need the professional to do something that for some reason you cannot or do not want to do yourself. However, how do you know that the professional did the *right* thing (i.e., the thing that was necessary and appropriate in your situation) in the *right* way (i.e., the most professional and cost-effective way)? It is always possible that the professional took advantage of your lack of expertise to defraud or cheat you in some way.

Talking about doing the right thing in the right way is obviously vague. So, consider as examples two situations involving professionals that most everyone encounters at some point in time—buying a home and going to the doctor. Buying a home can be a daunting experience, not only because it is for most of us the most expensive thing we will ever buy, but also because it is a very complicated process, involving lots of forms and paperwork (listings, offers, loan applications, titles, insurance, etc.) and lots of different people (realtors,

DOI: 10.4324/9781003175322-2

appraisers, mortgage brokers, surveyors, originators, loan officers, lenders, etc.). Indeed, the process is so complicated that many home buyers simply trust the professionals who work in the home mortgage industry to guide them through it, and they sign a myriad of papers involved in the transaction without reading or understanding them. Unfortunately, between 2005 and 2008, this blind trust in the integrity of the home mortgage industry was often misplaced as literally thousands of Americans fell victim to deceptive and fraudulent lending practices, in which they were misled by mortgage brokers into taking on loans that were not in their best interests. Besides marketing deceptive loans, professionals in the mortgage and banking industries also engaged in a host of other scams and schemes that we will explain more fully in Chapter 6.

Now, consider the health care industry. Suppose you have not been feeling well for a few days and decide to go to a doctor. She looks you over, asks some questions about your symptoms, and then recommends further tests in order to make a definitive diagnosis. You do not really know if you need more tests. Of course, you could go and get a second opinion, but that is going to take more time. Besides, the doctor is supposed to be an expert. You are likely to accept the doctor's advice and agree to get the tests. However, unbeknownst to you, the doctor knows exactly what is wrong with you, but, for financial reasons, she orders unnecessary tests. Perhaps she is part owner of the testing company and so is interested in directing business that way or has an agreement with the lab to split the fee when she sends business to them. Regardless of her motives, she has committed fraud, and you (her patient) are the direct victim. However, it is important to point out that you are not the *only* victim in this particular transaction. Because a substantial portion of your costs for the tests are likely covered by insurance, your insurer is also a victim, and, because medical costs rise as a consequence of medical fraud, society as a whole is victimized.

Both of these examples illustrate different forms of fraud. In both cases, a professional uses his or her superior knowledge and expertise to take advantage of someone. Fraud is not limited to medicine and real estate. It can occur in every profession. It represents one of the most common types of white-collar crime, but there are many other types of white-collar crime that we will discuss in this book. For example, violations of environmental regulations, fraudulent accounting practices, exploitation of workers, securities violations, and antitrust violations are among a host of others that we will consider. Unlike the examples of fraud given here, many of these offenses do not involve a discrete interaction between an offender and a victim. Nevertheless, they are all forms of white-collar crime.

Although there are good reasons to believe that the frauds discussed earlier and other white-collar type of crimes are more common now than they have ever been (Weisburd et al., 1991), it would be a mistake to think that white-collar crime is a new invention of the criminal mind. Unfortunately, criminals have engaged in white-collar type crimes for literally thousands of years.

An Historical Look at White-Collar Crime

What we today would call white-collar crime is not new. It's been around a long time. For example, in the fourth century BC, the Greek philosopher Aristotle wrote about embezzlement of funds by road commissioners and other officials. The theft of public money by government officers was a crime under the Athenian constitution, and a jury could sentence someone convicted of such a crime to pay ten times the amount stolen (von Fritz and Kapp, 1950). The Bible and other ancient religious texts condemn a number of exploitative business activities as harmful and counter to the common good. They may not have been legally defined as crimes, but they were certainly regarded as morally wrong (Geis, 1988). For example, admonitions about the immorality of cheating in the marketplace can be found in Proverbs (11:25): "He that holdeth corn, the people will curse him: But blessing shall be upon the head of him that selleth it". Similarly, Deuteronomy (25:13) declares: "For every one practicing unfairness is abominable to the Lord your God". According to Talmudic scholars, "The Talmud excoriated those who hoarded food in order to resell it at a high price, tampered with weights and measures ... and raised prices unjustly" (Friedman, 1980, p. 47).

If we move forward several centuries to the late Middle Ages in England, we find that the common law outlawed three business-related activities: regrating, engrossing, and forestalling (Geis, 1988). Each of these activities represented a different way in which someone could try to corner the market on important commodities, especially foodstuffs, in order to charge high prices and make exorbitant profits. For example, engrossing involved buying up the entire stock of some commodity, say corn or wheat, in order to resell it at monopoly prices. This sort of behavior foreshadows what today we call antitrust offenses (Geis, 1988). Embezzlement by knights and other officers of the king was also a common offense during the Middle Ages (Pike, 1873), and in Dante's *Inferno* the eighth circle of hell is reserved for the counsellors of fraud and the betrayal of trust (Chevigny, 2001).

Continuing our journey through time, in the early twentieth century, the noted American sociologist E. A. Ross railed against "the criminaloid", that is, powerful business owners and executives who exploit people and manipulate the marketplace out of an uninhibited desire to maximize their profits, all the while pretending to be pious and respectable. As examples of economic duplicity combined with the appearance of respectability, Ross noted that

> [t]he director who speculates in the securities of his corporation, the banker who lends his depositors' money to himself under divers corporate aliases, the railroad official who grants a secret rebate for his private graft, the builder who hires walking delegates to harass his rivals with causeless strikes, the labor leader who instigates a strike in order to be paid for calling it off, the publisher who bribes his textbooks into the schools, these reveal in their faces nothing of the wolf or vulture.
>
> (Ross, 1907, p. 50)

Ross accused these individuals of moral insensibility and held them responsible for cheating, injuring, and even killing workers and consumers. Thus, long before the term *white-collar crime* was coined, depredations committed by the rich and powerful in the pursuit of profit and wealth have been recognized and denounced.

Many of the themes that run through this book and that permeate the study of white-collar crime can be found in the historical record. For example, the crime of engrossing involves a perversion of legitimate business activities to serve illegitimate ends and to exploit others. As we will see, a defining feature of white-collar crime is its link to legitimate business or economic activities. Another important theme is the observation that supposedly respectable people commit these offenses. These people are not thought of by others as ordinary criminals and they certainly do not think of themselves that way. Aristotle complained about road commissioners and public officials who embezzle public funds, not about ordinary thugs. Also prominent is the idea that these crimes are committed out of greed and a lust for power, not out of desperation or any sort of psychological abnormality.

As E. A. Ross argued, the criminaloid's obsession with profit makes him morally insensitive but not crazy.

But what exactly is white-collar crime?

Defining White-Collar Crime

Throughout his career, Sutherland used several different definitions of "white-collar crime". In his most famous book, *White-Collar Crime*, he defined it "as a crime committed by a person of respectability and high social status in the course of his occupation" (Sutherland, 1983, p. 7). He went on to note that this definition "excludes many crimes of the upper class, such as most of their cases of murder, adultery, and intoxication, since these are not customarily a part of their occupational procedures". In a footnote, he added that the term "white-collar is used here to refer principally to business managers and executives". This definition has provoked both admiration and condemnation for more than 60 years. It continues to be a source of debate and controversy, but we will get to those issues a little later.

Sutherland expanded on, and further clarified his conception of, white-collar crime in a 1949 entry in the *Encyclopedia of Criminology* (Branham and Kutash, 1949, p. 511). In the encyclopedia article, he wrote that "the white collar criminal is defined as a person with high socio-economic status who violates the laws designed to regulate his occupational activities". Sutherland continued that the

> white collar criminal should be differentiated, on the one hand, from the person of lower socio-economic status who violates the regular penal code or the special trade regulations which apply to him; and, on the other hand, from the person of high socio-economic status who violates the regular penal code in ways not connected with his occupation.
>
> (p. 511)

Note that according to this definition, some of the people involved in the mortgage fraud we described earlier might not be considered white-collar criminals by Sutherland. We discuss this issue of who is and who is not a white-collar criminal in more detail further on, but for now let us return to an examination of Sutherland's definition.

As a way to define a particular type of crime, Sutherland's definitions are unusual in that they refer to characteristics of the actor. Legal commentators addressing other sorts of crimes typically take great pains to establish clear definitions of the acts that must take place and the state of mind that an individual must possess in order for a crime to be committed, but little is said about the characteristics of the actor. Sutherland's approach, however, tells us that only certain types of people can commit white-collar crimes, those with "respectability and high social status". It also specifies that the act must arise out of the course of the actor's occupation. For Sutherland, both the status of the actor and the occupational location of the act determine whether it is a white-collar crime.

The Controversy Surrounding Sutherland's Approach

From the outset, Sutherland's approach to white-collar crime provoked criticism and controversy. One issue concerns the legal status of white-collar type offenses. A distinguishing feature of Sutherland's approach was his willingness to include acts that had been sanctioned through civil or administrative legal proceedings as part of white-collar crime. This decision provoked extensive comment and criticism from legal scholars who contended that only acts that were punished under criminal laws can rightly be called crimes (Tappan, 1947). In Sutherland's view, however, including other types of violations was justified because many civil laws deal with practices that are fundamentally similar to criminal offenses. In addition, many illegal business practices can be sanctioned under either criminal or civil law or both. To exclude offenses that are pursued under civil law arbitrarily limits the range of white-collar offenses. This limitation is especially important in the context of white-collar crime, because the organizations and individuals who commit these offenses often use their political power and economic resources to avoid criminal prosecution. As many white-collar crime commentators have noted, it is important to investigate how and under what circumstances business activities are criminalized (Cullen et al., 2006).

Another major point of contention that arose out of Sutherland's approach is whether the offender's social status should be a defining characteristic of white-collar crime. Sutherland included respectability and high social status in his definition precisely because he wanted to draw attention to the criminality of business groups. He argued that the criminological theories of his day were class biased and incomplete because they equated crime with lower-class individuals and ignored crime by upper-class individuals. In addition, he was morally outraged by what he regarded as the lenient and preferential treatment afforded to business offenders in the criminal justice system.

Sutherland undoubtedly was correct about the narrowness of criminological theory and the unfairness of the criminal justice system of his day. Nevertheless, including social status and respectability in the definition of white-collar crime creates problems for research and analysis. One problem that arises when social status is a defining element of crime is that it cannot then be used to explain or predict the occurrence of the crime. In other words, social status cannot be used as an explanatory variable because it is not allowed to vary independently of the crime. Thus, by definitional fiat, white-collar crime researchers are prevented from investigating how the social status of individuals influences the types or the seriousness of the white-collar offenses they commit. Similar offenses may be committed by corporate executives and by employees at the bottom of the corporate hierarchy, but only the former meet Sutherland's definition of white-collar crime.

Suppose, for example, that a top corporate executive participates in a meeting about his company and learns about a development that will drive the value of the company's stock up in the next few weeks. Hoping to take advantage of this inside information, the executive buys a large share of the company's stock while it is still cheap. Suppose also that a low-level typist who transcribes the minutes from the meeting notices the same information and she also decides to buy company stock just as the executive did. Both the executive and the typist have committed what is called *insider trading*, and it is illegal. In Sutherland's eyes, the executive is clearly a white-collar criminal, but what about the typist? Along with other white-collar crime scholars, we believe it does not make sense to focus only on the corporate executive and to ignore the typist. It is important to investigate how social status is related to white-collar crime, just as we investigate how it is related to ordinary street crime. The question of how social status is related to white-collar crime should not be decided arbitrarily by definitional decree. Indeed, a major theme of this book is that social status is important precisely because it influences access to opportunities for white-collar crime and it is likely to influence offender motivation, too. People with high social status may also be able to influence the content of the laws that address their behavior and the way in which law is administered by criminal justice and regulatory agencies.

We need to pay attention to status not only in regard to how it influences access to opportunities but also in regard to who has it and who does not. Those without high social status have fewer opportunities to commit white-collar offenses. In the example given earlier, the executive was a man. Although women have made great strides in the corporate world over the past few decades, they are still under-represented in leadership positions in major corporations. According to a recent report by Catalyst, a non-profit research and advisory organization working to expand opportunities for women, women constituted 29 percent in senior management roles globally in 2019 (Catalyst, August, 2020). In the United States, among Fortune 500 companies, only 30 (6 percent) are run by a woman (Catalyst, June, 2021). Women are even rarer in leading roles in Standard & Poor's 500 companies, where they make up only 4 percent of chief executives and 10 percent of chief financial officers (Davidoff, 2013). As we show later, partially because of gender stratification in the labor force, women do not commit as many white-collar crimes as men, and the crimes that women do commit are not as serious as those committed by men (Daly, 1989; Steffensmeier, Schwartz, and Roche, 2013). The same is true of African-Americans, Hispanics, and other peoples of color. They, too, are underrepresented in leadership positions, and their access to white-collar crime opportunities is similarly limited in societies that are stratified by patriarchy and white racial privilege. In short, white-collar crime opportunities are differentially distributed by gender, race, ethnicity, and status.

Including social status in the definition of white-collar crime also rules out the possibility of exploring how variation in the status of offenders influences societal reactions to their offenses. For example, it is important to investigate whether acts of insider trading by corporate executives and by clerical staff are treated the same or differently by authorities. Are small businesses that engage in consumer fraud treated the same in court as multinational corporations that cheat the public? In order to investigate these issues, white-collar crime must be defined in a status-neutral manner.

Offender-Based Approaches to Defining White-Collar Crime

Sutherland's definition is the most well-known and influential example of what we call the *offender-based* approach to defining white-collar crime. Offender-based definitions emphasize as an essential characteristic of white-collar crime the high social status, power, and respectability of the actor. Despite its shortcomings, Sutherland's offender-based approach has remained popular. Numerous attempts have been made to define the concept in a manner that is faithful to Sutherland's intentions but that clarify or expand upon his definition. For example, Albert J. Reiss and Albert D. Biderman proposed that

> white-collar violations are those violations of law to which penalties are attached that involve the use of a violator's position of significant power, influence, or trust in the legitimate economic or political institutional order for the purpose of illegal gain, or to commit an illegal act for personal or organizational gain.
>
> (Reiss and Biderman, 1981, p. 4)

Another Way of Looking at White-Collar Crime: Offense-Based Definitions

Sutherland's approach to defining white-collar crime is the one that resonates best with the popular image of the white-collar offender, but after Sutherland's address a competing conceptual approach soon emerged (Benson, Van Slyke, and Cullen, 2016). We call it the *offense-based* approach, because it defines white-collar crime based on the nature of the illegal act. In 1970, Herbert Edelhertz, then an official at the U.S. Department of Justice, proposed a highly influential offense-based definition of white-collar crime. He defined white-collar crime as "*an illegal act or series of illegal acts committed by non-physical means and by concealment or guile to obtain money or property, to avoid the payment or loss of money or property, or to obtain business or personal advantage*" (Edelhertz, 1970, p. 3). This definition defines white-collar crime according to the means by which the offense is carried out—specifically, nonphysical means that involve concealment or guile. Any illegal act or series of acts committed by any person that meets these formal requirements is considered white-collar crime.

Edelhertz (1970, pp. 19–20) went on to identify four basic types of white-collar crime:

1 Personal crimes: crimes by persons operating on an individual, *ad hoc* basis, for personal gain in a nonbusiness context—for example, individual income tax violations and credit card frauds.
2 Abuses of trust: crimes in the course of their occupations by those operating within businesses, government, or other establishments, or in a professional capacity, in violation of their duty of loyalty and fidelity to employer or client—for example, embezzlement, commercial bribery, and mistreatment of clients by professionals.
3 Business crimes: crimes incidental to and in furtherance of business operations, but not the central purpose of such business operations—for example, antitrust violations and food and drug violations.
4 Con games: white-collar crime as a business, or as the central activity of the business—for example, advance fee swindles and home improvement schemes.

Another example of the offense-based school of thought on defining white-collar crime was provided in 1990 by Susan Shapiro. She argued that the essential characteristic of the acts that are commonly called *white-collar crimes* is that they involve the violation or abuse of trust. She proposed that the concept of white-collar crime be liberated by "disentangling the identification of the perpetrators from their misdeeds" (Shapiro, 1990, p. 346). In Shapiro's view, offender-based definitions create an imprisoning framework. This framework leads scholars to misunderstand the structural sources of white-collar offenses, the problems they create for social control agencies, and the nature of class bias in the justice system.

Offense-based definitions have proved popular with researchers for several reasons. Because no mention is made of the social status of the actor or the social location of the act, both status and location are free to vary independently of the definition of the offense and can be used as explanatory variables. Researchers who use an offense-based definition have the freedom to explore how variation in the social status of the actor influences characteristics of the white-collar crimes committed and how the status of the actor influences societal reactions to offenses. Researchers can also investigate whether white-collar offenses committed in occupational settings differ from those committed outside occupational settings. Finally, offense-based definitions make it easier for researchers to draw samples of white-collar offenders from official data sources, such as court conviction records. Researchers need only identify a set of statutory offenses that meet certain formal criteria—for example, offenses that are not physical and that are based on deception. Then, it is just a matter of sampling individuals convicted of those offenses. A number of well-regarded studies published in the 1980s and 1990s used this strategy to identify and investigate white-collar offenders in the U.S. federal judicial system (Benson and Walker, 1988; Hagan and Nagel, 1982; Wheeler, Weisburd, and Bode, 1982).

Despite its popularity with some researchers, the offense-based approach to white-collar crime raises troubling issues for many other white-collar crime scholars (Geis, 1996, 2016; Pontell, 2016). The very ease with which offense-based definitions can be used to draw samples becomes a trap for investigators, leading them to ignore the most important aspects of the white-collar crime phenomenon. Investigators who use offense-based definitions often end up studying the relatively minor misdeeds of ordinary people of very modest financial means who somehow become caught up in the criminal justice system. Indeed, if you construed Edelhertz's definition loosely, it would permit an unemployed single mother who lied on an application for welfare to claim the status of white-collar criminal. In addition, if white-collar crime is defined on the basis of crime characteristics, then criminal justice officials can brag about fighting white-collar crime when really all they are doing is harassing telemarketing fraudsters and employee thieves (Geis, 2016; Shover and Cullen, 2011). Offense-based definitions trivialize the whole concept of white-collar crime, leading researchers, politicians, and law enforcers to neglect the most serious forms of elite crime (Pontell, 2016).

Even more important, with its focus on money and property, Edelhertz's definition turns attention away from the types of white-collar crime that do physical harm to people (Braithwaite, 1985). For example, among the most serious white-collar crimes are illegal discharge of hazardous waste into the environment, manufacture of dangerous products, and the causing of death, injury, or illness of workers via unsafe working conditions. Such crimes rarely appear in studies that follow Edelhertz's approach to defining white-collar crime.

Offense-based samples drawn from the federal judicial system, which supposedly has a larger proportion of white-collar clients than is found in state courts, tend to be composed primarily of middle-class individuals who have committed banal and simplistic offenses (Wheeler et al., 1988a). Likewise, an analysis of cases from the Netherlands confirms this general portrait, suggesting that offense-based classification criteria—*even those that filter out less serious cases*—tend to capture mostly middle-class individuals (e.g., van Onna, van der Gueest, Huisman, and Denkers, 2014).

The powerful corporations and corporate executives that originally drew Sutherland's ire are largely absent. Offense-based approaches also tend inevitably to draw researchers toward the study of acts that have been officially defined as illegal. As a result, powerful individuals and corporate actors who are able to avoid official labeling in the first place never appear in the resulting samples. Indeed, it is almost impossible to use the offense-based approach to study the crimes of large multinational corporations, because they are almost never actually charged with criminal violations, let alone convicted. Thus, the major criticism of the offense-based approach is that in practice it misses the crimes of the powerful, who simply sidestep the criminalization process. The very people that Sutherland originally sought to bring to the attention of criminologists are ignored. In their place we find small-time con men and unemployed cheating welfare moms (Daly, 1989).

Reconsidering the Two Approaches

The critics of Edelhertz's offense-based approach to defining white-collar crime make an important point. In practice, the use of this approach has often (but not always) resulted in studies that do not include the very offenses and offenders that drew Sutherland's attention in the first place. As John Braithwaite (1985, p. 18) put it, perhaps a bit too strongly, the "practical consequences for empirical research have been that most white-collar criminals end up having blue collars". In addition, those who have used Edelhertz's approach have tended to ignore white-collar crimes that impose physical harm and violence on their victims. Both the manufacture of dangerous products and the maintenance of unsafe working environments are important types of white-collar crime.

We agree that it is important to avoid reducing the study of white-collar crime to small-time frauds by home repairmen and employee theft by retail clerks. If using an offense-based approach means that in practice high-status offenders are ignored, then criminology is just as class biased and incomplete now as it was in Sutherland's day (Benson et al., 2016). But we note that this "practical consequence", as Braithwaite calls it, is just that—a practical consequence. It is not a logical consequence of the offense-based approach. Rather, it is a consequence of how this approach has been used by some researchers (Hagan, Nagel [Bernstein], and Albonetti, 1980; Weisburd et al., 1991; Wheeler, Weisburd, and Bode, 1982). Because it relies on statutes to identify white-collar offenders, the offense-based approach simply makes it easier to find some types of offending and to miss others.

But there is nothing in the offense-based approach to defining white-collar crime that prevents researchers from examining the offenses of people with high social status or respectability or who hold positions of "significant power, influence, or trust". Suitably motivated researchers could use an offense-based approach to focus on the white-collar offenses of high-status *individuals* who occupy positions of power, influence, and trust. Likewise, suitably motivated researchers could examine how deceit and guile are used to manufacture dangerous products and to maintain unsafe workplaces for business advantage, or to commit civil and regulatory offenses. That this often does not happen reflects a failure on the part of researchers, not a fundamental weakness of the offense-based approach. The key point to keep in mind is that regardless of the characteristics of the individuals involved, white-collar crimes are committed using particular techniques. That is, they rely upon a certain modus operandi. The characteristics of the individuals who commit these offenses are important insofar as they influence access to the opportunities to use these techniques. As we argue throughout this book, many of the characteristics that are part of offender-based definitions (e.g., high social status, respectability, elite occupational positions) are indeed important precisely because they provide offenders with access to opportunities for white-collar crime.

The idea that white-collar crime involves particular techniques was well known to Sutherland. Throughout his major works on white-collar crime, he describes the techniques for specific misdeeds, as in this passage taken from the speech in which he first introduced the term:

> These varied types of white-collar crimes in business and the professions consist principally of violation of delegated or implied trust, and many of them can be reduced to two categories: (1) misrepresentation of asset values and (2) duplicity in the manipulation of power. The first is approximately the same as fraud or swindling; the second is similar to the double-cross.
>
> (Sutherland, 1940, p. 3; see also 1941, p. 112, 1949, pp. 152–158)

As Sutherland certainly understood, access to these techniques can be greatly facilitated by holding particular occupational positions. In a discussion of financial crime, he noted that "many corporate executives make strenuous efforts to secure positions in which they may have an opportunity to violate the trust for which they are legally responsible" (Sutherland, 1949, pp. 153–154). We would add to Sutherland's observation the caveat that both race and gender influence access to these lucrative positions. All other things being equal, in the Global North, white males are more likely to have access to these positions than women and racial or ethnic minorities.

The offender-based and offense-based approaches to defining white-collar crime are not contradictory or mutually exclusive. Rather, they simply emphasize different aspects of a general empirical regularity involving the characteristics or social positions of individuals and the types of offenses that they tend to commit. The techniques of white-collar offending tend to be used more by people who have high social status and hold certain occupational positions than by people who do not have these characteristics. This is not to say that people of low social status who work in menial jobs or are unemployed cannot use misrepresentation and duplicity to take advantage of others. Of course, they can. But they have much less opportunity to do so than people of high social status who hold positions of significant trust or power. Similarly, members of the middle and upper social classes could commit conventional property crimes, such as burglary and robbery, but they generally do not because they have access to other easier and less risky ways of making money by stealing.

The social and occupational characteristics of white-collar offenders are important in another way as well. These characteristics are related to the seriousness of the offenses that offenders commit. In regard to criminal offenses, seriousness has two primary dimensions: the harmfulness of the offense and the blameworthiness of the offender (Wheeler et al., 1982; Wheeler, Mann, and Sarat, 1988b). The white-collar offenses committed by high-status individuals who hold positions of power in large organizations tend to be more serious than those of other types of individuals. Consider, for example, an offense such as the illegal disposal of hazardous waste. It is true that many types of small businesses generate hazardous waste and then illegally dispose of it using midnight dumpers (Epstein and Hammett, 1995; Rebovich, 1992). As the name implies, midnight dumping involves the illegal disposal of hazardous waste under the cover of darkness somewhere where it is not supposed to go, such as an abandoned building or a vacant lot. These businesses often are owned by people who do not wear suits and ties and who operate on very thin profit margins. Examples include the electroplating, carpet cleaning, dry cleaning, and furniture-refinishing businesses. The potential harm to the environment posed by the illegal practices of small businesses is a serious problem. Indeed, some evidence from the Environmental Protection Agency (EPA) suggests that the environmental threat posed by all small businesses taken together may even exceed that posed by large organizations, simply because there are so many small businesses and they are difficult to track—in part because much of the regulatory oversight of small businesses is delegated to the states. A perfect example is the recent (2013) toxic spill of 10,000 gallons of coal processing compounds into the drinking water of hundreds of thousands of West Virginians from a poorly maintained and rarely inspected storage site along the Elk River owned by Freedom Industries. More than 30 people were hospitalized and hundreds more were treated as a consequence of the spill, and state regulators were left with "egg on their faces" (Barrett, 2014).

Although regulations have lessened industrial point source pollution from larger companies (Vandenbergh, 2001), the danger represented individually by your local dry cleaner pales in comparison to the danger that arises when large organizations illegally dispose of hazardous waste. The examples here are numerous. Consider, for instance, the Hooker Chemical Corporation (Tallmer, 1987), which was responsible for the infamous Love Canal tragedy; or Rockwell International Company, which contaminated Rocky Flats, Colorado, with nuclear waste (Rosoff, Pontell, and Tillman, 2013). The list could go on (for many examples, see chapter 4 in Rosoff et al., 2013).

The important point to recognize is that environmental offenses (and, obviously, many other types of white-collar offenses) are committed by the high-status executives and managers of powerful multinational corporations and by the economically struggling owners of small businesses (Barlow, 1993). Of course, we should not overlook all the businesses that fall somewhere between these two extremes. They are involved as well. Adopting a research strategy that ends up focusing only on small business owners is a mistake, but it is also a mistake to focus exclusively on multinational corporations. Similar offenses may occur at all levels of business activity.

We must be careful, though, not to overstress the notion of similarity. Just because similar offenses may occur across a broad range of levels of economic organization does not mean that they necessarily have the same causes and consequences. Nor does it mean that they can be controlled in the same way. That sort of one-size-fits-all type of thinking inevitably misses important aspects of the phenomenon of white-collar crime. The causes and consequences of white-collar crime are matters that must be settled through empirical investigation. Likewise, identifying the best response to white-collar crime requires careful analysis of the cost and effectiveness of different types of control strategies.

Measuring White-Collar Crime

Quantifying criminal behavior is not easy, and the difficulties of assigning numbers to behavior are especially pronounced in the case of white-collar crime (Benson, Kennedy, and Logan, 2016). Measuring white-collar crime poses both conceptual and practical challenges. Conceptually, the challenge is that what counts as white-collar crime depends on whether you define the term using an offense-based definition or an offender-based definition. Offense-based definitions result in a much larger number of cases than do offender-based definitions. With an offense-based definition, all offenses based on fraud or deception are counted regardless of who commits them or how trivial they are. As we noted above, someone who lies on a welfare application could be a white-collar offender under Edelhertz's definition. However, if an offender-based definition, such as the one proposed by Sutherland, is used, then the number of offenses is much smaller because only offenses committed by people of high social status that are occupationally related are counted. It is also important to recognize that organizations, as well as individuals, can be charged with and convicted of white-collar crimes, and it is not uncommon for both the corporation and individual executives to be charged in regard to a particular offense. When both individuals and organizations are linked in such a manner, determining the number of "offenders" and "offenses" becomes problematic.

On a practical level, the major challenge for those who would measure white-collar crime is that there is no single centralized agency responsible for recording instances of white-collar crime. Much of the enforcement of federal white-collar offending statutes, for example, is delegated to agencies such as the Securities and Exchange Commission, the Environmental Protection Agency, the Occupational Health and Safety Administration, the Surface Mining Administration, the Federal Trade Commission, and the Antitrust Division of the U.S. Department of Justice, as well as a host of other agencies and commissions. Not only are official data on white-collar offenses and white-collar offenders scattered across a bewilderingly large array of regulatory and law enforcement agencies (Benson et al., 2016), the mechanics required to merge these diverse indicators and measures into a single data source are considerable (Simpson and Yeager, 2015).

There are other practical problems that complicate the process of counting white-collar crimes committed in organizational or corporate settings. These types of crimes can be subject to three different types of control: criminal, civil, and regulatory justice. Should regulatory and civil violations be included, as Sutherland recommended? Or should the domain of corporate crime be limited to violations of the criminal law? In their famous study of corporate crime, Clinard and Yeager (2006, p. 113) reported that approximately 60 percent of the Fortune 500 companies in their sample had at least one "federal action" brought against them between 1975 and 1976, which on its face would seem to represent a rather high prevalence rate of offending among corporations. But "federal actions" included civil, regulatory, and criminal actions, and only 30 of these actions involved criminal fines. Indeed, criminal fines accounted for only 3.4 percent of all federal actions taken against the companies. Since the 1970s, criminal convictions of organizations have continued to be exceedingly rare. Indeed, according to the U.S. Sentencing Commission (USSC), in 2020 only 94 organizations were convicted in U.S. federal courts (USSC, 2021). This is down from 181 in 2015, which was the number we cited in the third edition of this book. For a variety of reasons, we agree with those who argue that civil and regulatory violations should be included as part of white-collar and corporate crime, but we note that this makes comparisons between white-collar and street crime difficult if not entirely inappropriate.

Concluding Thoughts on Defining White-Collar Crime

The definition of white-collar crime remains a matter of contention. Though we hope that our proposed reconciliation of the two definitional approaches will be seen as reasonable, we are not foolish enough to think that we have settled the matter once and for all. Criminologists should never forget Sutherland's fundamental insight that the upper social classes are not free from crime. In the course of their occupations, people of respectability and high social status commit serious crimes every day. Even though they often avoid apprehension and conviction, upper-class people lie, cheat, steal, and harm others with astonishing frequency. To ignore this reality is simply to misunderstand the problem of crime in the modern world. Yet, we believe it is possible to remain true to Sutherland's insight while at the same time adopting a more expansive perspective on the problem of crime in the modern world. In the chapters that follow, we often deal with offenders who do not fit the criteria imposed by Sutherland's offender-based definition. This is not because we think that Sutherland's definition is wrong. Rather, it is because, as we noted earlier, it is simply a fact that people of middle and lower social status can and do use the techniques identified by Sutherland himself—misrepresentation and duplicity—to commit illegal acts just as people of high social status do. Similarly, small businesses can engage in illegal activities just as national and multinational corporations do. In the coming chapters, we will spend considerable time in describing and analyzing the crimes of organizational behemoths and the powerful executives who run them. However, our overriding goal is to explore how variations in social status and organizational size influence the type, seriousness, and patterning of white-collar offenses.

Chapter 2

Who Is the White-Collar Offender?

In his definition of white-collar crime and in his many writings on the subject, Sutherland described the white-collar offender as a person of respectability and high social status who commits an offense during the course of his or her occupation. If we follow Sutherland's approach, then the question posed in the title of this chapter is already partially answered. The white-collar offender is a respectable person of high social status who uses his/her employment position as an opportunity to engage in illegal behavior. At the time Sutherland was writing, the offender in the United States would nearly always have been a middle-aged white male. Of course, what Sutherland meant by "respectable" and "high social status" is not completely clear, but he did indicate that by white-collar he meant to refer to "business managers and executives" (Sutherland, 1983). And, as discussed in Chapter 1, it is clear that Sutherland was uninterested in traditional or conventional offenses such as burglary or assault—which anyone could commit. Rather, the occupational roles held by managers and executives provided status and respectability as well as unique opportunities to commit crimes.

If we thought about it for a bit, we could probably come up with definitions for the terms *respectable* and *high social status* that would make sense conceptually. To answer the question of who is the white-collar offender, we would have to identify individuals who fit our definitions and who engage in occupationally related crime. We would want to know what it is that distinguishes respectable high-social-status people who are dishonest from those who are honest. Sutherland had a theory about the answer to this question. Other theories have been put forward by other scholars. We discuss these theories in the next chapter, but for now, we want to consider what happens if we do not use Sutherland's definition.

Suppose that instead of following Sutherland, we defined white-collar crime using Edelhertz's approach—that is, as a property crime committed by nonphysical means and by concealment or deception. How would taking Edelhertz's approach affect the answer to the question, who is the white-collar offender? If we follow Edelhertz's approach, our problem boils down to this: what do we know about the people who commit property crimes by nonphysical means and through the use of concealment or deceit?

Thanks to a series of studies at Yale University, we actually know quite a lot about these people. In the mid-1970s, a group of researchers led by Stanton Wheeler of Yale University conducted a study of white-collar offenders in the federal judicial system. From these investigations, an interesting picture of the people who commit crimes of deception has emerged. As we will show, some of these people clearly are white-collar offenders in Sutherland's sense of the term, but many of them are not.

DOI: 10.4324/9781003175322-3

The Yale Studies on White-Collar Crime

The Yale researchers began by identifying eight offenses in the federal criminal code that most scholars and lay people would agree were white-collar type crimes. For our purposes, what is important is that these are offenses that are committed by concealment and deception rather than brute physical force. The eight offenses were:

- Securities violations
- Antitrust violations
- Bribery
- Bank embezzlement
- Mail and wire fraud
- Tax fraud
- False claims and statements, and
- Credit and lending institution fraud.

All of these offenses fit Edelhertz's definition, and we believe that in many cases Sutherland would have no objections, either.

Obviously, the list does not include every white-collar crime in the federal code. Many others could have been used. Nevertheless, we think the researchers are correct in claiming that this set of offenses represents "a broad and heterogeneous view of white-collar criminal activity that is prosecuted in the federal courts" (Weisburd et al., 1991, p. 11).

The researchers identified all of the people who had been convicted of any one of the eight offenses named above in seven large federal district courts. From here on, we will call these the *criterion* offenses. From this pool of individuals, the researchers then selected a sample of offenders from the criterion offense categories in the seven districts. The total sample included 1,094 offenders.

In addition to the white-collar offenders, the researchers also selected a sample of 210 individuals who had been convicted of nonviolent financially oriented common crimes. This comparison sample of common criminals included individuals who had been convicted of either postal theft or postal forgery.[1] These federal offenses are similar to the better-known common property crimes of burglary and larceny. Burglary and larceny, however, are crimes that are governed by state rather than federal law, so they could not be used by the researchers for making comparisons.

The researchers gathered data from each offender's presentence investigation report (PSI). The PSI is a document prepared by a federal probation officer whenever an offender is convicted in federal court. Federal judges use PSIs when they make decisions about sentencing. As the majority of cases in the federal system are settled by pleas, judges often do not have an opportunity to learn much about the offender or the offense prior to sentencing. The PSI is designed to help judges overcome this information shortage. It helps the judge learn in detail about the offense and the offender.

Regarding the offense, the PSI informs the judge about the official charges to which the defendant has pled guilty (e.g., one count of violating 18 USC 287, which is a federal statute governing false claims or statements). But in addition to the official charge, the PSI contains a "defendant's version of the offense" and an "official version of the offense". The defendant's version is just that: it is the defendant's version or explanation of what happened. Some defendants write these statements themselves, but many rely upon their lawyers to help them craft a statement that will not be offensive to the judge and that may help them get a more lenient sentence (Rothman and Gandossy, 1982). Not surprisingly, defendants with the help of their attorneys often go to great lengths to present themselves in favorable terms. The overlap between what really happened and the defendant's *version* of what happened is never perfect.

For our purposes, the official version of the offense is more important and useful. It is supposed to present an unbiased and objective description of the acts that led to the filing of criminal charges against the defendant. It usually contains a detailed description of the offense, including information on what was done, who was involved, who was harmed, how much money was lost, how complex the offense was, and how long it lasted. This descriptive information about the offense tells us much more about what really happened than does the formal charge. In addition to information on the offense, the PSI contains information about the defendant. Much of this information focuses on the defendant's prior criminal record, including previous arrests, convictions, and sentences. However, the PSI also contains information about the defendant's social, economic, and demographic background. Typically, probation officers will describe the defendant's age, race, gender, family of origin, marital history, educational attainment, employment history, medical and psychological condition, financial status, place of residence, religious preference, alcohol and drug use, and standing in the community. Thus, the PSI can be used to find out who commits white-collar types of crimes and to compare these people to those who commit common street crimes. In short, we can use it to investigate important questions about white-collar offenders and white-collar crimes, such as, who commits the most serious crimes—people of high social status or those of low social status? Are the people who commit white-collar crimes really different from those who commit run-of-the-mill common crimes? If so, how are they different?

However, like all research methodologies, the one used by the Yale researchers is not perfect, as they were well aware (Weisburd et al., 1991, pp. 17–21). The researchers acknowledged four shortcomings in their research design.

First, they studied only eight federal offenses. There are many other federal offenses that could conceivably be called white-collar crimes. If the researchers had included a different mix of offenses, their results may be different. For example, neither environmental violations nor violations of workplace safety laws were included in the study, yet these are important and common forms of white-collar crime.

Second, the researchers studied only seven federal districts. These seven were selected because they were large and the researchers thought that they would have a lot of white-collar crime cases. As with the mix of offenses, it is possible that had a different mix of districts been selected, the results might have changed as well.

Taken together, the first two shortcomings raise the possibility that if we were looking at a different sample, we might see a different portrait of the white-collar offender. For example, it is certainly possible that the people who commit bank embezzlement in New York City are not like those who embezzle in, say, Amarillo, Texas. Whether a sample is representative of all the possible cases from which it is drawn is a common problem in social science research. The best way to address this shortcoming is to look at more than one sample. If the results from different samples converge, then we can have much more confidence in them than we could from a single observation point. Luckily, at the same time that the Yale researchers were conducting their study, several other investigations of white-collar offenders in the federal system were also under way (Benson and Moore, 1992; Benson and

Walker, 1988; Hagan et al., 1980). We will not describe these studies in detail now, but we will use them later as a check on the results of the Yale project.

The last two shortcomings are potentially more serious. They both involve the types of people and offenses that we end up looking at if our sampling strategy is restricted to convicted offenders. By including only cases that resulted in a defendant's being convicted in federal criminal court, the study missed all of the white-collar cases that were handled in other ways, such as, for example, in civil courts or in regulatory proceedings. The study missed all of the individuals whose cases could have been handled in criminal court but for some reason were not. This is not an insignificant issue. The picture that we get of the white-collar offender depends entirely on who gets drawn into the criminal justice system. If the process by which people are drawn into the system is biased in some way, then our image of the white-collar offender will be biased in just that way as well.

For example, imagine that at the time of the Yale study, two bank employees were caught embezzling by their employers. One of the individuals was an older white man who was a bank vice president, while the other was a young black woman who was a teller. Further suppose that for some reason, the white man's employer decides to fire the man rather than press charges. This apparent generosity on the part of the employer is not as unlikely or outlandish as it may seem at first. The bank owners may wish to avoid the embarrassment of having the bank officer's name in the paper, which would not reflect well on the bank. On the other hand, the black woman's employer calls the local U.S. District Attorney, who files charges against the woman in federal court. The woman is eventually convicted of bank embezzlement. The problem here is obvious. Our two bank embezzlers differ in their sociodemographic characteristics, but only one can possibly turn up in the Yale study. If something like this happens often, then using conviction records as our data source will give us a distorted view of the characteristics of white-collar offenders.

The final shortcoming of using court convictions to identify white-collar offenders also relates to the issue of who gets into the criminal justice system in the first place. All those offenses that are never detected in the first place are missed. In other words, conviction records give us only offenders who are unlucky or careless enough to get caught. For example, to return again to our two bank embezzlers, suppose that because of his position, the bank vice president is able to cover up his offense so that it is never discovered. If bank vice presidents often get away with embezzlement, while bank tellers rarely do, then conviction records will present a biased picture of who commits bank embezzlement. As we will see at many points in this book, detection is a big problem in the study and control of white-collar crime. It is always debatable whether the offenses and offenders whom we detect are the same as the offenses and offenders who escape detection.

On the other hand, we also do not really know whether the offenses that go undetected or that do not result in court convictions really are all that much different from those that do come to light. Some white-collar crime scholars argue that offenders of high social status and economic power use these advantages to avoid prosecution (Coleman, 1989; Reiman, 1979). Opposing this view are studies that suggest that prosecutors actually like to go after the "big cases", so to speak, and are eager to take on cases with high-profile defendants (Benson, Cullen, and Maakestad, 1990; Katz, 1980). For example, a former attorney general of New York, Elliot Spitzer, made a career out of taking on very high-profile white-collar cases (Cullen et al., 2006, pp. 329–330).

Taken together, the four shortcomings of the Yale study add up to this: we cannot be entirely positive that the offenders and offenses in this study represent all white-collar crimes. The reasons for our uncertainty are that: (1) a different mix of offenses might produce different results, (2) a different mix of districts might produce different results, (3) some offenders who could have been included in the study were not because their cases were handled in other ways, and (4) offenders who are convicted may not be the same as those who avoid detection in the first place. These are not trivial shortcomings, but we should not overstate their importance. We can address the first two by looking at other studies of federal offenders that use different offenses and different districts. Regarding the last two shortcomings, probably the best we can do is to acknowledge that what we see may not be all there is. Nevertheless, the Yale studies on white-collar crime at least can show us what persons convicted of white-collar type offenses look like.

The Social and Demographic Characteristics of White-Collar Offenders

In the late 1990s and early 2000s, big time financial scandals appeared to explode. The names of Andrew Fastow, Kenneth Lay, Bernard Ebbers, Dennis Kozlowski, Martha Stewart, and Bernard Madoff were plastered over the *New York Times* and *Wall Street Journal* for months at a time. These were high-profile people who were convicted of very high-profile white-collar crimes. Andrew Fastow, the former chief financial officer for Enron, pled guilty to accounting fraud in 2004 and was sentenced to federal prison. His boss, Ken Lay, was convicted of fraud in 2006 but died before he was sentenced. Bernard Ebbers was the former head of WorldCom and was convicted of accounting fraud. Dennis Kozlowski was the former head of Tyco International, a large conglomerate; he was convicted of stealing billions of dollars from his company. Martha Stewart was convicted of lying to federal authorities concerning a stock transaction and was sentenced to serve five months in a federal correctional institution. Finally, Bernie Madoff was the mastermind behind the largest Ponzi scheme in history and was convicted of stealing literally billions of dollars from his clients (Henriques, 2011). With the exception of Martha Stewart, these individuals represent the archetype of the white-collar offender. They are rich, powerful, male, and white. At the time that they committed their offenses, they held leadership positions in major corporations. Although they were not all born wealthy, none of them came from what could be called a disadvantaged or troubled family background.

It would be hard to find a group that more closely fits the common conception or stereotype of the white-collar offender than these people. You would never mistake them for common criminals. However, is this what most of the people who are convicted for white-collar crimes are like? The answer is partly yes and partly no.

The "yes" part of the answer relates to the age, race, and sex characteristics of white-collar offenders and to their employment status and level of education. The data in Table 2.1 are taken from the Yale study (Wheeler et al., 1988a). It compares the white-collar criminals to the common criminals and to the general population of the seven districts in which the study was conducted.

Let's look first at the gender, race, and age characteristics of the people who were convicted of white-collar crimes and compare them with the general public. The most striking and obvious fact is that the white-collar offenders are overwhelmingly male. About half of the general public is male, but nearly nine of ten white-collar offenders are male. The white-collar offenders also are more likely to be white (81.7 percent) than are members of the general public (76.8 percent), but the overrepresentation of whites in the sample is only little

Table 2.1 Demographic, education, and employment characteristics of white-collar offenders, common criminals, and the general public

	Common Criminals	White-Collar Criminals	General Public
Sex (male)	68.6%	85.5%	48.6%
Race (white)	34.3%	81.7%	76.8%
Age (mean)	30	40	30
Education			
High school graduates	45.5%	79.3%	69.0%
College graduates	3.9%	27.1%	19.0%
Employment			
Unemployed	56.7%	5.7%	5.9%
Steadily employed	12.7%	58.4%	Not available

Adapted from Tables III and IV in Wheeler et al., 1988a.

more than we would expect by chance. Finally, the average age of the persons convicted of white-collar crimes is 40, a good bit older than the average age of 30 of the general public in these districts. Compared with the general public, then, the people who are convicted of white-collar crimes are older, a bit more likely to be white, and much more likely to be male.

How do the white-collar criminals compare with the people who commit non-violent common crimes? Here there are substantial differences, especially in regard to race. While 81.7 percent of white-collar criminals are white, only about one of three common criminals is white (34.3 percent). Social scientists would put it this way: non-whites are grossly over-represented among common criminals and underrepresented among white-collar criminals. In contrast, whites are grossly underrepresented among common criminals and overrepresented among white-collar criminals.

There are other differences as well. The persons convicted of nonviolent common crimes are on average ten years younger than the white-collar criminals. It is also clear that common crime is more of an equal opportunity employer than is white-collar crime. More than 30 percent of the common criminals are female compared with less than 15 percent of the white-collar criminals. Overall, though, women are much less likely than men to commit any sort of crime.

Now we turn to the "no" part of the answer to our question regarding how well people like Bernard Madoff, Ken Lay, and Martha Stewart represent white-collar offenders in general. Advanced education and steady employment are two of the standard markers of success in our society, and they are two characteristics that are commonly associated with white-collar criminals. As should come as no surprise, white-collar offenders are indeed much more likely to be well educated than are common criminals. Almost 80 percent of white-collar offenders have at least graduated from high school versus less than half of common criminals. More than one-fourth of white-collar criminals are college graduates (27.1 percent) compared with less than 5 percent of the common criminals (3.9 percent).

In one sense, these results are exactly what we would expect. The white-collar offenders are more highly educated than the common criminals. However, in another sense, these results do not fit the standard view of the white-collar offender. Most of the white-collar offenders are *not* highly educated. More than 70 percent of them are *not* college graduates. It is true that white-collar offenders are more likely to have graduated from college than members of the general public (27.3 percent versus 19.0 percent, respectively), but the difference is not huge. In regard to education, then, the white-collar offenders are better off than the public in general, but it would not be correct to say that they are always highly educated.

With respect to the standard view of white-collar offenders, the finding that most of them do not have college degrees is important. Advanced education is an indicator of high social status. Offenders who have not completed a college education lack one of the badges of high social status that Sutherland and those who adopt his approach often identify with white-collar criminals.

The results on employment status also call into question the standard image of the white-collar offender. As was the case with education, white-collar and common criminals differ dramatically in employment status. More than half (56.7 percent) of the common criminals were unemployed at the time that they committed the criterion offense that brought them into federal court. In contrast, only 5.7 percent of the white-collar offenders were unemployed at the time of their offenses. This percentage corresponds almost exactly with the unemployment rate for the general public (5.9 percent). So far, so good. Again, this is what we would expect. It is not surprising to find that most common criminals are unemployed. But the picture gets more puzzling when we look at the rate of "steady employment" for the white-collar offenders. In the Yale study, steady employment meant that the individual had had uninterrupted employment during the five-year period preceding the conviction. Fewer than 60 percent of the white-collar offenders had been steadily employed (58.7 percent) prior to their convictions. Granted, that looks pretty good compared with the common criminals, who had a steady employment rate of only 12.7 percent. But it also means that *more than* 40 percent of the white-collar offenders were *not* steadily employed prior to their convictions.

It is easy to get lost in numbers and tables and to miss the forest for the trees. So, let's step back and try to summarize the main conclusions that we can draw from Table 2.1. First, as expected, the typical white-collar offender is a middle-aged white male. Second, as expected, on average white-collar offenders are better educated and more likely to be employed than common criminals. Third, however, and *not* as expected, most white-collar offenders have only a high school diploma, and a substantial proportion of them could not count on steady employment prior to their offenses. Thus, the people convicted of white-collar crimes in federal courts are indeed different from common criminals, but on average they do not appear to be social elites. They do not appear to have high social status.

The data presented in Table 2.1 apply to all of the white-collar offenders in the Yale study considered as a group. But recall that the Yale researchers selected individuals who had been convicted of eight different types of white-collar crimes, ranging from antitrust violators to bank embezzlers. Obviously, the people who commit antitrust violations may not be the same as the people who commit bank embezzlement. There may be substantial variations in the social characteristics of white-collar offenders, and these variations may be linked to the types of offenses they commit.

In Table 2.2, we again explore the social and demographic characteristics of white-collar offenders. However, this time, instead of looking at the group as a whole, we categorize offenders by the type of offense they committed. This cross-categorization results in a complex table that may look overwhelming, but if we proceed systematically, we should be able to make sense of it.

Table 2.2 Social and demographic characteristics of white-collar offenders by statutory offense

	Antitrust	Securities Fraud	Tax	Bribery	Credit Fraud	False Claims	Mail Fraud	Bank Embezzlement
Race (white)	99.1%	99.6%	87.1%	83.3%	71.5%	61.8%	76.8%	74.1%
Sex (male)	99.1%	97.8%	94.1%	95.2%	84.8%	84.7%	82.1%	54.8%
Age	53	44	47	45	38	39	38	31
Financial Standing								
Median assets	$650,000	$59,000	$49,500	$45,000	$7,000	$4,000	$2,000	$2,000
Median liabilities	$81,000	$55,000	$23,500	$19,000	$7,000	$5,000	$3,500	$3,000
Education								
College graduates	40.0%	43.0%	27.0%	27.0%	18.0%	29.0%	23.0%	13.0%
Homeowners	87.8%	62.1%	57.7%	57.0%	44.8%	42.1%	33.5%	31.0%

Adapted from Table VII in Wheeler et al., 1988a.

Let's begin by considering the standard demographic characteristics, starting with race, which is in the first row of the table. It would not be an exaggeration to say that in the decade of the 1970s, your chances of finding a non-white antitrust or securities violator were slim to none. More than 99 percent of both antitrust and securities violators were white. There were 117 antitrust violators in the Yale study, and 116 of them were white; astonishingly, of the 225 securities violators, 224 were white. On the other end of the spectrum, only 61.8 percent of the false-claims violators were white, which obviously means that almost 40 percent of them were non-white, and only 71.5 percent of those who committed lending and credit fraud were white. The percentage white in the other four offense categories falls between these two end points. Thus, at the time of the Yale study, antitrust and securities violations were almost exclusively white-only offenses. It is a striking finding that there are such large variations in the racial composition of the different offense types.

The story is similar when we look at gender. As with race, we find notable variations across the offense types by gender. With only very few exceptions, antitrust, securities, tax, and bribery violations are committed by males. In contrast, almost half of the bank embezzlers are females. Finally, there is age. Two numbers stand out. The average age of the antitrust violators is 53, while the average age of the bank embezzlers is 31. Relatively young people commit bank embezzlement, while people who are almost eligible for early retirement fix prices and rig bids.

Systematic variations, such as the ones we found here for race, gender, and age, are important. They are clues to how the world works. By definition, systematic variations do not arise randomly. They are the result of some sort of systematic causal process. If we can identify and understand these variations, then we are well on our way to understanding the underlying causal processes that produced them. In our case, this means understanding how and why particular types of people tend to commit particular types of white-collar crimes. By particular types of people, we mean people who have certain demographic characteristics. As we argued in Chapter 1, we believe that access to white-collar crime opportunities varies by race, gender, and age as well as other variables, and it is access to opportunities that explains patterns in the social and demographic characteristics of white-collar offenders. In Table 2.2, we see the first preliminary evidence in favor of this interpretation.

In order to commit certain types of white-collar offenses, it is virtually required that you have access to particular occupational positions. For example, it is much easier to commit a securities offense if you work in the securities industry as, say, a stockbroker or a stock analyst. Since most of the people who work in the securities industry are white males, we should not be surprised to find that most securities offenders are white males. Neither should we be surprised that most antitrust violators are white males. To commit an antitrust violation, you have to have an executive-level position in a fairly large company. As we document later in Chapter 9, these positions are held disproportionately by white males.

There are other indications in Table 2.2 that social characteristics influence access to white-collar crime opportunities. The bottom half of the table shows information on the financial standing, education, and homeownership of the white-collar offenders in each of the offense categories. Comparing the antitrust offenders with the bank embezzlers is instructive. The median assets for the antitrust offenders are a whopping $650,000. For the bank embezzlers, the median assets are a puny $2,000. Since their median liabilities are $3,000, many of them are actually in the hole, that is, their debts exceed their assets. The financial condition of the antitrust offenders looks rock solid, while the bank embezzlers look like they are just scraping by from paycheck to paycheck.

We see similar extreme differences between antitrust offenders and bank embezzlers in education and homeownership. Four of ten of the antitrust offenders (40 percent) were college graduates versus about one of ten of the bank embezzlers (13 percent). Close to 90 percent of the antitrust offenders (87.8 percent) owned their homes, whereas less than a third of the bank embezzlers did. The rest of the offense categories are arrayed between these two extremes. The securities offenders did not appear to be quite as well off as the antitrust offenders in financial standing or homeownership. Nevertheless, they were definitely better off in these regards than the people convicted of mail fraud, who more closely resembled the bank embezzlers. Less than one-fourth of the mail fraud offenders had a college degree; only one-third owned their own homes; and their average liabilities exceeded their average assets. Indeed, the only notable difference between those who committed bank embezzlement and those who committed mail fraud was gender. Almost half of the bank embezzlers were women, while eight of ten mail fraud offenders were male. Like others, we find race- and gender-linked differences in offending (Daly, 1989), which we interpret to mean that there are race- and gender-linked differences in opportunities to offend.

A Validity Check

As we noted earlier, it is always possible that the sample of offenders used in the Yale study is in some way unusual or not representative of white-collar offenders generally. Luckily for us, at approximately the same time as the Yale study was going on, another federally funded investigation of white-collar offenders was also under way. This study, conducted by Brian Forst and William Rhodes, used a similar methodology and sampled 2,643 individuals convicted of six ostensibly white-collar crimes from eight federal district courts.[2] The white-collar offenses were bank embezzlement, bribery, false claims, mail fraud, income tax violations, and postal embezzlement.

For our purposes, the important thing about the Forst and Rhodes study is that the offenders come from different federal districts, and the set of offenses is similar although not exactly the same. For example, postal embezzlement, which is in the Forst and Rhodes sample, was not included in the Yale study, and the Forst and Rhodes study lacks antitrust and

Table 2.3 Descriptive statistics on two samples of white-collar offenders

Sample	Tax Y	Tax F&R	Bribery Y	Bribery F&R	False Claims Y	False Claims F&R	Mail Fraud Y	Mail Fraud F&R	Bank Embezzlement Y	Bank Embezzlement F&R	Postal Embezzlement[a] F&R
Demographic Characteristics											
Mean age	47	48	45	47	39	38	38	37	31	30	34
% White	87.1	89.3	83.3	77.5	61.8	56.9	76.8	78.7	74.1	75.5	65.0
% Male	94.3	91.8	95.2	89.4	84.7	72.8	82.1	85.5	55.2	52.6	89.5
Personal History											
% College degree	27.4	23.5	28.9	24.3	29.2	18.4	21.7	13.1	12.9	9.3	1.4
% Homeowners	57.7	70.6	57.0	63.2	42.1	40.0	33.5	31.3	28.4	41.8	49.3

Notes: Y = Yale study sample data from table 3.1 in Weisburd et al. (1991); F&R = Forst and Rhodes.
[a] Postal embezzlement was not included in the Yale study sample.

securities offenders. We can see how the social and demographic characteristics of white-collar offenders convicted of similar offenses but in different federal districts compare. Are they similar or different?

The answer to that question is that they are remarkably similar (see Table 2.3). To keep things simple, we will discuss only the results for tax violators and bank embezzlers. The results for the other offenses parallel these closely. With respect to age, race, and gender, the tax violators in the Yale study are virtually identical to those in the Forst and Rhodes study, and the same is true of the bank embezzlers from both studies. The average age of a tax violator in the Yale study was 47 compared with 48 in the Forst and Rhodes study, while the average age of a bank embezzler in the Yale study was 31 versus 30 in the Forst and Rhodes study. The differences in race and gender are equally small. What is most striking is the similarity in the overall pattern of characteristics. In both studies, tax violators overwhelmingly were white males in their late 40s. This result probably stems from the predominance of males as heads of households and owners of small businesses who were the chief tax preparers in the 1970s. In both studies, we also find that bank embezzlement involved individuals who were younger and more likely to be female or non-white than were tax violators. These similarities in patterns extend to other characteristics, such as graduating from college and owning a home. In both studies, we find that tax violators were more likely than bank embezzlers to have attained these two markers of social success. Overall, the offenders in the Yale study match up well with their counterparts in the Forst and Rhodes study.

The similarity between the offenders in the two studies means that we can be reasonably sure that they generally represent the type of people who are convicted of these particular white-collar crimes in federal courts. In other words, we can have some confidence in the validity and generalizability of what we have learned thus far about white-collar offenders, at least those who were convicted in federal district courts in the 1970s.

What can we conclude from all these numbers and comparisons? Two points stand out. First, as a group, white-collar offenders are not like common criminals. The two groups come from different sectors of the population. Second, not all white-collar offenders are alike. They are not all highly educated or wealthy. Indeed, there is substantial variation in the social and demographic characteristics of the people who commit white-collar types of crimes. Some indeed do fit the stereotype of the white-collar offender as an educated, wealthy, employed, white male, but others do not share these attributes. Thus, white-collar criminals turn out to be more socially and demographically diverse than the standard view would have us believe.

Contemporary White-Collar Offenders

The Yale study and the Forst and Rhodes study represented important contributions to our understanding of the social and demographic characteristics of white-collar offenders. Both studies, however, relied on data from offenders who had been convicted in federal courts for crimes committed in the mid-1970s. Four decades have passed since then, and the United States has changed in many ways. Consider, for example, the subtle revolution involving women in the workplace. In 1970, women's labor force participation rate was just over 40 percent. By 2000, the female labor force participation rate had risen to 60 percent, a level it has held relatively steadily since then (U.S. Bureau of Labor Statistics, 2019). There were other changes involving working women as well. In 1970, about 11 percent of the women aged 25 to 64 in the labor force held college degrees, but in 2018 the proportion of women in the labor force holding college degrees had quadrupled to 44 percent (U.S. Bureau of Labor Statistics, 2019). Women were not the only ones who experienced changes in work and education in the late twentieth and early twenty-first centuries. The percentage of young men who went on to college also increased between 1970 and 2014 (Ingels et al., 2012). And young people of all races and ethnicities are more likely to graduate from college now than they were back in the 1970s (Kena et al., 2015). Thus, compared to the 1970s, more women are working now, and they are more likely to have college degrees, equipping them for different kinds of work than they did in the past. Likewise, non-whites also have more education and presumably have access to more white-collar types of jobs now than they did in the past. In short, the educational and occupational makeup of the U.S. population has evolved since the 1970s.

Since access to white-collar-type jobs is a prerequisite for many white-collar crimes, it is possible that changes in the occupational and educational characteristics of the U.S. population over the past four decades have been reflected in the social and demographic characteristics of those who commit white-collar crimes. In other words, it may no longer be true that older white males dominate white-collar crime as much as they did in the past. Fortunately, with data from the U.S. Sentencing Commission (USSC) and other sources we can make comparisons between the people convicted for white-collar crimes today versus those in the 1970s. It is always tricky to make comparisons over time involving broad offense categories because there may be other important factors that also explain changes, but nevertheless some trends can be observed. The USSC collects data on the age, race, sex, and educational characteristics of individuals convicted of several white-collar offenses such as antitrust, tax, bribery, and a category called theft/embezzlement/fraud (see Table 2.4, which summarizes data from 2015–2020). For comparison purposes, Table 2.4 also includes two other white-collar offense categories—environmental offenses, and food and drug offenses.

As Table 2.4 shows, in regard to race and ethnicity white-collar offenders have changed, and in some cases age and gender are also different. For example, whites no longer dominate antitrust to the same degree. In the 1970s, 99.1 percent of antitrust offenders were white, but only 55 percent of contemporary offenders are white, suggesting that access to the opportunity to commit antitrust offenses is now less segregated than it was four decades

Table 2.4 Descriptive statistics on contemporary white-collar offenders

	Antitrust	Tax	Bribery	Embezzlement	Fraud	Environmental	Food and Drug
Demographic Characteristic							
Mean age	53	50	47	44	41	46	47
% White	55	63	43	60	45	71	65
% Male	100	76	81	44	69	94	76
% College graduates	64	34	31	17	22	16	39
Convictions 2009–2015	117	4,398	1,557	2,623	55,256	1,220	457

Note: Although the Yale study includes "fraud" as one of its categories of white-collar crime, we believe it is not appropriate to compare the Yale fraud data to the Sentencing Commission's fraud data. The Sentencing Commission's definition of "fraud" includes a much broader array of statutes and behaviors than was used in the Yale study. The data for number of convictions varies slightly depending on the demographic characteristic. The numbers reported here come from the Sourcebook table on gender.

Source: U.S. Sentencing Commission, Interactive Sourcebook of Statistics, 2009–2015

ago. The race composition of tax and bribery offenders has also changed dramatically. Whites constituted over 80 percent of tax and bribery offenders in the 1970s, but they now make up only about two-thirds (63 percent) of tax offenders and less than half (43 percent) of bribery offenders. There has been little change in regard to the mean age or gender for white-collar offenders. The average age was 53 for contemporary antitrust offenders, the same as it was in the 1970s. The gender composition of antitrust has also remained virtually unchanged, with 92 percent of offenders being male. For tax and bribery offenders, the mean age for contemporary offenders is nearly the same as it was in the 1970s, with the average offender being around 50. For all four offenses, the proportion of offenders who are college graduates has risen, though not markedly. That there has been an increase in the proportion of white-collar offenders with college degrees is not unexpected in light of the growth in college attendance rates throughout the American population.

Taken together, Tables 2.3 and 2.4 suggest that over the past 40 years, white-collar crime has become more of an equal opportunity employer and is no longer the exclusive preserve of middle-aged white males. Both women and non-whites are more involved now, reflecting perhaps some of the social advances that these groups have made in American society toward the end of the twentieth century (Benson, Feldmeyer, Gabbidon, and Chio, 2020). However, we do not want to suggest that race and sex no longer matter in regard to white-collar crime. White males still predominate in most offense categories, and it is telling that for antitrust violations, the highest-level offense in our analysis, the demographic makeup of the offending population has changed less than the other categories of offending.

White-Collar Criminal Careers

The phrase *white-collar criminal career* seems like an oxymoron. Part of the standard view of white-collar offenders is that they are mainstream, law-abiding individuals. They are assumed to be one-shot offenders, not people who engage in crime on a regular basis. Unlike the run-of-the-mill common street criminal who usually has repeated contacts with the criminal justice system, white-collar offenders are not expected to have prior criminal

Table 2.5 Percent with prior arrests among white-collar and common offenders

Offense	Yale Study *	Forst and Rhodes Study **
White-collar	43	39
Antitrust	3	n.a.
Securities	32	n.a.
Income tax	47	42
Bribery	23	24
Lending and credit fraud	55	n.a.
False claims	56	49
Mail fraud	54	66
Bank embezzlement	29	18
Common	90	83

Notes: n.a. = not available.
* Adapted from table 2, Weisburd et al. (1991).
** Adapted from Benson and Moore (1992).

records. Thus, one of the more remarkable findings from the Yale and Forst and Rhodes studies concerns the prior criminal records of white-collar criminals. A surprisingly large proportion of white-collar criminals already had prior criminal records before they committed their criterion offense. Table 2.5 presents information on the prior arrests for all of the white-collar offense categories and for the common offense categories in both studies. In both studies, we find that about 40 percent of the white-collar offenders had a prior arrest. So, a substantial proportion of white-collar offenders have some familiarity with the business end of police work. But they probably do not know their way around a police station as well as the common criminals. As Table 2.5 shows, a much larger percentage of common criminals have prior arrests. Clearly, the white-collar criminals are not as experienced with the criminal justice system as the common criminals.

It may be surprising that four of ten white-collar criminals have had prior contact with the justice system, but are they really that unusual? Perhaps this is about average for the general public. It is hard to say for sure, because there are few studies on the criminal histories of the general population, and estimates of the overall prevalence of arrest vary between 10 and 25 percent (Singh and Adams, 1979; Tillman, 1987), although one study estimated that fully half of all males in the United States will be arrested at some point in their lifetimes (Christensen, 1967).

Although it is not uncommon for white-collar offenders in general to have a prior arrest, this is not true of those who commit particular types of white-collar crime. Just as we found when we investigated the social and demographic characteristics of white-collar offenders, we also find considerable variation in their criminal histories. In the Yale study, for example, only 3 percent of the antitrust offenders had a prior arrest. This figure is considerably below the norm for the general population. But more than half of the people convicted for lending and credit fraud, false claims, or mail fraud had a prior arrest, which is considerably above the population norm. Persons convicted of income tax violations, securities fraud, bribery, or bank embezzlement fell between these two extremes. A very similar pattern is found in the Forst and Rhodes study, with those convicted of bribery and bank embezzlement on the low end of the scale compared with those convicted of making false claims or mail fraud.

Table 2.6 Mean number of prior arrests for white-collar and common offenders*

Offense	Mean	At Least One Arrest, %
White-collar	1.79	39.0
Embezzlement	0.52	18.4
Bribery	0.65	23.6
Income tax	1.91	42.1
False claims	2.29	49.0
Mail fraud	3.90	65.9
Common	5.63	81.1
Narcotics	3.55	72.2
Forgery	6.49	82.6
Bank robbery	6.85	88.4
All offenders	3.41	57.8

* Adapted from table 1, Benson and Moore (1992).

It appears, then, that bribers and bank embezzlers have less extensive criminal histories than the people who make false claims or commit mail fraud, but even this latter group of white-collar offenders are substantially well below the prior arrest percentage among common offenders (90 and 83 percent for the Yale and Forst and Rhodes studies, respectively). There is evidence that in this case, appearances are not misleading. Table 2.6 shows the average number of prior arrests for each of the white-collar offense categories in the Forst and Rhodes study. On average, bribers and bank embezzlers have far fewer prior arrests than false claims and mail fraud offenders.

What general conclusions can be drawn from these numbers? Two conclusions mirror those we reached earlier on social and demographic characteristics. First, many of the people convicted of white-collar offenses do not fit the stereotype of the white-collar offender. A nontrivial proportion of white-collar offenders are repeat offenders—a finding confirmed in cross-national surveys from other countries (see, for instance, van Onna et al., 2014). Second, the people who commit some types of white-collar crime are much more criminally experienced than the people who commit other types of white-collar crime. Specifically, antitrust offenders, bank embezzlers, and bribers appear to be much less caught up in a life of crime than people who make false claims, commit lending and credit fraud, or use the U.S. postal system to commit fraud. Thus, it appears that different types of people who have different criminal backgrounds commit different types of white-collar crime.

As Tables 2.5 and 2.6 show, it is not uncommon for white-collar offenders to have what can be called criminal careers. But what do these careers look like? We know from the study of ordinary street criminals that most offenders start committing crimes sometime between the ages of 15 and 17, and they typically end their careers in their early 20s (Blumstein et al., 1986; Piquero, 2008). We also know that most offenders are generalists and commit different types of crime rather than specializing in one particular form of offending, such as burglary or auto theft (Piquero and Weisburd, 2009; Tracy, Wolfgang, and Figlio, 1990). A few studies have attempted to examine the criminal careers of white-collar offenders (see Benson and Moore, 1992; Piquero and Weisburd, 2009; Weisburd and Waring, 2001), and these studies clearly suggest that more "differences than similarities exist between the criminal careers of white-collar offenders and those of common offenders" (Piquero and Weisburd, 2009, p. 156). In an analysis of the Yale data, Weisburd and Waring (2001) found that white-collar offenders typically start much later in life than common offenders. The average age of onset for white-collar offenders was 35, and their careers tended to last longer, with an average career length of 14 years (Weisburd and Waring, 2001). However, white-collar offenders tend to commit relatively few offenses during their careers.

In addition to examining career length and rate of offending, Weisburd and Waring (2001) looked at the general shape of the trajectories followed by white-collar offenders. Their analyses indicated that there were three prominent offending patterns: low rate, medium rate, and high rate. The low rate offenders, who made up about 70 percent of the Yale sample, committed very few offenses. They offended very infrequently and only under certain conditions (Piquero and Weisburd, 2009). Weisburd and Waring suggested that these people were either "crisis responders" or "opportunity takers". Crisis responders are those who commit white-collar crime out of a sense of desperation (see also, Engdahl, 2011). Opportunity takers, on the other hand, are those who find themselves in an occupational position in which they figure out or learn from others that their jobs give them opportunities to enrich themselves illegally.

The medium rate group were about 25 percent of the sample (Piquero and Weisburd, 2009). This group also offended relatively infrequently but nevertheless more persistently than the low rate group. The medium rate group appeared to be made up of "opportunity seekers", that is, people who would actively look for opportunities and situations in which they could take advantage of others to make a buck.

Finally, the high rate group was small, only about 5 percent of the sample (Piquero and Weisburd, 2009), but they offended more often and more consistently over time than the other two groups. The people in the high rate group also committed a broader array of offenses. Their crimes involved a mix of white-collar and non–white-collar offenses, which raises an important point about the difficulty of identifying white-collar offenders. Indeed, a nontrivial number of them (5 percent to 30 percent) had arrests for non–white-collar crimes. In other words, these individuals do not necessarily specialize in white-collar crime. Rather, they appear to be stereotypical criminals who occasionally commit white-collar offenses. The lesson to be learned from this is that a single arrest may not be the best way to identify white-collar offenders. This lesson is confirmed by a recent study of 644 white-collar offenders in the Netherlands. Analysis revealed two broad types of white-collar offenders—low-frequency offenders who accounted for 78 percent of offenders and a smaller high-frequency offender group. The high-frequency group accounted for 22 percent of all white-collar offenders. In addition to the notable differences in offending frequency, the two categories of offenders also differed on when they first became involved in crime. The low-frequency offenders began their offending "careers" in adulthood while the latter started to offend in adolescence (van Onna et al., 2014).

In sum, the available data on the criminal careers of white-collar offenders suggests that most are from the middle class rather than the upper class. They tend to start and to desist from offending later in life than common criminals, and they are somewhat more likely to specialize in a particular type of offending than common criminals. In light of these differences, it seems likely that the causes of white-collar crime involve triggers and risk factors that are unique to white-collar offenders, including opportunities provided by occupations, business-related pressures, and adult problems (Piquero and Piquero, 2016).

What About Organizations and High-Status Offenders?

Up to this point, we have focused on the social, demographic, and criminal characteristics of the people convicted of white-collar crimes in the federal judicial system. But in our investigation thus far, we have taken an offense-based approach to white-collar crime, and as we saw above, this can sometimes lead to a mixed bag of offenders. How would things change if instead we followed Sutherland and focused on individuals who score high on respectability and social status and who hold positions of significant influence or power in legitimate public or private organizations?

Unfortunately, there are very few quantitative studies to guide us. Most of what we know about high-status white-collar offenders comes from case studies of particularly egregious offenders or offenses. Although case studies can be enormously informative, it is always risky to generalize from them. It is not surprising that there are so few quantitative studies. It is hard to study high-status individuals using standard research methodologies such as surveys or interviews. They often are unwilling to cooperate in studies, and it is even harder to get them to cooperate when the focus of the study is crime or wrongdoing. Hence, sometimes, it makes more sense to concentrate on organizations rather than individuals.

After all, as Sutherland (1949) demonstrated, many of the really egregious white-collar offenses, the ones that make the evening news and the newspaper headlines, are committed in organizations, often large, complex organizations. In large organizations, people often work in groups to accomplish intricate multifaceted tasks and goals. For example, consider the scandal that broke in 2015 involving the German automaker, Volkswagen, and its so-called "Clean Diesel" engines (Smith and Parloff, 2016). Clean diesels were touted as meeting U.S. emission standards for a collection of dangerous pollutants called NOx. NOx emissions from vehicles are regulated by the U.S. EPA, because they pose significant threats to air quality and human health in urban environments. Between 2008 and 2015, Volkswagen and its subsidiaries, Audi and Porsche, marketed 15 different models worldwide that were equipped with so-called clean diesels and touted them as being eco-friendly "green" alternatives to the smog-belching vehicles produced by other automakers. But it was a fraud. The cars were not really "green" at all. The engines actually emitted up to 40 times the allowable levels of NOx. Volkswagen was able to get away with this fraud because it had installed software in the engine's computers that could sense when the car was being tested in the lab. When the car was being tested by the EPA or other regulatory agencies, the software would turn up the engine's emission-reduction equipment to meet the EPA standards, and then turn the equipment off once the car was driving on actual roads. It was a complicated technical undertaking that involved engineers, software programmers, mid-level supervisors, and persons in higher-level management positions. But who exactly should be held responsible? Not surprisingly, when the fraud was uncovered, the company's chief executive officer (CEO), Martin Winterkorn, denied knowing anything and blamed the whole fiasco on a handful of "rogue engineers". But Federal prosecutors disagreed and, in a surprise move, filed criminal charges against six Volkswagen executives, including the head of development for the Volkswagen brand and the head of engine development (Tabuchi, Ewing, and Apuzzo, 2017), several of whom were later convicted and sentenced to imprisonment. In 2018, the CEO of Volkswagen, Martin Winterkorn, was also indicted on fraud and conspiracy charges in both the United States and Germany. Criminal investigations were also initiated by prosecutors in France, Italy, Sweden, and South Korea (Smith and Parloff, 2016), and the inquiry has been extended to other automobile manufacturers, such as Fiat Chrysler (Isidore, 2017; Tabuchi, 2017; Sorokonish, 2017).

The problem here is a general one that criminologists and prosecutors have long recognized when it comes to understanding and controlling crimes committed in organizational settings. In large, complex organizations, responsibility for projects often is diffused or spread out over a number of people. The diffusion of responsibility makes it difficult to single out a particular individual or group of individuals who ought to be held responsible when things go wrong. Indeed, the decision by Federal prosecutors in the Volkswagen case to file criminal charges against individual executives is unusual. Prior to this case, Federal prosecutors typically had not pursued criminal charges against individual corporate executives, preferring instead to concentrate on the organization itself and to reach what are called *non-prosecution* or *deferred prosecution agreements*, in which the corporation agrees to institute reforms to prevent future offending in return for not being criminally charged (Garrett, 2014). We will have more to say about deferred prosecution agreements in the last section of the book, but for now we return to the task of thinking about organizations as offenders.

The Characteristics of Organizational Offenders and Offenses

Assuming that companies can commit crime (a supposition, as we discuss below, that is challenged by some scholars), what do we know about organizational offenders and the types of crimes they commit? The USSC tracks case and offender information for organizations sentenced in federal courts. These data can offer insight into some of the attributes of sentenced offenders. For instance, the USSC data reveal that the majority of sentenced organizations are small. In fiscal year (FY) 2022, we can see from Figure 2.1 that 81.4 percent have fewer than 50 employees, while only 7 percent have more than 1,000 employees.

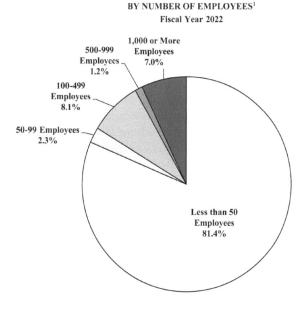

SIZE OF ORGANIZATIONAL OFFENDERS
BY NUMBER OF EMPLOYEES[1]
Fiscal Year 2022

1,000 or More Employees 7.0%

500-999 Employees 1.2%

100-499 Employees 8.1%

50-99 Employees 2.3%

Less than 50 Employees 81.4%

Figure 2.1 Number of employees of organizational offenders

[1] Of the 99 organizational cases, 13 were missing information on the number of employees in the organization. Descriptions of variables used in this figure are provided in Appendix A.

Source: USSC Annual Report and 2022 Sourcebook of Federal Sentencing Statistics

Using FY 2022 USSC data, the following image of the corporate offender emerges:

> There were 99 organizational cases in FY 2022. One-quarter of these involved environmental offenses (25.3 percent) but the most common offense was fraud (40.4 percent). The preponderance of fraud is unusual in the USSC data, but perhaps not surprising given the numerous opportunities for business fraud tied to pandemic relief funding. These two categories were followed by money laundering (8.1 percent) and import and export crimes (4 percent). Immigration, antitrust, drugs, food and drug categories were smaller categories off violations but collectively made up 15 percent of the total with other offenses rounding out the whole.
>
> Of the 35 organizational defendants sentenced pursuant to the Chapter 8 fine provisions guidelines, only one had a previous criminal or administrative record within the previous five years. Most were not—officially at least—recidivists.
>
> A notable number of the convicted organizations appear not to have substantial financial assets. Indeed, 35 percent of the sentenced organizations were deemed unable to pay and were therefore granted a reduced fine.
>
> Self-reporting is extremely rare or absent. A central component of the sentencing guidelines encourages a cooperative relationship between business and legal authorities (this is considered a mitigating circumstance); yet, in FY 2022 only two sentenced organizations self-reported the offense to authorities.[3]
>
> With only 99 cases sentenced under Chapter 8 during the fiscal year (compared with 64,142 felony and class A misdemeanor cases handled across all U.S. circuit and districts courts), criminal behavior by corporations would appear to be relatively rare.
>
> (U.S.S.C. *Annual Report and Sourcebook of Federal Sentencing Statistics*, 2022)

How does this picture of corporate crime and the typical organizational offender comport with what we have learned from other research, and how useful are the guidelines data to estimate the scope and character of corporate crime? The early Sentencing Commission data are problematic due to case-specific missing data and entire cases omitted from the database (Alexander, Arlen, and Cohen, 2001). After 2005, the case information, however, became more consistent and reliable. Most corporate offenses are litigated civilly or administratively and are not referred for criminal prosecution. Because the USSC data comprise criminal cases, extrapolating about the dark figure of corporate crime or offender characteristics from this source says nothing about the likely characteristics of corporate crime cases and offenders handled outside of the criminal justice system. Arlen (2012, p. 349) suggests that the guidelines' self-reporting provisions perversely reward, through mitigation points, the types of offenders that would be the easiest for authorities to discover and who are also the least troublesome. The self-reporting provision therefore is apt to attract less sophisticated offenders who are likely involved in less serious or less consequential crimes. It is unclear what the true distribution of serious versus minor cases of corporate crime would be in the general population, but Arlen's argument implies that using these data to project a dark figure of corporate crime will underestimate them. The guidelines data also capture offenders at the end of the criminal justice process, measuring convictions and not charges or crimes known to authorities. We know little about what happens to cases that are discovered but not investigated, or about which cases move from an "arrest" to some kind of diversion. Studies of traditional offenders suggest that those who begin the justice process are quite different from those who make it all the way through to the conviction and sentencing stages. It is likely that in the case of corporate crime, the organizations that travel all the way through the criminal justice funnel differ from those that are diverted or shunted out of the system along the way. However, at this point in time we know little about offender similarities and differences from one stage of the process to the next and how that may vary by justice system (criminal, administrative, or civil).

Small Businesses as Offenders

The crimes of larger businesses tend to dominate news headlines and draw global attention from politicians, law enforcement and the media due to their potential to have an outsized impact on society. Yet, it is worth asking whether the USSC data underrepresents the criminality of smaller firms. According to U.S. Census (2018) data, in 2016, 98 percent of all firms in the U.S. employed fewer than 100 people and 85 percent employed fewer than 20 people. While small businesses were the most commonly sentenced businesses in the USSC data, large businesses were overrepresented in the sentencing figures. Businesses with more than 1,000 employees comprise just 0.7 percent of all firms in the U.S., yet USSC data show that these firms made up more than 7 percent of sentenced organizations.

Historical data show that the distribution of businesses across size categories is relatively consistent over time. Importantly, the proportion of small businesses that make up the U.S. economy is similar to that found in the European Union, Latin America, and the Caribbean (Eurostat, 2022; OECD, 2019), and by some estimates around 90 percent of businesses across the globe are small and medium-sized (World Bank, 2022). While small businesses have ample opportunities to engage in crime, they may be less likely to face scrutiny when compared to their larger counterparts. For example, Between October 2021 and September 2022, the U.S. Occupational Safety and Health Administration (OSHA, 2022) conducted 17,361 facility inspections. OSHA issued 46,668 citations for violations of federal standards, generating fines of well over a $192 million. Small businesses represented 93.6 percent of all OSHA inspections. However, only 57.3 percent of all citations issued for federal violations were issued to small businesses. Large businesses (those with 100 or more employees) comprised just 6.4 percent of all OSHA inspections yet accounted for nearly 43 percent of the total fines levied.

Assuming similar trends in sentencing across firm size over time, we are left with only a handful of possible conclusions: (1) that there is something inherently criminogenic about larger businesses, hence their overrepresentation in sentencing data; (2) that there are no differences in the criminality of small businesses relative to larger firms, yet smaller firms are more likely to avoid criminal prosecutions or more likely to face prosecution at the local level—data that are not currently compiled; or (3) that there are no differences between small and large firm criminality, yet smaller firms are less scrutinized than larger firms.

Another possibility is that the legal structure, external perception/visibility, and operational dynamics of large businesses make crimes committed by these firms more easily attributable to firm behavior, whereas crimes committed by smaller businesses may tend to be associated with individual behavior. Many small businesses around the globe are sole proprietorships or employ only a handful of people. According to the U.S. Small Business Administration (2021), in 2021 the average newly formed business employed about three people, while 13.7 percent of all small businesses were sole proprietorships. While sole proprietorships tend not to offer the same legal protections as other types of corporate organizations (such as s-corporations, limited liability partnerships, etc.), the nature of offending occurring within these businesses is in many ways indistinguishable from that of larger businesses. Widespread corporate criminality as found in the cases of Enron, Tyco, Volkswagen, and other large corporations present a picture of large firms intentionally engaging in criminal behavior to protect or generate revenue. In larger firms we tend to look towards the organization as the offender (or at least a guilty party or co-conspirator with individual executives), yet in small business crimes we tend to look at the owner as the sole complicit actor.

Crimes committed within businesses that are operated solely by the owner, or by a handful of employees, can appear to be crimes committed by the owner rather than the business. Despite the fact that funds flow through the business and that the crime is committed as part of the business's normal operations, even co-occurring alongside legitimate business operations, individuals tend to be the target of enforcement actions. For example, in 2014 (CBS, 2014) a franchised location of the national retail chain Dollar Castle was raided by police who discovered counterfeit goods that would have been valued at nearly $500,000 if they had been legitimate. The business sold the items alongside legitimate merchandise and the revenue earned from the sales of these products flowed through the business's regular bank account. Store employees restocked the products and rang up customers when these illicit goods were sold. This store was literally in the business of selling counterfeits, yet it was the store owner, not the business who was charged with the criminal offense.

Distinctions in enforcement across small and large firms may create the perception that smaller businesses are less likely to be engaged in crime and this may affect researchers' ability to gather valid and reliable data on small business offending. Research conducted by the Center for Anti-Counterfeiting and Product Protection (Kennedy, 2019) found that just over 13 percent of individuals charged with federal counterfeiting offenses were owners or co-owners of a legitimate business that was used to facilitate the counterfeiting scheme. Furthermore, this research found that the most common crimes to co-occur with product counterfeiting offenses were white-collar crimes and occupational offenses such as money laundering, tax evasion, and fraud. All of the businesses involved in these crimes were small businesses, yet the offenses were most likely to be captured in the official record as personal offenses rather than organizational offenses.

In conclusion, many of the same criticisms raised about criminal data on individual white-collar offenders are equally relevant for organizational crime data. A recent report contracted by the Bureau of Justice Statistics to explore the feasibility of building a federal data series on white-collar crime revealed extensive challenges associated with such an immense task (Simpson and Yeager, 2015). As mentioned previously, the vast majority of corporate violations are processed and sanctioned through either administrative or civil legal processes, not the criminal justice system. Thus, information from all three primary sources would need to be integrated in order to capture the totality of offending and the extent of the federal response to it. However, even if the data could be collectively extracted, the unit of measure (case or defendant) and when/what type of information is captured within each agency varies considerably. And, we know too little about the funneling process (that is to say, which cases enter into the system and how they move within and between systems) to have a good understanding of data deficiencies and bias. Thus, it is important to recognize that any system that seeks to measure corporate offenders is likely to be incomplete.

Does It Make Sense to Think of Corporations as Offenders?

A corporation is a group of people authorized by a government to act as a unit, and as far as the law is concerned, a corporation is considered to be "a person", one that can be held legally accountable for its actions. But for criminologists, the idea of treating corporations as though they are criminal actors raises tricky ontological questions. Donald Cressey (1989) argues against treating corporations as criminal actors for the purposes of criminological theory and research. Cressey recognizes that as far as the law is concerned, corporations are treated as fictitious persons, but in his view, criminological analysis is different than legal analysis. Criminology should focus on real people, not on legal fictions. Corporations do not act, people do. Treating a corporation as if it was a person is misplaced anthropomorphism, and trying to explain corporate as opposed to individual behavior leads to conceptual confusion. Thus, according to Cressey, the distinction between corporate and occupational crime is unnecessary. Other scholars disagree. They contend that corporations do act and that corporate actions are more than the sum of the acts of individual organizational members. John Braithwaite and Brent Fisse (1990) provide an illustration. They note that in a corporation, each member of a board of directors can vote to declare a dividend, but only the board as a collectivity has the power to actually declare a dividend. The collective action of the board is qualitatively different from the actions of the individuals who make up the board. In addition, the board's collective decision may result from processes such as "groupthink" or the group risky shift phenomenon that do not apply when individuals make decisions in isolation from one another. Hence, for Braithwaite and Fisse, it makes sense to treat corporations as distinct objects of explanation.

Regardless which side of this philosophical debate is correct, a large body of research has focused on exploring the characteristics of organizations and industries that are related to corporate crime (for examples, see Clinard and Yeager, 2006; Ermann and Lundman, 1978; Gross, 1978, 1980; Simpson, 1986, 2002; Simpson, Garner, and Gibbs, 2007). We discuss this research in more detail in later chapters, but for now we note it is important to keep in mind that many white-collar crimes have an organizational dimension and cannot be reduced to individual-level propensities or characteristics. To understand why these offenses occur and how they can be prevented, we must recognize the dynamics of organizational behavior and develop theories that integrate and combine both individual and organizational levels of analysis (Vaughan, 2007). So, the term "white-collar offender" should be used with caution because at times it may make more sense to focus or organizations rather than individual wrongdoers.

Summary

The main objective of this chapter has been to describe what is known about the people and organizations who commit white-collar type offenses. Large empirical studies of offenders agree that the people who are convicted of white-collar types of crimes in the federal judicial system are not like the people who are convicted there of ordinary street crimes (Benson and Kerley, 2000; Weisburd et al., 1991). Those convicted of white-collar types of offenses come from a different social and demographic background than common offenders. Compared with common street-crime offenders, white-collar offenders are older, more likely to be male, and more likely to be white. They also are more likely to be married, to own their own homes, to be financially secure, and to be employed at the time of their offenses. Although data from the U.S. Sentencing Commission suggests that the social and demographic profile of white-collar offenders has changed since the 1970s, the people who commit white-collar crimes today also do not "look" like ordinary street offenders. These findings should not come as a major surprise to anyone. But it is surprising how many of the white-collar offenders in these studies do not appear to conform to Sutherland's definition of the white-collar offender as a person of respectability and high social status. As David Weisburd and his colleagues (1991) put it, these are primarily middle-class offenders. However, this picture of the white-collar offender is necessarily limited by the data on which it is based. Samples drawn from the federal judicial system miss all of those offenders who for whatever reason avoid being drawn into the system in the first place. It seems likely that if anyone is going to avoid the system, it will be Sutherland's type of high-social-status offender.

Finally, unlike ordinary street crime, white-collar crime often has an organizational dimension, that is, it is situated in an organizational context and involves people who are engaged in organizational roles or activities. Thus, both individuals and organizations can be thought of as white-collar offenders.

Notes

1 The crime of postal forgery may seem similar to white-collar crime in that it would appear to involve deception. However, most of the time, postal forgery is simply straightforward theft. Typically, the offender steals a government-issued check for a welfare or social security benefit from a mailbox and is caught when trying to cash the check by forging the recipient's endorsement. Whether the offender is charged with postal theft or postal forgery depends mainly on whether he or she is caught at the time of the theft or when trying to pass the check (Weisburd et al., 1991, p. 17).

2 The districts were New Jersey, Eastern New York, Connecticut, Northern Ohio, Middle Florida, Western Oklahoma, Northern New Mexico, and Northern California.

3 Arlen (2012, p. 325) shows that larger companies, where offenses are significantly less apt to be discovered by the government, have little to gain and much to lose by self-reporting. Further, deferred prosecution agreements—an increasingly common tool utilized by the Department of Justice for "dealing with large corporations that employ thousands and have a significant influence on the health of industries and the markets" (Bukh, 2012, p. 1) as long as firms admit wrongdoing, cooperate with an investigation, pay a fine, and improve internal compliance—reinforce the argument that the USSC data are biased toward smaller and likely less powerful firms.

Part II

Criminological Theory and the Opportunity Perspective

Most criminologists would be both delighted and astonished if their subject matter—crime—could be predicted and explained by one all-encompassing general theory. But whenever a theory is put forth that claims to be *the* general theory of crime, one of the first questions asked is "What about white-collar crime?" Indeed, sometimes this question is raised first and then answered by the general theorists themselves as a way of mounting a pre-emptive strike against the attack (see Hirschi and Gottfredson, 1987a, 1987b). The reason why white-collar crime is always raised as a counterfactual to self-styled general theories of crime is obvious. Neither white-collar offenses nor white-collar offenders fit common stereotypes of crime and criminals. Hence, it is reasonable to ask whether a theory of apples can also be a theory of oranges.

A number of attempts have been made by theorists to bring white-collar crime under the umbrella of mainstream criminological theory, and we review them in Chapter 3. Next, in Chapter 4, we focus on the psychology of white-collar crime and the role that psychopathy may play in these offenses. While there are important differences among the traditional theoretical and psychological approaches to white-collar crime, they all share one thing in common. They all focus on offenders and attempt to explicate the factors that cause offenders to do what they do. In essence, they are theories of criminality rather than theories of crime. But crime and criminality are not the same thing (Gottfredson and Hirschi, 1990). They are conceptually distinct. A crime is an event, something that happens at a particular time and place. Criminality, on the other hand, is a characteristic of a person or an organization. It refers to the likelihood that a person or entity will participate in a criminal act. Most criminological theories focus on criminality, but it is possible to think theoretically about crimes themselves as objects of study separate from criminals, which is what we do in Chapter 5, where we show how white-collar crimes differ from other types of crime and develop our opportunity perspective on white-collar crime.

DOI: 10.4324/9781003175322-4

Criminological Theory and the Opportunity Perspective

Explaining White-Collar Crime
Traditional and Modern Criminological Theories

One of Sutherland's professed goals in writing about white-collar crime was to reform criminological theory. In the 1930s, when Sutherland began working on what he would come to call white-collar crime, criminological theory was dominated by the view that crime was concentrated in the lower social classes and was caused by the personal and social pathologies that accompany poverty. Sutherland contended that this approach was wrong on two counts. First, it does "not even explain lower class criminality" (Sutherland, 1940, p. 10). As he correctly pointed out, many—indeed most—poverty-stricken people are not criminal. Therefore, poverty and the pathologies associated with it cannot be general or sufficient causes of criminal behavior. Second, theories that use data taken from the poverty-stricken classes are based on "a biased sample that omits almost entirely the behavior of white-collar criminals" (Sutherland, 1940, p. 9). Specifically, they ignore the many serious crimes committed by individuals in the upper social classes in the course of their occupations—in other words, white-collar crime. A truly adequate criminological theory should account for or explain crime in all its different forms (Sutherland, 1940). Accordingly, Sutherland proposed a theory of white-collar crime based on his famous differential association theory.

Sutherland has not been the only one to develop a theory of white-collar crime. Just as with conventional crime, many theoretical approaches have been tried in the search for a better understanding of this form of crime. The process of applying standard criminological theories to white-collar crime often involves what have been called "conceptual acrobatics" (Simpson, 2013b). Concepts and ideas that were originally developed to apply to traditional forms of crime must be adjusted to account for the special features of white-collar crime and the distinguishing characteristics of white-collar offenders. Despite these conceptual challenges, variants of differential association, anomie, control, rational choice, integrated and developmental theories have been proposed to explain white-collar crime.

Yet, for a variety of reasons, none of these efforts have achieved widespread acceptance, and there is little consensus on how best to explain white-collar crime. The subject matter, as defined by Sutherland, is multifaceted. For instance, "in the course of one's occupation" is inclusive of diverse professions (e.g., physicians and plumbers), non-profit organizations such as churches, and businesses from Mom-and-Pop operations to multi-national corporations. Empirical work in this area is difficult to conduct. Researchers rarely have access to the funding for research that is available to those who study traditional forms of street crime. There are few solid facts to work with, and none of the various theories of white-collar crime have been subjected to extensive empirical scrutiny. In addition, some theories of white-collar crime are constructed in such a way that it is difficult to test them. For

DOI: 10.4324/9781003175322-5

example, some theories use variables that apply at different levels of analysis. Individual-, organizational-, structural-, and cultural-level variables may all be cited as necessary parts of the overall explanation of white-collar crime (Coleman, 1987). Though this kind of approach is comprehensive and provocative, it is also virtually untestable as it is nearly impossible to measure or control for all of the factors that are cited in the explanation. Thus, the empirical validity of the theories of white-collar crime remains limited. Because it is not clear which theoretical approach provides the best or the most promising explanation, we have opted to provide an overview of the various efforts that have been tried. Although criminologists have not made a great deal of progress in testing theories of white-collar crime, they have continued to pursue Sutherland's goal of reforming criminological theory. They have explored whether standard criminological theories can account for white-collar crime, so we describe these efforts below.

Differential Association

Sutherland theorized that the general processes that cause other sorts of crime also cause white-collar crime. He argued that individual involvement in white-collar crime comes about because of a process called *differential association*. The theory of differential association postulates that

> criminal behavior is learned in association with those who define such criminal behavior favorably and in isolation from those who define it unfavorably and that a person in an appropriate situation will engage in white-collar crime if, and only if, the "weight of definitions favorable exceeds the weight of the unfavorable definitions".
>
> (Sutherland, 1983, p. 240)

Sutherland thought that attitudes and cultural orientations that define illegal business behavior in favorable terms are pervasive throughout the business world. Newcomers to the world of business are socialized to accept these attitudes and orientations. They learn how to commit certain types of offenses and how to rationalize these offenses so that, in the offender's mind, they are seen as acceptable, ordinary, and necessary business practices. Thus, a white-collar criminal culture permeates the world of business and is passed from one generation of executives and employees to the next.

Sutherland had many examples of how young people new to the world of business were socialized into the self-serving morality of the marketplace by their bosses. For example, the manager of a shoe store explained the rules of the game to a new employee this way (Sutherland, 1983, p. 243):

> My job is to move out shoes and I hire you to assist in this. I am perfectly glad to fit a person with a pair of shoes if we have his size, but I am willing to misfit him if it is necessary in order to sell him a pair of shoes. I expect you to do the same. If you do not like this, someone else can have your job. While you are working for me, I expect you to have no scruples about how you sell shoes.

Retail sales may be a cut-throat business, but it is not the only profession in which duplicity prevails. Consider another example from Sutherland (1983, pp. 244–245) regarding a certified public accountant who worked for a respected firm of public accountants. After the accountant had been on the job for several years, he had this to say about the morality of his profession (Sutherland, 1983, p. 244):

> While I was a student in the school of business I learned the principles of accounting. After I had worked for a time for an accounting firm I found that I had failed to learn many important things about accounting. An accounting firm gets its work from business firms and, within limits, must make the reports which those business firms desire. The accounting firm for which I work is respected and there is none better in the city. On my first assignment I discovered some irregularities in the books of the firm and these would lead anyone to question the financial policies of that firm. When I showed my report to the manager of our accounting firm, he said that was not a part of my assignment and I should leave it out. Although I was confident that the business firm was dishonest, I had to conceal this information. Again and again I have been compelled to do the same thing in other assignments. I get so disgusted with things of this sort that I wish I could leave the profession. I guess I must stick to it, for it is the only occupation for which I have training.

The attitudes and practices that Sutherland found during his research have persisted. For example, the owner of a public construction firm who was convicted of antitrust violations for bid rigging had this to say about how that practice was viewed in his industry:

> It was a way of doing business before we ever got into the business. So, it was like why do you brush your teeth in the morning or something. ... It was part of the everyday. ... It was a method of survival.
>
> (Benson, 1985, p. 591)

What this suggests is that Sutherland was right. The culture of business does not always promote morality or obedience to the law. Rather, it provides definitions of the world that are favorable to violation of law to those who come in contact with it (Hochstetler and Copes, 2001).

But the mere presence of definitions favorable to the violation of law is not enough by itself to cause white-collar crime. Definitions favorable to violation of the law must be of sufficient magnitude or "weight" so as to overwhelm competing definitions unfavorable to violations of law. According to Sutherland, in the world of business, this condition is satisfied because of isolation and social disorganization. Members of the business community are isolated from definitions unfavorable to their law violations because the government, entertainment industry, and news media have traditionally equated crime with the lower socioeconomic classes. Hence, businesspersons rarely are confronted with unfavorable definitions of their behavior, and they are unlikely to experience criminal labeling.

The ability of businesspersons to avoid unfavorable definitions of their behavior is enhanced because society is socially disorganized in regard to white-collar crime. Sutherland identified two types of social disorganization: *anomie* refers to a lack of standards regarding behavior in specific areas of social action; *conflict of standards* refers to conflict between social groups with reference to specific practices. Sutherland thought that anomie regarding harmful and illegal business practices was widespread for two reasons. First, business behavior is complex, technical, and difficult to observe. Second, because America was founded on the ideals of competition and free enterprise, the public is ambivalent about government control of business activity. Taken together, these factors impede the development of a strong public consensus on the wrongfulness and harmfulness of shady business practices. Lacking clear signals of concern from the public, law enforcers are not vigorous in their pursuit of business misconduct.

Also mitigating against control of business misconduct is an enduring conflict of standards between the business community and other interests in society. Sutherland thought the business community was tightly organized against regulatory control of business practices. Businesses vigorously contest any effort by government, consumer groups, labor unions, and environmental organizations to expand regulatory controls and to criminalize harmful business practices. The continual conflict between the business community and those who would control it weakens public outrage over business misconduct. The idea that regulations are "bad for business and the economy" has been a catchphrase for business leaders and their defenders throughout American history.

Anomie/Strain Theory

The concept of anomie has a long history in sociology and criminology. The famous French sociologist, Emile Durkheim, argued it was an important factor in suicide. For Durkheim (1951), *anomie* referred to a breakdown or lack of regulation in society that left individuals with a sense of normlessness and bereft of moral guidance. With respect to criminology, anomie theory was originally developed by Robert Merton. For Merton (1938), *anomie* referred not only to a sense of normlessness but to a distinctive feature of American society—its strong cultural emphasis on the desirability of material success and individual achievement. These goals are promoted as worthwhile, indeed, essential objectives that everyone should pursue. They are the foundational pillars of the American Dream (Messner and Rosenfeld, 2013). However, access to legitimate opportunities to achieve these goals is not equally available to everyone, and American culture says little about how these objectives should be achieved. Taken together, the emphasis placed on individual material success coupled with limited access to opportunities and limited attention on legitimate means of achievement creates societal strain—conditions that promote criminal behavior. People are expected to pursue material goals, but goal-seeking behavior is not well regulated or channeled. Hence, people who cannot achieve their goals via legitimate means look for other ways to get ahead and sometimes resort to criminal means. Merton used his version of anomie to explain why some societies have higher crime rates than others and why crime is concentrated in the lower social classes (Merton, 1938).

Merton's theory has sometimes been criticized as being class biased because as it was originally formulated, it ignored the crimes of the rich and powerful. But even Merton (1964) acknowledged that anomie and strain could be features of upper-class life with his observation that "less often than one might believe is there room for repose at the top" (p. 221). Just as anomie and strain may promote ordinary street crime, they may also incite white-collar and corporate crime (Messner and Rosenfeld, 2013; Vaughan, 1983).

Although business corporations can have multiple goals, in capitalist economies the dominant goal is always profit maximization (Vaughan, 1983). Corporations compete with one another to maximize profits in a game that is never-ending. There is no obvious stopping point at which enough is enough. Weak competitors may fall by the wayside, but new ones emerge to take their place. So, even companies that are leaders in their industries must always worry about potential competition. Hence, because of the competitive structure of capitalist economies, corporations are continually under pressure to do better.

Coupled with the cultural themes of success and ceaseless competition are uncertainty and confusion about where the line between acceptable and unacceptable business behavior should be drawn. In this anomic environment, there is constant pressure to engage in corporate deviance to achieve profit goals, and corporations often succumb to this pressure. The American Dream has a very pronounced downside (Messner and Rosenfeld, 2013).

Edward Gross takes a similar view of corporate deviance, but he focuses more on the culture and structure of organizations than on those of society as a whole (Gross, 1978). Gross argues that organizations are inherently criminogenic, because they are goal-directed entities, and their performance is evaluated according to their effectiveness in achieving their goals. Hence, they are continually under pressure to achieve. Further, organizations always confront competition and uncertainty in working toward their goals. The emphasis on performance combined with competition and uncertainty creates pressure to break rules and to achieve goals at all costs.

Gross hypothesizes that variation in organizational crime results from several sources. First, the degree of accountability of an organization or an organizational subunit is directly related to the likelihood of rule breaking. Organizations that are held accountable to specific criteria by which success in goal attainment can be judged are under more pressure to perform than organizations whose success in goal attainment is not as strictly judged. For example, it is easier to judge whether a private corporation is making a profit than whether a charitable organization is achieving its altruistic goals.

Second, pressure to engage in organizational crime is directly related to the objectivity of performance measures. Business corporations can be judged and compared against one another in terms of their profitability, and their relative level of profitability can be easily determined by others. For example, one very simple and objective measure of the relative success of a corporation is its "earnings per share". As the term implies, earnings per share can be roughly defined as the total earnings that a company has in a particular reporting period divided by the total number of shares outstanding in the company. If a company earned a million dollars and there were ten million shares outstanding, then the company would have earned ten cents per share. In general, the higher a company's earnings per share, the better it is doing for shareholders. So, this number is important to investors and Wall Street analysts. Not surprisingly, companies try very hard to reach their expected earnings per share numbers. Failure to generate significant earnings per share may cause investors to move their money elsewhere, which from the perspective of the company is not good. Companies that fail to profit are subject to failure, their survival depends on it. Thus, company executives are under a great deal of pressure to do whatever is necessary, including using fraudulent accounting practices to meet Wall Street's expectations regarding earnings per share.

In contrast to for-profit corporations, many other types of organizations, such as hospitals, universities, and government bureaucracies, are not subject to such a brutally simple and objective measure of their success. Like all organizations, they are goal driven, but it is more difficult to tell exactly how well they are doing relative to their goals and to one another. Hence, we expect the leaders of these organizations to be less pressured to break the law to achieve organizational goals.

Third, within corporations, the more a subunit interacts with the organizational environment, the more likely it is to deviate to achieve goals because of the uncertainty generated by the environment. The environment of an organization includes competitors, suppliers, government regulators, and customers. Thus, among manufacturers, we should expect to find more illegal or fraudulent activity in sales departments than in engineering departments. People in sales must interact regularly with competitors, suppliers, customers, and regulators. These environmental entities are a source of uncertainty. They can impede goal attainment and must, therefore, be managed. Engineers, on the other hand, are relatively isolated from environmental contingencies and hence have less need to resort to fraudulent or criminal means to reduce environmental uncertainty.

Fourth and finally, pressure to engage in organizational crime is inversely related to the availability of goal displacement. If an organization that is threatened by lack of success in achieving its manifest goals can shift to other more attainable goals, then the pressure to deviate is lessened. The ability to displace goals is probably less available to private for-profit corporations than it is to non-profit and governmental organizations. Consider, for example, a university that promotes itself as being one of the fastest growing and most popular universities in a region, but then for some reason enrolments decline. The university leaders could acknowledge that they are failing to meet their enrolment goals, but it is more likely that they will start to proclaim new goals, such as a higher graduation rate or success in job placements for graduates. In other words, universities can switch goals according to changing conditions. This sort of goal displacement is more difficult if not impossible for profit-making business organizations. They either must make money or go out of business. The option of just doing something else is not open to them.

Altogether, accountability, objectivity of performance measures, environmental uncertainty, and flexibility in goal displacement influence the degree of pressure that organizations are under to deviate. This pressure may rise and fall over time, but it never disappears entirely. It is always there, always demanding that organizations surpass their performance goals.

Self-Control Theory

By far the most commonly assessed and evaluated control theory in criminology is self-control. In the late 1980s and early 1990s, Travis Hirschi and Michael Gottfredson developed self-control theory (Hirschi and Gottfredson, 1987a, 1987b; Gottfredson and Hirschi, 1990). The basic premise of self-control theory is that crime and other forms of deviance result from the combination of low self-control and criminal opportunities. Low self-control is conceived to be a behavioral predisposition that inclines individuals to pursue their short-term self-interest with little regard for the long-term consequences of their actions or for the rights and feelings of other people. One's level of self-control is assumed to be established early in life and to remain relatively constant thereafter. Persons with low self-control are more likely to take advantage of criminal opportunities and, because they lack self-control, they are also more apt to engage in other risky (analogous) behaviors than persons with higher levels of self-control.

Hirschi and Gottfredson argue that self-control theory is a general theory of crime and that it applies to white-collar crime. Indeed, they argue that the pursuit of special theories of white-collar crime is misguided. Based on their theory of self-control, they contend that white-collar crime should be relatively rare compared with street crimes because persons with low self-control are unlikely to have white-collar occupations. Hence, people with low self-control have limited opportunities to commit white-collar offenses. Conversely, people who succeed in white-collar occupations have high levels of self-control and hence are not likely to take advantage of the criminal opportunities that their occupations provide them. The few white-collar persons who do engage in white-collar crime are assumed to have less self-control than their similarly situated counterparts, though they may have more self-control than ordinary street criminals.

The ideas that white-collar crime is rare and that it can be explained by the same control-based factors as other crimes have been vigorously contested by many white-collar crime scholars (Benson and Moore, 1992; Geis, 1996; Reed and Yeager, 1996; Steffensmeier, 1989; Yeager and Reed, 1998; Simpson and Piquero, 2002). There are three problems with self-control theory as applied to white-collar crime: (1) it underestimates the extent of white-collar law-breaking; (2) it misinterprets how self-control may work in business settings, and; (3) it misconstrues the nature of white-collar criminal opportunities.

First, whether white-collar crime is rare is debatable for both empirical and theoretical reasons. Sutherland himself documented extensive lawbreaking among America's leading corporations. Decades after Sutherland's pioneering work, Clinard and Yeager (1980) also found evidence of widespread lawbreaking in corporate America. As the past decade has demonstrated, scandals involving business organizations, both big and small, continue to be uncovered. For example, the past decade witnessed General Motors' cover-up of its faulty ignition switch (Ivory, 2014), the Volkswagen clean diesel scandal (Smith and Parloff, 2016), and widespread fraud at Wells Fargo Bank (Krantz, 2016). In short, lawbreaking among even the largest of corporations does not appear to be uncommon. As another indicator of the extent of corporate deviance, consider the spate of corporate earnings restatements that occurred in the late 1990s and early 2000s. Restatements soared after the exposure and criminal prosecution of the executives involved in accounting fraud at Enron, WorldCom, and a host of other major corporations (Lev, 2003). According to a report by the U.S. General Accounting Office (GAO) between January 1997 and June 2002, the annual rate of earnings restatements grew by 145 percent. During this five-year period, about 10 percent of the companies listed on the NYSX, AMEX, and NASDAQ stock exchanges filed earnings restatements because of accounting irregularities (U.S. General Accounting Office, 2002). While the GAO does not directly say that all of these restatements involved criminal activity, the strong implication from the report is that a notable proportion of the leaders of corporate America are not above deceiving investors—at least until they think they might get caught. If we consider that accounting fraud is only one type of white-collar offense that companies can engage in, then the figure of 10 percent becomes even more notable.

Other research suggests that the GAO may not be far off in estimating that one out of ten corporations engaged in accounting fraud between 1997 and 2002. Economists Dyck, Morse, and Zingales (2013) took advantage of the natural experiment that arose after the collapse of Arthur Andersen in 2002. Arthur Andersen was a large accounting firm that handled the auditing for Enron and was convicted of accounting fraud for its role in Enron's schemes. As one of the big five accounting firms in the world, Andersen had many large corporate clients. When Andersen collapsed, these companies had to find new auditors. Dyck, Morse, and Zingales theorized that the new auditors would be especially vigilant looking for corporate fraud and would want to clean house to avoid the fate that befell Arthur Andersen. Using sophisticated statistical techniques that looked at the rate of fraud detection both before and after the new auditors took over, the researchers estimate that the "probability of a company engaging in fraud in any given year is 13.8%" (Dyck, Morse, and Zingales, 2013, p. 1). Again, as with the GAO, this estimate of the pervasiveness of corporate fraud and wrongdoing applies only to accounting fraud. There is no telling how high the percentage would rise if we could somehow count all of the various offenses available to corporations. Clearly, however, it would not be in the range that we would ordinarily call *rare*.

In addition, there are theoretical reasons for believing that as extensive as the empirical record is, it may nevertheless greatly understate the amount of white-collar lawbreaking. This is because there are fundamental differences between white-collar crime and other forms of crime that affect the rate of detection. We will develop this theme more fully in a later chapter, but we briefly introduce it here. When an ordinary street crime is committed, such as, for example, robbery, burglary, auto theft, or assault, it is obvious that an offense has occurred. The offender may not be known, but the fact that there has been an offense is plain to see. Some sort of physical evidence is present. However, many white-collar crimes are not obvious in this way. They leave no obvious physical evidence such as a missing car, broken window, or bloodied body. White-collar offenders use deception to commit their offenses. If they are successful, then the fact that an offense has occurred may never be known, not even by the victim. For example, think back to the doctor introduced in the first chapter. If the victim in this case simply accepts the doctor's recommendations regarding further tests, then who will ever discover that the doctor committed fraud by deliberately ordering tests that were medically unnecessary? The fundamental problem here is that for crimes that are non-self-revealing, it is very difficult, if not impossible, ever to figure out the true number of offenses.

A second problem with self-control theory involves the concept of self-control. The theory assumes that self-control is always exercised for conforming or socially accepted ends. In other words, the theory assumes that people with high self-control always do the right thing. Yet, there is no logical reason why self-control and the abilities associated with it (intelligence, foresight, and persistence) could not be used to plan and execute a complicated criminal scheme, especially if the potential take was large and the potential risk of discovery small (Tittle, 1991). It seems perhaps a bit Pollyannaish to assume that people who have self-discipline are always nice people. Indeed, empirical tests of the theory as applied to potential white-collar offenders reveal that a substantial percentage of managers and managers in training are willing to commit offenses under the right set of circumstances (Simpson and Piquero, 2002).

Third, and finally, there is a problem with how criminal opportunities are conceptualized in the theory. Criminal opportunities are conceived as simple obvious things, such as an unguarded purse or an unlocked car that has the keys in it. The basic idea is that criminal opportunities arise whenever a criminally inclined person has access to some sort of object that he or she would like to have. In technical terms, a criminal opportunity consists of a suitable target and a lack of capable guardianship (Cohen and Felson, 1979). In self-control theory, it is assumed that targets such as the purse or the car are intrinsically attractive or desirable, and the only thing holding us back from trying to get them is our level of self-control. But is this really true? We would suggest that the attractiveness of a target depends at least in part on the potential offender's situation (i.e., on factors in his or her life that are independent of his or her level of self-control). Recognizing this feature of criminal opportunities is particularly important for white-collar crime, because situational factors can be important sources of motivation for white-collar crime. For example, would the executives at Enron have bothered to run the risk of accounting fraud if the company really was making a lot of money?

Additionally, research suggests there is a motivational route to crime that may be unique to white-collar offenders (Benson and Kerley, 2000; Benson and Moore, 1992; Weisburd and Waring, 2001; Wheeler, 1992). White-collar crime may result not only from the drive for material success but out of fear of losing what one already has. Some individuals may become involved in white-collar offenses because they fear that if they do not, they are at risk of losing their station in life. For people accustomed to the material comforts of a middle-class lifestyle, the prospect of losing it all because of a downturn in the economy or a miscalculation in a business transaction may create strong pressure to deviate to avoid a fall from grace. For example, consider a small business owner who is quite willing to abide by the law in return for a comfortable but not extravagant standard of living. However, if the business is threatened by competition or a downturn in the economy, the same individual may feel that the only option is to break the law in order to survive.

Thus, fear of failure may impel individuals to engage in white-collar crime. Indeed, the fear of failure may be a unique motivational cause of white-collar crime, because unlike many street offenders, white-collar offenders often have something to lose. It is not clear how self-control would influence potential offenders under these conditions.

Rational Choice Theory

Another theoretical perspective that has been applied to white-collar crime is rational choice theory (Paternoster and Simpson, 1993; Shover and Hochstetler, 2006). Rational choice theory assumes that all actors are self-interested and make decisions about whether to engage in criminal or conventional behavior according to an assessment of the costs and benefits associated with each line of behavior. In simplified terms, the theory posits that rational actors will choose to engage in crime rather than non-crime when the perceived net benefits of crime are larger than the perceived net benefits of non-crime (where net-benefits = benefits − costs). By non-crime, we mean the other things that a person could do, such as, for example, going to school, working at a job, or volunteering in a community. Both crime and non-crime have benefits and costs and these costs have subjective and objective dimensions. Sticking just with crime, for example, a subjective cost of crime might be feeling guilty or fearing apprehension, while a subjective benefit of crime would be the thrill and excitement of getting away with something illegal. An objective cost of crime would be formal punishment by the criminal justice system, while an objective benefit would be the gains made from the illegal act.

Paternoster and Simpson (1993) have explicated a rational choice theory of the decision to commit corporate crime. They call their approach a *subjective utility theory of offending*. It focuses on individual and organizational benefits and costs as they are subjectively perceived by individuals. Hence, their rational choice theory is aimed at individual decision makers rather than the corporation as a whole even though the corporate situation and context is considered part of the individual's calculus. According to their theory, the individual's decision to commit a corporate crime or violate a regulatory rule involves a series of factors. To calculate the potential costs of corporate crime, actors subjectively estimate the certainty and severity of formal legal sanctions, the certainty and severity of informal sanctions (for example, discovery and subsequent rejection by family members or business associates), and the certainty and importance of loss of self-respect. Actors also consider the benefits of corporate crime, which include the perceived benefits of noncompliance (i.e., higher profits, greater market share, or some other organizationally relevant goal) and the perceived cost of rule compliance (i.e., expenses that follow from complying with regulatory standards). Paternoster and Simpson argue that in addition to these standard rational choice variables, the strength of the actor's moral beliefs, whether he or she perceives rule enforcers as legitimate and fair, the characteristics of the potential criminal event, and prior offending by the person also influence the likelihood of offending.

Another attempt at applying the choice perspective to white-collar crime has been made by Neal Shover and Andrew Hochstetler (2006). The theory developed by Shover and Hochstetler, however, focuses less on the individual decision maker and more on the economic and political conditions that influence opportunities for white-collar and corporate crime. They argue that in order to understand why white-collar crime flourishes, we need to pay attention to the supply of "lure" and the lack of "credible oversight".

The concept of "lure" is not formally defined by Shover and Hochstetler. They describe it simply as "arrangements or situations that turn heads" (Shover and Hochstetler, 2006, p. 27) and note that it is not the same as "criminal opportunity" (p. 68). However, their discussion of lure suggests that it should be thought of as any situation in which people can enrich themselves by (1) gaining privileged and unjustified access to financial resources, or (2) gaining access to some means by which to enhance their own financial interests through the exploitation of others.

As an example of the first form of lure, consider federal health care programs, such as Medicare and Medicaid. These programs handle literally billions of dollars, dollars that can be powerfully alluring to people. By virtue of their positions in the health care industry, physicians and many others associated with the health care system have opportunities to obtain money through fraud. In short, because of the tremendous amounts of money spent on health care via these government programs, they lure or attract criminal entrepreneurs.

The second type of lure can be illustrated by the corporate exploitation of illegal immigrants who come to America in search of a better life. Because undocumented immigrants cannot go to authorities to file complaints on horrendously unsafe working conditions or scandalously low pay, they can be very attractive as employees in some industries. Employers can exploit them with little fear of legal consequences.

As another example of lure, consider the opportunities to make an easy dollar that arise after natural disasters, such as hurricanes, tornados, wildfires, and recently the COVID-19 pandemic. In their efforts to help those who are afflicted, government agencies and non-governmental organizations often pour millions of dollars into disaster relief programs. Because of the urgency of the need, these programs focus on getting help to people quickly without asking a lot of questions or checking carefully into the legitimacy of relief claims. For the unscrupulous, this is an ideal situation. Money is being handed out with few questions asked. Disaster relief fraud is now a well-known and perennial form of white-collar crime (National White-Collar Crime Center, 2009). Indeed, since it was established in 2005, the U.S. National Center for Disaster Fraud (2021) has received over 220,000 complaints of fraud, and as we will discuss in a later chapter, this is exactly what happened during the recent COVID-19 pandemic.

According to Shover and Hochstetler (2006, p. 76), "Lure becomes criminal opportunity in the absence of credible oversight". Oversight refers to the attention that others (such as customers, law enforcement officials, or regulators) pay to a person's or an organization's activity and to the ability of those others to impose some sort of negative consequence when they observe misconduct. Oversight can be generated either by private sources or through the state. Private oversight arises through such mechanisms as civil lawsuits or whistle-blowers. Customers, for example, can file class action lawsuits against companies. The threat of a lawsuit serves as a check on the misbehavior of private enterprises. Similarly, whistle-blowers can expose illegal or unethical conduct and bring unwanted attention to corporate wrongdoers. In addition, larger companies whose stocks are traded on a public stock exchange or via the over-the-counter-market are subject to another form of private oversight through their legal obligation to be audited by an external auditor. In theory, the external audit serves as a check on the truthfulness of a company's financial reports. Although private oversight can play an important role in the control of white-collar crime and in the calculus of white-collar offenders, it has limitations and is by no means perfect. Hence, in modern industrial and post-industrial societies, the state is called upon to provide additional oversight. State oversight occurs through criminalization, lawsuits brought by the government, and regulation. As we discuss more fully in Chapter 9, the state attempts to assert oversight and control over white-collar crime by criminalizing, regulating, or filing civil lawsuits over activities that it deems harmful, but it does so with only limited and often only temporary success.

Taken together, both private and state oversight expose potential white-collar offenders to the possibility that their illegal activities will come to light and be sanctioned. According to the rational choice perspective, if this possibility is perceived by potential offenders to be low, then the credibility of oversight is low and the choice to engage in white-collar crime becomes correspondingly more attractive. Like many white-collar crime scholars, Shover and Hochstetler (2006) argue that there is a lack of credible oversight in the United States and indeed throughout the modern world, creating conditions in which white-collar crime can flourish.

Of the theories presented here, rational choice, or simply "choice theory", as it is sometimes called, is the one most compatible with our opportunity perspective. It explicitly recognizes opportunity as an important cause and necessary ingredient of crime. It suggests that in order to understand patterns in white-collar crime, we need to pay attention to how changes in the organization and functioning of the legitimate business world can affect opportunities for white-collar crime (Shover and Hochstetler, 2006). Indeed, in some ways the future of white-collar crime looks quite bright, as new opportunities for fraud have emerged over the past few decades because of the expansion of government programs, the revolution in financial services, the growth of communications technology, and the rise of the global economy (Shover and Hochstetler, 2006).

Integrated Theory

All of the theories reviewed above seem to have at least some plausibility, but they also seem to be like the proverbial three blind men describing an elephant. They each contain only part of the truth regarding the causes of crime. Hence, criminologists have begun to explore ways to integrate standard criminological theories, such as differential association, anomie/strain, and control theories, in hopes of providing more comprehensive explanations of street crime. John Braithwaite (1989) has extended this line of thought to white-collar and organizational crime. He argues that to understand organizational crime, we need to integrate the insights of strain, labeling, subculture, and control theories. From strain theory, he draws the premise that failure to achieve highly valued goals, such as material success, creates pressure or strain to deviate. To relieve strain, corporate actors may resort to crime as an alternate means of achieving success. Whether actors do resort to crime depends in part on the availability of illegitimate means for achieving the blocked goal. Illegitimate means are made available through deviant subcultures. Business subcultures can transmit knowledge of how organizations and their leaders may successfully violate the law. In addition, deviant subcultures may attempt to force members to conform to the subculture's values and expectations. Taken together, strain, the availability of subcultural values that endorse illegitimate means, and enforced conformity to those values foster corporate crime.

Opposition to these criminogenic forces comes from social controls within the organization and from shaming imposed on offenders by the larger society. Drawing from control theory, Braithwaite argues that corporations can reduce the likelihood that their members will violate the law by strengthening internal controls against illegal behavior. This can be accomplished when organizational leaders promote pro-social values, socialize all corporate members to these values, and create strong internal control units to monitor corporate compliance with the law.

Braithwaite introduces the idea of differential shaming to explain how shaming by society may either promote or retard corporate crime. Shaming, which in the case of business corporations is carried out primarily by regulatory agencies, may be either stigmatizing or reintegrative. When illegal actors are stigmatized, they are treated as outcasts, and their involvement in deviance is treated as an indication of a true deviant inner character. Reintegrative shaming, on the other hand, is focused on the wrongfulness of the deed rather than the character of the actor. Those who administer reintegrative shaming attempt to maintain bonds of respect with the offender, and they try to reintegrate the offender back into the social whole after shaming is terminated. Braithwaite argues that stigmatizing shaming tends to create resistance to change in actors and to push them ever more deeply into their deviant subculture. Hence, stigmatizing shaming is counterproductive. It actually promotes rather than deters corporate crime. Reintegrative shaming deters offender recidivism because it clearly announces the wrongfulness of the act but then attempts to make the actor feel like a respected member of society, a member who has a vested interest in conforming to society's rules.

Another integrated theory has been proposed by Coleman who argues that white-collar crime results from "a coincidence of appropriate motivation and opportunity" (Coleman, 1987, p. 408). Motivation refers to symbolic constructions that define certain goals and activities as desirable. In the case of white-collar crime, it is especially important that the offender be able to define his or her behavior so that it is socially acceptable. Hence, white-collar offenders use neutralizations and rationalizations to justify or excuse behavior that is illegal. For example, business executives will complain that laws and regulations are unfair or unnecessary and that they interfere too much in the operation of the free market. Breaking a law that is unfair, unnecessary, and counterproductive is more acceptable than violating a standard that everyone agrees is just and necessary for society's survival. According to Coleman (1987, p. 406), the neutralizations that offenders use to justify their crimes are rooted in what he calls "the culture of competition".

The culture of competition refers to a complex of beliefs common in capitalistic societies that hold that the pursuit of wealth and success are the central goals of human endeavor. The idea here is that striving to make a profit, to get ahead, to be successful, and to be the best is the most appropriate and meaningful approach to life. As autonomous individuals, we are each responsible for our own success, and it is appropriate to try to get ahead by whatever means are available. In other words, chasing the American Dream is what we are supposed to do, and our success in doing so is a measure of our intrinsic worth as human beings (Messner and Rosenfeld, 2013). In Coleman's view, then, the culture of competition provides a source of rationalizations and neutralizations that white-collar offenders use as motivations for illegal behavior.

The other pillar in Coleman's theoretical framework is opportunity. An opportunity is a potential course of action that is made available by a particular set of social conditions and that the actor recognizes as being available to him or her. Opportunities vary in their attractiveness according to four factors: (1) the size of the gain to be obtained by the illegal act, (2) the risk of detection and punishment, (3) the compatibility of the act with the offender's own beliefs and values, and (4) the availability of other opportunities. In short, a white-collar crime opportunity will be considered attractive from the offender's point of view when it promises a worthwhile gain, involves little chance of being caught, does not violate the offender's own personal standards of behavior, and appears more likely to accomplish the offender's objectives than any other course of action.

Exactly how white-collar crime opportunities are distributed is difficult to say with certainty. Coleman identifies four factors that influence the distribution of opportunity: law and enforcement, industries, organizations, and occupations. The law obviously determines what is illegal and the level of resources allocated to enforcing the law determines the relative risk of detection and punishment.

A second factor that shapes opportunities is the structure of an industry. For example, antitrust violations should be more common in industries that are heavily concentrated than in industries where there are many small producers. It is harder to organize and control a conspiracy involving many participants than one involving only a few. The research, however, on market structure and the prevalence of antitrust violations is mixed (Coleman, 1987, p. 428).

Finally, occupations present different types of opportunities. For example, attorneys, physicians, financial advisers, and other independent professionals all have opportunities to take advantage of their clients that are built into their professions. The work of professionals often occurs without the direct supervision of the client (Shapiro, 1990). This situation gives unethical professionals the freedom to pursue their own interests at the expense of their clients. Occupational opportunities also vary according to one's position or status in an organization. For example, consider bribery of government officials. Many people work for the government, but most do not work in positions where they are likely to be offered bribes or be able to solicit bribes. Whether a government worker is likely to be offered bribes depends on the economic value of the services that the person controls (Coleman, 1987, p. 433). People in high positions in government, such as Congressional Representatives, exert control over enormous sums of money in the form of valuable government contracts. Hence, it should not be surprising that they are lobbied and cajoled by corporations for preferential treatment and are regularly caught selling their services to the highest bidder (Rosoff, Pontell, and Tillman, 2013, pp. 427–435).

To summarize, Coleman's theory works on multiple levels—individual, occupational, organizational, industrial, societal, and cultural. White-collar crime occurs when actors with suitable motivations encounter attractive opportunities. Motivations for white-collar crime are rooted in the culture of competition and are disseminated via organizational and occupational subcultures. The attractiveness of opportunities depends on their monetary value as compared to other courses of action, level of risk, and compatibility with the potential offender's beliefs and values. Opportunities are distributed differently across industries, organizations, and occupations.

Race-based Theories

Race has long been situated as an important factor in criminological theories, with much controversy surrounding its impact as a direct or indirect predictor of offending. Most of this research has focused on the over-representation of black Americans in ordinary street crime. Scholars disagree on whether the over-representation of black Americans in crime is due to structural conditions and cultural factors or to more vigorous enforcement of the law against racial minorities.

Theories that attribute racial differences in crime solely to structural conditions fall into what is called the "racial invariance" camp. Racial invariance scholars (e.g., Sampson and Wilson, 1995; Sampson et al., 2018) argue that blacks and whites would offend at the same rates if their community, familial, and economic conditions were equal. In other words, the fact that offending differences exist reflects the very different ecological situations of white communities versus black communities. In contrast, scholars who oppose the racial invariance perspective argue that structural conditions only partially account for offending differences (e.g., Unnever et al., 2016)—instead

> ...the unique history of slavery, subjugation, and ongoing discrimination experienced by Blacks in America leads to deeply felt feelings of anger and hostility toward the White authoritarian power structure. As a result, Blacks are less likely to develop, or have a strong investment in, attitudes, beliefs, and behaviors espoused by traditional American society and may develop alternative subgroup norms.
>
> (Benson and Kennedy, 2018, p. 255)

This view is sometimes called the racial exceptionalism perspective.

Theories on racial differences in white-collar and corporate crime have been absent until very recently, although the racial/ethnic distribution of white-collar offenders has been a subject of debate since the 1980s. Hirschi and Gottfredson (1987a) and Wheeler et al. (1988a) investigated racial differences among white-collar offenders and found that the results depended on the data source and definition being used. Hirschi and Gottfredson, for example, found that blacks were overrepresented among embezzlement and fraud cases—similar to the disproportionality seen among traditional offenders—even after controlling for occupational opportunities. Wheeler et al., on the other hand, found that black white-collar offenders were overrepresented in crimes that do not require occupational access (e.g., false claims or lending and credit fraud) while white offenders were overrepresented among more complicated and higher-status crimes (e.g., antitrust and securities fraud).

A recent study examined federal sentencing data for the years 2000–2015. It assessed whether changes in occupational access for racial/ethnic minorities at the state level is correlated with changes in white-collar crime convictions among black, Latino, and Asian Americans. Benson et al. (2020) demonstrated that as Latino and Asian Americans increased their representation in white-collar jobs, their representation in low-level white-collar convictions also increased. However, minority movement into any job level (low-, medium-, or high-level white-collar jobs) did not influence differences in middle- or high-level crimes. In other words, whites still dominate in middle- and high-level white-collar crimes. The authors frame their research in terms of opportunity theories (see Wilcox and Cullen, 2018), arguing—similarly to "racial invariance" theorists—that white-collar offending by racial and ethnic minorities appears to be growing more like that of whites as their structural conditions (i.e., access to better occupational statuses) have improved.

A theory that focuses on "elite" white-collar and corporate offending takes an approach closer to "racial exceptionalism"—but focuses on whites rather than blacks and argues that cultural differences among elite whites create motivations/justifications for white-collar offending. Sohoni and Rorie (2019) argue that whites grow up in environments that are racially, socially, and financially isolated from minority groups within society. Such isolation, along with unique childrearing practices emphasizing negotiation, is theorized to produce "broad cognitive frameworks" in which elite whites are more likely to be competitive, more likely to have feelings of entitlement, and are less likely to be empathetic toward others across all life domains. When it comes to offending, these broad cognitive frameworks—in conjunction with the indirect nature of elite white-collar and corporate crime victimization—enable would-be white-collar offenders to more easily adopt techniques of neutralization (Sykes and Matza, 1957) that, in turn, make it easier to commit such crimes.

Empirical evidence on Sohoni and Rorie's race-based theory of white-collar crime is lacking, although preliminary (unpublished) research provides mixed results (Rorie et al., 2020). Future research is warranted on the role of race in various types of white-collar offending. If it were purely a matter of opportunity, we would have expected to see more high- and middle-level white-collar crimes committed by non-white offenders as they entered high- and middle-class occupations over the 16-year period studied by Benson et al. (2020). It might be that non-white executives and upper-level employees are left out of the predominantly white male crime networks involved in elite corporate and white-collar crimes like accounting fraud and antitrust offenses (see Steffensmeier et al., 2013). Non-whites may also perceive white-collar crimes to be more serious than their white counterparts (Unnever et al., 2008; Simpson, Galvin, Loughran, and Cohen, 2022), reducing their relative willingness to commit the offenses in the first place. It could also be that non-white executives feel more scrutiny at that level and, therefore, the risk of offending is greater than for white personnel. Alternatively, given that non-white individuals have a harder time climbing the corporate ladder (see Collins, 1997; Fontaine, 1993), they may fear the consequences of committing crime and being caught more than whites. It remains an empirical question as to whether the cognitive gymnastics of white-collar offenders differ by race. Further, building on the work of Benson et al., much more work needs to examine non-white offenders outside of the black/white dichotomy. Within U.S. borders, questions about experiences with racial discrimination extend beyond those of African-American citizens, especially with the rise of immigration concerns over the past 40 years (see, e.g., Gassman-Pines, 2015). Internationally, most countries have some form of a racial/ethnic hierarchy that impacts a variety of employment, health, cultural, and structural outcomes (see, e.g., Jodhka and Shah, 2010; Thurber et al., 2021; Zick et al., 2008), yet little to no English-language research examines racial/ethnic differences in white-collar offending within European, Asian, South and Central American, Australian, Canadian, or African countries. Research assessing similarities and differences between the empirical patterns and theoretical observations made by U.S. scholars versus those working internationally remains an important scientific opportunity.

Developmental and Life-Course Theories

The central premise of the developmental and life-course paradigm is simple: human development must be viewed as a set of continuously interacting processes that occur throughout life (Elder, 1996). What happens at one point in time in a person's development influences, *but does not strictly determine*, what happens at later points in their development. With respect to crime, a distinctive feature of the life course approach is that it treats involvement in crime as both a dependent and an independent variable. For example, abuse in childhood influences the likelihood that one will become a delinquent in adolescence (dependent variable), and being a delinquent in adolescence (independent variable) influences the likelihood that one will be unemployed in adulthood (Benson and Kerley, 2000). The central questions that developmental and life course theories try to answer concern the processes involved in onset and desistance. When and why do some people start offending (onset) and when and why do some people stop offending (desistance)? And what do their offending trajectories look like between onset and desistance.

Unfortunately, little empirical research has investigated the processes of onset and desistance among white-collar offenders. This is likely due to the dearth of longitudinal data on these offenders—most life-course and criminal career research uses large longitudinal datasets of children and adolescents (e.g., Moffitt et al., 2002; Sampson and Laub, 1990). In contrast, white-collar offenders tend to offend in later ages. Studies that sample older offenders (especially those identified in criminal justice system data) must engage in retrospective methods that are limited in a variety of ways (see Kazemian and Farrington, 2005, for an excellent overview). For one, focusing only on offenders caught and subjected to criminal justice system processes results in selection bias such that truly "elite" offenders are not included because they are more likely to have evaded arrest or conviction through their ability to afford good defense attorneys. Hence, they are unlikely to appear in samples drawn from official data sources.

That said, some work within the white-collar crime domain uses longitudinal data gathered in the 1970s and 1980s on white-collar offenders by Forst and Rhodes (1987) as well as the Yale scholars described earlier (e.g., Weisburd et al., 1991; Weisburd and Waring., 2001; Wheeler et al., 1982). For example, Benson and Kerley (2000) used the Forst and Rhodes data to examine how white-collar offenders differ from traditional offenders in childhood, in terms of schooling, and in adulthood. They find substantive differences starting from childhood—white-collar offenders were less likely to have a family member with a criminal record, less likely to be abused, neglected, or abandoned by their caregivers, and were less likely to be raised in poverty. Regarding education, white-collar offenders were less likely to have poor academic performance or problems with social adjustment during their school years. In adulthood, they noted that differences become amplified—white-collar offenders were more likely to be married, have a college degree and steady employment, own a home, and have financial assets over $10,000. They were also more involved in their communities and more likely to have conforming friends. Nevertheless, Benson and Kerley noted that (despite this finding) most white-collar offenders are not heavily involved in community groups and hence not the "pillars of the community" so often portrayed in narratives about these offenders.

Piquero and Weisburd (2009) used the Weisburd and Waring (2001) longitudinal data to understand white-collar offending trajectories. Piquero and Weisburd subjected the data to "group-based trajectory modelling" (e.g., Nagin, 2010) and found three different offending patterns among those offenders. The first was a "low rate" group with infrequent offenders, analogous to Weisburd et al.'s initial "crisis responders" and "opportunity takers". Among these individuals, who made up 71 percent of the entire sample, situational factors seemed to explain offending. The second group consisted of a "medium rate" group, consisting of 25 percent of the sample, for which both situational factors and underlying criminal propensity seemed to play a role—these were similar to the "opportunity seekers" in Weis-burd et al.'s research. Finally, 5 percent of the sample made up the "high rate" group—or what Weisburd et al. called "stereotypical criminals". These individuals were very similar to traditional street offenders, continued offending throughout the follow-up period, and criminal propensity seemed to matter much more for these offenders than for those in the other two groups.

Benson (2012) reviewed both the Forst and Rhodes data as well as the Weisburd et al. data using a life-course lens. He finds that—although white-collar offenders are not necessarily the paragons of society so often portrayed in accounts of white-collar of-fending—these offenders do "… occupy distinctly different places in the American social structure than common offenders" (p. 201). In terms of criminal careers, white-collar offenders tend to desist far later in life (in their 40s and 50s), compared to the average traditional offenders' desistance in their early 30s. In fact, in the Weisburd et al. data, 10 percent of the sample who reached the age of 70 had arrests in their 70s. In contrast to typical thinking about white-collar offenders, the Weisburd et al. (1991) data indicates that crime specialization was far less likely among white-collar offenders than thought. For some high-level offenses, like securities fraud, offenders may stick to one offense—but they are generally more versatile than expected.

Scholars in the Netherlands used data from several different governmental agencies to create a longitudinal dataset (from age 12 onwards) examining the lives of 644 white-collar offenders prosecuted in the Netherlands between 2008 and 2012 (van Onna et al., 2014). Van Onna et al. (2014) found that the criminal careers of these white-collar offenders could be classified into four groups. The first group consisted of "stereotypical white-collar of-fenders" who committed one or two white-collar offenses as adults but otherwise did not offend during adolescence or early adulthood. Their offending peaks later, around the age of 50. The second group, "adult-onset offenders" began offending in early adulthood but maintained a relatively low frequency of offending before peaking at the age of 40. These two groups of relatively low-frequency offenders made up about three-fourths of the sam-ple (78.2 percent). The other two groups consisted of more frequent offenders. The third group of "adult persisters" offended during adolescence and peaked around the age of 40. Finally, the fourth group of "stereotypical criminals" exhibited the more well-known age-crime curve with highly-active offending behavior in adolescence, peaking in their early 30s, and then a sharp decline. Overall, this sample of offenders (who were selected because of their involvement in white-collar crime) demonstrates that classifying someone as a "white-collar offender" based on one adult offense may produce erroneous conclusions about their offending careers. As opposed to white-collar crime being a "one-off" offense, van Onna et al.'s research demonstrates that many adult white-collar offenders—in contrast to typical portrayals—may not have specialized in white-collar crime and may have begun offending in adolescence (see also Benson, 2021)

Overall, the life-course paradigm has implications for the study of white-collar crime and the study of white-collar crime has implications for the life-course par-adigm. Most white-collar offenders do not follow the same trajectories in crime that have been theorized regarding traditional offenders by well-known life course scholars such as Terrie Moffitt (1993). For instance, white-collar offenders typically start offending when they are considerably older than traditional offenders. In ad-dition, white-collar offenders often participate in conventional institutions of social control, such as marriage and employment, that are supposed to promote desistance according to prominent life course scholars Sampson and Laub (1993). Among many white-collar offenders, of course, conventional occupations provide opportunities for offending, not protection against it (see Benson et al., 2020). Finally, life-course theories often attribute criminal offending to both psychological and sociological factors, but white-collar offenders are thought not to suffer from personality deficits (Benson, 2012).[1]

So, is it possible to apply a life course approach to white-collar offending? Or are white-collar offending patterns better explained by situational factors? Overall, the patterns of offending for white-collar criminals do not appear to fit traditional patterns of criminal behavior, nor can these offenses be attributed to dysfunctional families in childhood or personality traits. These offenses seem to be related to adult events such as individual stressors or, perhaps, exposure to criminogenic corporate structures and cultures (Benson, 2012; Piquero and Piquero, 2016). We know that white-collar offenders often cite family or occupational events as their "trigger" toward offending—e.g., the loss of a spouse's job, being wronged by someone in authority, or other financial problems (Benson, 1985; Klenowski et al., 2011).

Desistance, at first glance, appears to be very different depending on the type of offender—the social factors cited by life-course theorists as promoting desistance (e.g., social bonds) tend to happen earlier than white-collar offending begins and so cannot explain white-collar desistance (Piquero and Piquero, 2016). It is also worth noting that, unlike traditional crimes, white-collar offending is far less likely to impede one from pursuing traditional opportunities or experiencing important transitional events since white-collar offenders tend to commit crimes after they have already established a conventional lifestyle. This still depends on one's social status, however—lower-level managers or workers are more likely to lose their job as a result of white-collar offending than executives, employers, or higher-level managers (Benson, 2012).

Further, given the later age of desistance for white-collar offenders, it's likely that the physical demands of offending are not as salient for white-collar offenders as for traditional offenders. Indeed, the opportunities for offending are probably more frequently presented to older white-collar offenders, as they move into positions of trust within their occupational environment (Piquero and Piquero, 2016). Weisburd and Waring argue that desistance among white-collar offenders may be related to cognitive changes—the cost-benefit analysis likely changes as one ages such that the risk of legal interventions is much greater as one nears the end of their lives.

Finally, it is also important to recognize that the changing demographics of white-collar offenders reflects the general life course principle of the importance of the place and time of one's birth (Benson, 2021). As non-white groups move into more middle-class lifestyles, their trajectories and transitions may reflect more similarities with previously-privileged groups than they have in the past. It's unclear whether "middle and upper-class culture" (e.g., fear of falling, competitiveness, entitlement; Piquero 2012; Sohoni and Rorie, 2019; Shover and Hochstetler, 2006) might play a role with the increased representation among racial/ethnic minorities among white-collar offenders—or whether it's purely a matter of opportunity, of being "in the right place at the right time".

Thus far, we have discussed the basic assumptions and empirical findings of the life course perspective as it pertains to individuals. However, an incipient literature has adopted a life-course approach at the organizational level, exploring how the "theoretical and methodological approaches of developmental and life-course criminology would translate into the realm of corporate crime" (Blokland, Kluin, and Huisman, 2021: 695).

Sutherland initially described corporate offending patterns over the life course of the firm (1949) revealing that corporations, like individuals, have criminal careers (see also Hunter, 2021; 2023). The life-course approach provides a framework for understanding offending onset during a firm's life course, the situations and circumstances that increase the risk of offending (pathways and turning points), reoffending, and the likelihood of desistance. Simpson (2019) and her colleagues (Simpson, Layana, and Galvin, forthcoming) link life-course to organizational life cycle theory to predict patterns of corporate illegality to identifiable life stages for firms (birth, growth, maturity, decline, and death). For example, newly formed companies (birth) lack established procedures, protocols, and internal oversight but typically experience highly competitive environments and thus are prone to risky decisions. The maturity stage is characterized by prior financial success, established rules and bureaucracy, and experienced management. The theory would suggest that firms will experience more corporate offending during the birth stage than during the maturity phase. Consistent with theoretical predictions, trajectory models and other longitudinal empirical analyses reveal that firms, over time, have multiple and distinct patterns of offending and that some of these patterns are affected by organizational life events (Simpson and Schell, 2009). As a new criminological approach, organizational life-course is in need of further conceptual refinement and empirical testing. Some concepts derived to explain individual continuity and change are difficult to operationalize at the organizational level (Simpson et al., forthcoming), but to paraphrase Blokland et al. (2021: 698) there is no a priori reason to expect that the approach will not assist in our understanding of corporate crime. It is simply too early to tell whether the approach offers a better understanding of this form of crime or whether, like many of the other theories described in this section, it comes up short.

A Note on the Importance of Critical and Postmodern Perspectives

The theories reviewed above all take the law as a given. By that, we mean that they do not ask questions about how the law got to be the way that it is. Why are some harmful acts regularly met with criminal sanctions (e.g., drunk driving), while other seemingly equally harmful acts are rarely prosecuted in criminal court (e.g., manufacturing dangerous products)? This is not a question that traditional criminological theories seek to answer. Rather, they focus on law breaking and for the most part ignore law making and law enforcement.[2] But how laws are made and how they are enforced should be fundamental concerns for the study of white-collar crime, because the structure and enforcement of law strongly influences opportunities for white-collar crime.[3] This fact has been most insightfully exposed and analyzed by theorists working in critical and postmodern perspectives.

The terms "critical" and "postmodern" are difficult to pin down explicitly and we make no attempt to do so here, because they have become umbrella designations for a variety of different theories and perspectives (Friedrichs, 2009). Rather, we wish only to identify and briefly discuss a couple of ideas that can be drawn from these approaches that will inform our opportunity perspective going forward. Two exceedingly important ideas found in virtually all versions of critical and postmodern thought are that (1) law making is a political process over which economic and political elites have a significant amount of influence (Friedrichs, 2009), and (2) social harm is produced through this intersection of private capital and governmental interests (Kramer and Michalowski, 1990). Indeed, state policy gives rise both to the corporate form as well as opportunities to engage in financial activities—legitimate and illegitimate (Prechel and Morris, 2010). Elites use their economic and political power to lobby, pressure, cajole, and sometimes simply bribe lawmakers to write laws in such a way that their economic and business-related activities are not characterized as criminal, no matter how harmful such activities may be (Cullen, Agnew, and Wilcox, 2014). Thus, critical criminologists draw our attention to the fact that "crime" is a social construct. An activity or type of behavior becomes a crime in the legal sense only when some government declares it to be so. And businesspeople fight hard against any efforts by government officials to criminalize their particular activities.

But sometimes these efforts fail, and statutes that outlaw the activities of elites eventually do get enacted into law. When that happens, elites switch their attention to the enforcement process and try to undercut either the way in which a law will be enforced or the resources devoted to enforcing it (Barak, 2012). The most glaring contemporary example of feeble enforcement concerns the billion-dollar frauds committed by the big investment banks (Goldman Sacks, JP Morgan Chase, and Citigroup to name but a few) in the run-up to the economic collapse of 2008. Even though the frauds went on for years, none of the banks and none of their executives have been charged with any criminal wrongdoing. They have paid civil fines and admitted misleading investors, but the companies have not been convicted in criminal court and no one has gone to jail (Barak, 2012). In short, oversight seems to have been far less than credible.

Critical perspectives also give us insight into the mechanisms that produce shifts in white-collar offending patterns over time. The political-economy approach treats markets, the capitalist state, and corporate structures as dynamic and symbiotic. In the case of environmental exploitation, for instance, harms and degradation emerged in the context of unfettered industrial development. Efforts to define, contain, and regulate the damage (officially beginning with the creation of the Environmental Protection Agency in 1970) created new and reconfigured opportunities for companies to engage in harmful activities. Firms can shift their operations to new areas of production that are less regulated (within the U.S. or abroad), develop new techniques that accomplish the same goals (say, deep-water drilling), or explore new markets that are less controlled (fracking). Thus, "the state may legitimate economic policies that promote continual economic expansion and ecological disorganization because such policies reinforce dominant economic relationships and power structures" (Stretesky, Long, and Lynch, 2013, p. 234).

For our purposes, the critical and postmodern perspectives are important because they draw attention to the complicity of governments in allowing white-collar criminal opportunities to arise in the first place and to persist over time. Indeed, through deregulation, the state can at times create criminal opportunities where none existed before (Headworth and Hagan, 2016; Calavita and Pontell, 1990). And to make matters worse, the pressure to deregulate comes mainly from the very people and businesses who will be in position to take advantage of the criminal opportunities created by deregulation.

Summary

Except for the critical and postmodern perspectives, the theories reviewed above share one thing in common. They all focus in some way on the offender's motivation for committing white-collar crime or on a person's situation or psychological makeup. Sutherland stressed the cultural norms and attitudes that prevail in the business world. Business executives are indoctrinated to these norms and attitudes, and they come to see illegal behavior as somehow an acceptable and necessary part of doing business. Anomie theory focuses on the widespread cultural emphases on competition and material success. These cultural emphases drive individual business executives and their organizations to constantly seek out innovative, sometimes illegal, ways to get ahead and stay ahead. Rational choice theory directs attention to the offender's calculus regarding the costs and benefits of illegal versus legal behavior. It is assumed that everyone, including white-collar offenders, is motivated to act in accordance with what they perceive to be their own best interests. Although control theories do not posit that any sort of special motivation is involved in white-collar crime, they do nevertheless draw attention to the offender's personal situation or his or her psychological makeup. It is the offender's lack of self-control that leads to offending. Integrated theories combine features from different theories but with the same overall objective of explaining why people break the law. Thus, in all of these theories, the focus is strongly on offenders and the factors that push or pull them toward offending.

In a similar vein, recent developments in racial and ethnically-based perspectives along with life course and developmental processes have opened up new ways of thinking about how individual and organizational situations influence offender motivations. It seems likely that these new perspectives will someday, perhaps soon, surpass traditional theoretical perspectives in garnering attention and effort from researchers. In the next chapter we continue our focus on individual offenders by delving more deeply into recent research on the psychological side of white-collar offending.

Notes

1 However, recent research is demonstrating the importance of personality traits and psychological factors (Benson, 2016; see also Harbinson and Benson, 2020; Ragatz and Fremouw, 2012).
2 Though to be fair, theorists working in the rational choice perspective do note that the penalties associated with a law and the level of enforcement given to it are relevant to the cost-benefit calculations of offenders. But rational choice theories have nothing to say in regard to why some harmful acts are criminalized and the laws against them vigorously enforced while other harmful acts are not often punished.
3 Indeed, one of Sutherland's main points about white-collar crime was that the offenders are "administratively segregated" from criminal proceedings, and the differential treatment of the offenders was, in his view, one of the reasons why white-collar crime flourished.

Chapter 4

Explaining White-Collar Crime
Individual Traits and Psychological Approaches

Early Views on the Psychology of White-Collar Offenders

Historically, researchers have not invested much time or effort investigating the psychology of white-collar offenders (Meier and Geis, 1982). However, recently the number of studies focused on the psychology of white-collar offending has started to grow, and some intriguing findings have emerged (for an early review, see Benson and Manchak, 2014). We review these new findings below. However, before we do that, we note that even though there has not been a lot of attention focused on the individual characteristics of white-collar offenders, the idea that elite white-collar offenders are somehow psychologically distinctive has been around for a long time. As mentioned in Chapter 1, over a century ago, the sociologist E.A. Ross wrote about what he called "criminaloids". He argued that the distinctive characteristic of the business leaders of his day, whom today we would call white-collar criminals, was *moral insensitivity*. In the pursuit of profit, criminaloids are not bothered by the harm that they inflict on others or on society in general. However, and this is an important qualification, criminaloids (i.e., white-collar offenders) are not the victims of any sort of serious psychological disturbance or abnormality (Ross, 1977). White-collar offenders may be boorish, but they are not crazy. Ross (p. 31) described them this way:

> The key to the criminaloid is not evil impulse but moral insensibility. ... Nature has not foredoomed them to evil by a double dose of lust, cruelty, malice, greed, or jealousy. They are not degenerates tormented by monstrous cravings. They want nothing more than we all want—money, power, and consideration—in a word, success; but they are in a hurry and they are not particular as to the means.

Sutherland held a similar view of white-collar offenders as more or less psychologically normal. Indeed, he used the apparent psychological normalcy of white-collar offenders to ridicule the criminological theories of his day. These theories typically presented the criminal as a person who grew up in poverty and who was psychologically damaged by the social pathologies that accompany a life of trouble and disadvantage. Poverty and the stressful conditions associated with it were seen as the root causes of crime. In a famous passage, Sutherland argued that this approach cannot be correct. Poverty and psychopathology cannot be general explanations of crime, because in regard to white-collar offenders, "With a small number of exceptions, they are not in poverty, were not reared in slums or badly deteriorated families, and are not feebleminded or psychopathic" (Sutherland, 1940, p. 10).

DOI: 10.4324/9781003175322-6

A good deal of anecdotal evidence indicates that Sutherland's understanding of the psychology of white-collar offenders has considerable merit. Interviews of persons convicted of white-collar crimes find that with only a few exceptions, they deny that they ever intended to commit a crime. They describe their crimes as normal business practices or at worst as honest mistakes. For example, two men who ran a public construction firm and had been convicted of bid rigging and other violations of antitrust law presented this interpretation of their activities: "It was a way of doing business. Like, you know, why do you brush your teeth in the morning? It was the way things were done long before we got into the business" (Benson, 1985, p. 591).

This theme often is repeated by white-collar offenders, particularly by high-status executives who commit offenses in the furtherance of legitimate businesses. They deny that their actions were intended to harm anyone directly, and they deny that anyone was directly harmed. In other words, they do not define their actions as morally wrong. Rather, they define them as economically necessary in order for their businesses to survive. If we take their words at face value, it appears that these executives view violating the law in order to protect their businesses as the lesser of two evils. Because their actions are not in their view harmful or morally wrong, it is acceptable for them to break the law in order to protect their companies. Indeed, for businesspeople whether a practice is defined as ethical depends in large measure on whether it is a standard practice. If something is normal practice, then it is ethical. It may not be legal, but it is ethical in the eyes of business executives (Chibnall and Saunders, 1977). Thus, two psychological characteristics of high-status offenders are (1) a wilful blindness to the criminality of their behavior and (2) a belief that the economic survival of the firm is more important than obedience to the law.

Business executives are not alone in denying the guilty mind. Medical and professionals of all sorts routinely commit fraud and, when caught, they vigorously deny that they knowingly broke the law. For example, a dentist who was convicted of fraud against the Medicaid system explained his offense by blaming others in the practice:

> Inwardly, I personally felt that the only crime I committed was not telling on these guys. Not that I deliberately, intentionally committed a crime against the system. My only crime was that I should have had the guts to tell on these guys, what they were doing, rather than putting up with it and then trying gradually to get out of the system without hurting them or without them thinking that I was going to snitch on them.
>
> (Benson, 1985, pp. 597–598)

Physicians who have been caught violating the laws governing their profession are especially unwilling to acknowledge that their actions are motivated by greed. Instead, they see themselves as "sacrificial lambs" who have fallen victim to idiotic rules and regulations or to mendacious employees (Jesilow, Geis, and Pontell, 1991). Like business executives, medical professionals often profess allegiance to a different set of priorities. As they put it, focusing on patient care is far more important than obeying some silly law or regulation. Consider this example from a physician convicted of fraud against Medicaid (Jesilow et al., 1991, p. 3321):

> They [the Medicaid officials] are the ones who eventually look over all this and say: "No, that was wrong." Now their idea of right and wrong is very different from what is considered right and wrong by normal people, or by physicians who are not necessarily

normal, but at least [have their own] ideas about what is right and wrong. And to us, right and wrong have to do with things like patient care, whether we give them the right treatments. It doesn't have anything to do with some Medicaid regulation.

Cognitive Landscapes

Sutherland argued early on that the world of business is characterized by a culture in which definitions favorable to law-breaking are widespread. Being part of the world of business exposes businesspeople to these definitions and that can sometimes lead them to feel justified in breaking the law via a process that Sutherland called differential association. Although the theory of differential association has fallen out of favor over time, the idea that the business community has a culture that may at times promote lawbreaking is still widely accepted among white-collar crime scholars. However, the term used to describe this culture has changed. It is now called a cognitive landscape.

Cognitive landscape is a concept that arose out of research on the relationship between race and traditional offending. It offers a new way of thinking about how workplace cultures may influence white-collar offending. As originally conceived, the phrase refers to the idea that community norms, and their adoption by individuals within a community, are influenced by structural advantages or disadvantages (Sampson and Wilson, 1995). Among traditional offenders, crime is seen as a "viable option" when choosing among behavioral responses to social disorganization within their communities. Sampson and Wilson (see also Sampson and Bean, 2006) make it clear that crime is not necessarily applauded or advocated by individuals in disorganized communities, but they argue that certain communities are isolated from mainstream culture, conventional role models, and social networks. As a result, opportunities for learning mainstream cultural norms are limited. In such communities "… a system of values emerges in which crime, disorder, and drug use are less than fervently condemned and hence expected as part of everyday life" (Sampson and Wilson, 1995, p. 50).

A similar idea has been the subject of attention from white-collar crime scholars who have investigated workplace isolation as a mechanism for learning that white-collar crime is an acceptable behavior under certain conditions. Recall that Sutherland's differential association theory holds that individuals not only learn how to commit crime from other people, but they learn the justifications for crime when they are isolated from people that would castigate such behaviors. Some recent empirical research supports workplace-level influences. For example, Patterson et al. (2010) showed that workplace safety culture varies across Emergency Medical Service (EMS) agencies above-and-beyond the variation in safety values among individuals. They explain that such agency variation might be due to underlying cultural variations resulting from regional differences, economic resources available to the agencies, leadership styles, and/or the leadership structure. In another study, Jordanoska (2018) conducted qualitative research examining the "social ecology" of white-collar and corporate crimes. Although she framed the research in terms of situational action theory (Wikström et al., 2017), the concept of "criminogenic exposure" seems analogous to the concept of cognitive landscapes. She describes criminogenic exposure as "… the person's encounter with settings whose (perceived) moral norms and their (perceived) levels of enforcement (or lack of enforcement) encourage criminal actions in response to particular opportunities to offend" (pp. 1428–1429). Jordanoska goes on to discuss how the hierarchical structure of a workplace may socialize employees into "criminogenic moral contexts" that produce offending. For example, the values that a company director manifests may be translated into workplace priorities, policies, and practices. It follows that if the director's values are criminogenic, then this creates a criminogenic moral context for subordinates.

Recent research details how, even outside of the workplace, community-level structural factors (i.e., in the form of legalization, deregulation, and criminalization) impact the cognitive landscapes of citizens and promote "everyday-life crimes" such as insurance fraud, cheating fellow consumers when selling items second-hand, and tax evasion. Karstedt and Farrall (2006; see also Farrall and Karstedt, 2020) argue that deregulation efforts produce "market anomie", which is described as occurring

> ... when a mood of lawlessness and cynical attitudes towards rules and regulations are spreading that increase both victimization and offending, which, in turn, feed into such a mood. The shift in the balance of obligations between consumers and business, as well as obligations toward legal and other rules, cuts into the normative fabric of trust, fairness, and legitimacy that regulates the moral economy, thus reducing conformity as well as consensus on acceptable practices.
>
> (Karsdtedt and Farrall, 2006, p. 1017)

At the individual level, this cognitive landscape manifests into a "syndrome of market anomie" in which individuals experience distrust toward legal institutions and the legal rules as well as feelings of insecurity about the ability of the law to protect them. They argue that "... individual and group perceptions are grounded in the structural and institutional landscape of the market that defines 'winners' and 'losers' as well as powerful and powerless groups" (p. 1017). Such perceptions, in turn, shape the ability of people to justify their own offending—e.g., through perceptions, their own experiences, and social messaging (i.e., others' experiences) about offending that lends itself to a belief that "everyone is doing it".

Cognitive landscapes have also been evoked in research on public perceptions of white-collar and corporate crime. For example, Unnever et al. (2008) note that African-Americans and whites differ in their opinions about the seriousness of corporate crime and the appropriate mechanisms for punishing such crime. These differences arise because of African-Americans' experiences of discrimination—especially by the criminal justice system—as well as the portrayal of corporate crimes committed predominantly by elite whites. Such factors promote a cognitive landscape among members of the African-American community that impacts their normative values as they pertain to white-collar and corporate crime. The researchers found that African-American respondents were more likely than whites to favor stricter regulations to prevent financial corporate crimes as well as more punitive sanctions, such as longer prison terms and higher fines, for corporate offenders. A recent study by Simpson, Galvin, Loughran, and Cohen (2022) found that white survey respondents were less likely than persons of color to rate organizational white-collar crimes as more serious than burglary when the white-collar offenses were tied to official justice system responses (civil, criminal, and regulatory). The authors suggest that specifying the different ways in which the state responds to organizational offending possibly activates perceptions among non-whites that white-collar offenders are treated differently (more leniently) than street offenders.

Psychological Traits

The idea that the world of business is pervaded by a criminogenic cognitive landscape has a certain surface plausibility. But it suffers from the same deficiency that Sutherland noted when he criticized theories based on the supposed pathologies of poverty as the root cause of crime. It overpredicts the rate of offending in the business community (Levi, 2010). Just as not everyone who lives in a poverty-stricken neighbourhood is a criminal, neither is every small businessowner nor every business executive a criminal. In other words, a criminogenic cognitive landscape by itself cannot explain why some corporate leaders commit corporate crimes while others do not. In order to explain variation in corporate and white-collar crime at the individual level, we must turn to individual level factors.

Case studies of well-known and egregious white-collar offenses suggest several psychological factors that may be involved in high-status white-collar crimes. One of these traits is the offender's relish of a *sense of superiority over the victim* (Stotland, 1977). For example, Bernard Madoff, who orchestrated the largest Ponzi scheme on record, had this to say about the people who lost their life savings as a result of his fraud: "Fuck my victims. I carried them for twenty years, and now I'm doing 150 years" (Fishman, 2010, p. 32). In the Enron case, a telephone call between two California energy traders was taped as they discussed how they had illegally manipulated the price of energy that Californians had to pay. The exchange begins with the traders talking about California's demand that Enron refund $8 million in overcharges for energy (Roberts, 2004, p. 1):

> *Trader 1*: They're [expletive] taking all the money back from you guys, all the money you guys stole from those poor grandmothers in California?
> *Trader 2*: Yeah, Grandma Millie, man.
> *Trader 1*: Yeah, Grandma Millie, man. But she's the one who couldn't figure out how to [expletive] vote on the butterfly ballot.
> *Trader 2*: Yeah, now she wants her [expletive] money back for all the power you've charged right up, jammed right up her [expletive] for [expletive] $250 a megawatt hour.

As disgusting as this may sound, the traders appeared to take a perverse delight in manipulating and making fools of their victims. In effect, their victims meant nothing to them. The feeling of power and superiority that arises out of the offense is psychologically rewarding to the offender and may become a source of motivation for continued offending (Shover, 2007; Stotland, 1977).

The white-collar offender's sense of superiority is often accompanied by arrogance (Shover and Hochstetler, 2006, pp. 66–67). Elite white-collar offenders seem to believe "they don't have to follow the rules because they made them" (Swartz, 2003, p. 302). As Shover and Hochstetler (2006, p. 67) note, the arrogant are accustomed to being in charge and to doing things their own way. Convinced of their own superiority, they assume that whatever they want to do must be right. They do not have to be bothered with the minor technicalities of the law, because in their view their personal integrity is beyond question. Like old-time Calvinists, they seem to believe that their personal success in reaching the top of the corporate hierarchy indicates that they have been chosen by a higher power. Thus, they are entitled to do as they please and to take what they want (Shover and Hochstetler, 2006).

Related to arrogance and a sense of superiority is the gratification that comes from mastering a complex situation. Stotland (1977) calls this source of motivation "ego challenge". It may be a particularly important and prevalent aspect of long-term frauds that are carried out in large organizations and that require highly specialized skills. For example, many of the offenses that were committed during the Enron scandal involved highly complex schemes designed to manipulate and misuse the standard accounting rules and practices as well as the reporting requirements of the SEC (McLean and Elkind, 2004). The schemes had to make Enron appear to be more profitable than it really was. Further, the schemes had to be constructed so that they did not raise the suspicions of regulators at the SEC or Wall Street investors or industry analysts. In short, the executives at Enron had to fool a lot of very smart people and it took some ingenuity to accomplish this. Although we must acknowledge the possibility that the people who were supposed to be watching the barn door, the so-called gatekeepers, fell down on the job (Coffee, 2002). Nevertheless, it took smart people with a good deal of skill to come up with the accounting schemes used at Enron. The executives who carried it off clearly were proud of their skills and enjoyed exercising them (McLean and Elkind, 2004).

Some scholars believe that large organizations, especially large for-profit private corporations, are inherently criminogenic, and they tend to be led by individuals with particular personality traits conducive to crime (Gross, 1978, 1980). According to Edward Gross (1978), the people who end up as leaders in large organizations tend to be "organizational strainers". They are ambitious, shrewd, and morally flexible. They are ambitious in the sense that they have a strong desire to get to the top, to be seen as persons of importance, power, and status. Ambition alone is not enough, however. It must be coupled with shrewdness, the ability to spot organizational opportunities for advancement. They understand that talent alone does not ensure success. It also involves the ability to fraternize with and to make a good impression on people with power, that is the people who can help your career advance in the political infighting that characterizes large organizations. Finally, organizational strainers tend to be morally flexible. They are not troubled at the prospect of putting organizational goals ahead of ethical principles and legal mandates. Once they are in charge, they want to be seen as successful leaders of successful organizations, and if organizational success requires cutting a few regulatory or legal corners then they are comfortable with doing just that.

Psychopathy and White-Collar Crime

The idea that certain personality characteristics may help someone rise to a leadership role in a corporation and that these same characteristics may be associated with corporate crime is beginning to receive some empirical support. The most intriguing research concerns psychopathy (Dutton, 2012). Psychopathy is a multifaceted personality disorder that includes traits such as superficial charm, insincerity, ego-centricity, manipulativeness, narcissism, and grandiosity (Board and Fritzon, 2005; Benson and Manchak, 2014), but the core characteristic of psychopathy is lack of emotion and remorse (Gao and Raine, 2010). Psychopaths are intelligent and they can be very charming and engaging, but at bottom they lack a sense of morality and do not care about others (Hare, 1993). In the evocative phrasing of Babiak and Hare (2006), they are "snakes in suits".

Psychopathy is often associated with persistent aggressive and criminal behavior, so it is not surprising that the rate of psychopathy is higher among people in prison than in the general population (Babiak, Newmann, and Hare, 2010). But it is surprising that the rate of psychopathy is also higher among people in leadership positions in the corporate world

(Dutton, 2012). Corporate psychopaths, however, are usually able to avoid contact with the criminal justice system, and hence they have come to be known as "successful psychopaths". Successful psychopaths manifest the core personality traits of psychopathy, most notably narcissism and lack of empathy, but they have better self-control than the psychopaths who end up in prison (Gao and Raine, 2010). Some scholars have suggested that this combination of characteristics allows psychopaths to gain access to and take advantage of vulnerable people and corporations (Babiak and Hare, 2006; Babiak et al., 2010; Boddy, 2011). As Hare famously put it, "not all psychopaths are in prison, some are in the boardroom" (quoted in Babiak et al., 2010, p. 174).

Babiak and Hare (2006) argue that many psychopaths have excellent communication skills and are good at reading other people and situations. Their verbal fluency and lack of social inhibitions enable them to speak up in meetings, which helps them to appear to be capable of leadership. In theory, they can use their charm and psychological insight to manipulate others so as to advance their own interests and rise in corporate hierarchies. In addition, their narcissism and lack of empathy enable them to make decisions that advance corporate interests at the expense of others without feeling the pangs of conscience that trouble most people (Dutton, 2012).

It is difficult to know, of course, exactly how prevalent psychopathy is among business leaders. One small study, however, suggests that the rate is higher in corporations than in the general public, though less high than you would find in prison (Babiak et al., 2010). The researchers studied 203 individuals involved in management development programs in several different companies. They administered a standard psychopathy checklist and found that approximately 3 percent of the management trainees scored high on the checklist. Three percent is significantly above the estimated 1 percent rate of psychopathy in the general population, though far less than the 15 percent psychopathy rate found in prisons (Babiak et al., 2010). Another study compared senior business managers in the United Kingdom to persons with diagnosed personality disorders on a variety of personality traits. Compared to persons with diagnosed personality disorders, the business managers scored the same on narcissism and higher on histrionic personality disorder (which comprises superficial charm, insincerity, manipulativeness, and ego-centricity). But the managers scored significantly lower than the comparison group on all other personality disorders, such as paranoia and schizophrenia (Board and Fritzon, 2005). These corporate psychopaths appear to have the psychopathic traits that may facilitate occupational advancement without displaying obvious signs of other mental disorders. In other words, they wear a "mask of sanity" (Cleckley, 1982).

All in all, several potentially important characteristics of the psychology of white-collar offenders appear to stand out. They include the offenders' unwillingness to define their behavior as crime, belief that economic survival is more important than obeying the law, sense of superiority over victims, need for ego challenge, lack of social conscientiousness, arrogance, and perhaps most disturbingly, psychopathic characteristics, such as superficial charm and lack of empathy. Although plenty of anecdotal evidence suggests that some or all of these characteristics play a role in many white-collar crimes, we must be careful how we interpret this evidence. It is important not to overstate the causal importance of these psychological factors. Just because people who commit white-collar crime appear to have a sense of superiority over others, it does not follow that people who think that they are better than everyone else are white-collar criminals. Similarly, even though some white-collar offenders appear to find intrinsic gratification in orchestrating complex illegal schemes, we cannot conclude that people who like solving complex problems will resort to white-collar crime when they are bored and in need of a thrill. These cautionary remarks hold even for full-blown psychological constructs, such as psychopathy. People can be insensitive and manipulative without necessarily doing anything criminal (Dutton, 2012). In addition, we must remember that almost all the research on the psychology of white-collar offenders involves case studies or very small samples of offenders. These studies have been based almost exclusively on high-status offenders. How strongly we can generalize from this empirical base is not at all clear. Whether they would apply, for instance, to low-status offenders is an open question. Nevertheless, it would seem not too much of a stretch to speculate in one way. If individuals with the characteristics identified earlier find themselves in situations that offer opportunities to enrich or empower themselves by means of some kind of white-collar crime, we should not be particularly surprised when at least some of them take advantage of those opportunities. It may also be the case that these very same traits may, under certain conditions, help people advance in the world of business. This is not to say that all corporate leaders are crooks, but on the other hand being a crook may not necessarily disqualify one from getting ahead in the corporate world.

Finally, we note that strictly psychological approaches to explaining white-collar crime suffer from a problem that is the reverse of the problem that besets explanations based on cultural factors and cognitive landscapes. Whereas cultural explanations overpredict the rate of offending, theories based on individual psychological traits do the opposite. They under predict the rate of offending (Levi, 2010). Some of the people who commit white-collar and corporate crimes, indeed probably most of them, do not suffer from psychopathy or other serious psychological conditions. Their offending is more likely to be a response to the stresses or strains brought about by external events, such as a downturn in profitability that might lead to an offense arising out of a fear of falling. Thus, by themselves psychological and other individual traits do not fully account for the overall rate of offending in regards to any particular type of white-collar or corporate crime. Exactly how individual traits and cognitive landscapes interact to produce white-collar offending remains a matter for continued research. In addition, as we will discuss in the following chapter, there is another factor to consider and that is the availability of white-collar offending opportunities.

Gender and Thinking about White-Collar Crime

Before we turn to opportunity structures, however, it is important to note recent research on how gender appears to influence thinking about white-collar crime. The question is: do female white-collar offenders differ from male offenders in how they think about white-collar crime? Until recently, the limited research on gendered differences in criminal thinking was primarily qualitative, and it was based on small samples (Zeitz, 1981; Klenowski, Copes and Mullins, 2011). A new study by Harbinson and Benson (2020) has extended this research on gendered differences in criminal thinking by applying the Psychological Inventory of Criminal Thinking Styles (PICTS) to a large sample of white-collar offenders. The PICTS is an 80-item self-report measure that assesses what are called criminal thinking styles (Walters, 1995, 2014; Walters and Geyer, 2004). Factor analyses have identified two major PICTS factors. That is to say, the analyses suggest that there are two general styles of criminal thinking called Reactive and Proactive Thinking. Reactive criminal thinking leads to spontaneous, emotional, and impetuous criminal actions. For example, someone who feels justified in lashing out physically at someone else who has disrespected them illustrates reactive criminal thinking. Proactive criminal thinking, on the other hand, precedes planned and goal directed crimes, such as a carefully orchestrated bank robbery. The two styles of criminal thinking can be combined mathematically to create an overall measure for criminal thinking. Previous research using the PICTS has found some differences in criminal thinking styles between persons convicted of white-collar type crimes versus those convicted of non-white-collar offenses (Ragatz, Fremous, and Baker, 2012; Walters and Geyer, 2004).

To investigate whether gender influences the criminal thinking styles of white-collar offenders, Harbinson and Benson (2020) used data from the Office of Probation and Pretrial Services of the Administrative Office of the U.S. Courts. The sample included over 10,000 women and over 20,000 men convicted of various types of white-collar crime in federal courts. Most of the convictions were for generic crimes such as tax offenses, mail and wire fraud, and false claims.

The results of this study were surprising. Contrary to expectations, on all three scales (i.e., Proactive, Reactive, and General) women scored higher than men. The differences were small but they were statistically significant.[1] Since PICTS scores can be influenced by various demographic and social variables such as age, race, education level and social class, the researchers conducted additional multivariate analyses to see if the results for gender could be accounted for by these variables. They could not. Even in a complex multiple regression model, gender still distinguished criminal thinking styles with women scoring slightly higher than men.

What should be made of these results? The researchers expected to find gender-based differences in criminal thinking styles. And they did, but not in the direction they were expecting. At least as measured by the PICTS, female white-collar offenders manifest slightly higher levels of Proactive, Reactive, and General criminal thinking styles than male offenders. Considering men's greater prevalence in white-collar crime, the finding that female white-collar offenders differ from male offenders in the wrong direction is perplexing.

There are a couple of possible reasons for women's higher scores on the PICTS. The first is that women may simply be more truthful and attentive when they complete the survey than men are. In other words, women may be less likely to lie than men and their scores reflect their thinking styles more accurately than do men's scores. If so, this would mean that the PICTS as a measuring tool does not truly reflect the relationship between gender and criminal thinking. The second possible explanation is that because crime is less socially acceptable for women, the women who are not inhibited by social disapproval are as deviant in their thinking as men. There may be a certain threshold in criminal thinking that leads to actual offending, and men are more likely to pass this threshold than women. But the women who do cross the threshold and engage in crime are by necessity like men in their thinking styles. Another possibility is that only women who commit more serious offenses get sent to prison, while men are more likely to get sent to prison for less serious offenses. If this is the case, then the women in this sample may be on average more criminally minded than are the men simply because only the most criminally minded women get sent to prison. These explanations are not necessarily mutually exclusive (Walters, 2002).

Overall, we do not know whether men and women in general score the same on the PICTS. If the PICTS were administered to a random sample of the general population, it might reveal that men on average score higher than women, and that only a subset of women score the same as men. This possibility would suggest that there are factors—biological, psychological, and social—that hold women in general back from offending more so than men. But women who are not deterred by such factors resemble men in their criminal thinking styles. Unfortunately, at this point we are left with the cliché that more research is needed.

Summary: Individual Traits and White-Collar Crime

Sutherland was adamant that white-collar offenders were normal people who offended primarily because they fell prey to the criminogenic culture of the world of business. It appears, however, that he may not have been entirely correct about this. A small but growing body of work suggests that at least some of the people who commit white-collar type crimes have personality characteristics that distinguish them from the average person. They may, for example, be arrogant narcissists who lack feelings of empathy for others. Or they may habitually indulge in certain patterns of thinking that enable them to justify the pursuit of their own interests by taking advantage of others. In other words, individual traits appear to play some role in white-collar offending.

But we need to be cautious in how we interpret these results primarily because the differences in traits between white-collar offenders and non-offenders are not large. It is true that some research suggests that the rate of psychopathy among corporate executives may be higher than in the general population, but psychopathy is not nearly as prevalent nor as pronounced among executives as it is among the violent offenders housed in maximum security prisons. Successful psychopaths may lack empathy, but they are not extremely impulsive or violent. Likewise, the research on criminal thinking styles finds that white-collar offenders, both male and female, tend to score on the low ends of the various thinking style scales, certainly lower than people convicted of serious street crimes. Similarly, the research showing that white-collar offenders often deny their criminality and use neutralizations to justify their offenses must not be overstated. Most people have tried to excuse their own misbehavior at one time or another in their lives.

Thus, regarding the psychology of white-collar offenders, it is probably safe to say that the vast majority of them do not view themselves as criminals or their activities as crimes. With few exceptions, they go to great lengths to deny having any intent to commit a crime against anyone (Benson, 1985). It also seems clear that the perpetrators of really big-time white-collar crimes possess an exaggerated sense of self-confidence and entitlement, and they may share some personality traits that are found among psychopaths. Indeed, recent research makes E.A. Ross seem particularly prescient. Recall that nearly a century ago he asserted that the key characteristic of white-collar criminaloids was their insensitivity to the moral implications of their actions. They may also have other characteristics, such as shrewdness and extraverted personalities, that enable them to fare well in the competition for high-level jobs where opportunities for white-collar crime are plentiful.

Focusing on offenders is, of course, perfectly appropriate. Indeed, it has been standard practice throughout the history of criminology. We need to understand what causes some people to violate the law while others conform to its demands. However, motivations or personal characteristics by themselves do not explain why offenders violate the law at one time but not another, or in one place but not another. In other words, the motivations and personal characteristics of offenders cannot fully explain why they commit particular crimes at particular times and places. There is another factor that comes into play, and that factor is the presence or absence of a criminal opportunity.

Without some kind of criminal opportunity, even the most habitual career criminal cannot commit a crime. Bank robbers cannot rob banks if there are no banks available, and bank embezzlers cannot embezzle if they do not have a job in a bank. Banks provide opportunities for both bank robbers and bank embezzlers. Thus, to understand crime requires an analysis of both offenders and their opportunities. In the next chapter, we take up the topic of white-collar criminal opportunities. Of course, we are not the first to recognize that opportunity plays a role in white-collar offending. All of the theoretical approaches that we have discussed in this and the preceding chapter have something to say about opportunity, but previous approaches toward opportunity have been more broad-based and less focused than the perspective that will be presented in the next chapter, where we argue opportunities both ignite motivations to offend and shape the types of offending that individuals choose to pursue.

Note

1 Although we do not report the results here, the researchers also looked at various sub-scales that can be constructed out of the PICTS and found the same pattern of results. Women scored either the same or slightly higher than men.

Chapter 5

Explaining White-Collar Crime

The Opportunity Perspective

Criminologists spend an enormous amount of time and energy studying criminals. They want to know what kind of person is likely to become a criminal. Why do they do it? When do they start? When do they stop? How many crimes do they commit? What kind of crimes do they commit? What are their families like? Where do they live? What kind of friends do they have? The list could go on, and of course, these are important questions. We hope that by answering them, we will eventually understand why individual involvement in crime seems to vary so much. For a lot of reasons, we need to know as much as possible about the factors that affect involvement in crime. Indeed, throughout this book, we ask and try to answer many of these questions regarding the people who commit white-collar crimes. Nevertheless, it is important to keep in mind that knowing about criminals is not the same as knowing about crime. People often confuse the problem of explaining crime with the problem of explaining criminals, but the two should be kept separate (Gottfredson and Hirschi, 1990). Crime is an event, something that happens. A criminal, on the other hand, is an individual who behaves in a way that society has defined as unacceptable. Explaining why people behave one way or another is not the same as explaining why a particular event happens at a particular time and in a particular place.

To understand why a particular crime occurs at a particular time and place, it is necessary to pay attention not only to the person who commits the crime but to the situation in which the person is located. Obviously, it is important to know about an offender's motives or reasons for committing an offense. But suppose that we know that an offender has a strong motive to steal money. The desire for money, however, does not explain why he robs a liquor store as opposed to a bank that is located next to the liquor store. Both places have the money that the offender needs. Why choose one instead of the other? From the offender's point of view, however, there may be several reasons to select a liquor store over a bank. Banks often have security guards who have guns. Banks have video cameras that take pictures. If it happens to be after business hours and the bank is closed, the chances of breaking in and stealing anything are practically nil. Nowadays, bank vaults are virtually impregnable. Liquor stores, on the other hand, are open for longer hours than banks. They may be staffed by only one person, and, best of all, the money is right there in the cash register. So, if you look at the situation from the offender's point of view, the liquor store presents a better *criminal opportunity* than the bank, especially if the criminal is working alone and in a hurry.

DOI: 10.4324/9781003175322-7

Understanding Criminal Opportunities

Criminal opportunities are now recognized as an important cause of all crime (Felson, 2002), because without an opportunity, there cannot be a crime. In the past few decades, the study of crime has increasingly focused on the situational and ecological factors that create or facilitate opportunities for street crime (Clarke, 1983; Cohen and Felson, 1979; Felson, 2002). Opportunities also are important causes of white-collar crime. However, as we will show, the opportunity structures of many white-collar crimes differ dramatically from those for ordinary street crimes. These differences generate a double-edged sword. They create both difficulties and openings for controlling white-collar crime.

What exactly is a criminal opportunity? According to routine activity theory, a criminal opportunity comprises two elements: a *suitable target* and a *lack of capable guardianship*. A target can be a person or some kind of property. What makes a person or a piece of property suitable as a target for crime? That depends on a lot of factors. Without exploring all of them, we can identify some of the main considerations. From the offender's point of view, the attractiveness or suitability of a person as a target depends on that person's vulnerability and in some cases on the person's symbolic or emotional value to the offender. All other things being equal, we assume that violent offenders would rather attack someone who is not well equipped to fight back (i.e., someone who is vulnerable). As one researcher puts it, big people hit little people (Felson, 1996). In addition, we assume that violent offenders would prefer to go after someone they have a grudge against or someone who has disrespected them as opposed to a random person. In other words, it seems likely that it is more satisfying to shoot someone you are mad at than someone you don't have strong feelings about one way or the other. Thus, two important factors that determine the suitability of people as targets are vulnerability and emotional value.

There are also many factors that can make one piece of property more suitable than another. Property becomes attractive to an offender if it is valuable, portable, and fungible. The importance of value for property offenders is obvious. Portability is important because if you are going to steal a physical object, then by definition you have to move it from one place to another. That being the case, an iPad is a lot easier to steal than a refrigerator. Last, it matters whether the object is fungible or not. Something is fungible when it can be exchanged for something else. Money is very fungible. You can exchange it for just about anything. Property offenders look for things that are fungible, because ordinarily they are not interested in using the things they steal. Rather, they want to sell them for money. Thus, smart thieves try to steal things that are easy to exchange for money (i.e., easy to sell). For example, suppose you need some cash, and you break into a house to steal something. Inside, you have your choice of a valuable painting or a brand-new iPad. The painting may actually be worth much more than the iPad, but which one is going to be easier to sell? To sum up, all other things being equal, thieves look for property that is valuable, easy to carry, and easy to sell for money or exchange for something else, such as drugs or alcohol.

The other component of a criminal opportunity is capable guardianship, or rather the lack of capable guardianship. You may think of capable guardianship as a big strong person who can defend you or your property, but the term *guardianship* should be interpreted in a broader way. By capable guardianship, we mean anything that can either physically prevent the offender from getting to the target or that can make the offender decide it is too risky to go after the target. Guardianship takes two main forms: blocking access and surveillance.

Techniques of guardianship that can physically block an offender from getting to a target include walls, locks, and bars on windows as well as anything else that has the effect of restricting the offender's access to the target. Property offenders can be prevented from carrying out their intentions if they cannot get to their desired target because of a locked door or a barred window. Of course, offenders can always try to break through whatever is blocking their attack. But the general point remains: blocking access makes it more difficult for an offender to carry out his or her intentions, and this makes the criminal opportunity less attractive to the offender.

Besides having their access to a target blocked, offenders can also be put off if they feel that it is too risky to attack a particular target. By risky we mean the risk to the offender of being observed or otherwise detected, either while committing the crime or afterward. So, if a target, be it a person or a piece of property, is under surveillance by a police officer, a neighbor, a security camera, an alarm system, or anything else, potential offenders have to take this into account. Surveillance increases the likelihood that the offender's actions will be noticed, and accordingly, the offender faces an increased risk of being caught. Thus, surveillance reduces the attractiveness of criminal opportunities. This is why, of course, security cameras are now ubiquitous in retail establishments, government buildings, private residences, and increasingly, public streets.

As ways of thinking about criminal opportunities, the concepts "suitable target" and "lack of guardianship" have obvious similarities to "lure" and "lack of credible oversight" as articulated by Shover and Hochstetler (2006), but they are not identical. For street crime, a suitable target is usually a concrete physical object such as a piece of jewellery or cash in a register. In contrast, lure refers less to physical objects and more to particular types of situations in which a person can take advantage of certain types of economic transactions in such a way as to enrich herself without necessarily directly stealing from another person. Likewise, guardianship and credible oversight are related but not identical concepts. Guardianship usually involves some effort to directly block access to a target or some way of putting the target under direct and constant surveillance. As applied to white-collar crime, oversight usually does not involve blocking access to or directly watching some potential target. Rather, it involves developing mechanisms to review the activities of business-men and -women in order to ascertain whether their behavior complies with legal or ethical standards. For example, to prevent burglary, we lock doors, install alarm systems, and hope that our neighbors will keep an eye on our homes when we are away. To prevent insider trading, we review the stock-trading activities of corporate executives to determine whether they were based on inside information. Regarding white-collar crime, lure and the credibility of oversight may be the most appropriate ways to conceptualize criminal opportunities, because white-collar crimes almost always represent perversions of legitimate economic activities.

Recent research on how guardians work in relation to some white-collar crimes has uncovered a disturbing phenomenon (Chan and Gibbs, 2022). It is called guardian-offender overlap. Guardians are supposed to exercise credible oversight. That is, they are supposed to review the activities of potential offenders to make sure they comply with legal standards. For example, consider accounting fraud. Public companies are required to submit various financial reports that are prepared by independent external auditors based on material submitted by internal financial personnel. The reports that are supposed to provide an objective and accurate picture of the company's financial situation. The company's managers, chief officers, and board of directors can be thought of as internal guardians in that they have a duty to protect the interests of shareholders by making sure that financial reports are accurate. Chan and Gibbs (2022) studied firms that had been subjected to enforcement actions by the Securities and Exchange Commission (SEC). They found that in many of these cases, the internal guardians actually participated in shaping the financial material so that a misleading or fraudulent picture of the company's financial situation was reported. In other words, the persons charged with guardianship had themselves participated in the offense of accounting fraud.

The Nature and Techniques of White-Collar Crime

Criminal opportunities are exploited through the use of particular techniques. That is, in order to take advantage of a criminal opportunity, the offender often must know how to use a particular technique. Indeed, sometimes it is the availability of a technique that determines whether a situation presents a criminal opportunity or not. For example, an auto thief who knows how to hot-wire a car has many more opportunities to steal cars than does a thief who does not know the technique of hot-wiring. The unskilled thief must look for a car with the keys in it, while the skilled thief can go after any car that is unguarded. Thus, in order to understand criminal opportunities, we have to learn about the techniques that offenders use to commit particular types of crimes. This is especially true in regard to white-collar types of crimes. The techniques of white-collar crime are distinctly different from the techniques of other sorts of offenses. Thus, we need to consider techniques in a more systematic fashion.

The dictionary definition of technique that is most appropriate for our purposes here is "a method for accomplishing a desired aim". Thus, a technique is a way to get something done. Obviously, depending on what you want to get done, there may be different techniques that you can use. For example, a burglar's technique for breaking into a house might involve carefully drilling a hole in a door, then using a needlepoint saw to enlarge the hole, then reaching inside to unlock the door, and then sneaking in to steal silver or jewellery. Most burglars don't do this. They use a simpler technique: kick the door hard until the doorframe or the lock breaks, then dash in and grab whatever is out in the open, looks valuable, and is small enough to carry.

There are several important points to notice about this example. First, regardless of which technique was used, the burglar employed physical means (drilling a hole or kicking in the door) to accomplish the goal. Second, the burglar was somewhere he or she was not supposed to be and doing something that is obviously and clearly illegal. Third, the burglar was in direct contact with the victim or target of the offense, which in this case would be the homeowner's property. Fourth, the victim is a specific identifiable individual—in this case, the homeowner. Finally, the illegal activities that made up this offense (kicking in the door, grabbing the stuff, running away from the house) took place at a discrete point in time and space. We can specify the address, day, and maybe even time that the crime took place.

Many conventional street crimes are like this. They involve physical actions. There is direct contact between the offender and a specific target or victim of the illegal activities. They are obviously illegal while they are occurring, and they occur at a particular place and time.

White-collar offenses, on the other hand, often are not like this. They do not involve physical actions except in the most trivial sense that we move our bodies or parts of our bodies whenever we do anything. The physical activities of white-collar crime are very simple, commonplace activities such as writing, or talking on the phone, or entering information into a computer. Compared to our burglar, white-collar offenders do things differently. They often have a perfect right to be where they are and where the offense occurs. The offense itself may not involve any direct physical contact between the offender and the victim or the target of the offense. Finally, the offense typically will not be obviously illegal while it is occurring. In short, many white-collar offenses manifest the following three properties: (1) the offender has *legitimate access* to the location in which the crime is committed, (2) the offender is *spatially separated* from the victim, and (3) the offender's actions have a *superficial appearance of legitimacy*.

Legitimate Access

An important difference between white-collar crime and common crimes is that the white-collar offender has legitimate access to the target or the victim of his actions. All offenders have to solve the problem of how to get access to their targets in order to commit their offenses. For instance, in the example above regarding burglary, the offender had to figure out some way to break into the house in order to burglarize it. However, for white-collar offenders, this problem often never arises, because the offender has legitimate access to the target as a result of their occupational position. For example, a corporate executive who wants to engage in illegal insider trading does not have to break into the New York Stock Exchange; he can simply use his computer to buy or sell company stock. Likewise, a business owner who wants to cheat on her taxes can fail to report all her business income on her tax form. In both examples, the offenders have legitimate access to their targets—the stock market or the local tax department, respectively.

Spatial Separation from the Victim

Unlike ordinary street criminals, white-collar offenders often do not have to come into direct contact with their victims. The corporate executive who engages in insider trading, for example, does not take money directly from anybody. The crime of insider trading has victims, but they are not directly contacted by insider trading offenders. Even in the most serious types of white-collar crime that involve actual physical harm to people, such as workplace safety violations, there often is no contact between the offender and the victims. For example, miners who are injured or killed as a result of cave-ins caused by illegally unsafe working conditions probably have never met the mine owner who decided to skimp on safety equipment and training. This distance between offender and victim is true of many of the offenses that we will be discussing in this book. Only occasionally for particular types of offenses is there any sort of face-to-face interaction between white-collar offenders and the people who are harmed by their actions.

Superficial Appearance of Legitimacy

Finally, the physical actions of white-collar offenders almost always have the superficial appearance of legitimacy. When a burglar breaks into a house or a robber pulls a gun on a victim, it is obvious that something illegal is happening, and we can infer the offender's state of mind, his evil intent, from his actions. This is often not true for white-collar crimes.

Viewed from the outside, the offender's actions look normal. Consider again the corporate executive who illegally trades on inside information. It is perfectly legal for executives to buy and sell stock in their own companies. It only becomes illegal when they do so knowingly on the basis of information that is hidden from or not available to other investors. But how can outsiders know what the executive did or did not know? This fact means that we cannot necessarily judge the offender's state of mind from his actions, and as we will explain later, that makes it difficult to prosecute and convict white-collar offenders.

To illustrate how these properties come together in a particular example of white-collar crime, consider the famous case of Bernie Madoff, who orchestrated a Ponzi scheme that resulted in losses of billions of dollars to thousands of individuals (Henriques, 2011). Madoff was the founder of Bernard L. Madoff Investment Securities, a company that received money from individuals, pension funds, and other types of organizations for purposes of investment. Like all investment advisors, Madoff promised to invest money for his clients. He claimed to have a secret and highly sophisticated strategy that would produce consistent returns over long periods of time. If you were accepted by Madoff as a client (and he did not accept everyone), you were going to see your money grow more reliably than anywhere else. For many years, this was exactly what happened. His clients gave him their money and received periodic statements reflecting how much their accounts had increased in value during good times and bad times in the market. To his clients and to Wall Street, Madoff seemed to be a financial wizard. Unfortunately for his clients, however, Madoff was not a wizard but a charlatan. He was running a very sophisticated Ponzi scheme, and the "profits" that clients thought they were making existed only on paper. When a client wanted to withdraw funds, Madoff would take money from other accounts to pay off the client making the withdrawal. The scheme worked until 2008, when too many of his clients demanded their money back at the same time and he did not have the funds available to cover all the redemptions. His scheme collapsed and billions were lost. Madoff was arrested and eventually convicted of investment fraud. His scheme illustrates the properties of white-collar crime. First, he had legitimate access to other people's money. Indeed, they willingly gave it to him to invest on their behalf. They did so because he had a superficial appearance of legitimacy. He was a famous investor on Wall Street who ran a business investing other people's money. Finally, as for spatial separation, most of Madoff's clients never actually saw or met him. They were spread across the country and around the globe.

Of course, not all white-collar crimes manifest all these characteristics. Some, for example, do involve direct contact between the offender and the victim. White-collar crimes come in a bewilderingly large variety. Nevertheless, it is important to try to identify the key characteristics that appear in white-collar offenses. They are important because they affect how white-collar offenses are carried out as well as our ability to develop effective prevention strategies.

So, how do white-collar offenders carry out their crimes? They use three main techniques. In order of importance, the techniques are: (1) *deception*, (2) the *abuse of trust*, and (3) *concealment and conspiracy*. For analytical purposes, we consider each of these techniques separately, but in the real world, more than one of them may be involved in any particular white-collar offense.

The primary technique used by white-collar offenders is deception. It is their master modus operandi. Indeed, the other two techniques that we will be discussing—abuse of trust and concealment—are in a sense simply very important ways in which deception may be accomplished or situations in which it is particularly easy to deceive others.

Deception

Deception is a commonplace word, and we do not need to make it too complicated. However, because it is such a familiar word, it is easy to gloss over some of the conceptual subtleties that are involved in deception. For the study of white-collar crime, it is important to think carefully about exactly what deception is and how it is accomplished. Deception occurs when one person misleads another by making things appear other than they really are. Or, more formally, we could say that deception occurs whenever one person or organization causes another to experience a discrepancy between appearance and reality (Rue, 1994, p. 84). From the point of view of the person who is doing the deceiving, deception is "the advantageous distortion of perceived reality" (Bowyer, 1982, p. 47). On the other hand, for the person on the receiving end, the distortion of reality definitely is not advantageous.

Deception occurs in relationships. That is, deception is a type of interaction between two entities—the deceiver and the deceived (Rue, 1994). The relational nature of deception complicates its analysis. In order to be sure that deception has occurred, we have to know the intentions of the person or organization that is creating the deception. We also have to know the perceptions of the person or organization that is the object of deception. Deception occurs only when two conditions are met. First, one person must deliberately intend to mislead another about the nature of reality, and second, the other person must be misled about reality; they must misperceive it. As we will see later, the relational nature of deception makes it difficult to control the offenses which use this technique.

Deception requires a deliberate attempt by one person to mislead another into doing something that the person would not do if he or she had all the facts (i.e., if he or she hadn't been deceived). We say deception requires one person's misleading another only for rhetorical convenience. Obviously, deceptions can be carried out by groups of people working together to take advantage of other individuals or groups. But to continue with an example, suppose the owner of a business applies for a loan from a bank and, on the loan application, the owner deliberately overstates her financial assets and understates her financial liabilities. She does this in order to make her financial status appear better than it really is in hopes that the bank loan officer will approve her loan application. Obviously, she is deceiving or attempting to deceive the bank. She is also committing the crime of making false statements on a loan application.

Deception by virtue of false or misleading statements is a common technique of white-collar crime. It underlies all consumer fraud-type cases, not to mention a good bit of most advertising. There is no shortage of examples of false and misleading advertising by major manufacturers in which the goal is to convince consumers that a particular product is better than its competitors. Although examples of false and misleading advertising can probably be found in almost every industry and trade, many of the most well-known and publicized cases involve companies that manufacture or process food items, pharmaceuticals, and health related products. For instance, in March 2020, the Federal Trade Commission (FTC) fined a company called Teami, LLC for misleading consumers by claiming without reliable scientific evidence that their products would "fight cancer, clear clogged arteries, decrease migraines, treat and prevent flus, and treat colds" and "would help consumers lose weight" (US FTC March 6, 2020). Teami attempted to carry out their deceptions by secretly paying well-known social influencers, such as Cardi B and others, to promote their products without revealing that the influencers were being paid. What is interesting about this case is that rather than putting ads in magazines or other traditional marketing outlets, Teami took advantage of the popularity of social influencers to deceptively promote its products. Likewise, Kim Kardashian was recently fined by the Securities and Exchange Commission for promoting a cryptocurrency on social media without revealing that she was being paid by the currency's issuer.

Another example of how fraudsters attempt to take advantage of current events and social trends can be found in the multitude of companies that marketed worthless products and services in response to the COVID-19 pandemic. As of January 19, 2022, the FTC has issued warning letters to 405 companies and individuals who were making baseless claims that their COVID-19 services and products could prevent or treat COVID-19. Like Teami, many of these companies used social media platforms to sell their products (US FTC, January 19, 2022). These cases illustrate how white-collar offenders attempt to pervert legitimate economic and business practices for their own ends.

Exactly what counts as being deceptive can be complicated to determine, because deceptiveness is subjective. What fools one person might not fool another. Deception can be complex or simple. It can involve an orchestrated advertising campaign by a large company or a simple misstatement of fact by an individual applying for a bank loan or a government benefit. It can involve the actions of individuals against large organizations, or the actions of large organizations against individuals, or individuals against individuals, or large organizations against other large organizations. These variations in the nature of the relationship between the person or organization being deceived and the person or organization doing the deceiving will be important to consider when we come to the topic of preventing white-collar crime. However, for our purposes now, the important point to note is that the use of deception is one of the standard techniques of white-collar crime. As we review different types of white-collar crime in subsequent chapters, we will want to identify how they are based on deception, to think about how the form of deception is possible, and to explore how we can reduce the likelihood that the deception will be successful.

Abuse of Trust

An important form of deception is the abuse of trust. Abuses of trust occur in what are called "agent–client relationships" or simply "agency relationships". An agency relationship arises whenever an individual or an organization is authorized to "act for" or "on behalf of" another individual or organization (Shapiro, 1990). We call the person or organization that acts for someone else the *agent*. The other party to the relationship is called the *principal*. Typically, agents provide principals with some sort of specialized service based on the agents' expertise or training. Agents do things that we don't have the ability, expertise, time, or willingness to do for ourselves. As principals, we place our trust in agents and hope that they will act in our best interests. But agents sometimes abuse the trust that we place in them through the use of some form of deception. For example, suppose you have some money you want to invest in the stock market but you do not feel confident about picking stocks yourself. So, you contact a stockbroker and ask her for some advice in picking stocks and help in buying them. The stockbroker agrees to take you on as a client. You give her your money with the understanding that she will invest it in the market for you. You are now in an agency relationship based on trust, and you hope that the stockbroker, your agent, will take good care of your money and invest it wisely. It is her duty to use her professional skills to invest your money to help you achieve your financial goals. However, she may not do this at all. She may simply take your money and run off with it. She may foolishly gamble with it in high-risk stocks and lose it all. She may advise you to buy stock in a company that has promised to pay her a kickback for every new client she brings in. In short, she could do a lot of things that would violate the trust you placed in her when you asked her to be your broker.

Agency relationships can vary in many ways (Shapiro, 1990). In some relationships, the principal exerts a great deal of control over the agent, which reduces the chances that the agent can take advantage of the principal. Some agency relationships involve a one-to-one interaction between the agent and the principal, as in our example above with you and the stockbroker. Other relationships involve an agent who acts on behalf of a large number of principals. For example, if you work for a company that has a retirement plan for its employees, the people who manage the pension fund are agents for all the employees who participate in the retirement savings program. These variations in agency relationships influence opportunities for fraud and abuse by agents.

The main trouble with agency relationships is that they are unbalanced (Shapiro, 1990). Agents typically have access to much more information than principals do. Thus, the agent's actions may be based on factors that you as the principal have no way of knowing. In the stockbroker example given above, the broker obviously has access to a lot more information than you do about the stock market. That's why you went to her in the first place. In addition, what the agent does for you is hidden in the sense that you usually don't watch the agent as he or she works. You assume that your broker is taking your money and investing it for you, but you probably don't sit in her office and look over her shoulder as she makes transactions. Next, agents often have control over your property, which they can use to their advantage. Finally, there is a built-in ambivalence in agency relationships. This ambivalence arises out of the potential conflict between the principal's interests and the agent's self-interests. The people who act as your agents—stockbrokers, accountants, financial advisors, doctors, pension fund managers, and so on—all must make a living themselves. Thus, in addition to looking out for you, they are also looking out for themselves. They're trying to make a living, and sometimes what is good for their interests may not be good for yours and vice versa, but agents usually try to keep this conflict of interest to themselves. The need to obscure the fact that agents are looking out for themselves may explain why so many companies and professionals claim to treat their customers like family. As Susan Shapiro (1990) notes, in the modern world, agency relationships are problematic but unavoidable. Hence, we are all potential victims of the abuse of trust.

The degree to which agency relationships are unbalanced and to which the agent's actions are hidden from the principal can vary. Large public corporations, for example, are almost always run by professional managers who in effect act as agents for the owners of the company, that is, the stockholders in the company. Most stockholders have no idea what the professional managers are doing. Indeed, they probably don't even know who most of the managers are. Stockholders are at an extreme information disadvantage. On the other hand, the owner of a private company may take a very active role in her company's day-to-day operations. She may know as much about what is going on as the company's professional managers. In this type of situation, the managers, as agents, may not have an information advantage over the principal, the owner. Active, participatory owners make it difficult for managers to hide what they are doing. This type of agency relationship is not as unbalanced as one in which the principal has less power over the agent and is more likely to be disadvantaged in information.

Concealment and Conspiracy

Concealment and conspiracy are the final techniques of white-collar offenders and are important ways in which deception is achieved. Concealment and conspiracy are also used by ordinary street offenders but for a different purpose than that of white-collar offenders. For ordinary street offenders, concealment may be used to hide the offender's identity. In the case of white-collar crime, it is used to hide the crime. For example, a couple of robbers might work together to rob a liquor store. Perhaps one would hang around outside the store and observe traffic patterns, while the other would go inside and check out the layout of the store: where the cash register is located, how many people are working there, whether there are any security cameras, and whether there is any sign that whoever works in the store has a firearm. Then, the robbers might meet and compare notes to decide the best time for their attack, presumably when the store is relatively empty and the cash register relatively full. They might also decide to wear masks to hide their identities. They try to do whatever they can to ensure that when they initiate the robbery, it will go as quickly and efficiently as possible. They want to get in and out fast, and they hope that no one will recognize them in the process. In this case, the would-be robbers are conspiring to hide the true nature of their activities until the time of the robbery, and then they hope to hide their identities from the victims and the police. Once the robbery gets started, however, it becomes blazingly obvious that a crime is under way. It is easy to imagine other sorts of crimes in which offenders engage in similar clandestine activities before the offense occurs.

White-collar offenders also conspire to hide the true nature of their activities but in a way different from that of conventional offenders. In the case of many white-collar crimes, the conspiratorial activities of the offenders are designed to hide the crime itself. The object of the conspiracy is to conceal and coordinate activities so as to illegally benefit the members of the conspiracy without ever revealing that anything illegal has taken place. Price fixing is a good example. In his famous study of price fixing in the heavy electrical equipment industry, Gilbert Geis (1977) describes how executives from the major manufacturers of electrical equipment would meet and communicate with one another in secret to coordinate the bids that they gave to the purchasers of heavy electrical equipment. Rather than competing against one another by submitting their bids without comparing notes, the executives would decide among themselves in advance who was going to win each contract. The chosen company would then be allowed to submit the "low" bid on the contract, while the other companies submitted slightly higher or otherwise less competitive bids.

This case eventually came to light and the executives were charged and convicted, but it went on for several years before the price-fixing conspiracy was uncovered. Only after detection did it become apparent that laws had been broken and crimes committed. Indeed, the conspiracy came to light only because the executives apparently made the mistake of submitting identical bids in sealed envelopes to the Tennessee Valley Authority (TVA) (Geis, 1977). The TVA officials thought it was highly unlikely that they would receive identical bids for the exceedingly technical and complex electrical equipment that they wanted to purchase. The officials complained to the federal government, which then initiated a grand jury probe that eventually uncovered the facts of these antitrust violations. If the conspirators had been cleverer and submitted bids that were not identical but just similar, there is no telling how long the price fixing would have gone undetected.

Bid rigging is not limited to big corporations. It can also occur among much smaller businesses. For example, in 2019, nine real estate investors were convicted of rigging bids for properties that were being sold at public real estate foreclosure auctions (U.S. Department of Justice, 2019). When properties are sold at auction, the proceeds can be used to pay off the mortgage with any remaining proceeds going to the homeowner. Instead of making competing bids against each other at the auctions, the real estate investors designated a winning "high" bidder in advance for particular properties. The non-winning "low" bidders then received payoffs from the winning bidder. This conspiracy resulted in both the mortgage holder and the homeowner losing money.

Concealment and conspiracy also were instrumental to the longevity of the accounting scandals that rocked corporate America in the late 1990s and early 2000s. The most famous case concerned a company called Enron. Enron was a giant energy trading company that was forced into bankruptcy after its accounting frauds were revealed. The story of Enron is bewilderingly complex and included many different types of fraud, but one of the cleverest schemes involved creating and then misusing what are called "special purpose entities" (SPEs). SPEs are set up by companies who want to hedge risk. By law, SPEs are required to have a certain degree of independence from the company that established them. In other words, an SPE is not supposed to be wholly owned or controlled by the company that sets it up. However, the SPEs set up by Enron were not independent and were used illegally as a way of hiding some of the company's debt. Enron would "sell" its debt to the SPEs that it set up and thereby remove the debt from Enron's books. By conspiring to conceal the true level of the company's debt, executives at Enron could make the company appear to be much more profitable than it really was (McLean and Elkind, 2004, pp. 157–158).

Another example of a white-collar offense that is based on concealment and conspiracy is stock manipulation. Stock manipulation comes in many forms that we will discuss in greater detail in a later chapter (Comerton-Forde and Putnins 2014). In one form called "pump and dump", a group of individuals secretly work together to orchestrate the buying and selling of a particular stock in a manner designed to drive up its price—the pump. Misleading publicity and posts on social media platforms about the stock are used to reinforce the appearance that the stock is becoming a hot item that will continue to rise in value. At some point, when the price has risen high enough, the conspirators sell the stock that they had previously bought at a low price and take their profits—the dump (Shapiro, 1984, pp. 14–15).

In these cases, and in others that rely on concealment and conspiracy, the perpetrators of the offense try to take advantage of how our economic system works by mimicking legitimate activities. In a capitalistic free-market economy, such as ours, we assume that the costs of goods and services are set through competition between producers and the principles of supply and demand. We assume that stock prices reflect objective evaluations of the value of stocks that are made by honest buyers and sellers. And we assume that when a company, such as Enron, reports its assets and liabilities, the figures are accurate. Based on these assumptions, we make decisions to buy products, or sell stocks, or invest in a company, or in some other way part with our money. By using concealment and conspiracy, white-collar offenders can take advantage of our reliance on these assumptions to enrich themselves or their organizations illegally.

By definition, conspiracies involve at least two people working together to accomplish some sort of objective in a clandestine manner, and that means that the people involved have to cooperate and figure out who is going to do what. In other words, conspiracies entail roles, a division of labor, and a coordination of activities. Consider, for example, the long history of organized crime groups such as the Mafia or the gangs who traffic in illegal drugs virtually everywhere in America. These groups have been the subject of considerable attention from both law enforcement agencies and researchers focusing on how they are organized and how they operate (for an overview, see Paoli, 2014). These groups often appear to be structured in a loosely hierarchical fashion with a "big boss" at the top and various levels of specialized subordinates ("lieutenants" and "soldiers") arrayed below them (Albanese, 1999).

Conspiracies are also commonplace in white-collar crime, and this makes some of them similar to organized crimes. However, white-collar conspiracies are different from those found in organized crime, because unlike organized crime gangs that operate in illicit markets (e.g., the provision of outlawed goods and services such as drugs, prostitution, or loan-sharking), white-collar crime groups operate in legitimate markets and involve people who hold legitimate occupational positions within organizations (Lord and Levi, 2017). In these conspiracies, people who occupy different occupational positions in a commercial enterprise play different roles in carrying out the illegal scheme. For example, a number of major corporate accounting frauds were uncovered and prosecuted by the U.S. Department of Justice in the late 1990s and early 2000s (Brickey, 2008). These frauds were complex undertakings that were designed to deceive investors, auditors, and government regulators. While a few of the frauds were committed by solo offenders, most were conspiracies involving anywhere from two to ten or more individuals playing different roles in the schemes. For example,

> *ringleaders* initiated or orchestrated a scheme or played a major leadership role; *major players* proactively furthered a scheme but did not initiate or orchestrate it; *in-between players* executed a part of a scheme or its cover-up as directed or encouraged by a superior but with some diligence or inventiveness once involved; and, *minor participants* were mostly reactive, acting at the behest of a superior, or in some minor capacity, such as following orders or acting in other complicit ways.
>
> (Steffensmeier et al., 2013, pp. 456–457)

The division of labor in other white-collar crimes may be different than it was for the corporate accounting frauds of the early twenty-first century, but the general principle holds. As Sutherland (1949) noted long ago, white-collar crimes are often like organized crimes (Lord and Levi, 2017). Thus, as we will see in future chapters, an important aspect of the opportunity structure for many white-collar crimes is the availability, knowledge, and skills of potential conspiracy members.

The Many Facets of Deception

All white-collar crimes are in some way based on deception. That is, the offender in some way tries to hide the crime itself. However, the nature of the deception varies in terms of its intended longevity, potential victims, and form. Regarding longevity, sometimes the deception is meant or intended by the perpetrator to be permanent. The offender endeavors to design or commit the crime in such a manner that it will never be discovered. As we discuss in the following chapters, non-self-revealing frauds in the health care system are like this, and many other white-collar offenses, such as insider trading and price fixing, also are based on the idea of permanent deception. However, not all white-collar crimes are intended to remain hidden forever. In some cases, the offender aspires only to fool the victim long enough to get whatever he or she wants from the victim and then get away. The perpetrators of these scams understand that eventually their schemes will be exposed. Accordingly, they tend to move around and not stay put in one place too long.

The targets of deception in white-collar crime include individuals, organizations, government programs, the community in general, and law enforcers. The target sometimes is a specific individual whom the offender has somehow identified as a potential victim and who is approached directly by the offender. At other times, the victims may be individuals, but they are not individually targeted by offenders. False advertising is a classic example. Here the offender advertises some product or service in a misleading manner, hoping that someone will be fooled by the come-on. It does not really matter who falls for the scam as long as there are enough people who do, so that the scheme becomes profitable for the offender.

The victims of white-collar crime, however, are not always individuals. Some of the most profitable targets for white-collar offenders are government programs. These programs, such as the federal Medicare and Medicaid programs, distribute enormous sums of money. They make very attractive targets for those who wish to pick up some easy cash. Like government programs, business organizations can be targeted by individuals or other businesses. For example, in certain antitrust conspiracies, the victims are other businesses who have to pay more for the products or services because of price fixing among their suppliers. For example, in 2012 Japanese automobile parts suppliers were charged with fixing prices for their products. The direct victims of this scheme were automakers and auto repairers who had to pay artificially high prices (Trop, 2013). Of course, some of these costs were passed on to consumers, so they are indirect victims of this offense.

Finally, for some white-collar crimes, there really may be no specific identifiable targets or victims. The target is the system of economic exchange itself. Consider, for example, insider trading, whereby a corporate insider makes some sort of advantageous stock trade on the basis of inside information. The offender uses the inside information to exploit or take advantage of the naturally occurring fluctuations in the price of stocks. The offender is not out to hurt any other stock trader or organization or government program. Rather, he or she is making a trade based on superior information about what is likely to happen in the future. Other investors may, of course, be hurt if they happen to be the ones who bought or sold the stock that the offender is involved with, but they are not specifically targeted by the offender, and they may have made the same decision to buy or sell regardless of what the inside trader did. This kind of diffuse victimization is a characteristic feature of some white-collar crimes.

Deception can be achieved in different ways. Recall that deception is the advantageous distortion of perceived reality (Bowyer, 1982). It is a relational concept that always involves two organisms or entities—a deceiver and a deceived. Deception occurs when one person or entity (the deceiver) somehow defeats the ability of another person or entity (the deceived) to perceive reality as it really is. How the deceiver goes about accomplishing this objective depends in part on who or what the victim is and on what the offender is trying to do to or get from the victim. The cases that we will be reviewing in this book suggest that there are three general forms or ways in which deception in white-collar crime is achieved: embellishing, mimicking, and concealment.

Consider first the strategy of embellishing. In many consumer and investment frauds, the offender tries to lure the victim into buying a product or service or investing in a project by somehow suggesting that the product or service is like others in its category—only better. The investment scheme is presented as solid and reliable, like other good investments, but better because it has a higher or more consistent rate of return. The fraudulent home repair contractor who does shoddy work or uses substandard materials presents himself as competent and reliable, like other good contractors, but better because he is cheaper. Offenders who use embellishment hope to entice victims by making them think that buying a product or investing in a scheme is in their best interests when it really is not. Embellishment depends on that part of human nature that always seems to be looking for a good deal or a free lunch. It is a good strategy for white-collar offenders to use, because the line between being justifiably proud of your product and lying about it is often not clear. Distinguishing between the person who is presenting his or her product in the best possible light and the person who is an outright liar is the problem for both victims and law enforcers.

Successful embellishment depends on making something stand out from the ordinary and thereby bringing attention to yourself. Mimicking, on the other hand, depends on doing just the opposite. The object is to make something appear normal rather than exceptional. As we will show, fraud in the federal Medicaid system is a perfect example. In these frauds, a physician or other type of health care professional submits an unjustified claim for reimbursement to the Medicaid program. To be successful, the offender must make his or her claim appear to be normal and legitimate. The idea is not to draw attention but rather to blend in by mimicking the millions of other legitimate claims that are paid every day. Fraud in other government programs works in much the same way. The government provides a benefit to some qualified group. The trick for the white-collar offender is to appear to be qualified for the benefit. Besides fraud in government programs, there are other white-collar offenses that depend on mimicking (e.g., some types of insider trading in the stock market and some antitrust offenses such as bid rigging and price fixing). Successful inside traders are those who make their moves appear to be part of normal market activity. Likewise, successful antitrust offenders are those who make their pricing decisions look normal and reasonable.

Concealment is another strategy that white-collar offenders use. It often underlies some of the more serious forms of white-collar crime. Consider, for example, environmental and workplace safety offenses. In many of these crimes, offenders try to conceal their illegal activities from outside observers. They do not try to entice potential victims into spending their money, nor do they try to obtain money illegally from government programs. Rather, offenders engage in clandestine activities that work to their financial benefit but are also illegal and potentially harmful to others. In the following chapters, we will present many examples of serious white-collar offending that involved large corporations hiding their activities from the government and their local communities.

Reconsidering Sutherland: Techniques and Power

Sutherland urged criminologists to acknowledge and to investigate the crimes of the powerful, and he is rightly remembered and venerated for this. Regardless whether you agree or disagree with his approach to white-collar crime, there is no doubt that without his fundamental insights, criminology would be impoverished and our society would be even more vulnerable to the abuses of the rich and powerful than it already is. Thus, we should never forget Sutherland's basic point that wealthy and powerful individuals commit occupationally related crimes that cause great social harm.

However, we believe that Sutherland's analysis can be extended by investigating not only who the white-collar offender is, but also how white-collar offenses are committed—that is, we must pay attention to the techniques used by white-collar offenders. We believe that this focus on techniques will permit us to develop a firmer understanding of how and why these crimes occur. We also believe it will shed new light on the problem of control by directing our attention toward the strategy of fighting white-collar crime by manipulating situational conditions that affect the attractiveness of opportunities for crime.

Even though we intend to concentrate on techniques and opportunity structures, we will not ignore Sutherland's concern with power. Indeed, the economic and political power of white-collar offenders is important precisely because it provides them with access to white-collar crime opportunities and facilitates their ability to deceive, to conceal, and to abuse trust. As critical and postmodern theorists have demonstrated, elites also use their economic and political power to shape the legal environment—both criminal and regulatory—within which they operate (Friedrichs, 2009). Their ability to shape the legal environment directly affects opportunity structures for white-collar crime by reducing the credibility of oversight and giving offenders more freedom to operate with impunity (Ruggiero, 2009). Thus, social and economic power plays a central role in the rest of our analysis.

Summary

White-collar crimes are different than ordinary street crimes in regard to their opportunity structures and the techniques that are used to commit them. Three important features of white-collar crime are (1) specialized access, (2) the superficial appearance of legitimacy, and (3) spatial separation from victims. Of these features, specialized access is probably the most important (Felson, 2002). It is the offender's occupational or organizational role that provides him or her with access to the crime target. Specialized access helps offenders to paint their actions with a superficial appearance of legitimacy and often allows them to separate themselves from any direct contact with individual victims.

White-collar crimes are based on deception, which can be defined as the "advantageous distortion of perceived reality" (Bowyer, 1982, p. 47). The trick for the offender is to hide the crime, to make what is illegitimate appear legitimate. Offenders who are in trust relationships with their victims often are in particularly good positions to accomplish this task. Deception can be achieved in different ways. As we show in the following chapters, some offenders try to make their illegal activities blend in with legal activities, while others simply try to conceal what they are doing.

Part III

Applying the Opportunity Perspective to White-Collar Crime

The opportunity perspective assumes that particular crimes have particular opportunity structures (i.e., conditions that make a particular type of crime possible and attractive to potential offenders), and this applies to white-collar crimes, but the necessary conditions may vary substantially from one white-collar offense to another. For example, the conditions that make health care fraud feasible and attractive to offenders differ from those needed for price fixing. Thus, the opportunity perspective prompts us to focus on highly specific forms of crime. Obviously, there are many different forms of white-collar crime, and we cannot cover all of them here. So, instead we take a representative sample of well-known and important types of white-collar crime and use them to illustrate how our approach would work. Our goal is to focus on how the different offenses are committed. We hope that understanding how an offense is committed will suggest ways in which to prevent or reduce similar offenses in the future.

Because we are focusing on "how" particular white-collar offenses are committed, we leave aside, for the time being, the issue of "why" they are committed. That is, at this point, we assume that a motivated offender is present without attempting to understand exactly what his or her motivations are or what causes him or her to engage in the offense. However, in many cases, it is safe to assume that the underlying motivation for white-collar crime is financially based. Indeed, white-collar offenders often are motivated by one or more of four objectives: (1) to benefit themselves financially, (2) to benefit the financial standing or competitive position of a company or an employer, (3) to stay in business, or (4) to avoid losing financial assets. However, even though white-collar and corporate offenses may be motivated by financial considerations, some of them can have serious physical effects on the health and well-being of workers, consumers, and the public in general.

In Chapter 6, we explore crimes whose effects are primarily financial. Specifically, we focus on health care fraud, mortgage fraud, securities violations, antitrust violations, and frauds related to natural disasters, including COVID-19. The perpetrators of these crimes can range from individuals or small businesses to huge multinational corporations. For each offense, we first present some background material that explains the structure of the industry or business activity out of which the offense arises. Then, we examine the opportunity structure for each offense. In all cases, there are a variety of different types or subtypes of each offense within each of our general categories. For the sake of brevity, we concentrate on only a few of the subtypes. In Chapter 7, we follow the same approach to cover offenses that often cause physical harms and that raise more complicated issues with respect to their opportunity structures—environmental offenses, workplace safety offenses, and manufacturing offenses. We end with a brief introduction to atrocity crimes.

DOI: 10.4324/9781003175322-8

Applying the Opportunity Perspective to White-Collar Crime

Financial Crimes in Health Care, Mortgages, Securities, Markets, and Crises

Health Care Fraud

The health care industry is the largest single industry in the U.S. economy. In 2020, it accounted for roughly 19.7 percent of the United States gross domestic product, or $4.1 trillion dollars (Centers for Medicare & Medicaid Services, 2023). Besides being large and expensive, the health care industry is also complex, involving many different types of professionals and organizations. Obviously, physicians and hospitals are a part of the industry, but the industry also includes treatment centers, nursing homes, outpatient clinics, home health care businesses, testing laboratories, and a host of other health-related facilities and programs. Any sort of organization that provides any kind of medical service is part of the health care industry. Included as well are the companies that provide medical equipment and supplies, which can range from Band-Aids to advanced magnetic resonance imaging machines. As we will see, there are also companies that provide record keeping, accounting, and billing services for health care providers and organizations. Finally, of course, there are the pharmaceutical companies. So, it's a big industry, with lots of different kinds of suppliers and customers, involving a lot of money. Unfortunately, a lot of the money that goes into the health care industry does not go to treat patients. Rather, it is lost to fraud and abuse.

Just how much is lost? Nobody knows for sure, and estimates vary widely from $80 billion to over $250 billion (Sharp, 2011). In the late 1990s, Sparrow (1998) estimated that as much as 10 percent was lost annually to fraud and abuse, but other estimates peg the figure at 3 percent. Considering that currently around $4.1 trillion is spent annually on health care, the amount lost to fraud may exceed $320 billion per year if the 10 percent figure is accurate (Martin et al., 2017). This works out to about $877 million per day.

Any of the many different types of professionals and organizations involved in the health care industry can engage in fraud, including physicians, pharmacists, physical therapists, health care organizations, nursing homes, psychiatric units, substance abuse programs, mental health facilities, testing laboratories, medical suppliers, as well as the companies that manage billing and records for health care organizations. All these organizations potentially can be sites for fraud. Finally, there is evidence that organized criminals and con artists have gotten into the lucrative business of fraud in health care (U.S. Federal Bureau of Investigation, 2010).

In order to understand why fraud is such a huge problem in the health care industry, we must first understand how the industry works. The most important thing to know is that most of the money spent on health care is not spent by individual consumers. That makes

DOI: 10.4324/9781003175322-9

health care unlike most other industries that provide services and products to consumers. If you go to a restaurant and order a meal, you pay for it. If you buy a car, you pay for it. If your car needs to be fixed, you go to a mechanic and you pay for it. In all these transactions, you have a vested interest in making sure that you get your money's worth. But for most of us, health care doesn't work like this. Most health care costs are covered by insurance. The costs are paid, at least in part, either by a private insurance company or by one of the two big government insurance programs—Medicare and Medicaid. Thus, the people who pay are not the people who receive the medical service, whatever it might be. This difference in the structure of the industry is crucial to understanding the opportunity structure for different forms of health care fraud.

To demonstrate the significance of the structure of the health care industry, let's consider a few diagrams. The first diagram (Figure 6.1) is an idealized illustration of how the health care system is supposed to work.

In Figure 6.1, here's what happens. An elderly patient goes to a doctor and receives some sort of medical service. Let's say it is a minor surgical procedure performed in the office. The doctor's office submits a claim for reimbursement to Medicare. (Note: keep in mind that any number of health care providers and health care organizations could take the place of the physician and submit the claim. Our example uses a physician only to keep things

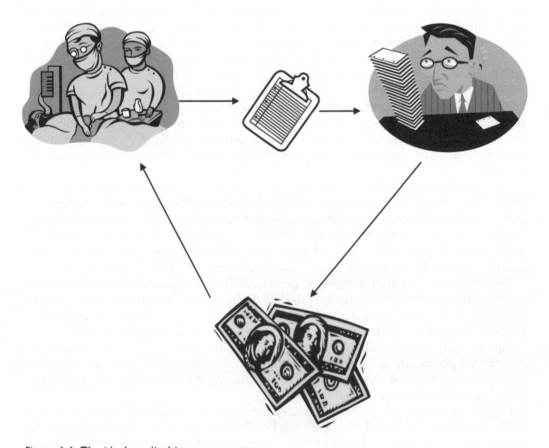

Figure 6.1 The ideal medical insurance system

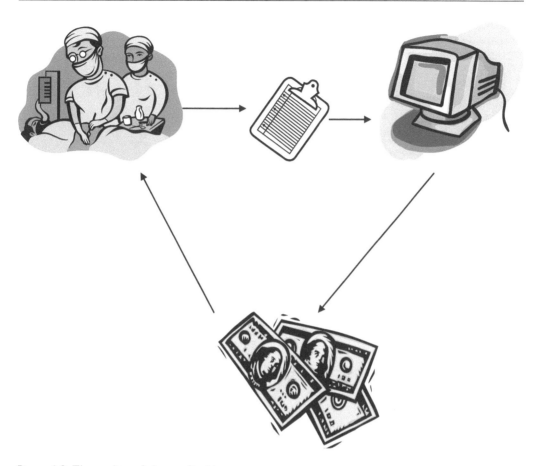

Figure 6.2 The reality of the medical insurance system

simple.) The claim is reviewed by an agent at Medicare. After the agent has determined that the claim form is acceptable, a check is sent to the doctor's office.

You may have noticed that the agent in Figure 6.1 does not look very happy. That's because he's got a lot of work to do. On average, the Medicare system receives more than a billion claims per year, far too many to be checked individually by real people. As a result, the Medicare system really operates as depicted in Figure 6.2, where the agent has been replaced by a computer. The computer reviews the claims and, based on certain decision rules, decides whether it should be paid.

Considering how the health care industry is organized, where are the opportunities for fraud? The key point in the cycle presented in Figure 6.2 occurs when the health care provider submits the claim to Medicare. That is the point at which fraud can occur. Figure 6.3 shows a simple example of how an ill-intentioned physician could take advantage of this system. In Figure 6.3, the physician simply sits in his or her office and submits a claim form even though he or she did not actually treat a patient. However, the form submitted in Figure 6.3 looks just like the form submitted in Figure 6.2. That is, it looks legitimate, and the computer authorizes payment to the doctor. There are many variations on this scheme and many ways of subtly changing the fraudulent information that is submitted

Figure 6.3 Ripping off the medical insurance system

as well as how it is submitted (Moffat, 1993). However, in a nutshell, that is how many health care frauds work. A claim is filed with Medicare, Medicaid, or a private health insurance company that does not accurately reflect what actually happened in the field or what should have happened in the field.

A more systematic variation on the physician's scam and one that can produce a lot of money in a short period of time is called the "rent-a-patient" scheme (Hast, 2000). The scheme involves a network of individuals, often including legitimate physicians (see Figure 6.4). For example, in one recent scheme two clinics located in Michigan advertised that they provided physical therapy services, but in reality, the clinics served as the largest pill mill operation in the Detroit-metro area. The clinic owners paid recruiters to bring "patients" to their physical therapy clinics to see physicians who wrote medically unnecessary prescriptions for oxycodone, Xanax, and other controlled substances for which the patients were charged fees. The owners billed Medicare and private insurers for physical therapy services that were never provided. The patients in turn filled the prescriptions and then sold the drugs on the streets of Detroit and elsewhere (U.S. Department of Health and Human Services and Department of Justice, 2021).

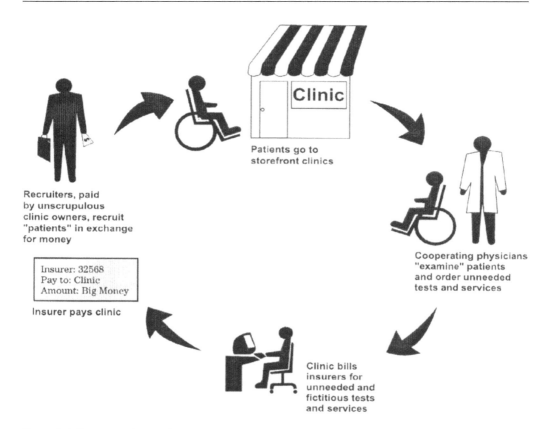

Figure 6.4 Rent-a-patient scheme

Source: Hast (2000)

Physicians are not the only ones defrauding the health care system. The Federal Bureau of Investigation (FBI) has investigated a number of high-profile cases of massive fraud by large organizations. For example, in 2011, the owners of a company called American Therapeutic Corporation (ATC) located in Miami, Florida, were convicted of filing approximately $205 million worth of fraudulent claims with Medicare. ATC operated the largest community mental health centers in Florida. In a ruse that is a variation on the rent-a-patient scheme, ATC paid kickbacks to assisted living facilities in order to recruit patients for group therapy programs that the patients didn't really need. In 2010, Glaxo-SmithKline, one of the largest pharmaceutical companies in the world, pled guilty and paid criminal fines for charges relating to the manufacture and distribution of adulterated drugs (U.S. Federal Bureau of Investigation, 2011). In another case, 20 individuals were convicted for their involvement in a sophisticated scheme to defraud Medicare. The convictions involved the largest certified home health agency in Miami (Anonymous, 2007). The agency was paid more than $100 million in Medicare funds for reimbursement of services, including nursing and home aide visits. These services either had not been provided, were not necessary, or were provided to people who were not eligible. In another case, Fresenius Medical Care North America, Inc., the world's largest provider of kidney dialysis products and services, agreed to pay the U.S. government $486 million to resolve an investigation of fraud at National Medical Care, Inc., a subsidiary of Fresenius (Rowland, 2005). The list of cases could go on, but as these examples indicate, the amounts of money involved can be huge.

More importantly, health care fraud can impose serious physical harm on patients, including death. For example, in 2014, Dr Farid Fata, a haematologist-oncologist, was convicted of administering unnecessary chemotherapy to patients, putting their health and lives at risk, and was sentenced to 45 years in prison. Dr Fata came to be known as "Dr Death" after his case was exposed by federal investigators (Stafford, 2015). He routinely gave chemotherapy to cancer-free patients. His crimes came to light when whistle-blowers in his office reported him to federal authorities.

Health care fraud illustrates to perfection the defining characteristics of white-collar crime. All health care providers and health care organizations have legitimate access to patients and to the various government programs and private companies that provide health care insurance. Even though the offenders are stealing from the government and insurance companies, they are spatially separated from them. Finally, their actions have the superficial appearance of legitimacy. Indeed, they depend on the appearance of legitimacy, because to get paid, those who commit fraud must submit claims that look routine and legitimate.

As we noted earlier, the key point in the opportunity structure for health care fraud is when the health care provider submits a claim to an insurer. As a thought experiment, imagine that insurers could instantly verify whether the information submitted on the claim truly represented what happened in the field, and furthermore, whether it was medically necessary. If this were the case, then health care providers would have no opportunity to commit fraud. However, for a number of reasons, this ideal situation is far from reality.

Part of the problem stems from the size, complexity, and structure of our health care system. For example, in 2021 close to 64 million people were enrolled in Medicare and another 76 million were enrolled in Medicaid (Centers for Medicare & Medicaid Services, 2021). Because there are so many claims, it is impossible to review all of them carefully to make sure that they are legitimate. So, most claims are reviewed by computers. On the one hand, this is good because computers are fast and they can process claims quickly. On the other hand, it is bad because computers do only what they are told to do and, in the past, have not been very good at looking for unusual patterns in data, making life easy for people who want to defraud health care programs. Another part of the problem is that controlling fraud takes time, personnel, and money away from processing claims (Sparrow, 1996). Government programs such as Medicare and Medicaid and private insurance companies are under a lot of pressure from physicians and the rest of the health care community to process claims as quickly as possible. Honest physicians want to be paid fast and with a minimum of hassle. Thus, for health insurers, there is a constant tension between using resources to control fraud and using resources to process and pay claims quickly. In the past, computers could be programmed to catch simple obvious frauds, such as when a doctor claimed to have operated on 100 patients in a day, but until recently, computers have been less adept at catching fraudulent claims that were not obvious. Sophisticated fraudsters could deliberately design their schemes so that they looked legitimate. They would test the system and learn from their mistakes about what is acceptable and what is not. For example, when a claim comes in that the computer recognizes as not acceptable, this does not automatically trigger an investigation that might uncover fraud. Instead, the claim is simply rejected. Unfortunately, this means that the offender has an opportunity to learn what does not work and gets away to try another day.

The passage of the Affordable Care Act in 2010 improved the situation regarding the control of health care fraud because it included measures to crack down on illegal activities involving Medicare and Medicaid. Early in its tenure, the Obama administration created a cabinet-level anti-fraud task force. The administration then created "strike force teams" with personnel from different agencies that were tasked with investigating fraud in areas that had unusually high rates of Medicare and Medicaid billings. Currently, strike force teams operate in South Florida, Los Angeles, Detroit, Houston, Brooklyn, Chicago, Dallas, Newark, and the Gulf Coast. Rather than using the standard "pay and chase" mode of enforcement in which claims are paid and then investigated to see if they are fraudulent, the strike force teams use a proactive approach to enforcement. They use data analytics to identify suspicious patterns and clusters of billings and then use special investigative techniques, such as undercover agents, surveillance, and wiretaps, to build cases against large-scale defrauders (Iglehart, 2010). For example, the case against the pill mill operation in the Detroit area cited above was the product of a strike force investigation.

Mortgage Fraud and the Global Financial Collapse

More so than other forms of crime, white-collar crime evolves over time. New forms emerge and old ones die away. Every few years there is a new scandal in which some previously unrecognized form of financial wrongdoing in the business world explodes onto the public stage, generating widespread public outrage, fervid political posturing, and improved job security for investigative journalists. Indeed, as we discuss in Chapter 10, the cycle of scandal, public outrage, and political response drives the evolution of legal controls over misconduct in business and the professions. In late 2008, the largest ever of these financial scandals slammed into the American economy like a tsunami. It involved a bewildering variety of interrelated frauds and financial crimes arising out of the real estate, mortgage, and investment banking industries.

As with fraud in health care, to understand the crimes that occurred in these three industries, it is necessary to get a handle on how these industries work, that is, how they are interconnected and how money is made in them. Over the past three decades, the home mortgage industry has changed in ways that have had both positive and negative effects on American society. On the positive side, the changes promoted greater access to homeownership for people of low to moderate incomes. However, on the negative side, the changes also created new opportunities for fraud (Barnett, 2013; Simpson, 2012). To illustrate these criminogenic conditions, we begin by tracing what typically happens when someone sets out to buy a home.

In the early 2000s, the real estate market was hot. Homes were selling fast and home prices were rising rapidly. In most cases, the process followed by the typical home buyer would go something like this. First, the prospective buyer would contact a real estate agent for help in finding homes for sale and in navigating the byzantine form-filled process of purchasing a home. After an acceptable home at an acceptable price was found, the buyer would get in touch with a mortgage broker, who would help the buyer find and apply for a home loan. The home buyer often needed help because applying for a loan could be a confusing process that involved a variety of different loan products. Before 1970, most mortgages were simple. They had fixed terms and required a certain size of down payment in relation to the value of the loan (called the loan-to-value rate), which was often 20 percent. The loan would then be paid off over the course of a set number of years (usually 15 or 30) at a fixed interest rate. To get a loan, potential buyers would go to their local bank or savings and loan association, fill out the necessary paperwork to apply for a mortgage and work with them if their application was approved.

However, beginning in the 1970s, lenders began to offer new forms of mortgages, such as *adjustable rate mortgages* (ARMs). As the name implies, the interest rate on an ARM loan is adjustable depending on various economic indicators. It changes over time, often starting out very low and then increasing later. ARM loans came in several different shapes and sizes. Other types of loans included *buy-downs*, where the seller subsidizes the borrower for a short period of time. *Graduated payment mortgages* start with low payments that rise over time. *Negative amortization loans* are loans where the payment is less than is needed to pay off the loan over time, and so the loan gradually gets larger over time. Another very important form of loan that developed during the 1990s was the *subprime* mortgage. These are loans made to people who normally would not qualify for regular loans because of their inadequate credit. Finally, starting around 2004, lenders developed what were called *alternative documentation loans*. These were designed for people who had complicated finances and who could not provide traditional financial documents, such as pay stubs or W-2 forms, to verify their creditworthiness. Self-employed people, for example, might fall into this category.[1] In addition to the profusion of loan products, interest rates fluctuated dramatically during the 1990s and 2000s, and lenders competed viciously to attract borrowers. The job of the mortgage broker was to help the borrower navigate this treacherous financial terrain and find the most appropriate loan product at the best price given the borrower's individual financial situation. The broker would also help organize the process of closing the loan. In return for providing these services, the broker would receive a fee, which could be paid by either the borrower or the lender.

As far as the home buyer is concerned, once the loan is closed, he or she can take possession of the house, move in, and say goodbye to the real estate agent and mortgage broker. As long as the buyer makes the monthly mortgage payments, there typically is nothing else to worry about.

You might think that when the buyer sends in the monthly mortgage payment it would go to the bank that made the loan, but that is not what actually happens. Rather, the loan takes on a life of its own and becomes part of a meandering river of financial transactions that disappears into the secretive and convoluted world of investment banking. To illustrate the process, let's assume that the loan was made by a local bank. The bank does not keep the loan and receive the payments from the borrower. Rather, the bank sells the loan on what is called the *secondary mortgage market*. So, for example, if the loan was for $100,000, the bank might sell it on the secondary market for $105,000. The $5,000 would be the bank's profit on the loan, and the bank would then have $100,000 to loan to a new borrower.

The secondary mortgage market involves large private financial institutions, such as Countrywide Bank, and semi-public institutions known as government-sponsored entities (GSEs). Two that you might have heard of are the Federal National Mortgage Association (FNMA), popularly known as "Fannie Mae", and the Federal Home Loan Mortgage Corporation, or "Freddie Mac". These two institutions were created by the federal government to increase liquidity in the mortgage market. In simplified form, the process worked in this manner. A bank lends a home buyer $100,000 to buy a home. The bank then sells the loan and its documentation to Fannie Mae for $100,000 plus some profit. The bank then has $100,000 available to lend to another home buyer and the process continues with subsequent buyers. Fannie Mae can hold the loan and receive the loan payments from the buyer or it can sell the loan as a security to another investor, in which case the investor would be paid interest or a dividend for as long as he or she held the security.

However, rather than selling individual loans as securities, Fannie Mae and the other institutional players in the secondary mortgage market usually create *mortgage-backed securities* (MBSs), which are securities based on a collection ("pool") of mortgages, and sell them to investors. The investors receive what is called the "pass through", that is, the interest and principal payments that the borrowers make each month on the loan. In the early 1980s, the relatively simple MBS idea was transformed when Fannie Mae and others began creating and selling *collateralized mortgage obligations* (CMOs). CMOs are complicated debt securities that can operate or perform in different ways. Simplifying greatly, a CMO is a collection of mortgage-backed securities that is divided into different classes (also called "tranches") based on the creditworthiness of the borrowers and is offered for sale by what is called a *special purpose entity* (SPE). The SPE sells bonds based on the different tranches in the CMO, with the bonds paying different rates depending on the creditworthiness of the mortgages that make up each particular tranche. Some tranches are less risky than others, and so the bonds based on these low-risk tranches pay lower rates. For example, the least risky tranche in a CMO might be based on mortgage loans made to people who can afford a 20 percent down payment and who have excellent credit histories, stable employment, and good incomes. The riskiest tranche, on the other hand, would be based on a collection of subprime or alternative documentation loans. These are loans made to borrowers who cannot afford much in the way of a down payment, who do not have good credit, and who are at much greater risk to default. The investors in CMOs are usually large banks, hedge funds, pension funds, or insurance companies. As long as borrowers make their payments on time, CMOs represent a good investment opportunity. However, if enough borrowers in any of the tranche's default on their loans, then the CMO becomes worthless and investors lose some or all of the money they have invested in the bond. This is precisely what started to happen in 2008 when the housing market collapsed. It might be helpful at this point to recap in outline form the steps involved in buying and financing a home when everything goes right:

1 The buyer works with a real estate agent to find the right home.
2 The buyer contacts a mortgage broker for help in identifying an appropriate loan product (say a subprime ARM loan) and finding a lender.
3 With the help of the mortgage broker, the buyer fills out the application for a loan and submits it to the lender.
4 After reviewing the loan application, the lender loans the money to the buyer and takes control of the title to the house and all the loan documents.
5 The lender sells the loan and documentation on the secondary market, say to Fannie Mae.
6 Fannie Mae creates an MBS and then bundles it into a CMO, which is then offered for sale by a SPE to investors.
7 Investors (usually pension funds, insurance companies, and investment banks) buy shares in the CMO.
8 The buyer makes his or her loan payments on time for the life of the loan and at the end of the term gets the title to the house.
9 The investors receive the rate of return promised to them for their shares in the CMO.
10 Everyone is happy.

Unfortunately, all too often the happy scenario outlined above was not what actually happened. At any number of points along the way, there were opportunities for fraud and other forms of financial malfeasance, involving in different ways all the players in the process, from home buyers up to the investment bankers who sold MBSs and CMOs. Indeed, between roughly 1990 and 2008, the housing, mortgage, and banking markets generated a tremendous amount of lure coupled with an astonishing lack of oversight.

Let's start with the home buyer. In the example given above, the buyer was presented as a responsible person who wanted to pay off the loan in a timely manner. However, in the 1990s and 2000s, not all buyers were responsible or honest. Buyers could engage in what was known as "fraud for property or housing" (Financial Crimes Enforcement Network, 2006). In a fraud for property scheme, the buyer would make false statements on the application for the loan in an attempt to secure a house. The false statements might include lies about his or her income, debts, or employment. This type of fraud was relatively easy to get away with during this period because the housing market was booming and there was little oversight of the loan application process by either lenders or regulators. This lack of oversight happened in part because the Internet made it easy for customers to apply for loans online and for banks to approve applications—sometimes within hours of the application. In other words, no one was checking carefully to see if what was on the loan application regarding the buyer's ability to repay the loan was accurate. Lenders were willing to make subprime loans that required no down payment, no proof of income, and interest-only payments (Barnett, 2013), because they profited not by making loans but rather by selling loans on the secondary market. The more loans they had to sell, the more profits they made. Black (2010) has referred to these kinds of loans as "liar's loans", noting that "liar's loans are optimal for only one group of lenders—those engaged in accounting control fraud".

Buyers, however, did not always act alone. Rather, they were often aided in carrying out this scheme by unscrupulous mortgage brokers who were more interested in earning a commission than in making sure the buyer could really afford the house and repay the loan. Indeed, sometimes mortgage brokers would conspire with real estate agents, appraisers, and others to engage in more sophisticated schemes, called property flipping, where the object was not property but profit. In simplified form, the scheme works like this. The real estate agent and the mortgage broker recruit a straw buyer, that is, a person who only pretends to want to buy a house. The agent, broker, and straw buyer work together to get a mortgage loan and buy the house for, say, $100,000. A little while later, the buyer puts the house up for sale, and an appraiser who is involved in the scheme appraises the house at, say, $150,000. The house is then sold at this inflated price, and after paying off the original loan, the conspirators now have $50,000 in profit (minus a few fees that must be paid). This "flipping" of the property could continue for a few more rounds until one of two things happened: Some unsuspecting buyer is left with a house for which he or she grossly overpaid, or the last buyer could also be a straw buyer and simply walk away from the house and default on the loan. Either way, the conspirators would make a nice profit for just a little paperwork. As with fraud for property schemes, property flipping was also easy to get away with because of lax oversight and competition among lenders to originate as many loans as possible. No one in the system spent much time checking the accuracy of loan documents.

In the previous two examples, the not wholly blameless victims of the fraudulent schemes were lenders, as the fraud was perpetrated against the financial institutions that made the loans. However, there were other schemes in which the victims were just ordinary people. These schemes involved mortgage brokers, banks, and other insiders who used their expertise to take advantage of unsuspecting home buyers. These schemes illustrate how legitimate financial transactions can be distorted to commit white-collar crimes. For example, consider the marketing of subprime loans in the years running up to 2008. Recall that subprime loans were developed in order to make it possible for people with low to moderate incomes to qualify for mortgage loans and to own their own homes. Subprime loans typically required applicants to provide lower down payments and less proof of income than ordinary prime loans. They were often packaged as ARMs, which meant that the interest rate started out low but eventually rose to a higher rate than that charged for traditional prime loans. Compared with prime loans, subprime loans also have higher fees and prepayment penalties. Because of their higher fees, penalties, and interest rates, these types of loans are very profitable for banks and a good source of income. Although the idea of giving low-income people a chance to own a home seems commendable, there is substantial evidence that this noble idea was perverted for illegal ends by many players in the mortgage and banking industry. Mortgage brokers would use fraud and deceit to entice unsophisticated low-income buyers to apply for loans that they really could not afford and that would end up in default (Calem, Herschaff, and Wachter, 2004). A disproportionate number of these low-income buyers were African-American or Hispanic, and the targeting of minority group members to steer them toward subprime loan products was standard practice among some mortgage brokers and bankers—so much so that even middle-income African-Americans and Hispanics who could have qualified for normal loans were steered toward subprime products to their disadvantage (Faber, 2013). When their loan payments ballooned after the buy-down period expired, many subprime buyers could no longer afford the new monthly mortgage payment and they defaulted. Because so many of these loans targeted low-income African-American and Hispanic homeowners, the collateral consequences to poor urban neighborhoods were catastrophic.

But the question can be raised, why would a mortgage broker or a banker want to loan money to someone who might not repay it? Why would lenders seek out borrowers who posed more rather than less risk? The answer to these questions lies in the structure of the mortgage industry outlined above, especially as it relates to the securitization of mortgages, that is, the practice of bundling mortgages together and selling them as mortgage-backed securities or collateralized debt obligations. Securitization disconnected lenders from the risks posed by subprime borrowers (Faber, 2013). Banks and other mortgage lenders did not have to worry about loans defaulting, because they sold the loans to other financial institutions that then securitized them. The risks associated with subprime loans were passed onto and borne by the investors in mortgage-backed securities. Thus, the broker and the lender that originated the loan would collect their fees and their profits from the sale of the loan, but they would not have to worry that the home buyer might eventually default on the loan. In addition, technological changes in the processing of loan applications that were adopted to speed up the approval process made it easier for applications based on fraudulent information to slip through unnoticed. Because competition for new loans was fierce, many lenders adopted *automated underwriting systems*. These software systems would review the loan application and either approve or reject it based solely on the information in the application. No attempt was made to verify that the information was accurate—for example, by checking to see whether the applicant really did have the income stated on the application (Barnett, 2013).

After loans moved on to the secondary market, new opportunities for fraud and deception opened up, but they were much more complicated than the schemes cooked up by real estate agents, mortgage brokers, and appraisers. The world of mortgage-backed securities, collateralized mortgage obligations, and collateralized debt obligations (CDOs) can be mind-numbingly complex. But at its core, fraud is always the same. It always involves a distortion of reality that is advantageous to one party and disadvantageous to another. In the case of mortgage-backed securities, the distortion involved the description of the risks associated with the various forms of mortgage-backed securities. Although the legal and financial details involved here require close attention to follow, it is worth the effort in order to understand how fraud and deception in the highest ranks of the financial world put the entire American economy on the very edge of total collapse.

Recall that a CMO is a collection of mortgage-backed securities that are grouped into different tranches based on the quality of the loans in the tranche. The different tranches pay different rates of return depending on their risk rating. Risk ratings are determined by big credit rating agencies, such as Standard & Poor's and Moody's. These agencies rate the risk associated with MBSs and with the different tranches in CMOs. The ratings typically range from "triple A" (AAA) to lower ratings, such as "double B" (BB). The rating of AAA indicates that there is little chance that the mortgages that underlie these instruments will end in default. Ideally, investors face a very small chance that they will lose money on instruments that are rated AAA. On the other hand, a rating in the BB range indicates that there is a greater risk that some percentage of the mortgages in the instrument will end in default and investors are more likely to lose money. In theory, credit rating agencies are supposed to provide an objective and independent analysis of the risks associated with different investments so that investors can make informed decisions. However, from 2000 to 2006, the objectivity, independence, and accuracy of the judgments made by the credit rating agencies were often less reliable than the subprime mortgages that they were supposed to be evaluating. Investors who thought they were putting their money into AAA-rated instruments found out later that they had been living in a fool's paradise and had been misled about the risks associated with the MBSs and CMOs they had invested in.

Large investment banks bought and securitized subprime loans in MBSs and CMOs and then sold them to investors without telling investors that a worrying percentage of the loans were likely fraudulent (Barnett, 2013), even though they knew or should have known that such was the case. Of course, when investment banks put together these investment vehicles, they are aware that a certain percentage of the loans involved will go bad and that reality is factored into the structure of the instrument. But selling MBSs and CMOs is a highly profitable and competitive business, and the investment banks that competed in this market had little incentive to look deeply into the mortgages on which they were based. Since it is more difficult to sell an instrument with a rating in the B range than one with a rating in the A range, investment banks were drawn toward presenting overly optimistic views of their loan pools. To put it in simple terms, they bought junk, dressed it up, and sold it as rock-solid investments. They were aided in this process by the credit ratings agencies, which simply accepted the data provided by the investment banks to rate MBSs and CMOs and as a result underestimated the percentage of likely fraudulent subprime loans that were involved and that were likely to end up in default.

The analysis of fraud in the American mortgage market presented above tells only part of the story. There were other forms of fraud and other players involved besides appraisers, brokers, lenders, and investment banks (for a more complete description of the mortgage process, see Simpson, 2012; Rorie and Simpson, 2012). But regardless of what role an individual or an institution played in the process, it is easy in retrospect to see that the overall structure of the mortgage industry strongly contributed to the prevalence, longevity, and seriousness of fraud. As Simpson (2012) notes, the industry was organized in a series of interlocking tiers such that pressures and constraints felt at one level influenced or affected other levels. For example, the competitive pressures felt by lenders to make as many loans as possible influenced their dealings with brokers, whom they pushed and encouraged to bring in subprime borrowers.

The incentives in the system were all pointing in the wrong direction. People wanted to own their own homes. After all, owning a home is a fundamental part of the American Dream, and during this period it seemed like everyone was buying a new home. As a result, many people were eager to trust the advice of brokers about the terms of complicated mortgage products that they did not understand. From the point of view of fraudsters, eager buyers make easy targets. At the same time, brokers and lenders were "incentivized" to make as many loans as possible and give little consideration to the ability of borrowers to repay their loans. Further up the food chain, investment banks needed loans to securitize, and the ratings agencies made their money by providing deceptively attractive ratings that made it easy for investment banks to sell CMOs. As long as the housing market was growing and home prices were rising, everybody, including investors in CMOs, made money. But eventually, of course, the bubble burst. The housing market became saturated, home prices stopped rising, subprime mortgage holders started defaulting, and CMOs started failing.

From the perspective of opportunity and choice theories, we can see that starting in roughly 2000, the mortgage industry became a source of lure, drawing in thousands of people seeking to work in this rapidly growing and richly rewarding industry. Between March 2001 and December 2005, employment among mortgage and nonmortgage loan brokers grew by 136 percent, more than in any other industry in the U.S. economy (Miller, 2006). Although most of the people who took up work as mortgage brokers during this period probably tried to conduct themselves honorably, it would be naïve to think that all of them were saints. Rather, it seems not unreasonable to suspect that a notable proportion of the people who worked in the mortgage industry during this period either were criminal opportunists to start with or became ones after they recognized the high-profit and low-risk nature of many mortgage fraud opportunities (Nguyen and Pontell, 2010).

Securities Offenses

Some of the offenses discussed in the preceding section on fraud in the mortgage market involved securities, specifically mortgage-backed securities, and collateralized mortgage obligations, but the securities industry encompasses much more than just mortgage-related financial instruments. And it has long been a prominent site of high-level white-collar crime.

Technically, a security is evidence of ownership, creditorship, or debt (Shapiro, 1984). To put it more simply, a security is a piece of paper, or an account number, or something that indicates that you have a financial interest or stake in some sort of economic undertaking. For example, stocks, bonds, shares in a mutual fund, promissory notes, and U.S. government savings bonds are all securities. In a sense, securities are symbolic commodities, and like all commodities, they have an exchange value. That is, they can be bought and sold.

People buy securities to make money or to avoid losing money. For example, you can buy shares in a mutual fund and make money through dividends or increases in the share price for your fund. Or you could buy stock in an individual company and make (or lose) money the same way. When people buy securities, they are in effect making a bet or taking a gamble that the security will pay off for them. They hope that the stock will go up in value. Publicly traded securities are bought and sold on exchanges, such as the New York Stock Exchange, and most of the stock in publicly held companies is owned by people who do not work in the company. Because most stock owners are outsiders, they have to trust what the company tells them when they make their buying and selling decisions. Trust is an intrinsic and unavoidable part of the system. And it is the requirement of trust that creates opportunities for white-collar crime in the securities industry, because people make their investment decisions based on what they think is trustworthy information about the securities in which they are interested.

There are five major types of security offenses (Shapiro, 1984). They all involve taking advantage of people's trust in one way or another.

Misrepresentations involve lying about the value or condition of a security. For example, suppose a stockbroker told you about a company that was planning to develop some land in the west on which oil and gas deposits had been discovered and invited you to get in on the ground floor of a great opportunity by buying stock in this company. However, in reality, the land had not even been surveyed and there was no way of knowing whether there really was gas and oil out there. That would be misrepresentation. In this case, the stockbroker could make money on the commissions she gets for selling the stock and maybe also by receiving a kickback from the company.

Misappropriation is old-fashioned stealing. Many people don't actually buy securities themselves. Instead, they use an intermediary, a stockbroker, to make purchases for them. Typically, then, this offense is committed by brokers or other financial advisors who simply take the money that their clients have given them to invest and instead steal or appropriate it for their own use.

Stock manipulation involves artificially manipulating the price of a security. This can be a complex offense, but basically it involves trying to create the impression that a stock is about to increase rapidly in value. If you can create that impression, then people are likely to rush to buy the stock and hence drive up the price. If you bought when the stock was low and then sold after its price had gone up, you could make a great deal of money very quickly.

Stock manipulators typically operate in teams involving multiple co-conspirators and proceed through a series of steps to orchestrate their schemes. First, the conspirators target and take control of a small or marginal company that operates in an industry in which breakthroughs or sudden advances seem possible, such as, for example, pharmaceuticals, green technology, biotechnology, hair restoration, or other esoteric technologies, products, or services. The plausibility of the breakthrough or discovery is an important part of the scheme, because it can be used to explain any sudden increase in the trading volume or price for a company's stock. Second, once the manipulators are in control of the target company, they can engage in a variety of activities designed to make it appear as though the company has made a breakthrough that will cause the company's stock to rise rapidly in price. Fraudulent and misleading news stories can be released to or planted in the news media, or posted on the Internet; slick brochures can be sent to potential investors. To solidify the impression that the company's trading volume is starting to boom, the conspirators can set up fake accounts or use nominee buyers to trade shares back and forth. Third, as unwary investors start buying shares and as prices start to peak, the conspirators take the money and hide it in private bank accounts rather than using it to expand or run the business. Eventually, the lack of any real breakthrough or product becomes apparent, prices start to fall, and the conspirators walk away with the investors' money.

A similar type of scheme was often used in the 1990s and 2000s when technology companies, the so-called "dot coms", were booming. The astonishing financial success of companies such as Microsoft, Apple, Google, Oracle, and Amazon, as well as a host of other, lesser known but nevertheless wealthy, technology-based companies, created the widespread impression that fortunes could be made investing in Internet startups through initial public offerings (IPOs). When these companies initially went public, investors who got in on the ground floor made millions, and many investors were frantically looking for the next big thing. Almost anything associated with technology or the Internet could be made to sound like a sure fire path to riches, precisely because the technology of the Internet was so new that few people understood it. Under these conditions, unsophisticated investors made easy targets for scam artists and boiler room operators who would fraudulently market IPOs for companies that had little to no chance of succeeding (Tillman and Indergaard, 2005).

Insider trading is perhaps the most publicized security offense. It arises when "insiders" trade on the basis of nonpublic information that is relevant to the price of a stock. There is nothing wrong with someone who works for a company buying its stock. This happens all the time. Indeed, for good reason we want insiders to buy stock in their own companies, because then they will be motivated to work hard in order to make the company as profitable as possible. But it is illegal for insiders to buy or sell stock on the basis of information that is not available to the public.

For example, in the famous ImClone Systems case that sent Martha Stewart to prison, the leader of the company, Dr Sam Waskal, was convicted of securities fraud for insider trading. ImClone was a biopharmaceutical firm working on a drug called Erbitux that was supposed to be a breakthrough in cancer treatment. The company's stock was being touted by analysts and was on its way up as the drug was undergoing review for approval by the Food and Drug Administration (FDA). Unfortunately for Waskal, the FDA eventually decided not to approve the drug. Waskal learned that Erbitux would not be approved on Christmas Day, December 2001, before the FDA had made a formal public announcement. He knew immediately that the price for ImClone stock would plummet as soon as the announcement was made, and anyone holding the stock would lose a lot of money. Waskal, his family, and his friends, including Martha Stewart, were among those who held significant interests in ImClone. Even though he was prohibited from doing so by law, Waskal tried to sell large blocks of his own stock holdings in ImClone to avoid losing money, and he alerted his family and friends to do the same. Word that ImClone was about to lose much of its value eventually reached Martha Stewart through an intermediary, and she sold off her holdings, too. For the record, we should note that Ms. Stewart was not actually convicted of insider trading. Rather, she went to jail for perjury because she lied to federal agents about why she sold her shares in ImClone when she did so (Stewart, 2011).

The law governing insider trading is exceedingly complex and has continued to evolve through both legislation and judicial opinion since the 1930s (Perez, Cochran, and Sousa, 2008; Reichman, 1993). However, the basic moral principle underlying the prohibition of insider trading is simple. When insiders have specialized access to information that is not available to the general public, they have an unfair advantage over other traders in the market. The laws against insider trading are designed to penalize and thus deter those who would act upon this unfair advantage to the detriment of others. Although the moral principle involved here is straightforward, using the criminal law to enforce it is difficult, and insider trading is an excellent example of the problems raised by the superficial appearance of legitimacy in white-collar crimes. To convict someone of insider trading, prosecutors have to show that the person bought or sold the stock in question *because and on the basis of* nonpublic material information. Perpetrators, of course, can claim that they did not know about the privileged information or that they traded for other reasons (Szockyj, 1993).

Investment schemes are deliberate attempts to trick people into investing in order to steal their money. Ponzi or pyramid schemes are the classic example here. In these schemes, investors are recruited through promises of extraordinarily high returns on investments. For example, the person in charge of the scheme tells potential investors that he has a great investment opportunity and offers to let the investor get in on it for only $10,000. The schemer promises to double people's money in just six months. Someone invests, and soon thereafter the schemer starts sending out dividend checks. The initial investors think the investment looks great and proceed to tell their friends and relatives about this fantastic opportunity, encouraging them to take advantage of it as well. As more people invest, the schemer is able to continue to send out dividends from the money he gets from new investors. He is also able to keep some extra for himself. But no new money is being generated from the so-called investment opportunity. Rather, the schemer is robbing Peter to pay Paul. Eventually, as more and more investors join, the number of members grows larger than the number of new investors, and there's not enough new money to pay everyone. The charade collapses—and everybody who invested loses money, except perhaps the ones who got in early.

The most famous recent example of a Ponzi scheme, of course, is that of Bernard Madoff (Henriques, 2011). Madoff's case is unusual for several reasons. First, Bernie Madoff was not a fly-by-night operator. Rather, he was a well-known and highly respected trader, investment advisor, and money manager on Wall Street, who once served as chairman of the Board of the National Association of Securities Dealers. Second, he did not actively recruit individual investors. Indeed, many people heard about Bernard L. Madoff Investment Securities by word of mouth. Madoff was Jewish, as were many of his investors who learned about him through informal networks. Third, rather than trying to recruit clients with promises of high returns, Madoff offered very steady returns to an exclusive clientele. Many of the investors in his company were money managers and investment firms, who were handling money for unions, pension funds, and the retirement savings of ordinary citizens. Fourth, while it is difficult to know the exact date at which Madoff's frauds began, it is clear that they lasted for at least a decade and perhaps much longer. This is unusual for Ponzi schemes, which usually collapse under their own weight much more quickly. The longevity of Madoff's scheme may have been facilitated by the high level of trust that his investors had in him because they shared a Jewish identity. Madoff's reputation and his ability to hide his scheme from regulators enabled him to continue to get new clients and to persist in fraud. Finally, there is the sheer size of Madoff's scheme, which eventually resulted in losses in the tens of billions of dollars (Henriques, 2011).

Like almost all Ponzi schemes, Madoff's case illustrates all of the defining characteristics of white-collar crime. His reputation on Wall Street gave him both the superficial appearance of legitimacy and legitimate access to other people's money, most of whom he never met or had any face-to-face contact with. He would send fraudulent statements to his clients indicating that their accounts were growing steadily despite the inevitable ups and downs of the stock market. If anyone demanded to withdraw a large amount of their funds, Madoff would threaten to kick the investor out of his fund. Astonishingly, even though the Securities and Exchange Commission (SEC) was warned in 2000 by an analyst named Harry Markopolos that Madoff's returns could not possibly be that consistent, the SEC never rigorously investigated his activities (Henriques, 2011), and his scheme continued until December 2008, when it finally collapsed. It had started to come apart earlier in the year as the economy was crashing and as more and more of his clients demanded to take their money out of the market. Madoff eventually realized he could never fulfil all of the redemption requests, called his lawyer, and surrendered to the FBI.

Opportunity and Securities Fraud

Some types of securities offenses have opportunity structures that are quite similar to consumer frauds. Misrepresentations and investment schemes, for example, rely on the deception of individuals. They are in a sense like mislabeled products or misleading advertising. The offender presents misleading information about a security, and the victim falls for it. Whether the offense succeeds or not depends on who is contacted and how skillful the offender is in presenting a distorted picture of reality. Although the Madoff case is unique because of its complexity, size, and longevity, at bottom it is like all Ponzi schemes. To their detriment, the victims trusted Madoff and believed in the picture of reality that he presented. Madoff was also fortunate to be operating in a regulatory environment that provided little oversight of his activities and in an economy that was growing rapidly. This combination of economic growth and regulatory ineptitude were crucial to his success.

Other types of securities offenses have different structures. Insider trading, for example, does not require the offender to deceive a particular individual in order to take advantage of her. Rather, the offender is attempting to hide or disguise a prohibited transaction. Whether the offense succeeds depends on how well the offender can hide transactions that are illegal but personally beneficial. The offenses must be hidden from outside observers, such as the SEC. The same problem confronts those who would manipulate the stock market. The key to successful stock manipulation is to make it appear as though the price of the targeted stock is moving as a result of the normal buying and selling decisions of investors in the market, but the offender does not need to contact or interact with the eventual victims at all. Done correctly, the offender makes a killing and nobody is the wiser.

Antitrust Offenses

Antitrust offenses are sometimes called *offenses of the marketplace*. They depend on the market in the sense that they are impossible to commit without a free market or something close to it being present. Hence, to begin our discussion of antitrust offenses, we first have to say a few things about this so-called free market. According to economists, a free market is one in which the prices of goods and services are arranged by the mutual non-coerced consent of sellers and buyers. In theory, prices are determined by the law of supply and demand with no government interference in the regulation of costs, supply, or demand (Downes and Goodman, 2006). Free-market economies can be contrasted with controlled economies, in which prices are set by a central authority. Soviet-style communism was an example of a controlled economy.

Although we call ourselves a free-market society, there is no such thing as a totally free market. There are all sorts of laws and regulations governing what and how things are produced, marketed, and sold. But relatively speaking, ours is a free-market economy, and that is one reason why we have antitrust laws and outlaw certain practices in the marketplace. We outlaw certain activities because we think that they somehow damage or negatively affect how the free market operates.

In theory, the free market is the most efficient form of economic organization. Businesses produce based on what they think the market (i.e., buyers) want, and buyers have the freedom to spend their money as they see fit. Businesses compete with one another for the attention of buyers. If a business firm meets the needs of buyers, they will buy the firm's products or services and it will make money. The firm's competitors will have to match or better its performance if they want to stay in business. Everybody is supposed to benefit from this arrangement, but it often does not seem to work out that way.

One of the most important forms of antitrust violation is the restrictive trade agreement. A restrictive trade agreement is just that: some form of illegal agreement between producers or sellers in an industry to restrict how the industry works. Recall that in a free market, prices are supposed to be determined by the mutual non-coerced consent of *sellers and buyers*. In theory, this means that sellers are not supposed to cooperate or work together to determine prices. There are three basic forms of restrictive trade agreements: price fixing, bid rigging, and market division or allocation schemes. *Price fixing* refers to agreements between competitors to set or in some way manipulate prices so that they are held at a certain level. For example, Apple Inc. and five major book publishers were recently accused of conspiring to raise the prices of e-books. According to a civil lawsuit filed by the U.S. Department of Justice, Apple and the book publishers were unhappy that Amazon was offering e-books at deeply discounted prices. The conspirators were alleged to have agreed among themselves to raise the price of many of the most popular books from $9.99 to $12.99 or $14.99 and then to force this model on Amazon (Catan, Trachtenberg, and Bray, 2012). In another recent case, nine Japanese automotive suppliers pleaded guilty to fixing the prices of auto parts sold in the United States and paid $740 million in criminal fines (Trop, 2013). *Bid rigging* refers to situations where competitors agree in advance who will submit the lowest bid as part of a competitive bid process for a contract. The purchasers in bid rigging cases often are federal, state, or local governments. Finally, *market allocation* occurs when competitors get together and divvy up an area so that only one of them operates in any one area at a time. For example, in the late 1970s and early 1980s, much of the collection of residential and commercial waste in and around New York City was controlled by a cartel made up of small cartage companies. These companies were often family owned and passed on from one generation to the next. The carters engaged in a sophisticated and long-running customer-allocation scheme in which customers were treated as assets that could be bought and sold. Prices were established and enforced by the cartel, and this conspiracy is estimated to have raised the prices paid by commercial customers by as much as 50 percent. An interesting feature of this market-allocation scheme was that organized crime was involved in enforcing the allocation of customers, and the knowledge that organized crime was involved helped to deter large national waste-collection firms from entering the local market (Reuter, 1993).

Although there is no shortage of restrictive trade agreements that involve ordinary products and services, such as auto parts and garbage pick-up, the most important and serious instances of bid rigging and price fixing have occurred in the arcane world of international finance. Recently, one of the most egregious cases of bid rigging involved what is known as the London Interbank Offered Rate or, as it is called, Libor (Tillman, Pontell, and Black, 2018). Even though Libor may seem far removed from the day-today concerns of ordinary citizens, it affects the lives of everyone on a daily basis. For example, Libor influences the interest rate that people are charged if they want to get an auto, student, or home loan. Over half of all adjustable-rate mortgages in the United States are linked to the Libor rate (McBride, 2016). It also influences the abilities of cities and towns to issue municipal bonds to finance new schools and road repairs.

The Libor rate is simply a number that is published daily which banks use to set short-term interest rates. It is determined by a straightforward procedure. Every week-day morning at around 11:00 a.m., a panel of global banks submit estimates of how much they think it would cost them to borrow money from other banks for different periods of time ranging from overnight to one year. The estimates (technically known as "fix rates") are submitted to the Thomson Reuters data collection service. The top and bottom 25 percent of submissions are discarded and then the average for the remaining submissions is calculated. The resulting number is then the official Libor rate for different currencies and different time periods (McBride, 2016). For example, there is one Libor rate for borrowing U.S. dollars for three months and another for borrowing German deutschmarks for a year and so on. Around the world, financial institutions use the Libor rate to set the rates they will charge their customers for loans. So, if the Libor rate is high when you apply for a loan, you may be charged a higher interest rate than you would be charged if the Libor rate were lower.

Importantly, Libor is also used to construct very complex financial instruments called derivatives and credit default swaps, which are also sold to customers. These products are too complicated for us to explain in detail, but it is important to know that they are used by big investors in financial markets, such as pension funds, governments, municipalities, and investment banks, to hedge their investment portfolios against various forms of risk. In theory, a derivative can be designed so that if one type of investment loses value, the derivative would gain in value. For example, the managers of a pension fund may invest some of their money in ordinary stocks and bonds, but then also invest in derivatives to counterbalance the risks posed by the unpredictable fluctuations in the value of the stock and bond investments. Done correctly, the overall value of the pension fund is enhanced by the combination of different types of investments, but it all depends on the validity of the Libor numbers underlying the derivatives.

Ideally, the Libor estimate that each bank on the panel submits reflects the bank's honest and objective opinion on what it would have to pay to borrow money for any particular period of time. Unfortunately, beginning in 2006, a group of traders and bankers figured out that by colluding together they could manipulate the Libor rate for their own benefit and to the detriment of consumers, businesses, and governments around the world. And they started doing just that. By the late 2000s, it became clear to regulators that traders and brokers in big investment banks in the United States, England, Switzerland, Germany, and Japan were conspiring to submit inaccurate information to Libor so that the resulting Libor rate would sometimes be artificially high and sometimes artificially low. As a result of these manipulations, the traders, brokers, and bankers got richer, while everyone else either lost money or made less than they should have on their investments, or were charged more than they should have been for a loan.

Eventually, regulatory and criminal justice authorities in the United States, England, and elsewhere filed charges against a number of individuals and 16 investment banks. As of 2013, the banks had collectively paid over $9.7 billion dollars in penalties and fines (Tillman et al., 2018). Even though there is substantial evidence that many higher-echelon bank executives knew what their traders and brokers were doing and approved of it, only a handful of mid-level individuals were ever convicted and sent to prison. During the investigations, the higher-level executives all feigned ignorance and blamed the fiasco on a handful of rogue traders (Enrich, 2017; Jordanoska and Lord, 2019).

Opportunity and Antitrust Offenses

Restrictive trade agreements are based on collusion between competitors in an industry, and they are more likely to arise under certain conditions. To be successful in their collusion, competitors must communicate, ensure compliance, and maintain secrecy. They must share information regarding how prices are to be set, markets divided, or bids rigged. The participants to the conspiracy also must have some method of ensuring that everyone complies with the terms of the agreement. Finally, they have to somehow hide their activities from purchasers and the government. Because of these requirements, restrictive trade agreements are more likely to arise in industries where there are few rather than many competitors. It is easier to share information, ensure compliance, and maintain secrecy among a small number of participants than it is among a large number.

Collusion is also more likely with some types of products than with others. In the case of the Libor scandal, for example, the bid riggers were aided by the fact that Libor was very poorly understood by the vast majority of investors. Outside of the conspirators, very few people knew how Libor was set and how it influenced the value of different types of investments. Fluctuations of less than one-tenth of 1 percent could have huge effects on the value of different derivatives. The traders, brokers, and bankers understood this, but their customers almost always did not.

Two other important features of the opportunity structure of restrictive trade agreements are the standardization of the product and its replaceability. The probability of collusion increases if the product or service in question is standardized and if other products cannot be easily substituted for it. The more standardized the product is, the easier it is for competing firms to reach an agreement on prices. Likewise, if other products cannot easily replace the product in question, then sellers do not have to worry that purchasers will simply buy something else if the price gets too high. Consider, for example, the natural gas industry and the retail pizza industry. Natural gas is natural gas. There is not much to differentiate between one kilogram of gas and another. Pizza, on the other hand, comes in an extraordinarily large number of permutations. It would be very difficult to agree upon a standard price, and even if the owners of pizza joints in a town could agree on a common price pattern, there would be limits on how high the price could be set. If it gets too unreasonable, consumers can simply switch to frozen pizza or another food entirely. For homeowners, however, switching from natural gas to some other form of energy is certainly a much more difficult undertaking than switching from pizza to spaghetti. Not surprisingly, therefore, bid rigging in natural gas prices is not unheard of (Tillman et al., 2018).

Finally, the nature of the relationships between competitors in an industry influences the likelihood of collusion. If competitors know one another well through social connections, trade associations, business contacts, or the movement of employees from one company to another, collusion becomes easier. For example, if a governmental agency makes repetitive purchases of a particular product or service, then over time vendors may come to know one another and decide to share the work for future business.

Fraud During Crises

Crises, such as natural disasters or the global pandemic that started in 2020, create new opportunities for fraud against consumers, businesses, and governments. To explain how crises facilitate fraud, we focus first on consumer fraud, a form of white-collar crime that has likely been practiced ever since people started selling and trading things. Consumer fraud involves deception via false or misleading information about a product or service (McCormick and Eberle, 2013). As a general rule, anything that can be sold or marketed legitimately can also be sold or marketed fraudulently, though it is easier to cheat consumers with some products and services—or in some situations—than others. Given the broad reach of this crime type, victimization costs are substantial. For example, Federal Trade Commission (2022) data indicates that consumers reported aggregate losses of $5.8 billion in 2021, with the top types of consumer frauds involving imposter scams; online shopping scams; prizes, sweepstakes, and lotteries; internet services; and job opportunities. Since 2018, reports of fraud to the FTC have ranged from 792,000 in the first quarter of 2018 to a high of 1,811,000 in the first quarter of 2021 (US Federal Trade Commission Sentinel Network, 2022).

Although criminologists have not devoted a lot of attention to frauds associated with natural disasters or pandemics, a few studies illustrate how offenders use the unique characteristics of crisis situations to take advantage of others. Studies on contractor fraud after weather-related disasters in Texas (Davila, 2005; Davila et al., 2005), for example, found that 3 to 6 percent of potential consumers were victims of contractor fraud. The authors theorized that the people who were most likely to be victimized were those who had a strong desire to return to normal as opposed to those who were more tolerant of the ambiguity and disruptions that follow a disaster. People with a strong desire to return back to normal may be more likely to be willing to accept *anyone* who offers to do needed repairs without checking on the contractor's reputation or prior experience. From the point of view of a fraudster, someone who is willing to accept the fraudsters words at face value makes for an ideal victim.

Just as natural disasters do not respect international boundaries neither do disaster-related frauds. For example, a study of Fijians living in poverty examined whether natural disasters increased job recruitment fraud (Takasaki, 2013). It found that two years after a cyclone hit, individuals who had experienced more housing damage during that event were more likely to be victimized by fraudulent agencies seeking fees to process job applications. The author argued that poverty restricted the mechanisms by which victims could cope with the stress of the cyclone's impact. People who experienced high levels of damage were more likely to pursue "risky migration" to foreign countries for employment, and that made them more susceptible to job-related frauds.

A common theme in this literature is that fraud victimization occurs as people try to get their lives "back to normal" and as they attempt to manage the anxiety that comes from the disruptions caused by disasters. Because it was a uniquely global, disruptive, and unprecedented modern-day event, it is worth examining how the COVID-19 pandemic of 2020 influenced fraud victimization. As of December 2022, more than 6.5 million people worldwide and more than one million people in the US have passed away due to COVID-19

(World Health Organization, 2022). At the pandemic's height in 2020–2021, various polls indicated that fear of getting COVID-19 was high (see, e.g., Anderson and Fingerhut, 2021; Gallup, 2022), and people around the world tended to see their government's handling of COVID-19 as confusing and inconsistent (see Lee, 2021; Silver and Connaughton, 2022). This combination of widespread harm, widespread fear, coupled with ambiguous and confusing official information created an ideal environmental for those who wanted to take advantage of people's anxieties.

Most of the existing research on fraud during COVID-19 consists of narrative reviews of fraud types and theories about why certain frauds would be more likely during the pandemic (see, e.g., Brooks et al., 2021; Chavda et al., 2022; Cross, 2020; Ma and McKinnon, 2022; Murrar, 2022). This research demonstrates that early on COVID-19 frauds included fake testing kits, fake vaccines, fraudulent assistance obtaining stimulus checks or other benefits, cyber-related frauds, and romance frauds (Chavda et al., 2022; Murrar, 2022). These sorts of frauds exploited people's fears about catching COVID-19 or their desire to return to "normal" more quickly.

Extensive research on fraud victimization more generally, that is fraud not related to COVID-19, has found that individual lifestyles and routine activities predict the likelihood of fraud victimization. Recent studies of COVID-19 frauds confirm this relationship. Even though many people changed their routine activities in response to the pandemic, people who engaged in certain types of routine activities were more likely than others to either be targeted by fraudsters or actually victimized by fraud. For example, Kennedy et al. (2021) found that measures of Routine Activity Theory predicted both targeting by fraudsters (i.e., contact by individuals or small businesses selling fraudulent products or services) as well as actual victimization (i.e., the purchase of fraudulent goods). For example, the survey by Kennedy and colleagues found that those who spent more time on the internet and who had responded positively to telemarketers prior to the pandemic were more likely to be targeted and actually victimized by pandemic related frauds. These findings reflect the increased reliance on online commerce during periods of mandated or self-imposed isolation and accords with other research demonstrating a marked increase in online shopping fraud (Kemp et al., 2021) as well as online romance frauds during the pandemic (Buil-Gil and Zeng, 2022). Online, there are fewer guardians monitoring financial transactions, the pool of potential targets is much larger (especially during COVID-19, when more people than ever before were using the internet to do their day-to-day tasks or find romantic partners), and the anonymity of the internet means that potential offenders are better able to feign legitimacy.

Changing opportunity structures could also explain increased crimes by organizations against governments during COVID-19 (see, e.g., Dilanian et al., 2021; OECD, 2020). In the United States, the Payroll Protection Program (PPP) passed by the U.S. Congress as part of the Corona Virus Aid Relief and Economic Security (CARES) Act was established to protect businesses and their employees from the disruptions associated with COVID-19 shutdowns and restrictions. Many businesses sought relief under the program, but the opportunity to access government relief resulted in substantial amounts of fraud. Companies inflated payroll expenses to receive more funds than they were eligible to receive, or business owners used the monies to benefit themselves rather than their employees (e.g., by purchasing luxury goods such as houses, cars, and jewelry) (United States Department of Justice, 2021).

It's worth noting, however, that although perpetrators may use routine activities to find targets, research also suggests that individual characteristics, such as self-control/

impulsivity, intersect with lifestyle and activities to impact the likelihood of victimization (Kennedy et al., 2021; see also Holtfreter et al., 2008; Nolte et al., 2021). This may be because individuals with lower self-regulation capabilities are less able to cope with anxiety (see Bertrams et al., 2010; Hamama et al., 2000; Powers et al., 2020) or are more strongly affected by other negative emotions (e.g., loneliness) brought on by crisis situations (Javaras et al., 2012). As such, people lower in self-control or higher in impulsivity may be more likely to engage in behaviors or purchase products that help alleviate feelings of worry or concern. In a pre-pandemic world, this might have taken the form of drugs, alcohol, going out to bars, or the like. During the pandemic, some of those risky activities were constrained (Acuff et al., 2020). Impulsive people may have been more susceptible to advertisements they saw while on social media sites and more likely to purchase products that they thought would help them via the online commerce environment available to them (see Nolte et al., 2021).

It is clear that increased use of the internet created new fraud victimization opportunities, and social media outlets likely facilitated connections between offenders and victims more so than other types of media, such as online news sources and business websites. The FTC (2021) analyzed their database of COVID-19 fraud-related warning letters to false advertisers and found that about half of individuals and businesses receiving cease-and-desist letters made claims on just four of the largest social media platforms—Facebook, Instagram, Twitter, and YouTube. They note that social media platforms' primary goal is to "amplify content" which enables everyday users to reach a large number of potential victims. Unfortunately, the administrators of these platforms are usually delayed in removing misleading information until after it has already been seen by thousands if not millions of people. The U.S. Department of Health and Human Services (2022) issued public warnings detailing how fraudsters seek personal information through social media outlets (e.g., through social media advertisements for testing or treatment, survey scams, via posting photos of vaccination cards on social media) and then using that information to commit medical identity fraud.

Some people may ask "How could someone possibly fall for fraudulent social media posts?" An analysis of fraud design strategies encompassing two natural disasters in Australia—the Black Summer Bushfires in the Fall of 2019 and Spring of 2020 as well as the first year of COVID-19 in 2020—found that fraudulent social media campaigns during these crises relied on mechanisms of "authority" and "scarcity" as well as the building of "social proof" inherent in online communities (i.e., seeing that people you know "liked" a product or page) to facilitate successful scams (Taodang and Gunder, 2022). The authors note that crisis-specific frauds "… bank on the notion that people may be less sure of what 'normal' and 'legitimate' transactions and communications are…" (p. 2) and that "…individuals experiencing a crisis are less able to identify authoritative actors and sources of information correctly…" (p. 2) in addition to feeling more pressure to take corrective actions, as we noted above. Thus, advertisements indicating that a product is "selling fast!" or is "only available for a limited time!" may trigger purchasing among people experiencing crises more so than it would at another time. Further, establishing authority—in this study—was a function of effectively mimicking government agency or charity organizations' labels in fraudulent messages.

Something that remains relatively unexplored in the literature, but likely would fit in nicely with the notion of "authority", is the role of social media influencers (e.g., Dr Joseph Mercola; see Frenkel, 2021) in enabling the spread of frauds.[2] One study (Abidin et al., 2021) examined news media reports about influencers during COVID, noting that news coverage in Australia, China, Japan, and South Korea highlighted how influencers engaged in efforts to promote good social behaviors during COVID or even participated in formal campaigns with government health organizations to encourage the following of social distancing or other health recommendations. On the flip side, there were also many news reports about influencers spreading misinformation or discouraging compliance with governmental mandates. Thus, it seems that social influencers may be something of a double-edged sword in regard to crises. On the one hand, they may provide critical information for fraud protection, while on the other, they may help facilitate fraudulent behavior.

Building knowledge about how consumer frauds spread during times of crises will likely inform prevention efforts. Current research is lacking, but there is some indication that public service announcements may help prevent fraud victimization during crises. One study using a Chinese sample found that respondents who followed government social media accounts perceived the threat of COVID scams to be more severe and felt more confident in taking prevention actions – and in the effectiveness of those actions – against such scams (Tang et al., 2021). In another manuscript, Holtfreter et al. (2008) discusses the success of a public awareness campaign in the state of Florida during the summer of 2004 related specifically to price gouging after hurricanes. Here, the number of consumer fraud complaints decreased by almost 84 percent during the 2004 hurricane season. In addition to promoting knowledge about fraud, the Florida announcements specifically mentioned the state's legal sanctions for committing this type of fraud. Ultimately, the authors concluded that "... the low victimization rate observed in this study may be a result of heightened awareness of consumer fraud schemes among potential victims as well as a general deterrent effect on potential offenders" (p. 198, footnote 9). Much more research is needed on the efficacy of public media campaigns on fraud prevention during crises, but such prevention mechanisms seem promising.

Summary

In this chapter, we have applied our opportunity perspective to a selection of white-collar crimes. There are many other types that could have been chosen, and even among those that we did explore, there are subtypes and variants that we did not address. Although each of the crimes discussed here is based on a specific opportunity structure, there are general themes that pertain to all of them.

For example, as Marcus Felson (2002, p. 99) has correctly pointed out, all predatory offenders have to solve the basic problem of gaining access to their intended crime target or victim. White-collar offenders have an advantage over street criminals in this regard, because by virtue of their occupational positions, they have legitimate access to their target or victim (Felson, 2002). In none of the offenses examined here did the offenders have to break down a door or jimmy a lock or hide in the bushes and grab passers-by. Rather, their access to the crime target was perfectly legal and normal.

The offender's specialized access to the crime target has profound implications for the problem of preventing these offenses. One of the major strategies used to prevent other forms of crime is to block the offender's access to the target. The whole point of locks, fences, and walls is to keep people with bad intentions away from you or something you value. For white-collar offenses, however, this strategy often is not feasible for obvious reasons. At least, it is not feasible in the form of physically blocking offenders from getting to a physical target. However, as we discuss in later chapters, there are ways to reconfigure the strategy of blocking access as applied to white-collar crime. Nevertheless, the problem of controlling white-collar crime remains enormously complicated.

All of the crimes that we have discussed in this chapter depend on the offender's conveying for some period of time a superficial appearance of legitimacy. The offenses involve behaviors or activities that look normal or routine when viewed from the outside. They somehow mimic or are based in normal economic activities. For example, during the housing boom of the 2000s, hundreds of thousands of subprime loans were made, packaged, and sold as mortgage-backed securities. Many, indeed probably a majority, of these activities were perfectly legal and appropriate, but a certain percentage was not. In these cases, buyers, brokers, lenders, and investment banks engaged in fraud—on their loan applications, via broker and lender targeting and deception of buyers, and by selling securities that held a much greater investment risk than advertised. The same was true throughout the Libor scandal. The sale of derivatives can be perfectly legal and financially prudent provided that the derivatives are not based on fraud. In many health care frauds, a health care provider submits a claim to a health care insurer. There is nothing unusual about that. Illegality arises when the claim does not reflect what actually happened in the field. In price fixing, a product or service is offered for sale, which is perfectly normal. It becomes a crime when the price of the product has been set by collusion among sellers rather than by free and open competition. Finally, successful fraud schemes perpetrated during crises depend on making fraudulent services or products appear legitimate to potential victims. Thus, white-collar crime depends on and is intimately linked to legitimate economic activities.

Like specialized access, the superficial appearance of legitimacy has implications for crime prevention and control. Besides blocking access, another major prevention strategy is surveillance. Security cameras, private guards, and neighborhood watches are all based on the idea that offenders will refrain from committing crimes if they think they are under surveillance. In the case of white-collar crimes, however, surveillance is problematic. The problem is that what the offender is doing physically is not obviously illegal or perhaps even suspicious-looking. Thus, although surveillance can play an important role in white-collar crime prevention, it involves more than simply looking for something that is obviously out of place or suspicious. It requires piercing the appearance of legitimacy.

Earlier we defined deception as the "advantageous distortion of perceived reality", with the advantage devolving to the offender. All of the offenses examined here somehow involve an advantageous distortion of reality, but the nature of the distortion and the way in which it is advantageous to the offender differ among crimes. There are two broad types of deception. They involve the presentation of misleading information and the concealment of information.

First, in many of the white-collar offenses examined here, the offenders in some way present misleading or false information about some aspect of a product or service. On the basis of that information, victims make decisions to relinquish control over economic resources to the benefit of offenders. The term *victim* needs to be construed broadly to include individuals, other organizations, and governmental programs. For example, in mortgage fraud, the victim may be an individual who buys a loan based on misleading information. Although they may seem different, many health care frauds work the same way, but here the victim is a health care insurer that pays for (in effect, buys) a service from a health care provider based on bad information.

Second, offenders can hide their activities and benefit by gaining control over economic resources that arise through the natural operation of the marketplace. For example, in price-fixing cases, offenders collude to set the price of some product or service above what it would be if the price were determined by competition. After the artificial price is set, the offenders benefit through the normal decisions of purchasers to buy products or services. Similarly, in stock manipulations, the offenders engage in clandestine actions that create a misleading image of the value of a stock or other type of security. They benefit if other players in the market behave normally in terms of their buying decisions.

Both kinds of deception—presenting misleading information and hiding information—have implications for the problem of control, which we briefly identify here and discuss more fully in future chapters. White-collar crimes based on the presentation of misleading information can be reduced if those who receive the information become better able to see through the misleading image that offenders try to create. To reduce offenses based on hiding information, we must become better at recognizing patterns of activities or at making the hiding of information riskier.

Notes

1 The idea behind the creation of these new loan products was at the start commendable. It was hoped that ARMs, subprime loans, and all of the other new products would expand the housing market to previously underserved segments of the population. They were designed to make it possible for people of low to moderate incomes to buy their own homes. But the subprime loans were profitable, and lenders' representatives were encouraged to sell the product to people who were not financially positioned to pay once the loan readjusted to a higher interest rate. But, by then, the mortgage companies had received their fees and the mortgage had been sold and bundled with other toxic securities on the secondary market.

2 Although at least one case demonstrates how being a social media influencer can backfire if you post pictures of your illegal gains online (United States Attorney's Office, District of Massachusetts, 2021).

Chapter 7

Corporate Violence

Environmental, Workplace, and Manufacturing Offenses

In the previous chapter, we examined crimes that impose financial or pecuniary costs on their victims, be they individuals, government agencies, or other businesses. In this chapter, we apply the opportunity perspective to environmental, workplace safety, and manufacturing crimes. These offenses are potentially much more serious in that they can and often do impose physical costs on individuals. This is not to say that the perpetrators deliberately set out to harm other people. They do not. The physical harms that they cause are unintended in the sense that they are not what the offender is trying to achieve. The motivation for the offense is not to impose harm on others but rather to gain a financial advantage. Physical harm, however, is always a potential side effect. Thus, we examine what has been called the "quiet violence" of corporations (Frank, 1985).

Much like the concept of white-collar crime, corporate violence can be defined in different ways. For instance, Punch (1996) refers to corporate violence as a legal or illegal business action that results in death, injury, or illness to people. Hills (1987) defines it as

> actual harm and risk of harm inflicted on consumers, workers, and the general public as a result of decisions by corporate executives or managers, from corporate negligence, the quest for profits at any cost, and wilful violations of health, safety and environmental laws.
>
> (Hills, 1987, p. vii)

More recently, Klein (2014) describes corporate violence as business corporations (through their policies and actions) causing injury or death to living beings via exposure to harmful conditions, products, or substances. Note that each of these scholars emphasize different elements of corporate violence in their definitions: wilful violation of law, legal or illegal actions, specific victims (consumers, workers, general public versus living beings) and means (policies and actions, exposure to harmful conditions, products, or substances). Such definitional variations affect how the concept is understood, counted, and measured, its costs and consequences, and the kinds of policies proposed or put into place to mitigate and control the behavior.

Rather than select a specific definition, in this chapter, we discuss the nature of the harm imposed by these behaviors and also emphasize that these offenses differ from those examined earlier in another way as well. Their legal status as crimes is more ambiguous. In the previous chapter, we applied the opportunity perspectives to offenses that involve some kind of fraud. Recognition of the harmfulness of fraud and of the need to proscribe fraudulent behavior has deep roots in legal history, going back to biblical times and probably farther

DOI: 10.4324/9781003175322-10

(Podgor, 1999). Although many of the specific offenses that we discussed earlier, such as subprime mortgage fraud and fraudulent billing in the health care industry, are new in the sense that they have come into being only relatively recently, their underlying illegality, nevertheless, is based on ancient legal principles. In this chapter, we deal with offenses that do not have such long historical pedigrees. These are modern offenses in the sense that they developed out of the industrialization and modernization of production in the past few centuries. Their legal status as crimes is still evolving. Many environmental, manufacturing, and workplace-related offenses are illegal in the sense that they violate various regulations, but they are not necessarily criminal. Indeed, an important part of the opportunity structures for these sorts of offenses is the ambiguous and debated nature of their legal status.

Environmental Crime

In an influential book, *The Closing Circle: Nature, Men, and Technology*, environmental activist Barry Commoner linked rising levels of industrial pollution to the development of new technologies (Commoner, 1971). He observed that though new technological developments typically increase profits for business, they frequently are accompanied by detrimental environmental side effects. Extra profit for business was often at the expense of environmental degradation, and the cost of this degradation was borne by society as a whole and not the business *per se*. Commoner's work gave rise to a form of environmentalism that has affected *what* is defined as environmental crime and *how* to "fight" the crime problem.

During the 1970s, Americans started to become increasingly sensitive to the high costs of pollution and to demand action against it. The case against the agricultural pesticide DDT for its harmful effects on wildlife and human health (documented in *Silent Spring* by Rachel Carson [1962]); the unforgettable sight of the Cuyahoga River, a tributary of Lake Erie, catching fire in 1969 as a result of petrochemical dumping by Cleveland and other Ohio cities; and the headlines garnered by 20 million Americans celebrating Earth Day in 1970 led the federal government (with President Nixon leading the charge) to mandate the creation of a centralized regulatory agency for environmental affairs, the U.S. Environmental Protection Agency (EPA). Joining the Environmental and Natural Resources Division (created in 1909) and the Environmental Crimes Section of the Department of Justice, the EPA was given control over the enforcement of federal environmental statutes. It was designed to assist and cooperate with state-level enforcement or, if pollution laws were not sufficiently enforced, to supersede state authority with federal enforcement efforts. Under this collaborative model, the states handle the bulk of environmental enforcement today. In 1997, for instance, while the federal EPA initiated 4,129 actions, state environmental agencies initiated 10,515 administrative actions and referred 379 cases to state courts (Scalia, 1999). A similar pattern can be seen in Figure 7.1, which captures state, federal, and local formal Clean Air Act (CAA) enforcement actions from 2014 through 2023 from stationary sources like chemical plants, utilities, and steel mills. We can see that federal enforcement efforts are dwarfed by those of the states. EPA data focused on drinking water, hazardous waste, pesticides, and wastewater violations also demonstrate that state enforcement efforts constitute the bulk of oversight activity.

The primary responsibility of the EPA is to clean up existing pollution problems and protect the environment and human health by enforcing environmental laws enacted by Congress. The EPA has criminal investigative and civil enforcement powers, which means that

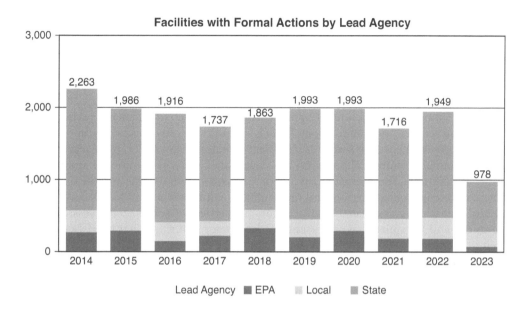

Figure 7.1 CAA formal enforcement, by lead agency, 2014–2023

violators may be prosecuted and jailed for environmental crimes or brought into statutory compliance through civil/administrative enforcement of regulations. Criminal enforcement is rare, especially for corporations. For instance, between 1994 and 1997, a total of 1,846 defendants were charged with a criminal environmental offense. Yet, only 314 (17 percent) of those criminally charged were *organizational* defendants, most of which were charged with an environmental protection violation (Scalia, 1999). By fiscal year 2021, the number of organizational defendants across all types of prosecutions had dropped to 90 from a five-year high of 131 in 2017. However, the most common offense for organizational offenders was environmental (25 percent of the total) and most of these were water related.

Criminal prosecution is typically reserved for the most egregious violations in which laws are knowingly and intentionally broken. In these kinds of cases, the goals of enforcement are to achieve both special and general deterrence. Compliance is the main goal of civil and administrative enforcement under the assumption that highly punitive sanctions are unnecessary (or because, as we discuss later, criminal legal standards are too difficult to meet). It is a much more common form of regulatory intervention. For example, of the 4,129 federal environmental enforcement actions initiated in 1997, 88 percent (3,634) were administrative or civil in nature (Scalia, 1999). Data from FY 2016 also reveal a split heavily weighted toward noncriminal cases: of the nearly 2,600 total cases opened, only 170 cases were handled criminally. For each of the next four years the overall total case counts fluctuated downward, dropping to 1,809 in 2020. The number of criminal cases opened yearly also fluctuated but with less of a linear pattern of descent. In 2017, for instance, 115 criminal cases were opened. In 2020, the number rose to 247. Still, the total number of criminal cases opened yearly remained relatively small vis-à-vis civil judicial and administrative cases (U.S. Environmental Protection Agency, 2016; 2022).

These statistics demonstrate that criminal intervention is relatively rare in the enforcement mix when violations are discovered. Yet, because we know so little about the hidden figure of environmental crime, it is difficult to estimate whether environmental enforcement effectively deters companies. The EPA, along with other federal agencies, is responsible for enforcing the law, which is continually expanding as new responsibilities and regulatory programs are added to the old (Portney, 2000). It is important to understand how these duties are carried out because criminal opportunities are tied to enforcement practices.

Individuals as well as organizations (which include not only businesses but also nonprofits and government agencies) can break environmental laws. Yet, until recently, most concern about environmental pollution has concentrated on organizational and industrial sources of pollution. Therefore, our discussion of environmental crime and the opportunity framework focuses on companies and the managers within them.

Recall that white-collar crime has three main properties: (1) specialized access, (2) spatial separation, and (3) superficial appearance of legitimacy. All these characteristics are illustrated in the tragic 1980s case of the W. R. Grace Corporation and a small working-class town in Massachusetts.

The case against the W. R. Grace Corporation began in the mid-1970s when the residents of Woburn, Massachusetts, started to realize that an abnormally large number of local children had contracted leukemia (Brown and Mikkelsen, 1990). For decades, the townspeople had noticed that a local lake, Lake Mishawum, often had a foul smell and an odd reddish color. They worried about the possibility of contaminated water because of the number of chemical and manufacturing plants in the area that produced toxic wastes. In 1978, two local wells were tested and had to be closed because of dangerously high levels of carbon-chloroform extract (CCE). At first, the problem was attributed to the method the town used to chlorinate water.

The problem with the water in Woburn, however, was much worse than an odd color and bad smell. The parents of the children diagnosed with leukemia eventually formed a committee to press for more testing. In 1979, the EPA tested the wetlands surrounding the two wells that had been closed and found elevated levels of arsenic, chromium, and lead—all known carcinogens. With help from researchers at the Harvard School of Public Health, the citizens group was able to document a statistically improbable cluster of leukemia cases in the Woburn area.

Eight families eventually filed a $100 million class action lawsuit against W. R. Grace. Of course, the company denied any wrongdoing. However, at the trial, it came out that the company's Cryovac Division had dumped toxic wastes on its property. The waste products had eventually filtered into the groundwater and from there into the homes and bodies of the people of Woburn. After a few years of legal maneuvering, W. R. Grace eventually settled with the families. In 1988, it was indicted and pled guilty in U.S. District Court of the crime of providing false statements to the EPA about its toxic waste disposal practices.

Unfortunately, what happened in Woburn, Massachusetts, is not an isolated case (for additional examples, see Rosoff, Pontell, and Tillman, 2013, pp. 149–210). There are literally hundreds if not thousands of similar pollution scenarios involving other companies and other communities, in the United States and worldwide. Indeed, a contemporary feature of toxic dumping is its transnational nature. Waste may be collected and moved from developed countries and dumped into less developed areas, such as the horn of Africa (Center for Global Development, 2016).

In all these cases, a legitimate business produces some type of toxic waste that is supposed to be handled and disposed of in a particular manner. However, instead of doing that, the company disposes of the waste illegally in some other way. There are several different ways. Like W. R. Grace, a company may simply dump the toxic waste on its own property. Alternatively, the company can truck the waste somewhere else and dump it, or more likely, hire someone else to do the same thing. Another strategy is to mix the toxic waste with other, nontoxic waste and dispose of all of it as nontoxic waste, which is much less stringently regulated and much less costly to handle (Rebovich, 1992). Similar dumping practices occur on a global scale. A recent case study by Bisschop (2015) emphasized asymmetries (cultural, knowledge, economic/political, and legal) between countries and communities that give rise to illegal e-waste disposal. Electronic waste, or e-waste for short, refers to end-of-life electrical goods that are discarded. Discarded items range from small smart phones to household goods such as laptops, televisions, and printers, to items as large as mainframe computers. Between 20 and 50 million tons of e-waste are generated each year (Yang et al., 2011). Focusing on the port of Antwerp in Belgium, Bisschop (2015) dissects the means through which *corporate and governmental actors* facilitate e-waste smuggling and illegal shipments into and out of the port—emphasizing such factors as active participation by firms (it is profitable), inattention to fraud and a lack of concern about where e-waste ends up by both parties, and weak enforcement on the part of government as central contributors to illegal flows. In addition to the extensive fraud associated with e-waste disposal, however, there may be significant health consequences associated with crude or improper dismantling via pollutants found in the air around disposal sites.

These highlighted cases display all the characteristic features of white-collar crime. The company has a legitimate right to use whatever chemicals or materials are involved and is, in effect, on its honor to dispose of them properly. Thus, it has specialized access. Those who will eventually be harmed may be miles or continents away from where the offense, the illegal dumping, occurs. Finally, because there often are no obvious signs that something bad has happened, the company appears to be doing nothing wrong, at least as viewed from the outside. Indeed, in the Woburn case, the families had to spend an extraordinary amount of time and effort gathering evidence to show that something illegal had happened. First, they had to demonstrate that there was a statistically improbable cluster of leukemia cases in Woburn. Then they had to prove that toxic waste from the Cryovac plant could filter into the groundwater and eventually into the drinking water of residents. Finally, they had to show that employees and managers at Cryovac did indeed improperly dispose of toxic waste. Although all these facts were proved, it was a complicated and difficult process to do so (Brown and Mikkelsen, 1990).

The opportunity structure of illegal hazardous waste disposal has two key features. First, companies are trusted to be responsible for disposing of waste in a legal manner. Hence, they are in control regarding whether they do so or not. Second, if they choose to dispose of toxic waste illegally, the effects of their illegal actions are not immediately obvious and indeed are often delayed for considerable periods of time. In the case of transnational environmental crimes, these problems often are exacerbated by pronounced legal and enforcement barriers associated with enforcement efforts in lesser developed countries (LDCs). Governments eager to attract investment are easily co-opted into lax or non-existent regulations. Governmental officials are susceptible to bribes, ultimately victimizing their own citizens in the name of development.

Companies such as W. R. Grace are able to engage in illegal disposal practices, primarily because of a lack of credible oversight (Shover and Hochstetler, 2006). As we noted at the start of this section, the enforcement system is an integral part of the opportunity structure for environmental crime. There are literally hundreds of thousands of business enterprises that produce some form of hazardous waste as a by-product of their normal operations. They range in size from behemoth corporations like the W. R. Grace Corporation to tiny mom-and-pop dry cleaning establishments. All these enterprises are supposed to handle and dispose of their waste as specified by law and regulations. And herein lies the problem. It is impossible to watch all of these organizations to make sure that they actually follow the law in disposing of their hazardous waste. The opportunity for environmental crime arises because it is difficult and costly to monitor whether companies are or are not complying with the law. Hence, the risk of the offense being exposed is low. Unfortunately, we do not really know how low the risk may be.

On the other side of the risk equation, many businesses—especially those in manufacturing sectors—are engaged in "productive" activities in which risk is an elemental component. For instance, the current manufacture of paper involves the use of bleach in pulp to strengthen paper and to keep it from yellowing when exposed to sunlight (https://purelypaper.co.uk/Environmental-FAQs/#:~:text=In%20the%20past%20chlorine%20gas,aquatic%20life%20and%20water%20quality). Thus, pulp and paper facilities must store large amounts of the chemical on site and, because the bleaching process also requires the use of sizable amounts of water, companies must successfully manage potentially hazardous contamination on a daily basis. Although firms are moving away from using bleach in pulp and paper processing by substituting fewer toxic chemicals and new technologies that offer better environmental options (U.S. Environmental Protection Agency, 2001), these still pose risks that need to be assessed and managed.

This important link between environmental risks and crime is central to conservation criminology, a newly developed theoretical perspective (Herbig and Joubert, 2006). This approach integrates criminology, natural resource management, and decision science to offer insight into why environmental offending occurs. It further unpacks how enforcement and compliance operate (including the politicized process through which law is created and applied); the relationship between human and natural ecosystems; the governance and management of natural resources; and the technical and perceived risks related to human and natural systems (Gibbs et al., 2010; McGarrell and Gibbs, 2014).

Conservation criminology ties in nicely with our opportunity perspective in several ways. First, both recognize that opportunities are shaped and distributed according to the nature of economic and productive activities of different industries. Second, as these legitimate opportunities expand and new laws emerge, so too do unintended criminal opportunity structures. Third, risks are often unknown (but conservation criminology offers tools to systematically assess risks and vulnerabilities). Fourth, in the environmental realm, not all harms are legally designated as crimes or even as offenses per se.

Keeping these similarities in mind, we now turn to an important case of environmental crime where a relatively new opportunity[1] in an established industry resulted in multiple deaths and extensive environmental degradation. In April 2010 an oil rig known as Deepwater Horizon exploded and sank into the Gulf of Mexico, unleashing an oil spill that is considered the largest spill in U.S. history (Congressional Research Service, 2014). The explosion killed 11 people and injured many others, and the pipe leaked oil and gas on the ocean floor for 87 days until the Macondo well was capped. In the interim, an estimated 4.9 million barrels of oil leaked into the Gulf, resulting in substantial deterioration of the ecosystem.

The primary corporate players in this disaster were British Petroleum PLC (BP), the Swiss company Transocean Ltd., and Halliburton. Several lesser-known companies were also named in court documents. BP pleaded guilty to criminal charges, admitting 11 counts of felony manslaughter, obstruction of Congress, and a series of environmental crimes, and agreed to a $4 billion fine. Class action claims by individuals and businesses who were economically harmed by the spill were settled by BP (which then challenged the settlement and lost). The company ultimately agreed to put aside $9.2 billion for claims (Trefis Team, 2014). In 2015, BP agreed to pay $18.7 billion to settle all remaining federal and state claims (Schlanger, 2015). Transocean agreed to pay $1.4 billion in civil and criminal fines and penalties, primarily related to federal Clean Water Act civil penalty claims. In a move to settle most claims against the company and avoid future liability regarding legal claims filed on behalf of thousands of potential victims whose "lives and livelihoods were ruined by the spill", Halliburton, who contracted with BP to provide cement for the well (*USA Today*, 2014) pleaded guilty to destroying evidence after the incident and agreed to settle claims for $1.1 billion without admitting negligence.

Only four individuals were charged in the Deepwater Horizon oil spill case. Prosecutors brought criminal charges ranging from obstruction of justice (deleting e-mails and voice mail communications) and lying to Congress, to seaman's manslaughter and involuntary manslaughter. Seaman's manslaughter is a special type of manslaughter charge in which criminal penalties (fines or up to ten years' imprisonment, or both) may be levied when loss of life results from a wrongful act related to misconduct, negligence, or inattention to duties by "captains, engineers, pilots or other persons" (Akpinar, 2010). In addition, some defendants were also charged with violation of the federal Clean Water Act (https://www.epa.gov/enforcement/transocean-settlement). Kurt Mix, a BP engineer, was found guilty in 2013 of obstructing justice but was granted a new trial based on his claim of juror misconduct (Fisk et al, 2014). The two supervisors charged with manslaughter (Robert Kaluza and Donald Vidrine) brought a motion to dismiss the manslaughter charges, but a judge ruled against their argument. The judge did agree, however, to drop the seaman's manslaughter charges, as neither Kaluza nor Vidrine had navigation functions in their jobs (Stempel, 2014). In 2015, however, the manslaughter charges were dropped by Federal prosecutors (with judicial concurrence). After two postponements, the trial of David Rainey (BP's former vice president of exploration for the Gulf of Mexico), charged with lying to Congress (obstruction) and making false statements to investigators, finally began in 2014. He was found not guilty of making false statements and the obstruction charge was dismissed (Associated Press, June 5, 2015). Because of these decisions no one went to prison for the BP disaster (Kravets, 2015).

The cause of the disaster has been linked to several factors: (1) a corporate culture of recklessness, (2) failure to utilize proper safety procedures once indicators of well instability were identified and noted by supervisors Kaluza and Vidrine, and (3) a weak system of regulation. The culture of recklessness is apparent in e-mail communications exchanged between the well engineer and his boss during the construction of the Macondo well. The engineer noted significant production problems. He observed that the drilling crew was "flying by the seat of our pants" under a "huge level of paranoia" that was "driving chaos", concluding that "the operation is not going to succeed if we continue in this manner" (Rushe, 2013). Because of the depth of the Macondo well and the use of new technology, the risks of the drilling operation well were relatively unknown. Yet, these very characteristics *should* have produced a full environmental assessment and review—at least according to the 2004 Minerals Management Service (MMS) Guidelines.

The MMS is the federal regulatory agency in charge of overseeing the offshore oil and gas industry. However, the MMS granted a "categorical exclusion" from the National Environmental Policy Act (NEPA) to certain oil and gas activities in the Gulf of Mexico during the Bush administration, which exempted this site (along with others) from extensive environmental review. The MMS also discounted any substantial environmental damage from oil spills in the region where the future well would be located. For instance, the agency predicted that offshore oil spills resulting from a proposed action would not likely significantly damage any wetlands along the Gulf Coast; that impacts to wetland habitats from an oil spill would be expected to be low and temporary; and that at the expected level of impact, the influence on commercial fishing activities would be negligible and indistinguishable from variations due to natural causes. Taking extant empirical data on loss of well control and blowouts into account, they concluded that these were rare events and of short duration—thus, their potential impacts to marine water quality were not expected to be significant (Cleveland, 2013). It would belabor the obvious to note that this assessment was wrong in every regard. Of course, even if a full environmental report had been submitted and assessed, and the well approved in spite of its deficiencies, it is not at all clear that the regulatory system could have prevented the disaster given that the MMS has about 60 inspectors to cover nearly 4,000 offshore facilities in the Gulf of Mexico (Cleveland, 2013).

In a commissioned post mortem report by the National Academy of Engineering, it was revealed that the blowout preventer technology utilized by Deepwater Horizon "was neither designed nor tested for the dynamic conditions that most likely existed at the time that attempts were made to recapture well control". The report also suggests that the shortcomings of Deepwater's equipment "may be present" at other deep water drilling operations (National Academy of Engineering, 2011, p. 71). Although the Obama administration put a moratorium on Gulf drilling and committed to following the recommendations of experts (including those of the National Academy of Engineering), drilling resumed at an accelerated pace in the Gulf, while few of the recommendations have been implemented—especially those related to blowout preventers (Birnbaum and Savitz, 2014).

The conservation criminology perspective offers analytic insight into the Deepwater Horizon case (McGarrell and Gibbs, 2014) by providing answers to some critical questions such as: (1) Why were the MMS regulations regarding deep water drilling in the Gulf mitigated during the Bush administration? And (2) Why did the MMS discredit the risks associated with drilling? The risk literature suggests that political action depends on an alignment between actuarial and public perception of risk. In effect, effective legislation requires strong public support. Because environmental regulators operate in a politically charged sphere with powerful corporate actors (and jobs) on one side and environmentalists on the other, it would appear that public opinion had not been swayed in the direction of legislative restrictions. In fact, the "evidence" presented by MMS suggested little risk associated with the deep-well drilling and the potential for blowouts. The risk assessments that were conducted did not appear to balance the likely costs to people, wildlife, and the environment (i.e., the natural resources perspective) but instead focused primarily on the consequences for commercial fishing interests. Finally, in the wake of the disaster, conservation criminology would expect fraud and other crimes to accompany new regulations and controls. Evidence clearly suggests that this has occurred. The Department of Justice, for instance, has committed to thoroughly investigate "all meritorious reports of fraud related to the oil spill and its aftermath, including fraudulent claims, charity fraud, identity theft, insurance fraud, and procurement and government-benefit fraud" (U.S. Department of Justice, 2014).

The BP case was discovered only after a spectacularly noticeable explosion. But environmental offenses may be exposed in a variety of different ways, including self-reports, inspections, whistle-blowing, and accidental discovery. Companies are required to keep track of how they handle hazardous waste and to self-report any instances of noncompliance. Although W. R. Grace certainly did not disclose its offense, some companies do make such reports, perhaps because they fear the negative publicity that would result if the offense were to come to light via other means. The ratio of reported to non-reported instances of noncompliance, however, is not known. Offenses can also be discovered by the EPA inspectors. Unfortunately, inspections are relatively rare because waste-producing enterprises vastly outnumber inspectors. Two other mechanisms of exposure are accidental discovery by the general public, such as an oil spill or fish kill, and whistle-blowing by knowledgeable employees.

Whistle-blowing is a potentially important source of exposure and hence risk for companies that violate environmental regulations. When a company *knowingly* engages in environmental crime, efforts are made, of course, to conceal the activity. Yet, within the company, multiple parties may be privy to the knowledge that a crime has occurred. From the point of view of company managers, these individuals are potential sources of risk because they could expose the offense. Because businesses vary greatly in size and structure, who and how many within a company may know about illegal activity also varies. Larger companies, compared with smaller ones, are more likely to be divided into specialized areas that make it easier to hide illegality from managers and employees in other areas. Smaller firms, on the other hand, are more likely to have a "flat" management structure (Barlow, 1993; Makkai and Braithwaite, 1994). Such a structure increases the likelihood that top managers will have actual knowledge of an illegal activity when it occurs. Legally, however, top managers are held liable for illegal activities that they *should* have known about but did not (Cohen, 1998).

Finally, it is important to recognize that in the case of environmental crimes, the potential offenders—businesses—have a great deal of influence over the nature of the oversight that is imposed on them. The system of enforcement that we have now came about as a result of a negotiated political process. The business community resisted the establishment of the EPA, and since they failed, they have continually attempted to restrict its size and legal mandate (Burns and Lynch, 2004, p. 71). Indeed, in the 1980s, during the Reagan administration, efforts were made to deregulate the environment and to reduce the EPA's budget (Burns and Lynch, 2004); and the appointment of Scott Pruitt, a longtime adversary of the agency, by then President Trump to head the EPA suggests that environmental regulation and enforcement were under siege by business during that administration (Eilperin, Mooney, and Mufson, 2017). To a degree, then, businesses can shape the opportunity structures for their offenses through their influence over the enforcement process. Large, well-established companies generally have more economic and political power than those that are smaller and newer. This translates into influential congressional and corporate friends, community leaders, and other stakeholders who make it more difficult for regulators to investigate and pursue offenders even if violations somehow come to light (Shover and Hochstetler, 2006).

These mechanisms produce a certain number of known instances of environmental crime every year. Yet, because many environmental offenses are not obvious, we never know how many offenses go undiscovered. The executives at W. R. Grace may have reasonably assumed that the benefit of their "crime" (saving money that would normally be spent on environmentally sound disposal of toxic waste) outweighed its costs (low risk of discovery). Yet, it is important to recognize that there are countervailing forces that business must contend with and that can potentially raise the costs of environmental deviance. As we know from the Deepwater Horizon/BP oil spill, the victims of environmental crimes are not always just individuals. Other organizations or groups may be harmed as well as wildlife. For instance, the Love Canal section of Niagara Falls in New York and the city of Times Beach, Missouri, were evacuated and, in the case of Times Beach, purchased by the government and destroyed after toxic chemicals were found in the soil. Illegal use, storage, and disposal of toxic chemicals by companies (Hooker Chemical and Northeastern Pharmaceutical and Chemical Company) were implicated in both cases. The municipal, state, and federal governments got involved—as they did in the 2010 BP oil spill, suing the industrial giants for redress on behalf of the victims and for financial assistance to help the federal government clean up the waste sites (Superfund). In these cases, the power relationship between offenders and victims is more balanced and less asymmetric than is often the case between environmental offenders and their victims. For example, an employee of a large petroleum company accused of illegal waste disposal once acknowledged that power asymmetries can vary when he observed, "I don't think the company is too awfully worried about suits filed by their own employees. They were more worried about the state because it has clout" (Trost, 1981).

Finally, we note that the cost of pollution weighs more heavily on some segments of society than others. Research has suggested, for instance, that minorities and the poor are disproportionately affected by pollution (Checker, 2005). Indeed, some suggest that victimization occurs precisely because these groups have less economic and political power to protect their communities from environmental polluters in the first place, and these same groups lack the resources to force environmental cleanup once pollution has occurred (or to move out of areas that have higher pollution levels). The term *environmental injustice* has been coined to describe the unequal distribution of environmental risks and hazards to which members of disadvantaged groups are subjected. We talk more about environmental injustice in Chapter 9.

Workplace Crimes

Many crimes occur in the workplace, but only some fit with our definition of white-collar offending (Friedrichs, 2002). For instance, an angry spouse can shoot his wife while she is working, or one worker may steal another's wallet. These traditional kinds of crimes can occur anywhere. The workplace is merely the setting in which the event transpires. However, some kinds of white-collar offenses arise out of the unique opportunities that are presented by a particular organizational structure or by a particular occupational position. In this section, we focus on work conditions that are hazardous for employee health and safety.

A good number, but not all, of workplace safety and health violations are regulated by the Occupational Safety and Health Administration (OSHA). Others may fall under more specialized agencies, such as the Mine Safety and Health Administration (MSHA) (Shover, Clelland, and Lynxwiler, 1986) or the Nuclear Regulatory Commission. Like the EPA, OSHA is a fairly new regulatory agency. The Occupational Safety and Health Act of 1970 established a federal program to protect most workers from job-related deaths, injuries, and illnesses. Established by the then Secretary of Labor, James Hodgson, on April 28, 1971, the task of the new agency was to administer the provisions of the OSH Act (MacLaury, 2008).

Although OSHA was established only 50 years ago, the dangers associated with working conditions were recognized long before that. In this country, laws governing the safety of working conditions started to appear during the mid-nineteenth century (Frank, 1993) and served as a rallying point for organized labor in the United States in the 1900s. Sadly, however, despite the laws and OSHA, work-related diseases, injuries, and deaths are estimated to number over a million annually, even though deaths on the job have decreased dramatically since OSHA was created (Payne, 2017). Some of these tragic outcomes are accidents or due to negligence on the part of workers; yet evidence suggests that firms too often fail to properly warn employees about hazardous conditions and neglect to train or equip them to safely negotiate the workplace. One estimate holds that up to one-third of all on-the-job injuries are due to illegal working conditions (Reasons, Ross, and Paterson, 1981). Unfortunately, taking precautions to protect workers is viewed by some firms as overly burdensome and costly to the company's bottom line (Clinard and Yeager, 1980, p. 69; Szasz, 1984).

When workplace violations do occur, there are regulatory, civil (tort), and criminal enforcement actions that can be brought against offenders (Frank, 1993). However, as is true in the case of environmental enforcement, criminal prosecution of OSHA cases is the legal intervention of last resort (Hawkins, 2002). For example, a careful review of OSHA data by the *New York Times* found that between 1982 and 2002, there were 2,197 cases in which a worker had died because of a willful violation of safety laws by the employer. Only 196 of these cases (less than 10 percent) were referred for criminal prosecution. Of these, only half led to convictions, and only 20 percent of the convictions led to sentences of incarceration. All in all, the likelihood that someone will be imprisoned when a worker dies as a result of a willful safety violation is less than 1 in 100 (Cullen et al., 2006).

In many ways, the opportunity structure for workplace offenses is similar to that for environmental crime, but there are some unique characteristics as well. As with most environmental crimes, in the case of workplace crimes, the criminal actors (whether the firm or officers of the company) are engaged in legitimate economic activity. Since a primary goal of owners and managers is to make a profit, they are always looking for ways to reduce the costs of production. Holding everything else constant, if costs can be reduced, then profits go up. For most businesses, the cost of labor has a significant impact on overall profitability. Hence, there is a built-in incentive to cut labor costs whenever possible. One way of doing this is by skimping on safety and in the process endangering workers.

For example, a case exposed by the *New York Times* involving McWane Inc., a privately held company headquartered in Birmingham, Alabama, provides a textbook example of the link between cutting costs and dangerous workplaces (Barstow and Bergman, 2003). McWane Inc. makes pipes, and it has profited enormously using "the McWane way" of running things. The McWane way is to cut labor costs to the bone by reducing the number of workers to the bare minimum, requiring the workers who are left to work extended hours, and avoiding as many safety-related costs as possible. These measures have made McWane one of the most profitable pipe manufacturers in America and one of the most dangerous employers in America. According to the *Times*, between 1995 and 2003, at least 4,600 injuries were recorded in McWane foundries. Nine workers were killed, and the company was cited for more than 400 federal health and safety violations. This is far more than all six of their major competitors combined (Barstow and Bergman, 2003).

Let's consider the story of McWane and the Tyler Pipe Company in more detail. In 1995, McWane bought Tyler Pipe, a foundry located in Tyler, Texas, and using the McWane way, turned it into a hellhole for the most disadvantaged and vulnerable of workers. After McWane bought the plant, it cut nearly two-thirds of employees while insisting that productivity remain the same. Safety inspectors, pollution control personnel, relief workers, cleaning crews, and maintenance workers were all eliminated. Rather than have three 8-hour shifts, the company instituted two 12-hour shifts and often required employees to work even more hours seven days a week. Conditions at the plant in Tyler got so bad that the company had to recruit employees from local prisons, and "only the desperate" would seek work at Tyler Pipe (Barstow and Bergman, 2003).

Not all types of work carry the same potential for harm. Employment in unskilled jobs, especially those in mining, manufacturing, and production, increases the risk of illegal exposure to hazardous substances or unsafe conditions on the job (although repetitive stress injuries can occur in clerical/secretarial and other forms of service work). Because these jobs are stratified by gender, race, and class, the chances of victimization are not distributed evenly within society, nor is the opportunity or means for redress (Szockyj and Fox, 1996)—a point we return to in Chapter 10.

A key property of white-collar offending is the spatial separation of victim and offender. In our environmental crime example, we noted how difficult it can be to trace victimization to its source. In the workplace, there is less separation between offenders and victims than in the case of environmental crime because both work for the same organization. Yet, the top managers who make health and safety decisions are unlikely to work "on the floor" in a plant or in the mine, where exposure risks are greatest. And in cases where the corporation is separated into divisions, separate facilities, or subsidiaries, top management may work in a corporate headquarters located hundreds or thousands of miles away from where employees are actually working. Moreover, because the risks of working with hazardous and toxic substances may not be apparent for many years and may be confounded by other "risk" factors (e.g., smoking), employees may never know that their ill health is caused by unsafe working conditions (Calhoun and Hiller, 1992). In mining and textiles, black and brown lung disease has been firmly established as an occupational health hazard associated with these lines of work. This risk has been ascertained after decades of medical research. Thus, for this type of white-collar crime, there is a physical and symbolic division of labor between the offender and victim that is akin to the kind of spatial separation that we have discussed earlier.

Our framework suggests that companies that violate OSHA regulations will try to maintain the appearance of legal compliance. They try to do so in a variety of different ways. Some may provide limited, but not sufficient, training or safety equipment to employees, perpetrating the illusion that health and safety provisions for employees have been met and are taken seriously. A firm also may purposively keep knowledge about toxic exposure and its consequences from employees, in some cases referring workers to "company" doctors who dismiss illnesses or fail to "connect the dots" that implicate toxic exposure in the workplace (e.g., liver cancer is caused by alcohol consumption and not by exposure to vinyl chloride). Indeed, corporations have a long history of knowingly exposing their employees to hazardous substances on the job while maintaining the illusion of ignorance (Calhoun and Hiller, 1992).

A famous example in this regard involves the Johns-Manville Corporation and asbestos (Brodeur, 1985). The potential dangers of exposure to asbestos, a mineral highly valued and useful for its resistance to heat, have been recognized since the first century of the

Common Era. Breathing asbestos-laden dust can lead to asbestosis, a crippling and usu-ally fatal lung disease. The Johns-Manville Corporation produced and marketed asbestos products for decades. Since at least the 1930s, the company had internal medical reports of asbestosis among its workers. Yet, it hid this information about health hazards from its own workers for decades (Brodeur, 1985; Calhoun and Hiller, 1992). By the 1970s, thousands of former Johns-Manville workers were dead or dying because of asbestos exposure (Friedrichs, 2010).

Knowingly exposing employees to unsafe working conditions also seems to be more com-mon in certain industries—both within the United States and globally. For instance, unsafe conditions are a feature of mining operations. The Sago mine in West Virginia, where 12 miners were killed in an explosion underground in 2006, was issued more than 270 safety citations in the two years prior to the explosion. Some of these citations were known to management in the Massey Energy Company (who owned the mine) and were related to problems that could result in shaft collapse and explosions. Several years before the Sago mine exploded—an incident that was followed two weeks later by a fire with two fatalities at an-other mine also owned by Massey—the U.S. Mine Safety and Health Administration (MSHA) adopted a cooperative health and safety partnership with labor, mine operators, and industry associations ostensibly coupled with strong enforcement against unsafe operators. But crit-ics of the cooperative tactic suggested that the regulatory strategy adopted by MSHA failed. It failed to effectively step-up enforcement after cooperative interventions did not work; the agency became less transparent as the cooperative strategy was implemented; and MSHA may not have effectively condemned the violations—i.e., it was overly lenient in its regulatory style (Simpson, 2006). A *New York Times* (2006) editorial noted,

> [S]adly, in the way mines are often run, the $24,000 in fines paid by the Sago managers last year constituted little more than the cost of doing business. In the Appalachian rou-tine, miners balking at risky conditions down below can quickly forfeit their livelihood if they have no union protection.

The U.S. record, however, is much better than mining operations in other countries. The MSHA realized a 35 percent decrease in fatal accidents after 2000 (Simpson, 2006). In Tur-key, on the other hand, there have been 1,308 fatal accidents since 2000; in 2013, 13,000 miners were involved in accidents and 10.4 percent of all work-related accidents in Turkey were in the mining industry (Senerdem, 2014). However, unlike in the United States, where supervisors and executives are rarely criminally prosecuted for negligence and manslaugh-ter, in 2014, after 301 miners were killed in a mining explosion in Turkey, prosecutors arrested and charged seven mine executives and supervisors with negligent death. This oc-curred in the context of significant public protest amid news reports that high levels of toxic gas were noted by sensors inside the mine several days before the disaster but company officials took no action (Associated Press, 2014).

These examples demonstrate that the opportunity perspective can be usefully applied to workplace safety offenses. Next, we see how the techniques of white-collar crime (de-ception, abuse of trust, and concealment) are utilized by OSHA violators. To do so, we draw from a well-known corporate crime case involving Occidental Chemical Company. Occidental workers were found to be sterile as a result of handling the pesticide DBCP (Simon and Etizen, 1990), a chemical used to control fruit pests.

DBCP was banned by the EPA in the late 1970s, but the damage had already been done. The company knew DBCP caused testicular atrophy in animals but took no action to warn its employees of potential consequences. A lawsuit was brought against the three largest producers of the chemical (Dow, Shell, and Occidental) by 57 employees. Twenty-five of these claims were ultimately settled by Occidental for $425,000 (Gold, 1989).

This case demonstrates how the white-collar offending techniques discussed throughout this book can inform our understanding of unsafe production. From all accounts, Occidental management knew the results from numerous studies by scientists at Shell and Dow Chemical that suggested alarming reproductive consequences associated with DBCP exposure. Occidental deceived its employees, failing to "connect the dots" even after an unusually high level of childlessness was noticed among male workers. The callous disregard for the safety of its employees is obvious in a remark made by one Occidental official in a film made about the case, *The Song of the Canary* (New Day Films, 1978). He said, "Heck, we just didn't draw the conclusion that there'd be sterility from the fact that the testicles were shrivelling up".

Concealment, the last technique to be discussed, is a critical element of unsafe productions. In the Occidental case, management knew of the hazards but concealed the evidence. If the true dangers of the workplace were revealed to employees, it might be hard to attract and keep them, or firms might need to raise wages in order to attract willing workers. The cost of cleanup, added safety training and equipment, and the risk of medical bills and potential lawsuits almost guarantee that many, if not most, companies will conceal rather than reveal violations and employee risks.

There are two key features to the opportunity structure for workplace crimes. First, like environmental offenses, they occur incidental to and as a by-product of legitimate economic activities that are conducted for the most part in private spaces, that is, within a private company's workplace. Hence, the offense is difficult to observe from the outside. The enforcement of workplace safety laws suffers from the same weakness as environmental enforcement. OSHA, like the EPA and the MMS, is not up to the task. There are too many potential offenders and far too few inspectors. Second, the victims are either not aware that they are being exposed to hazardous substances or working conditions, or they are powerless to do anything about it. Workers may be powerless simply because they have no other employment opportunities and are desperate for work. From the perspective of the company, both of these factors reduce the risk that their illegal and harmful treatment of workers will be exposed.

The twin problems of ignorance and powerlessness often are exacerbated for workers outside of the United States, particularly those in less developed countries. For example, in 2013 a building collapsed in Bangladesh killing more than 1,000 garment workers (mostly poor young women). The size and scale of business operations affect economic and political power not just in this country but worldwide. Large and profitable companies from the United States and other capitalist industrialized nations that stoke the economic engines of the developed world have significant environmental and workplace safety consequences in lesser developed countries.

Manufacturing Crimes

The foundations of early capitalism rested on the idiom "buyer beware", implying that the ultimate responsibility for protecting oneself from flawed products in the marketplace rested with the customer. In the United States, Americans most likely were formally and collectively introduced to manufacturing wrongdoings when Upton Sinclair published his treatise on the trials of working-class and immigrant life in the United States. In *The Jungle*, Sinclair (1906) exposed how the meat packing industry sold rotten and diseased meat to unsuspecting customers. Not long after the book was published, the 1906 Pure Food and Drug Act was passed, and a fledgling consumer movement was given momentum that did not fully materialize until the 1960s (Mayer, 2012).

Manufacturing crimes are those in which unsafe products are knowingly marketed to consumers (Clinard and Yeager, 1980) or those in which manufacturers put products on the market before they have been properly tested and their safety established. Pharmaceutical companies may, for instance, falsify drug testing results or even fabricate them (Braithwaite, 1984). These kinds of offenses are consistent with our definition of white-collar crime in that: (1) there is spatial separation between the offenders and victims, (2) the production of the flawed product occurs under the guise of legitimacy, and (3) the manufacturer has specialized access to consumers.

There are many known instances of manufacturing crimes, but, as we have discussed earlier, known cases are likely a small percentage of the total number of offenses that occur in any given year. The discovery of manufacturing crime often depends on someone getting injured and being able to track that injury back to its source. Oftentimes, making this connection—especially against powerful corporate actors—is difficult.

Although one of the most infamous cases of manufacturing crime is the Ford Pinto case (Cullen et al., 2006; Dowie, 1987; Swigert and Farrell, 1981), nearly 40 years later, General Motors (GM) Corporation found itself in the midst of its own scandal. In 2014, GM issued a recall for 2.6 million vehicles that had a dangerous defect associated with the ignition switch, including the popular Saturn, Pontiac, and Chevrolet brands, and an additional three million or more larger automobiles thought to have a separate ignition defect. The faulty automobiles marketed by GM have been responsible for 124 consumer deaths and 275 injuries (Woodyard, 2015). In addition, research by the Center for Auto Safety (CAS) has identified a total of 303 fatalities associated with airbags that failed to deploy—a likely consequence of the defective ignition switch (Boudette and Fuller, 2014).

GM chief executive officer Mary Barra, who in testimony to Congress cited results from an internal investigation, identified a single engineer in the firm who was able to approve the use of a switch that didn't meet company specifications, and who, years later, ordered a change to that switch without anyone else at GM being aware (Click On Detroit, 2014). In her testimony, Barra repeatedly noted that the "culture of secrecy" that gave rise to the production and dissemination of faulty automobiles was a problem in the "old GM" but not in the 2014 GM.

The GM case highlights a tactic often adopted by companies that are under litigation threat. General Motors filed for bankruptcy in 2009, which puts any lawsuits brought against the firm on hold until the bankruptcy is complete. The legal argument adopted by General Motors is that the defective ignition was a "product of the old GM" and the new GM should not be liable. In this way, the new corporate entity would avoid the costs associated with any lawsuits (Boudette and Fuller, 2014). Luckily for victims, the tactic failed this time around. The U.S. Second Court of Appeals overturned a bankruptcy judge's "protective" ruling concluding that shielding GM violated victims' "constitutional rights to due process, since they had not been notified of the defect prior to GM's bankruptcy" (Dye, 2016).

The pharmaceutical industry has provided a plethora of manufacturing crime examples, in the U.S. and abroad. Many of these were expertly documented and analyzed by John

Braithwaite in his classic work *Corporate Crime in the Pharmaceutical Industry* (1984). Drawing from interviews with 131 senior executives, Braithwaite showed how multinational companies employed a variety of techniques—including unsafe manufacturing processes, bribery, false advertising, and fraudulent testing—to undermine and circumvent drug safety requirements so firms could broadly and profitably distribute their products. Although his work was completed more than 30 years ago, the pharmaceutical industry continues to generate cases. In a case that has had wide ramifications a compounding pharmacy in Massachusetts (New England Compounding Center) was associated with the deaths of 64 people and more than 750 others who were sickened from drugs tainted with fungal meningitis in 2012 (Bidgood and Tavernise, 2014). Compounding pharmacies fill a particular role or niche in the pharmaceutical industry by making drugs prescribed by doctors for specific patients whose needs cannot be met by commercially available drugs. This sector of the industry, however, operated in a regulatory gap between the Food and Drug Administration and state oversight of the pharmacies.

In the case of New England Compounding Center (NECC), investigations launched by state and federal health authorities, Congress, and the Justice Department revealed that although the company was licensed only to sell medications to fill individual prescriptions, it was *conducting business like a manufacturer* by selling large shipments of drugs without prescriptions. Fake scripts were created to justify holding drugs in stock without a specific dosage linked to a patient, and drugs were compounded in a filthy processing room without proper sterilization—because the sterilization process was deemed too time consuming and cut into profits. Drug safety tests, required after the compounding process was completed, were ignored or only conducted on small amounts of a batch (Eichenwald, 2015). In addition, employees and managers knowingly mislabeled, sold, and shipped medicine to patients—even after it had expired.

NECC executives and pharmacists had criminal indictments brought against them for racketeering, fraud, conspiracy, financial crimes, and violating federal drug laws. The supervising pharmacist (Glenn Chin) and NECC President and Head pharmacist Barry Cadden also faced murder charges in seven states—Florida, Indiana, Maryland, Michigan, North Carolina, Tennessee, and Virginia (Bidgood and Tavernise, 2014). A federal jury found Cadden guilty of fraud and racketeering but not murder (Valencia and Lazar, 2017). Chin was convicted by a federal jury of all 77 counts against him, including racketeering, racketeering conspiracy, mail fraud and introduction of misbranded drugs into interstate commerce with the intent to defraud and mislead. Ultimately, Chin was sentenced by U.S. District Court Judge Richard G. Stearns to 126 months in prison plus an additional three years of supervised release. Chin was also ordered to pay forfeiture of $473,584 and $82 million in restitution. Cadden received 174 months in prison and was ordered to pay forfeiture of $1.4 million and restitution of $82 million (DOJ US Attorney's Office Press Release District of Massachusetts, July 21, 2021). Others charged in the case: (1) pleaded guilty to illegally transferring assets after the meningitis outbreak; (2) pleaded guilty to conspiring to defraud the Food and Drug Administration; (3) had some charges dismissed (three defendants). As part of the NECC bankruptcy agreement, a federal judge agreed to a $200-million settlement to compensate victims of the fungal meningitis outbreak (McGovern, 2015). Finally, Massachusetts tightened regulations on compounding practice. Compounding pharmacies are now required to obtain an appropriate license that fits their business regardless of whether they are operating within the state or they ship compounded preparations into the state. In addition, license renewal will entail unannounced inspection of the pharmacy and its sterile products. Regulators will have the authority to fine pharmacies for violations or, when the public is endangered, to suspend the license pending a hearing. Finally, the state Board of Registration in Pharmacy in Massachusetts will include more experienced pharmacists from various practice settings to provide better oversight. It remains to be seen how effective these new laws and procedures will be.

In addition to the three types of corporate violence mentioned above, atrocity or gross human rights crimes are emerging as an important new area of study and practice. These types of offenses include acts of genocide, crimes against humanity, war crimes and the crime of aggression; they qualify as corporate violence when atrocities are tied to corporate involvement (van Baar, 2019).

The subject of corporate involvement in war crimes was of interest to Sutherland (1949). Indeed, he included a chapter in *White-Collar Crime* that tracked the war-related violations of a 70-company sample. These offenses included violations of special war-related regulations during the two world wars, company avoidance of war taxes, treasonous behaviors, and other acts related to war-time restrictions (e.g., such as restraint of trade and interference with war policies to remain competitive). Most of us are familiar with the many ways in which German Industry supported the Nazi regime, prior to and in further of its war efforts. At the end of World War II, corporate leaders were prosecuted and their companies ordered liquidated (I.G. Farben) for their respective roles in the Holocaust.

The historical record of atrocity crimes, however, is much longer than this. Scholars trace corporate involvement in these crimes back several centuries, to the creation of national trading firms such as the Dutch or British East India Company. These companies were created to protect their respective countries' trade interests abroad but, in doing so, they participated in mass killings, looting and burning villages, and support of the slave trade (Huisman, Karstedt, and van Baar, 2022). Although the history is extensive, the topic of corporate involvement is rarely studied (van Baar, 2019). This inattention has begun to change. For instance, a recent article by Huisman and colleagues (2022, p. 399), reviewed and systematized 105 cases of atrocity crimes since WW II. Their study (post-WWII through 2019) revealed that "90 corporations were involved in crimes against humanity, 51 in war crimes, and 18 in genocide". The majority became involved in these acts through the nature of their business.

Many conceptual and empirical developments in this area focus on regulation and, in particular, the challenges of regulation. Various nations have adopted regulations and statutes to punish mass atrocity crime. As of 2016, at least 149 states maintained such legislation according to the U.S. Law Library of Congress. In addition, the International Criminal Court (ICC) is designated to investigate and prosecute atrocity cases but can only begin the process when a State Party refers the crimes to the Court (State Party Referral), where the UN Security Council refers the crimes to the Court (UN Security Council Referral), or instances in which the ICC Prosecutor initiates a preliminary examination into the crimes (Propio Motu Investigation). For a description of the ICC and how it works, we refer you to the ABA-ICC project (https://how-the-icc-works.aba-icc.org/). We do not cover this area of corporate violence in depth, but mention it here as an important new development for future consideration.

Summary

In this chapter, we have offered several definitions of and explored three forms or types of corporate violence. Like the financial crimes that we examined in the previous chapter, environmental, workplace safety, and manufacturing crimes have their own opportunity structures that are based on the characteristics that we have identified as important for white-collar crime. These characteristics include specialized access, spatial separation, and superficial appearance of legitimacy. In addition, like all white-collar crimes, these offenses involve the use of deception, concealment, and the abuse of trust. Yet, these offenses also have several unique features that need to be noted. These features influence our ability to detect and control these forms of white-collar crime.

First, even though manufacturing offenses, workplace-safety violations, and environmental crimes can have potentially devastating physical effects, they are, oddly enough, not predatory crimes. That is, the offenders do not intend to deliberately harm another person or persons, although they may show a callous disregard for potential victims as in the Sago mine or NECC pharmacy examples. Indeed, the offenders would prefer that no one be physically harmed because the lack of obvious physical harm makes it easier to conceal the offense. When consumers die, as happened in the GM recall case, or children fall ill with leukemia, as happened in Woburn, it draws attention and may eventually lead to the discovery of the offense. One implication of this feature is that if the crimes do come to light and are brought into court, the offenders can reasonably claim that they never intended to harm anyone.

Second, the offenses may be hidden within the businesses, making their discovery especially difficult. For example, the safety violations that plagued the workers in McWane's pipe foundries all occurred on premises controlled by McWane, as did the mining violations of the Sago corporation. The Cryovac Division of W. R. Grace dumped toxic waste on land that it owned. In these cases, the offenses were shielded from the scrutiny of outsiders. Unless and until something obviously bad happens, the only way in which the offense is going to be discovered is through either a regulatory inspection or a complaint by an inside whistle-blower. For employers, like McWane, who attract only the most vulnerable and desperate employees, the likelihood of a whistle-blower stepping forward is low. Also low is the likelihood of frequent and vigorous regulatory inspections. Recall that the Sago mine had many regulatory inspections and citations prior to the deadly explosion, but none serious enough to shut it down. Thus, the offender's ability to control the space within which the offenses occur is an important feature of the opportunity structures for workplace safety and environmental offenses.

A third, and final, feature of these offenses also involves the opportunity structure. In a sense, the opportunity structure is shaped at least in part by the offenders themselves through their influence over the regulatory regime that governs their activities. We elaborate on this idea in more detail in Chapter 10, where we focus on legal remedies for corporate crime. So here we provide only a brief overview.

One way to see how the business community shapes the very opportunity structures that it takes advantage of is to consider how law making in regard to street crime differs from law making for white-collar crimes. Have you ever seen or heard of your state legislature inviting in burglars or robbers to comment on proposed changes in the law governing burglary or robbery, such as, for example, an increase in penalties? Of course not. Indeed, we are sure the question strikes you as ludicrous. Yet, something very similar to this happens whenever legislative authorities contemplate changing the laws or implementing new criminal laws regarding business activities. CEOs, industry representatives, and lobbyists are invited or invite themselves to meet with legislators and to address committees to give their input on how the law should be written and enforced. The influence of the business community over regulatory agencies and the development of regulatory codes is even more pronounced, and this is especially the case with respect to the EPA and OSHA (Burns and Lynch, 2004; Calavita, 1983). In effect, the business community exerts a direct influence on the degree of the oversight that will be imposed on it. Less oversight equals better opportunities for crime. Ordinary street criminals should be so lucky.

Note

1 The first successful 3,000-meter well was drilled in 2003 (https://www.visiongain.com/report/deepwater-ep-market-2022/). The Deepwater Horizon well was substantially deeper: 18,360 feet—or approximately 5,596 meters below sea level (https://www.justice.gov/sites/default/files/criminal-vns/legacy/2013/01/18/2013-01-03-transocean-plea-agreement.pdf).

Part IV

The Symbolic Construction and Social Distribution of Opportunities

The opportunity perspective assumes that white-collar crime opportunities arise out of legitimate business activities and that all areas of economic activity create some type of opportunity for white-collar crime. That is, opportunities are ubiquitous, or to put it another way, lure is everywhere. Even though opportunities to engage in white-collar crimes would appear to be all around us, not everyone takes advantage of these opportunities. Thankfully, most people obey the law most of the time. That conformity to the law is widespread throughout society raises an important question for the opportunity perspective advanced here and for any criminological theory based on rational choice. If opportunities are ubiquitous, then why do only some people take advantage of them, while other similarly situated individuals do not?

In Chapter 8, we argue that one answer to this question can be found in how potential white-collar offenders conceive or symbolically construct opportunities, paying particular attention to the processes of neutralization, moral disengagement, and normalization of deviance. In Chapter 9, we present a different answer to the question, one that focuses on how the sociodemographic characteristics of social class, gender, and race influence access to white-collar crime opportunities. Opportunities for white-collar crime may, indeed, be ubiquitous throughout the business world, but access to these opportunities is not ubiquitous and not the same for everyone. In the United States and most of the Global North, people of a certain social class (high-level executives), gender (male), or race (white) are more likely to end up in occupational positions that provide access to white-collar crime opportunities than people of other class backgrounds (low-level employees), gender (female), and racial or ethnic identities (African-American or Hispanic).

DOI: 10.4324/9781003175322-11

Part IV

The Symbolic Construction and Social Distribution of Opportunities

The Symbolic Construction of Opportunity

Neutralization, Moral Disengagement, and Normalization of Deviance

One of the main points made in the preceding chapters is that white-collar crime arises out of legitimate business activities. Indeed, it is the structure and organization of business activities that create opportunities for particular white-collar crimes. The types of fraud that we see today in the health care system, for example, are possible in part because of the way in which health care in the United States is organized. Imagine for a moment that consumers paid for health care directly out of their own pockets instead of having costs paid mainly by insurance companies and government programs. There would still be opportunities for fraud, but they would not be the same types of opportunities that we have today. For instance, it is difficult to imagine how one could carry off the "rent-a-patient" scheme described in Chapter 6 if individual consumers paid for doctors' visits. All businesses and industries present opportunities for white-collar crime, and opportunities are, in a very real sense, everywhere.

Even though all businesses and industries create opportunities for white-collar crime, this does not mean that everyone involved in those economic activities is a white-collar criminal. We assume, or at least we hope, that a large majority of men and women in business obey the law as best they can. In short, some individuals who, because of their occupational positions, have access to white-collar crime opportunities do not take advantage of them, but then other individuals do not hesitate to get away with whatever they can.

Exactly how large or small the ratio of offenders to non-offenders is with respect to white-collar crime is a hotly debated issue. According to self-control theory, we should expect the proportion of individuals who take advantage of white-collar crime opportunities to be relatively small (Hirschi and Gottfredson, 1987a, 1987b). That is, controlling for access to opportunity, the rate of white-collar offending is predicted to be low according to self-control theory, because the people who occupy white-collar jobs are presumed to have high levels of self-control and hence able to resist the seductions of criminal opportunities (Hirschi and Gottfredson, 1987a). Other scholars disagree with self-control theory on this and other points (Benson and Moore, 1992; Geis, 2000; Reed and Yeager, 1996; Simpson and Piquero, 2002; Steffensmeier, 1989). Although we cannot settle the debate here, we note that both sides implicitly agree on a couple of points. Not everyone is an offender, and not all opportunities are taken advantage of. They disagree, of course, on the proportion of potential offenders who become real offenders and the proportion of potential opportunities that result in real offenses.

If we assume that opportunities for white-collar crime are ubiquitous in the business world, then why do some potential offenders take advantage of them, whereas other individuals in similar situations do not? Why do some people decide to act on some white-collar

DOI: 10.4324/9781003175322-12

crime opportunities but not others, at some times but not others, and in some places but not others? As we showed in Chapter 2, white-collar offenders come from a social stratum that is not the same as that of ordinary street criminals. They may not all be economic or social elites, but a large majority of the people who commit white-collar offenses are nevertheless solid middle-class citizens. They don't appear to suffer from the personal or social pathologies that plague so many of the people who commit street offenses. However, as we discussed in Chapter 4, research suggests that some people may be predisposed to white-collar crime because of their innate psychological traits. Thus, individual differences in personality may explain in part why some people become involved in white-collar crime while others who have the same opportunity do not succumb to its seductions. Even though people may vary in their susceptibility to the lure of white-collar crime, we do not think that individual differences are all that matters. White-collar offenders often have intact families, financial assets, ties to their communities, and good reputations as law-abiding, upstanding citizens. In short, they have a lot to lose if they are caught committing a white-collar offense (Wheeler, 1992). So, the question remains, why do they become involved in white-collar offending?

In this chapter, we argue that part of the answer to this question lies in how white-collar offenders conceive or symbolically construct opportunities. For many white-collar offenders, it is not enough merely to have access to an illegal opportunity to enrich themselves, or to avoid losing money, or to gain a business advantage. Rather, before committing the offense, many white-collar offenders need to somehow justify their illegal actions to themselves so that they can maintain a noncriminal identity. That is, they must look at their situation in such a way that they see their behavior as justified or at least as not improper. We also argue that symbolic constructions are influenced by gender, race, and social class (Klenowski, Copes, and Mullins, 2011; Maruna and Copes, 2005; Shover and Hochstetler, 2006; Willott, Griffen, and Torrance, 2001).

The White-Collar Offender's Sense of Identity

While testifying before a congressional committee, one of the executives involved in an antitrust case was asked whether he knew that his meetings with his co-conspirators were illegal. He replied, "Illegal? Yes, but not criminal. I didn't find that out until I read the indictment. ... I assumed that criminal action meant damaging someone and we did not do that" (Geis, 1977, p. 122). This executive is typical of many of the people involved in white-collar crime. He did not define his actions as criminal, even though he knew, as he admits in his testimony, that they were illegal. Most certainly he did not see himself as a criminal.

Many white-collar offenders are like this executive. Even after they have been convicted, most white-collar offenders are loath to admit that they meant to commit a crime. They go to great lengths to deny having a criminal mind (Benson, 1985). They say that they really did not intend to harm anyone and did not have a criminal intent. Although most will grudgingly admit that their actions may have violated the law somehow, they nevertheless describe their offenses as "oversights", "mistakes", or "technical violations". They present themselves as upstanding, law-abiding, moral individuals. They are committed to conventional moral values and have a respectable self-identity (Box, 1983). In their own eyes, they are not like real criminals. Indeed, because they see themselves as upstanding citizens, white-collar offenders often argue that they should be spared harsh punishments for their crimes because they have "suffered enough" as a result of having their name and reputation dragged through the mud during the criminal justice process (Benson, 1984, 1985; Benson and Cullen, 1988).

It is easy, of course, to pass off white-collar offenders' protestations as merely after-the-fact rationalizations and as attempts to put their untoward behavior in the best possible light. Undoubtedly, this interpretation is correct in some cases. Some white-collar offenders surely know that what they are doing is criminal, and they decide to go ahead and do it anyway. After they are caught, they try to lessen the stigma attached to their behavior by presenting an account that puts it in a favorable light. But we do not think this is true of all white-collar offenders. We believe that most people most of the time accept the major conventions of the moral order. Before they can violate these conventions, they must first convince themselves that the violations are for some reason acceptable (Sykes and Matza, 1957). White-collar offenders do this by using accounts and techniques of neutralization or engaging in processes of moral disengagement (Bandura, 1999).

An account is a statement made by someone to explain unanticipated or untoward behavior (Scott and Lyman, 1968). There are two general forms of accounts: excuses and justifications. In making an excuse, the person admits that he or she did something wrong but denies having full responsibility for the action. For example, someone who is convicted of income tax evasion might try to excuse his behavior by saying that he was confused by the complexity of the tax codes and just made a mistake.

The second general form of accounts—the justification—is important for understanding white-collar crime from an opportunity perspective. In justifying untoward behavior, the person accepts responsibility for the act but denies its pejorative content. For example, a teller who embezzles money from a bank might contend that she was really owed the money because she had worked overtime, and her boss had refused to pay her for it. Although justifications are typically delivered after the untoward action has occurred, they nevertheless reveal something about how actors view their situations before committing their offenses. For white-collar offenders, it tells us something about how they symbolically understood or conceived of the criminal opportunities that they took advantage of. White-collar crime opportunities have a cognitive dimension in the sense that offenders must conceive of the opportunity in such a way that they can maintain a noncriminal identity.

Cognitive Dimensions of Opportunities: Neutralizations

The world of business is imbued with a set of values and ideologies that can be used to define illegal behavior in favorable terms (Box, 1983; Sutherland, 1983). These values and norms are not directly antisocial, and they do not actively endorse lawbreaking. Rather, they operate as extenuating conditions under which crime becomes permissible (Box, 1983, p. 54). The availability of these norms and customs is important because they enable potential white-collar offenders to interpret their criminal intentions and behavior in noncriminal terms. They help offenders soften the harshness of their criminal acts to make them appear either as "not really" against the law or as somehow justified by a morality higher than that contained in the criminal law (Box, 1983, p. 54). In short, they help offenders symbolically construct the opportunities they confront as part of their normal occupational activities in ways that make illegal behavior seem acceptable.

It is possible for white-collar offenders to paint their illegal behavior in saintly colors because their environment provides them with an inventory of verbal techniques for avoiding and undercutting the moral bind of the law (Box, 1983, p. 54). These techniques are called *neutralizations* (Sykes and Matza, 1957). They permit offenders to engage in illegal behavior while at the same time not thinking of themselves as criminals. The type of neutralization used by offenders depends in part on the nature of the opportunity structure they confront. Certain types of neutralizations are more likely to be used for certain white-collar crimes than for others.

A technique often used by white-collar offenders has been called *denying responsibility* (Sykes and Matza, 1957). In these cases, offenders know or suspect that what they are doing is illegal, but they do not conceive of themselves as directly responsible for the act or its consequences. Two ways of doing this are by maintaining "concerted ignorance" (Katz, 1979) and "acting under orders". Both practices allow individuals to prepare what Katz (1979) calls a "metaphysical escape" plan so that they can engage in illegal activity but protect themselves in advance if it should later be exposed.

The laws regulating many industries can be enormously complex and difficult to understand. They often are vague and contain ambiguous definitions that can be interpreted in different ways, especially by individuals who would prefer not to be bothered with the trouble of conforming to regulatory requirements. Small business owners in particular may find the regulations governing their enterprises daunting and troublesome. They may feel overwhelmed by regulatory unreasonableness (Bardach and Kagan, 1982). Rather than spending time and energy to learn and understand the regulations, it is simply easier and more convenient not to know what is condoned and what is condemned. Even the officials who run well-endowed corporations often complain about the complexity of the regulatory environment. They contend that any violations their companies committed were done out of ignorance and not intentionally. If you do not really know what the law is, then you cannot really intentionally break it.

Corporate leaders can also avoid taking responsibility for their actions by maintaining ignorance about the risks that they impose on others (Friedrichs, 2010, p. 11). As we noted in Chapter 7, it is certainly fair to assume that in most cases where workers are sickened, injured, or killed by their work, their bosses do not intend for these tragedies to occur. Neither do corporate executives intentionally put dangerous products and drugs on the market. Their primary motive when these unfortunate events happen is always for the good of the company. They want to make the company more efficient and more profitable. Surely, efficiency and profitability are worthy objectives in a society governed by free-market principles. These objectives can be achieved by cutting costs, delaying repairs to equipment, avoiding unnecessary testing, and a host of other means. If these cost-cutting measures mean that someone accidentally gets hurt in the process, well—that is unfortunate, but executives will claim that it was not what they intended nor thought would happen. By focusing on their intentions and interpreting all harmful consequences as accidents, corporate officials can commit corporate crimes without even acknowledging that they are crimes in the first place (Box, 1983, p. 55; Friedrichs, 2010).

Those in leadership positions in large corporations can practice concerted ignorance in another way besides failing to learn regulatory requirements and ignoring risks. They can simply avoid knowing what their subordinates are doing. As corporations grow larger and more complex, lines of communication between different levels in the corporate hierarchy become longer and more difficult to maintain (Vaughan, 1990). Corporate leaders cannot be expected to directly supervise everyone under their command or to have an intimate knowledge of everything that goes on in their organization. What leaders can do is set general goals and objectives for the organization and hold their subordinates accountable for achieving them. Exactly how the subordinates go about achieving the objectives is not the leader's concern. If someone in the organization breaks the law while pursuing a corporate goal, corporate leaders can, with a clear conscience, claim that they never intended that to happen. With some plausibility, they can claim that they never directly ordered or authorized lawbreaking. Hence, they should not be held responsible for somebody else's misdeeds.

Unfortunately, in some cases, this strategy works. For example, in the Libor case that we introduced in Chapter 6, the man at the center of the scandal was a mathematically gifted but socially awkward trader named Tom Hayes (Enrich, 2017). Using trading strategies that were based on manipulating Libor rates, he made literally hundreds of millions of dollars for several different investment banks over the course of a decade. Because of his success, he was lauded by executives and courted by several different firms who wanted him to join them as a trader. It was no secret in the banking industry that Libor was being manipulated and that Hayes was using these manipulations to make money better than almost everybody else. But after the scandal broke and Hayes was charged with fraud and bid rigging by both the U.S. Department of Justice and the United Kingdom Serious Fraud Office, his former managers and supervisors claimed that they had no idea that his success was based on fraud. Prosecutors and juries apparently bought this story. Few senior executives were charged and none were convicted, even though the banks that they ran were fined hundreds of millions of dollars (Enrich, 2017).

Employees and subordinates can sometimes avoid responsibility by using another means. They can view themselves as simply subjects who must obey orders they receive from above. Though corporate leaders may claim that they did not know what was going on, subordinates feel that they are simply following orders. They are doing what their bosses want and what the corporation needs. Thus, employees may engage in actions that they know or strongly suspect are illegal without feeling responsible for the consequences. They are simply doing their jobs, and if they don't do so, then the company will find others who will. In this way, the underlings who commit white-collar crimes in organizational settings can still think of themselves as essentially law-abiding and morally upstanding people.

This pattern of behavior may be common in large organizations and may result from subtle negotiations between the occupants of different ranks in the organizational hierarchy as to how they are going to relate to one another. Both supervisors and their subordinates may exercise information control as a means of managing their relationships and avoiding culpability for illegal behavior. For example, managers and supervisors sometimes have a vested interest in not knowing too much about what their subordinates are doing, because if deviance should come to light, it could reflect poorly on their leadership. In addition, there may be times when managers really do not want to know if their subordinates are not following company policies exactly as written, because if they did know, then they would have to do something to enforce the policies, and this might make them unpopular with subordinates. Similarly, subordinates might not want to know exactly what their boss is thinking, because then they would be responsible for conforming to his or her wishes. Such "bilateral information control" in hierarchical organizations facilitates the continuation and cover-up of organizational deviance (Katz, 1979, p. 303).

A second general technique for sanitizing criminal opportunities in business settings is to *deny the victim*. The burglar who breaks into a home knows that he is taking someone else's property. Likewise, the robber who accosts someone on the street can see the fear in the victim's eyes. These offenders know beforehand that they are going to cause an innocent person to suffer some sort of harm or loss. White-collar offenders, however, often do not have to look their victims in the eye. Indeed, the "victim" may not be an individual at all but rather a vast governmental agency, such as Medicare in the case of health care fraud. In price-fixing cases, there may be millions of victims, each of whom loses only a trivial amount of money, or the victim may be another large corporate entity. Similarly, in the Libor scandal, Tom Hayes's primary victims were other traders and investment banks. At least that is the way that he viewed the situation (Enrich, 2017). But he blissfully ignored the reality that the traders and investment banks he was cheating were using other people's money and that these other people were also being victimized because of his actions (Enrich, 2017). In these types of cases, the victims come from an amorphous class of individuals whose investment and other financial decisions might have been different if they had had access to all the information. In all these cases, it is possible for white-collar offenders to convince themselves that no real person will suffer because of their actions, and therefore there is no real criminal victim. For example, a businessman convicted of price fixing looked at his offense in this manner:

> It certainly wasn't a premeditated type of thing in our case as far as I can see. ... To me it's different than [his partner] and I sitting down and we plan, well, we're going to rob this bank tomorrow and premeditatedly go in there. ... That wasn't the case at all. ... It wasn't like sitting down and planning I'm to rob this bank type of thing.
> (Benson, 1985, pp. 592–593)

This reasoning is plausible because it conforms to our common-sense construction of crime as involving a premeditated act that harms a real person. Many white-collar offenses fail to match this common-sense stereotype because the offenders do not set out intentionally to harm any specific individual. Rather, the consequences of their illegal acts fall upon impersonal organizations or a diffuse and unseen mass of people.

As Sutherland noted long ago, the laws that govern business behaviors in the United States define what lawyers call *mala prohibita* rather than *mala in se* offenses. That is, the behaviors are considered crimes only because they have been declared so by a legislative authority, as opposed to being universally recognized as innately evil and wrong. The laws that define *mala prohibita* offenses are not universally endorsed. Rather, there is, as Sutherland put it, a conflict of standards regarding just how much the government should intervene in a free-market society (Sutherland, 1983). People disagree about the need for government regulations in a whole host of areas and about how much businesspeople can be trusted to voluntarily regulate themselves. This conflict in standards gives rise to a third technique used by white-collar offenders to maintain a noncriminal identity: *condemning the condemners*. If the law itself is not legitimate or necessary and if those who enforce it are incompetent or untrustworthy, then our moral obligation to obey the law is undermined. In a free-enterprise system, businesspeople can argue to themselves that government has no business regulating economic behavior. In their view, the competitive processes of the market should decide what is or is not acceptable, not some bureaucrat who has never had to make a payroll or a profit. If business executives think that the law is unfair and that it unreasonably restricts the free play of economic forces, then they are free to violate the law (Conklin, 1977, p. 94).

Another technique used by corporate leaders is claim allegiance to a higher morality than that contained in the narrow legalisms of the law. There are several different forms that this *appeal to higher loyalties* can take. Employees who are asked to do something illegal may recognize that their behavior is wrong but argue to themselves that being loyal to their employer or organization is more important. Offenders can also make a distinction between morality and the technical requirements of the law and claim that it is more important to do the "right" thing than the legal thing. An example of this reasoning comes from one of the executives in the great electrical conspiracy:

> One faces a decision, I guess, at such times, about how far to go with company instructions, and since the spirit of such meetings only appeared to be correcting a horrible price level situation, that there was not an attempt to damage customers, charge excessive prices, there was no personal gain in it for me, the company did not seem actually to be defrauding … morally it did not seem quite so bad as might be inferred by the definition of the activity itself.
>
> (Geis, 1977, p. 123)

The key point is that the offenders see themselves as doing something for the good of the company while not directly harming or taking unfair advantage of anyone else. From this point of view, saving or protecting the company is the moral thing to do, and it claims a higher allegiance than obeying technical requirements of the law.

Businesspeople sometimes take an even broader view of the relationship between the law and business ethics. In a free-enterprise system, the pursuit of profit is seen as the generator of employment and wealth. It is the engine that drives our standard of living upward and ensures social welfare. Thus, the pursuit of profit can be viewed by businesspeople as the ethical thing to do. Indeed, it is the primary value on which our free-enterprise system operates, and it can at times supersede the ethical imperatives of the law. If obeying the law would retard the pursuit of fair profit, then the law itself is contrary to our country's most basic values and is morally inferior to business ethics. By viewing the pursuit of fair profit as the true reflection of our country's values, businesspeople can free themselves from the moral constraints of the law and maintain a noncriminal identity even while breaking the law.

Although both males and females use techniques of neutralizations, they may do so in different ways. For example, a study of intentions to violate environmental regulations found that gender influences how actors subjectively perceive opportunities (Simpson, Alper, and Benson, 2012). The study involved environmental decision makers in organizations based in the U.S. The male and female subjects were asked to respond to a series of scenarios that described an actor not complying with environmental regulations under different organizational conditions. In one scenario, a superior asked a subordinate to violate the law. For the men in the study, being *asked* to violate the law decreased the desirability of the behavior and increased the perceived shame associated with the behavior. This was not the case for women, where being asked to do something increased the social desirability of the act. The results here suggest that the potential loss of agency is more threatening to men than to women and that it may influence how both groups subjectively construct potential criminal opportunities. These and other subtle differences in how gender identities align with criminal behavior may play some role in the generally lower levels of female participation in white-collar crime.

All these techniques—denying responsibility, denying the victim, condemning the condemners, and appealing to higher loyalties—are available to potential white-collar offenders. They provide offenders with a perspective or viewpoint on their behavior that enables them to violate the law without feeling guilt or tarnishing their self-images as respectable people. In addition, the white-collar offender's efforts to maintain a noncriminal identity benefit from the stereotypical view of crime as a lower-class phenomenon in which predatory men prey upon innocent victims. For white-collar offenders, neither they nor their offenses resemble how the news media portrays crime. The white-collar offender's crimes are, in his or her view, different from street crimes. They are technical violations that harm no one and are committed for good reasons. Hence, white-collar offenders can view their actions as not tainted by the moral stigma that attaches to lower-class crime.

Moral Disengagement and the Structural Dimensions of Opportunity

Moral disengagement is a psychological construct that is related to the techniques of neutralization discussed above. However, it applies more broadly to white-collar crime in organizations than neutralization theory because it explicitly recognizes the social sources of many of the self-justifying cognitions of white-collar offenders. Moral disengagement refers to the psychosocial manoeuvrers that individuals and organizations use to selectively disengage moral self-sanctions when they undertake actions that harm others (Bandura, 1999). In other words, moral disengagement refers to the ways in which we can turn off our own moral standards against harming others. Once our moral standards are disengaged, we can then partake in harmful behavior without feeling bad about ourselves.

When someone is morally disengaged from a harmful or unethical act, they do not experience the self-censure that usually accompanies reprehensible conduct. Disengagement can be accomplished in several different ways. It may center on (1) reframing the conduct so that it is not seen as immoral, (2) minimizing the actor's role in causing harm, (3) minimizing the harmfulness of the conduct, or (4) devaluing or dehumanizing the victims of harm (Bandura, 1999). There are obvious similarities between the theory of moral disengagement and neutralization theory discussed earlier. Both theories seek to explain why seemingly good people can do bad things. But techniques of neutralization are typically thought of as linguistic or cognitive tools that permit offenders to temporarily free themselves from the constraints of moral conventions by providing them with a way to define their harmful behavior as acceptable under certain circumstances. The techniques are not thought of as aspects or parts of an individual's psychological makeup. Psychological research, however, suggests some people may be inherently more likely to use neutralizations or to morally disengage than others. The inventor of moral disengagement theory, Albert Bandura, suggests that people vary in their proneness to moral disengagement, and those who are highly prone are more likely to be involved in crime and deviance (Bandura, 1999).

In addition, moral disengagement has been shown to operate in organizations or groups, where individuals can participate in collective moral disengagement (White et al., 2009). Collective disengagement is not simply the aggregation of the cognitions of individuals in an organization or a group. Rather, it is an emergent phenomenon that arises out of the interactions of individuals within a collectivity, where each individual not only deactivates his own moral standards but also at the same time reinforces the exonerations made by other team members. Moral disengagement theory has been used to analyze terrorist atrocities as well as other inhumanities (Bandura, 1999, 2004), but for our purposes, we are interested in how the theory applies to white-collar crimes committed in corporate settings.

White and colleagues (2009) studied industries whose products or production practices are damaging to human health, including the tobacco, lead, vinyl chloride, and silicosis-producing industries. Their examination of internal documents and public state-ments uncovered evidence of a variety of modes of moral disengagement in the research and promotional activities of each industry. Companies in these industries (and most likely oth-ers that produce harmful products) attempt to shape how scientific findings are interpreted. They try to socially construct scientific evidence and public debate so that their products and production practices are seen as beneficial rather than harmful to individual and social well-being (Bero, 2005). This happens in part for the obvious reason that companies need to make their products acceptable to consumers to be profitable, but also because the people who work in these companies need to feel that their behavior is justified and morally accept-able. In other words, moral disengagement theory suggests that company leaders have to engage in a form of self-deception in order to engage in harmful practices. By manipulating scientific research and expert opinion, leaders attempt to construct social reality for them-selves and everyone else.

For example, one well-documented case of the manipulation of scientific research in-volves the tobacco industry (Bero, 2005). This case illustrates how industries that produce harmful products attempt to avoid government regulation and prevent public awareness of the dangers that their products pose to individuals and the environment. Starting in the 1950s and continuing to the 1990s, the tobacco industry devoted enormous resources to undermining scientific research showing the harmful effects of active smoking and second-hand smoke. The strategies and tactics used by tobacco companies to manipulate scientific research were eventually exposed through a lawsuit filed by the attorneys general of 46 states that forced the companies to release previously secret internal documents as part of a Master Settlement Agreement (Bero, 2005).

The tobacco wars ended in 1998 and the smoke from the battlefield has cleared, so to speak. In some ways the tobacco industry lost.[1] The harmfulness of tobacco is now well-known. Its dangers are taught in schools throughout the U.S. and gruesomely described in nationally televised public service announcements. In addition, laws protecting people against exposure to second-hand smoke are now common. As a result of the terms of the Master Settlement Agreement, we can now see what the industry was trying to do and how it was trying to do it. These are lessons that need to be learned because the techniques used by the tobacco industry to hide the harmfulness of its products continue to be employed in other industries. As noted above, the lead, vinyl chloride, and silicosis-producing industries have all engaged in the strategies and tactics of moral disengagement.

The tobacco documents show that the major goal of the companies was to generate con-troversy and confusion about the health risks of smoking tobacco and the risks of being exposed to second-hand smoke. To accomplish this goal, the industry used several different tactics. First, the industry funded research that supported its position that tobacco smoke was not harmful or not more harmful than other substances in the environment. To do this, the industry set up research institutes with scientific sounding names, such as the Tobacco Industry Research Committee (TIRC), which was promoted to the public as an organiza-tion that funded independent scientific research. In reality, however, the research funded by the TIRC was not independent, and it typically did not go through the normal processes of peer review used by federal organizations and large foundations. Rather, projects were reviewed by lawyers and company executives who selected those that were likely to produce results favorable to the industry (Bero, 2005). A second tactic was to publish research that supported the industry's position in outlets that were not peer reviewed, such as symposium proceedings or in special issues of journals. These non-peer reviewed articles could then be cited by industry advocates as demonstrating that the science on the harmfulness of tobacco smoke was unsettled. Third, the tobacco industry went to great lengths to criticize the methodologies and conclusions of studies that were not favorable to its position. It would recruit scientists to send letters to the editors of academic journals complaining that studies harmful to the industry's position were "junk science" or "obviously biased" by the activist leanings of the researchers. The goal of these tactics was not so much to prove that tobacco was safe but rather to cast doubt on the science showing it was unsafe. If that goal could have been accomplished, then policymakers most likely would have waited until a clearer empirical picture emerged, and the tobacco industry would have escaped more onerous regulation (Bero, 2005).

Even though the tobacco industry lost the scientific battle, the techniques that it used can be potentially valuable and effective for other companies. It is not hard for companies to find scientists who are willing to challenge the conclusions of other scientists, because scientists are supposed to be sceptical, and they also need money to support their research. Thus, in-house scientists can conduct their research without violating their scientific training or their personal ethics. In addition, many dangerous products do not produce injuries or illnesses immediately or all the time. Rather, their harmful effects are often delayed and spread out over a large population of exposed individuals, only some of whom are stricken (Calhoun and Hiller, 1992). These structural characteristics make it difficult for victims as well as regulators to prove a cause-and-effect type of relationship, and they make it plausible for in-house scientists to disengage from the moral implications of their work.

Risk and the Normalization of Deviance

A weakness of the opportunity perspective as applied to white-collar crime, particularly crimes committed in organizational settings, is that it implies that offenders are on some level aware that their actions are wrong or illegal. To say that offenders use techniques of neutralization to protect their sense of identity implies that they are aware that their behavior could be construed as illegal or morally objectionable. Neutralizations imply intentionality. Potential offenders are seen as convincing themselves that no one really will be hurt, or it's not really my fault, or the law is unfair to begin with, I need to save the company and the workers' jobs. However, this image of the offender as intentionally and knowingly violating the law may not be accurate regarding some types of deviance that occur in large organizations.

Some white-collar crime scholars argue that large organizations are characterized by conditions in which deviance can become normalized (Vaughan, 2005). Normalized deviance is deviant behavior that is not recognized by actors as being deviant. This occurs when individuals must decide what to do in a risky but complicated situation. The individuals involved may reinterpret information that could be seen as a sign of potential danger in such a way that the dangerousness of the situation is obscured or disappears altogether. A potential course of action that might have originally appeared as quite risky is transformed into one that appears acceptable and non-deviant. This reinterpretation of evidence leads to a decision that has unintended but very harmful outcomes and that in retrospect looks foolish if not criminally negligent on the part of the decision makers.

There is a difference between neutralized deviance and normalized deviance. In neutralized deviance, actors recognize at some level that what they are doing could be viewed as illegal, but they convince themselves that they have a good excuse for going ahead anyway.

In contrast, normalized deviance arises out of a more profound process of collective self-deception, in which actors really do not see their decisions as being risky with potentially harmful consequences. How does this happen?

The best example of the process of normalizing deviance comes from the space shuttle *Challenger* tragedy. In 1986, *Challenger* exploded shortly after take-off, killing all astronauts on board. After the tragedy, an investigation discovered evidence that appeared to indicate that officials at the U.S. National Aeronautics and Space Administration (NASA) had been forewarned about the possibility of a catastrophic failure on the shuttle. Yet, despite the warnings, they decided to authorize the launch anyway. It appeared that because they were under a lot of pressure to keep the shuttle program on schedule, NASA officials had deliberately ignored warnings and launched *Challenger* even though they knew it was risky. If this scenario were true, then all those involved in the *Challenger* decision would be guilty of misconduct or criminally negligent behavior. After a detailed investigation of the events leading up to the launch decision, however, Diane Vaughan (2005) argues that this interpretation is not accurate. In her view, the disaster was the result of mistakes in judgment rather than misconduct.

The explosion that doomed *Challenger* was caused by cold weather and a faulty O-ring. The O-rings were part of the solid rocket booster that launched the shuttle into space. The boosters were made in sections that were connected at joints that were sealed by O-rings. In the *Challenger* disaster, the O-rings failed. Rather than sealing the joints between the sections of the solid rocket booster, they allowed hot gases to escape, leading to the explosion. The outer O-rings failed in part because they were stiff owing to the cold temperature at the launch site. In the post-tragedy investigation, it was learned that during a pre-launch conference call, some engineers had argued against the launch. The engineers had protested that the cold temperatures that were predicted for launch time could cause the O-rings to fail. NASA managers, however, overrode the recommendations of the engineers and authorized the launch. Thus, the original interpretation of the tragedy was that NASA managers had been warned that the launch was risky but had nevertheless succumbed to political pressure and violated safety rules by authorizing the launch.

In contrast to this damning interpretation, Vaughan argues that the decision to launch *Challenger* was taken within an historical and structural context in which it was not seen as being unreasonably risky. The decision makers came to this erroneous conclusion because of a complex set of factors that included: (1) the context within which they received the information about the potentially faulty O-rings, (2) the organizational culture and political environment of NASA, and (3) the structural secrecy inherent in large organizations.

Information Context

Everyone knew that building and launching the space shuttle was inherently risky. Much of the technology involved was new, and the overall design of the shuttle vehicle had never been tried before. In this context, technical problems were expected, and it was understood that the risks associated with flying into space could never be reduced to zero. To handle the technical problems that occurred continually throughout the shuttle program, NASA established standardized procedures to analyze and correct them so that risk would be reduced to an acceptable level but not to zero. Therefore, the problem with the O-rings and cold weather was simply one of many technical problems that NASA engineers had encountered before.

A second aspect of the context that influenced how the problems with the O-rings were interpreted involved the accumulation of information over time. *Challenger* had completed nine missions before the explosion. When shuttle flights returned from space, they were examined carefully for signs of wear and failure. Erosion of the O-rings had been observed in some of the flights that preceded *Challenger*, but not in all of them. Sometimes the cause of the erosion was identified, such as, for example, a piece of lint on an O-ring, and corrected. After the fix, O-ring erosion in subsequent flights was either reduced or not observed for a while. Importantly, there was no convincing evidence that cold temperatures could cause the O-rings to fail. In 1985, erosion began occurring regularly but did not result in any explosions. NASA engineers interpreted these results as evidence that they understood the potential risks posed by the O-rings. Taken together, these factors led NASA officials to grossly underestimate the risks posed by the O-rings.

Organizational Culture and Political Environment

The organizational culture and political environment of NASA also played a role in the *Challenger* disaster. NASA was accountable to Congress, which agreed to fund the space shuttle program in part because NASA argued that it would eventually pay for itself. Thus, in making decisions to launch or not to launch the shuttle, NASA officials had to be sensitive to how these decisions would play to Congress. If the shuttle launches fell too far behind schedule, Congress presumably would not be happy and might reconsider its decision to fund the shuttle program.

In addition, to build, launch, and maintain the shuttle was an enormously complex task, involving hundreds of contractors. To keep track of the contractors, the millions of shuttle components, and the thousands of pre-launch activities, NASA became a very bureaucratic place with lots of rules. Following the rules contributed in an odd way to the normalization of deviance, because the rules conveyed a sense of safety and security. If you follow the rules and the shuttle flies successfully (which it had in all previous flights), then obviously following the rules meant that the shuttle is safe to fly. This kind of thinking led managers and engineers to downplay the significance of anomalies (such as warning signs that the O-rings were not working properly) that cropped up periodically in the shuttle program.

Thus, political accountability and reliance on bureaucratic procedures shaped how managers interpreted signs of potential danger in the shuttle program and specifically how they interpreted the conditions preceding the launch of *Challenger*. Based on what had happened during previous flights, everything looked normal or acceptably close to normal. At the time it was made, the decision to launch represented conformity. Only afterward, in retrospect, did it appear to indicate deviance and rule breaking.

Structural Secrecy

Like all large organizations, NASA is a complex place, and it suffers from a problem that is common to large organizations: structural secrecy. According to Diane Vaughan (2005, p. 264):

> [S]tructural secrecy refers ... to how organizational structure, division of labor, hierarchy, complexity, geographic dispersion of parts—systematically undermines the ability of people situated in one part of an organization to fully understand what happens in other parts.

Inevitably, as organizations grow large, knowledge about what is going on becomes compart-mentalized in subunits. Communication between subunits becomes difficult, as the people in one unit lack the expertise to really understand what people in another unit are doing. Even within subunits, individuals may have only partial knowledge about tasks and goals because of the specialized division of labor. The problem of structural secrecy becomes particularly pro-nounced when the people at the bottom of the organizational hierarchy are highly specialized experts. It is difficult for organizational leaders at the top to understand all the information that those below them have on any given issue. Organizations try to develop mechanisms for keeping track of what is going on and for exchanging information. They require people to fill out forms and file reports regularly. But these efforts often only add to the problem. As the flow of reports and files grows ever larger, the time that organizational leaders have for reading and mastering information remains fixed. The more information there is, the less that can be mastered. Ironi-cally, too much information can be as bad for organizational decision-making as too little.

In the case of the *Challenger* disaster, structural secrecy contributed to the normalization of deviance because it helped to conceal from decision makers the seriousness of the O-ring prob-lem. The actual process by which NASA made launch decisions was very formal and rigorous. It involved a four-tiered hierarchical process called a Flight Readiness Review. The work groups in charge of different components on the shuttle would submit their reports on the readiness of their particular component. These reports could be challenged at every stage of the Flight Readiness Review, but the engineering analyses were not replicated outside of the work group.

This was a key weakness in the decision-making process. The people who made the deci-sion to launch were dependent on information they received from those below them. They could criticize the information in a general way, but they did not analyze each component in the same detail as did the work groups. They did not conduct their own analyses. Most of the time, the process worked. Errors were caught and corrected. Engineers were sometimes asked to redo their analyses and make them more rigorous. Unfortunately, however, if a work group made an error but still recommended a launch that was based on tight engineer-ing analyses, no one outside the work group was likely to see the mistake and intervene.

The *Challenger* disaster involved a combination of all these factors—complex and am-biguous information, political and bureaucratic pressures, and structural secrecy. Together they created a situation in which a decision was taken that seemed reasonable at the time but that had disastrous consequences. According to Vaughan, the conventional interpreta-tion that the disaster was caused by reckless NASA officials who repeatedly ignored obvious warning signals is simply misguided. It does not accurately reflect what happened.

We end up, then, with two contrasting perspectives on the role of risk and responsibility in the *Challenger* disaster. The conventional interpretation says that NASA officials were responsible. They recklessly ignored risks that they knew existed, because they were more concerned with the success of the shuttle program than the safety of the crew. The alterna-tive interpretation puts the blame on faulty organizational structures and dynamics. The risks posed by the faulty O-ring design were not fully recognized because of organizational factors outside the control and understanding of anyone.

The Normalization of Deviance in Other Organizations

The space shuttle program officially ended on August 31, 2011, with only one other major accident, the breakup of *Columbia* on February 1, 2003. The shuttle program was obviously an enormously complex, risky, and one-of-a-kind undertaking. Much of the technology on which the shuttle was based had to be invented and tested along the way. Because of the unique nature of the shuttle program and the *Challenger* disaster, it is difficult to know how much we can generalize from what happened at NASA to other organizations. Yet, it is certainly possible that something like the normalization of deviance that occurred at NASA happens in other large organizations.

All large organizations suffer to some degree from the problem of structural secrecy. Large organizations naturally divide into specialized subunits and become more hierarchical, and these tendencies apply to organizations regardless of the country or culture in which they are located (Miller, 1987). Hierarchy and the division of tasks among subunits make it more difficult for information to flow and be accurately interpreted throughout the organizational structure. What happens in one part of an organization may be neither known nor fully understood in another part. Although organizational leaders can try to set up mechanisms to ensure that they know what is going on, there are limits to the amount of information that anyone, as a fallible human being, can absorb.

All large organizations also suffer from the problem of being accountable to external parties and forces. For NASA, the external accountability came from Congress, which expected a return on its investment of taxpayers' dollars in the shuttle program. Large private business organizations are accountable to their investors and stockholders, who also expect a return on their money. Having to live up to the expectations of the marketplace does not automatically and inevitably make organizational leaders into amoral calculators, but it does color their interpretation of information. The need to make a profit to satisfy stockholders and investors must always be considered in decision making. Private, for-profit organizations must always balance the fundamental requirement to make money against the risks and harms that may be imposed on others in the process of making money.

The degree to which large organizations have to contend with an information context similar to the one that confronted NASA depends on whether they are developing new products as opposed to simply marketing tried and true ones. New products always pose potential risks that must be evaluated through testing. The testing process produces information that must be distributed throughout the organization and interpreted by decision makers prior to putting the product on the market. Even after a new product is placed on the market, it continues to generate information in the form of feedback regarding problems and complaints from salespeople, customers, and users. The interpretation of this information may be skewed by its context. Whether a product is regarded as posing acceptable versus unacceptable risks depends on how information about its performance is captured and interpreted relative to all sorts of other feedback that an organization is receiving.

One of the most tragic examples that appears to illustrate the importance of information context, structural secrecy, and external accountability involves the Ford Pinto. The complete story of the Pinto is complex and involves technical details beyond the scope of this book. Accordingly, as its rise and fall has been ably reviewed elsewhere (Cullen et al., 2006), we present only a summary of events here.

The Pinto was a subcompact car that the Ford Motor Company introduced in 1970. It was designed to compete with small cars produced by Japanese manufacturers, such as Honda and Toyota. Lee Iacocca, then chairman of Ford, had instructed his engineers to design a car that weighed less than 2,000 pounds and that cost less than $2,000. To get the car to market quickly, the normal production time of 43 months was slashed to only 25 months (Cullen et al., 2006).

The Pinto was a popular car with consumers. More than 1.5 million units sold in its first six years of production. It suffered, however, from a serious design flaw. The gas tank had been placed too close to the rear wheel axle. It was in a position where it could be easily ruptured in a rear-end collision at moderate speed. Under the right conditions, a ruptured fuel tank could leak gasoline, leading to a devastating fire in the vehicle. Tragically, this happened repeatedly during the years that the Pinto was in production, and thousands of people died or were grotesquely disfigured in fiery crashes (Cullen et al., 2006, p. 146). The most famous accident and the one that led to the landmark criminal prosecution of Ford occurred in Elkhart, Indiana. Three teenage girls were burned to death after the Pinto they were driving was hit from behind by a van.

In retrospect, what made the Pinto story so outrageous was the discovery that Ford apparently had known since early in the production process that the design of the gas tank was flawed. The Pinto had been crash-tested, and the results of some tests indicated that fuel tank ruptures were likely to occur at moderate speeds. It also appeared that Ford had known that several relatively cheap technological fixes were available that could have made the car much safer. Officials at Ford, however, appeared to have chosen not to make any changes to the design of the gas tank after a cost-benefit analysis indicated that improved safety was not warranted financially. To put it bluntly, in Ford's view, it was cheaper to pay off a few crash victims than to fix the gas tank on thousands of cars.

The conventional interpretation of the Pinto case is in many ways similar to how the *Challenger* disaster was interpreted. In both cases, decision makers appear to have ignored obvious warning signs and put lives in danger in pursuit of organizational goals. Yet, there is an alternative interpretation of the Pinto decision that resembles Vaughan's reanalysis of the *Challenger* decision (Gioia, 1992; Lee and Ermann, 1999). The Pinto was brought to market after a lengthy process of development that involved hundreds of employees working in different subunits. Although some crash tests indicated that the gas tank design was flawed, the results of other tests fell within the normal range. In short, the crash tests were inconclusive. In addition, the car met federal safety standards that were in force at the time and appeared to be as safe as other subcompacts then on the road.

Thus, according to the alternative interpretation, the employees and managers at Ford were subject to organizational forces and situational factors that resembled those involved in the *Challenger* disaster—structural secrecy, ambiguous information, and external environmental pressures. Caught up in the rush to produce the Pinto on time, managers simply did not see the problems with the gas tank design as serious safety anomalies. They followed standard procedures, and the car's overall safety was assessed according to routine practices. Unfortunately, however, by following standard practices, the people at Ford ended up "normalizing" the rear-end crash test results, that is, defining them as acceptable risks rather than recognizing them as serious safety anomalies.

The *Challenger* and Pinto cases should alert us to the potential limits of the opportunity perspective in the context of large organizations. The opportunity perspective assumes that rationality lies behind the decision to commit a white-collar crime. It assumes that people see or recognize criminal opportunities and choose to take advantage of them for their own benefit (or, in the case of some people in organizations, for the benefit of their organizations). Yet, in large organizations, people may make decisions in situations where they do not truly understand the implications of those decisions. There is a difference between ignoring or neutralizing a risk and simply not seeing the risk in the first place. There is also a difference between concerted ignorance and structural secrecy. Concerted ignorance arises when organizational leaders deliberately try to avoid learning about certain types of information in hopes of thereby reducing or eliminating their legal culpability. Structural secrecy, on the other hand, arises when certain types of information do not circulate through an organization and, as a result, organizational leaders are unaware of them. Both the *Challenger* case and the Pinto case raise the possibility that under some circumstances, people in organizations simply do not see that their decisions may impose unacceptable risks on others. They misinterpret and normalize warning signs.

Of course, this exculpatory reasoning should not be carried too far. Whenever corporate executives are confronted with charges of illegality, they argue that nothing was intentional, but this argument should always be viewed with great skepticism. As we showed in Chapters 6 and 7, people who work in large corporations often knowingly take advantage of criminal opportunities for their own benefit or the benefit of their companies. Likewise, it is certainly not uncommon for corporate executives to try to hide behind the sham of concerted ignorance.

Cases of what appears to be deviance or criminality in large organizations seem to generate competing narratives almost automatically. These narratives provide wildly different interpretations of the intentionality of actors in large organizations, regardless of whether the case concerns an unsafe consumer product or a dangerous workplace or a large-scale financial fraud. On one side are narratives produced by consumer advocates, unions, investigative journalists, and white-collar crime scholars that interpret the behavior of corporate executives in terms of the greedy and criminal pursuit of profits over people (Barnett, 2013; Cullen et al., 2006; McLean and Elkind, 2004; Pontell and Geis, 2014; Shover and Hochstetler, 2006; Tillman, Pontell, and Black, 2018). On the other side are corporate apologists who contend that mistakes happen and that untoward events are the result of some sort of system failure as opposed to intentional wrongdoing (Gioia, 1992; Lee and Ermann, 1999; Vaughan, 2005). Exactly which of the two narratives is correct in any given case depends, of course, on the facts. But regardless whether any given case involves a criminal act or an unfortunate accident, the organizational setting greatly complicates its moral and legal interpretation, both in the courtroom and in the arena of public opinion.

We suggest that this structurally induced ambiguity plays an important role in the continuation of corporate crime in modern society for several reasons. First, ambiguity makes it possible for corporate leaders to construct metaphysical escapes that reduce if not eliminate their culpability. Of course, executives may be mistaken in their belief that no one will hold them accountable, but that simply means that they have misjudged the potential costs or risks of their actions, as any offender may do. What matters is not that metaphysical escapes or efforts at concerted ignorance always work, but that corporate leaders have reason to believe that they work most of the time. This belief makes it easier for corporate criminals to morally disengage from their risky actions than would be the case if they knew that discovery would automatically bring individual culpability. Second, ambiguity contributes to the factual complexity of corporate crimes. Consider, for example, a case involving the deaths of 51 workers who were killed when scaffolding for a water tower that they were working on collapsed. It was clear that OSHA regulations had been violated when the scaffolding was constructed and it was clear that the 51 workers had died, but it was not clear that the regulatory violations caused the scaffolding to collapse. Other factors, such as weather conditions, may also have been involved. Prosecutors looking into the case eventually decided that the case was so complex that they did not believe they could convince a jury beyond a reasonable doubt that the company or any executive in it was guilty of a crime (Braithwaite and Geis, 1982). More recently, it is instructive that so far no one in the investment banks involved in the financial collapse of 2008 has been charged with criminal fraud. Despite the widespread public outrage over the public bailout of investment banks, the lack of prosecutions certainly sends a message to corporate insiders that there is safety behind corporate walls (Pontell and Geis, 2014).

Summary

In this chapter, we have argued that white-collar crime opportunities have symbolic as well as structural dimensions. The structure of a white-collar crime opportunity is determined primarily by the way in which a business or industry is organized. As we described in earlier chapters, different forms of organization create different types of opportunities. The symbolic dimension of white-collar crime opportunities refers to how potential offenders interpret their illegal activities. Almost without exception white-collar offenders do not conceive of themselves as criminals. Rather, they think of themselves as upstanding, law-abiding, and morally principled individuals. To break the law deliberately for one's personal benefit without having some sort of excuse or justification would be inconsistent with a conventional self-image. To avoid this inconsistency, white-collar offenders often use neutralizations and the techniques of moral disengagement to excuse or justify their involvement in illegal activity.

The neutralizations that are most prominently used to justify white-collar crime can be divided into four main types: denying responsibility, denying the victims, condemning the condemners, and appealing to higher loyalties. Because of the complex nature of large corporations, both those at the top and those at the bottom can deny to themselves that they are individually responsible for untoward behavior. Those at the bottom can say that they are just following orders; those at the top can argue that they cannot really be expected to know and to be held responsible for every little thing that goes wrong in a huge organization. Similarly, it is easy for white-collar offenders to think that their actions do not really harm anyone, that there are no victims in the traditional sense of an individual who suffers some sort of loss or harm. Denying the victim is easy when the "victim" is a faceless government bureaucracy such as the Medicare system. In the eyes of business executives and professionals, government bureaucracies deserve to be condemned because they create burdensome regulations that get in the way of honest people trying to make an honest living. Finally, white-collar offenders can rationalize to themselves that sometimes obedience to the law is not their most important moral obligation. They have obligations to their shareholders, employees, and customers. It is more important to make a profit and to protect people's jobs than it is to obey some obscure and probably misguided government regulation. All these techniques of neutralization serve the same function. They help make it morally acceptable to offenders to take advantage of white-collar criminal opportunities.

Techniques of neutralization are necessary for white-collar offenders if they are aware that their actions could be characterized as illegal or unreasonably risky. It is the awareness of potential illegality that provokes the offender's use of neutralizations to undermine the moral stigma that would accompany involvement in criminal activity. However, as the cases of the space shuttle *Challenger* and perhaps the Ford Pinto show, sometimes it is not clear that organizational leaders have this level of awareness. In large organizations, deviance may, under certain circumstances, become normalized. That is, deviant or risky behavior may not be recognized as such. Rather, information that should be interpreted as a warning signal is misunderstood or reinterpreted as normal.

The normalization of deviance involves three factors. First, there is an information context that makes it difficult to separate out important messages and signals from those that can be safely ignored. This problem may arise because the information itself is ambiguous or because there is simply too much of it for people to assimilate and evaluate effectively. Second, structural secrecy hinders the flow of information to decision makers and throughout the organization. Because of the division of labor among subunits and because of task specialization, people in one part of an organization may not really understand the significance of what people in another part are doing. Third, the organization is subject to environmentally generated pressures or expectations to achieve some goal. For business corporations, the pressure comes mainly from the market and the need to make a profit. For other types of organizations, such as NASA, the expectations may be political in nature, but organizations are always under some type of pressure to perform (Gross, 1978). Regardless of the source, externally generated expectations shape the way that people in organizations evaluate information and make decisions. External expectations may lead decision makers to downplay risks, particularly when the risks are imposed on someone else (Friedrichs, 2010). Taken together, these factors—information context, structural secrecy, and the pressure to perform—can create conditions in which people in large organizations make decisions that from the outside appear to be obviously deviant or criminal. Yet, from the inside, they appear normal or routine and not out of the ordinary.

Note

1 But in other ways, the industry won. It is still in business and as of spring 2017, its profits are soaring despite a reduction in the number of smokers (Maloney and Chaudhuri, 2017).

Chapter 9

The Social Distribution of Opportunity
Class, Gender, and Race

In the preceding chapters, we have argued that opportunities for white-collar crime are shaped and distributed according to the nature of the economic and productive activities of different industries. Certain types of white-collar crime are more common in some industries than others because the opportunity to commit those types of crime is built into the organization of the industry. For example, the structure of the health care insurance system makes possible certain types of fraud, deception, and abuse of trust that would be difficult if not impossible to carry out in the retail clothing industry. As a general rule that has only a few exceptions, white-collar crimes are not spread evenly across industries or occupations. The exceptions involve activities that are common to all business undertakings. For example, all businesses must engage in accounting, and in the early 2000s accounting fraud appeared to have spread to all types of businesses and industries, indeed even to some municipal authorities (Partnoy, 2003).

Just as opportunities for white-collar crime are not distributed evenly across industries, they are also not distributed evenly across people. Some people are more likely to have access to opportunities for white-collar crime than others. In this chapter, we argue that access to opportunities for white-collar crime are shaped by social class, gender, and race. The reason why these social characteristics matter is not complicated. Most white-collar crimes are committed within occupational settings. Indeed, it is the offender's occupation that gives rise to the opportunity to commit different types of white-collar crime. Insider trading, for example, requires that one be an organizational insider of some sort or have access to inside information, which must come from some source inside the organization. Access to many white-collar crime opportunities is based, therefore, on having access to an occupational position. It follows that any characteristic that influences access to occupational positions will also, indirectly, influence access to opportunities to commit white-collar crime. This general rule is true even for occupational positions within the illicit markets of the underworld (Steffensmeier, 1983). Social class, gender, and race are just such characteristics.

You do not need an advanced academic degree to know that the occupational structure has long been stratified along class, gender, and racial lines (Kalev, 2009). Opportunities to commit white-collar crime also are stratified along these same lines. Depending on their gender, class, and race, some individuals will have more opportunities to offend while others will have fewer opportunities. By themselves or in conjunction with one another, these characteristics affect the white-collar crime opportunity structure.

Consider, for example, gender and the "glass ceiling". The glass ceiling refers to the barriers that women face moving into management-level positions within business. In 1991, the United States Department of Labor put together a group called the Glass Ceiling Commission to study the problem of women in business. The commission's report issued in 1995 found that despite more women moving into the labor force and in spite of substantial

DOI: 10.4324/9781003175322-13

advances in educational attainment by women (e.g., women held more than half the master's degrees awarded), 95 percent of senior managers were male. Since the mid-1990s, there has been some improvement, but women are still highly underrepresented in top management positions. In 2020, for instance, women held only 8.2 percent of leadership positions in Fortune 500 companies and they held an even smaller percentage (7.3 percent) of leadership positions in Fortune 1000 companies (Women Business Collaborative, 2021).

Women are not the only ones who bump their heads against the glass ceiling. Minorities also often are blocked from top leadership positions. The report of the Glass Ceiling Commission (1995) noted that African-Americans, Latinos, and Asians were nearly non-existent in senior management positions, with whites holding fully 97 percent of those positions. In 2014, only 4 percent of Fortune 500 CEOs were minorities (African-American, Asian, and Latin-American) and, as of March 2015 when McDonald's CEO Don Thompson stepped down, the percent of African-American CEOs at Fortune 500 companies dropped to 0.8 percent. To put this into perspective, African-Americans comprise 14.2 percent of the population. With Thompson's departure, the total number of African-American CEOs at Fortune 500 firms dropped from five to four (Berman, 2015).

Not surprisingly, when race and gender are considered together, it is easy to see that female non-white workers confront what has been called a "double-glass ceiling" in rising to executive level positions (Tim, Peck, and Gee, 2020). Using 2018 data from the Equal Employment Opportunity Commission, researchers from the Ascend Foundation calculated what they called an Executive Parity Index (EPI).[1] The EPI measures the degree to which individuals with a particular combination of race and gender characteristics are represented among executives relative to their representation in the population of professionally educated individuals. So, for example, the EPI for white males is 1.83, which means that white males are over-represented among executives by 83 percent compared to their representation among professionally educated individuals. For comparison's sake, the EPI for white women is .69, meaning they are under-represented by 31 percent. Even though they are under-represented, white women still fare better than non-white women. The respective EPIs for Hispanic, Asian, and black women are .41, .30, and .31. In short, non-white women, especially Asians and blacks, are greatly under-represented at the executive level in American workplace organizations (Tim, Peck, and Gee, 2020).

Thus, race, class, and gender are tightly coupled social characteristics that "reflect our nation's entire social history ... [and] our nation's present social structure, with income inequality and occupational immobility for some, but new levels of well-being and material success for others" (Harris, 1991, pp. 97–98). Although the position of women and minorities in the workplace has not remained entirely static, and there is evidence of some improvement in some companies and industries (Kalev, 2009), it is still the case that both groups are often segregated into low-level and undervalued positions.

Of course, not all occupations are equally stratified. Some occupations are more open to women and minorities than others. In this chapter, we explore how opportunities to commit white-collar crimes are stratified along class, gender, and racial lines. We also explore how these characteristics shape the risk of white-collar crime victimization.

Class, Status, and White-Collar Crime

Sutherland originally defined white-collar crime as crime committed by persons of "respectability and high social status". He set out to focus on "persons of the upper socioeconomic classes" (Sutherland, 1983, p. 7). Most of the examples and case studies presented in *White-Collar Crime* involved powerful men, including the leaders of such stalwarts of American capitalism as the U.S. Steel Corporation, Standard Oil Company, Procter & Gamble, and DuPont Chemicals (Sutherland, 1983, pp. 64–65). Sutherland's influential imagery resonated throughout the following decades. Even today, the common stereotype of the white-collar offender pictures him (yes, *him*) as a white businessman who occupies a position of power and prestige, a wealthy member of America's corporate elite. There is no shortage of examples of white male corporate elites involved in white-collar crime. Except perhaps for Martha Stewart and Theranos CEO Elizabeth Holmes, the ringleaders in the most recent string of corporate scandals are almost exclusively upper-class white males (Steffensmeier, Schwartz, and Roche, 2013).

People from other class and status backgrounds, however, are involved in white-collar crime. As we showed in Chapter 2, in the mid-1970s, most of the people convicted of white-collar types of crimes in the federal court system could not be described as upper-class corporate elites. Rather, they appeared to come primarily from the middle classes of American society (Weisburd et al., 1991). Many of the subjects in the Yale and the Forst and Rhodes samples were not exactly what Sutherland had in mind when he coined the term *white-collar crime*. The difference between Sutherland's white-collar offenders and those of more recent studies is explained in part by the changing nature of work in American society. In Sutherland's day, white-collar office work was high-status work, but that is no longer the case. Today, the labor market is dominated by low-status clerical and technical jobs. Wearing nice clothes to work and spending most of your working day in an office no longer guarantees high social status or financial success. Many white-collar jobs are little more than poorly paid dead-ends—known as "pink collar" positions for their tendency to be disproportionately filled by women (Weisburd et al., 1991).

Sutherland used the terms *status* and *class* interchangeably and did not make any sharp conceptual distinction between them. The contemporary view, however, is that although status and class are related, they are not exactly the same thing. *Social status* is a relative term in the sense that people can be ranked as having more or less of it, depending on their income, education, and occupation.

In contrast, *social class* refers to the nature and structural relationships of the occupational positions that people hold, not their standing relative to others. A widely used typology of class was developed by Erik Olin Wright. In Wright's typology, class position is based on three criteria: (1) ownership of capital assets, (2) control of organizational assets, and (3) possession of skill or credential assets (Wright, 1997). Wright distinguishes the owners of the means of production from non-owners, and managers and supervisors from others. Most of us fall into the non-owner class because we are simply employees who work for others and have no control over the means of production. Owners do have control over the means of production, but in advanced capitalist economies such as ours, they often do not actually exercise much day-to-day control. Rather, in most modern corporations, control is exercised by professional managers and supervisors. In regard to white-collar crime, the distinction between owners and managers is important. The most serious white-collar crimes are not necessarily committed by those who own corporations but by those who have access to and control over organizational resources, such as chief executive officers (CEOs), chief financial officers (CFOs), and upper-level line managers and supervisors (Wheeler and Rothman, 1980).

White-collar crimes vary in organizational complexity and in the severity of their consequences. More complex offenses have a discernible pattern, involve the use of organizational resources, are committed by multiple participants, and last for a long period of time.

The severity of an offense is determined by how many victims it has, the dollar value of the victims' losses, and the geographical impact of the offense. In the Yale study, the researchers found that the eight offenses they examined could be divided into a three-level hierarchy based on the components of organizational complexity (Weisburd et al., 1991, pp. 39–42). The offenses with high complexity included antitrust violations and securities fraud. Mail fraud, false claims, and bribery were moderately complex, while tax fraud, credit fraud, and bank embezzlement were usually of low complexity. Antitrust and securities offenses also ranked highest in severity, whereas false claims, credit fraud, bribery, tax fraud, and bank embezzlement ranked lowest. Mail fraud on average tended to have consequences for victims that fell between these two groups.

In the Yale study, then, the most serious and organizationally complex offenses were antitrust violations and securities fraud. Access to opportunities to commit these offenses appears to be heavily influenced by class position. Just over seven of ten of the antitrust offenders in the Yale sample were either owners or officers of their companies (71.3 percent). Among those convicted of securities fraud, a very similar percentage were owners or officers (68.4 percent). For all other offenses, only a third or less of those convicted were owners or officers (Weisburd et al., 1991, pp. 50–51). In other words, most of them were employees who probably had little or no supervisory authority and little or no power in the workplace. Opportunities to commit serious white-collar offenses, then, appear to be greatly enhanced for those who hold certain organizational positions.

The Yale study suggests that class position is more important than social status in determining access to white-collar crime opportunities. But social status and class position are linked in that social status provides access to organizational positions where there is greater potential for large-scale white-collar offending. Attending a prestigious university and garnering a business degree do not by themselves put one in a position to be a big-time white-collar criminal—but they may open the door to such positions. Wheeler and Rothman (1980, pp. 1420–1421) speculate on how organizational position and individual status combine to facilitate and augment white-collar offending:

> [A] portion of the organizational defendant's advantage accrues not through his organizational affiliation per se, but because the defendant's stature lends credibility to their claims. Occupational and organizational status tend to go together in our society—the stockbroker, for example, is also a vice-president of the firm and the lawyer is also general counsel to the corporation. This combination of organizational status and occupational position facilitates the theft of vastly greater sums of money than in the case of almost any other kind of crime, white-collar or not.

Large-scale white-collar offending depends on access to organizational resources, and access is facilitated by class position. Thus, professional managers and supervisors have the most opportunity to commit serious white-collar offenses. The patterns revealed in the admittedly dated Yale study are not aberrations. We see something similar in a 2008/2009 sample of 644 prosecuted white-collar offenders from the Netherlands (van Onna et al., 2014). Like the Yale offenders, the Dutch sample, while diverse, was decidedly middle class based on average income level and homeownership status. Among these offenders, only a few were business owners (17.9 percent), while another quarter (24.5 percent) were self-employed (typically small employers). Nearly 40 percent of the sample, however, were identified as directors, managers, or managing partners. These supervisory employees are, to use Wright's terminology (1997), in "contradictory class locations" because they share the opposite objective interests of two antagonistic classes (owners and employees). On the one hand, they hold significant positions of power within their firms by virtue of their occupational positions. But, on the other hand, they are still employees lacking ultimate control in contrast to direct ownership.

Van Onna and associates (2014) examined the kinds of white-collar offenses that were committed by different types of offenders in their sample. The group designated as "stereotypical" white-collar offenders (SWO = those more associated with Sutherland's definition) looked a lot like the securities and antitrust offenders in the Yale study.

> In terms of sociodemographic characteristics, as well as their selection offences, SWOs resemble the stereotypical image of white-collar criminals: They have higher incomes, assets, and liabilities; have relatively few benefits; and are over-represented in white-collar positions such as business owner, director, or manager. They are relatively often prosecuted for traditional white-collar crimes such as market abuse fraud (such as insider trading) and securities fraud.
>
> (van Onna et al., 2014, p. 773)

The Gender Gap in White-Collar Crime: Offending

One of the oldest and most widely accepted findings in criminology is that males are more likely to be offenders than females. Indeed, gender is regarded as the single best predictor of crime. This generalization appears to apply in all societies and in all historical periods (Steffensmeier and Allan, 2000). In regard to traditional street crimes, the gap between male and female offending is not the same for all offenses. It is smaller for some offenses than it is for others. For example, in 1995, the female percentage of arrests for minor property crimes was 35 percent. In other words, more than one-third of all the arrests for these offenses involved women. However, for crimes such as robbery, females accounted for only about 8 percent of arrestees (i.e., less than one in ten; Steffensmeier and Allan, 2000). The gender gap is narrower for minor property offenses and wider for more violent offenses. It is also wider for adults than it is for juveniles (Smith and Visher, 1980). Finally, research suggests that the male to female gap has narrowed over time, especially post-1985 (Heimer, 2000).

Gender is also a strong predictor of white-collar crime, and like traditional street crimes, the size of the gender gap depends on the type of white-collar crime. Recall from Chapter 2 that whereas women made up less than 5 percent of those convicted of antitrust or securities fraud in the Yale study, they accounted for almost half of the convicted bank embezzlers. And the data reported in Chapter 2 from the U.S. Sentencing Commission clearly indicate that this pattern has not changed recently. Between 2006 and 2012, women made up less than 1 percent of those convicted of antitrust offenses (see Table 2.4 in Chapter 2). In the Yale study, women offenders also were more apt to be unemployed, less educated, and single heads of households compared with their male counterparts. Their lower status vis-à-vis male offenders translated into less complex offenses, usually without co-offenders, that yielded lower financial benefits (Daly, 1989).[2]

Data from other studies show similar variations in the gender gap but they also suggest that for some types of offenses, the gender gap may be closing slightly. Recall that in the Forst and Rhodes study, women constituted just under 50 percent of the bank embezzlers but only about 10 percent of those convicted of bribery and tax offenses. More recent data from the Sentencing Commission suggests that women's involvement in tax and bribery offenses has increased somewhat so that women now account for about 20 percent of those convicted for tax violations and over 50 percent of those convicted for embezzlement (see Table 2.4 in Chapter 2).

While women's involvement in some forms of white-collar crime appears to be increasing slightly, they are still dramatically underrepresented in white-collar offenses that involve access to or control over organizational resources. For example, a study examined three different types of fraud (asset misappropriation, corruption, and fraudulent statements) using survey data collected by the Association of Certified Fraud Examiners (Holtfreter, 2005). Asset misappropriation is defined as the theft or misuse of organizational assets by employees. It is similar to embezzlement. Corruption involves the wrongful use of business influence for personal gain. Fraudulent statements involve the falsification of organizational records or documents. Of the three types of fraud, fraudulent statements require greater access to organizational resources and are more similar to organizational as opposed to occupational offenses. In regard to gender differences and consistent with the Yale study, Holtfreter (2005, p. 359) found that individuals who committed asset misappropriation "were significantly less likely to be male than those who committed fraudulent statements". In other words, females were more significantly represented among those charged with asset misappropriation as compared with those charged with fraudulent statements. However, she did not find any gender differences between asset misappropriation and corruption, or corruption and fraudulent statements.

Holtfreter's research reinforces the important link between the structure of organizations and white-collar offending opportunities. The three types of fraud differed with respect to organizational characteristics such as size, public versus privately traded firms, and internal compliance systems. For instance, she found that asset misappropriation was committed more often in smaller organizations, whereas corruption took place more often in larger (and generally publicly traded) companies. Audits and anonymous reporting systems discovered corruption (but not false statements or asset misappropriation) within firms.

Another study looked at the gender breakdown of defendants in the Enron and post-Enron financial scandals. It revealed an even smaller percentage of female defendants. Kathleen Brickey (2008) has collected data on all companies and their Officers against whom fraud charges were brought in the post-Enron era (i.e., between March 2002 and July 2007). Of the 355 total defendants in these cases, only 26 (7 percent) were women. A cursory glance at Brickey's data shows that the majority of cases had only one or no female defendants. A case involving an impropriety by KPMG, the big accounting firm, for instance, had one lone female among 22 male defendants. The well-known Adelphia case had six defendants, all of whom were male. The firm with the most women defendants in Brickey's study was Health-South, which also had a large number of individual defendants (25). One-fifth of these (five) were female. The Enron scandal, perhaps the most infamous financial fraud of the past decade, produced 33 individual co-defendants, but only three of these were female, including Lea Fastow, Enron assistant treasurer and wife of the former CFO (and co-defendant) Andrew Fastow.

Brickey's analysis has been expanded and deepened in a study by Darrell Steffensmeier and colleagues that sheds even more light on the gender gap in high-level corporate frauds in the post-Enron era (Steffensmeier et al., 2013). This study looked at 83 post-Enron corporate frauds that resulted in indictments and were prosecuted by the Department of Justice's Corporate Fraud Task Force (CFTF). The CFTF was formed after the Enron and WorldCom scandals, and it was explicitly focused on high-level corporate frauds. The CFTF compiled a database of indictments that contained information on the 83 cases and the 436 offenders involved in them. The researchers supplemented the information in the indictments with other data gathered from news sources as well as other government reports and press releases. They were able to identify the gender of the defendants, their occupational positions, and their roles in the various offenses. Of the 436 defendants, only 37 were women, that is, 9 percent of the sample.

A more significant finding perhaps than the small number of women involved in these cases concerns their roles in the fraud conspiracies. These high-level frauds always involved multiple conspirators who played different roles in the criminal networks. The researchers divided the roles into four levels—ringleader, major role, in-between role, and minor role. Of the 37 women, only three were ringleaders and only seven played a major role. The remaining 27 women played in-between (8) or minor (19) roles. Indeed, in over 70 percent of the cases, there were no women involved in the criminal group at all. This study is the first systematic gender-based analysis of high-level corporate frauds, the kind of white-collar crimes that would have interested Sutherland, and the results could not be more telling in regard to the gender gap in serious white-collar crimes.

As the studies cited clearly show, women are underrepresented in official statistics for certain types of organizationally based white-collar crimes. However, exactly what causes this pattern is open to interpretation. There are several possibilities. One interpretation is that because access to occupational and organizational positions is stratified by gender, women have fewer opportunities to engage in certain types of white-collar crime, specifically those types that allow offenders to use the organization as a weapon to deceive and conspire against victims; that is, criminal opportunities could be due to job incumbency. Hence, restricted access explains why it is unusual to find women charged with these types of white-collar crimes. Restricted access or lack of job incumbency may explain some of the underrepresentation of women in high-level corporate frauds, but it is not the whole story. Steffensmeier and colleagues (2013) argue that the proportion of women involved in post-Enron corporate frauds is considerably lower than the proportion of mid- and upper-level management positions held by women. In other words, based on their representation in management positions, more women should have been involved in these frauds if access to opportunity were the deciding factor. Since job incumbency does not seem to be the issue, some other factor or factors must explain the relatively low level of participation of women in these high-level frauds. Another possible explanation raised by Steffensmeier and colleagues (2013) is that women have restricted access to the informal networks that are found throughout large organizations. Thus, even though women's formal access to management positions is improving, they may still be discriminated against by men in regard to their inclusion in informal networks of power and, consequently, illegal activity.

The relationship between gender and crime is often treated in individualistic terms, but this ignores that many crimes are group undertakings that involve networks of people working together. Individuals not involved in these networks have reduced access to criminal opportunities. Research on street-level crime indicates that access to criminal networks is sex segregated, with women being largely excluded from networks or restricted to playing subordinate supporting roles (Maher, 1997; Miller, 2001; Mullins and Wright, 2003; Steffensmeier, 1983). The same sex segregation of roles appears to happen in white-collar crime, too. In the CFTF study, most of the women played only supporting roles and were included primarily for utilitarian reasons. The women who were included held strategic financial positions in the companies that were necessary for the frauds to be carried out. For example, since many of the frauds involved false statements about financial data that had to be made on official documents and reports, it was sometimes necessary for the ringleaders to secure the cooperation of women who held subordinate positions in the accounting department in order to carry out their crimes. Thus, the same processes of sex segregation found in street crime groups appear to be operating in regard to white-collar crime networks. Many white-collar crimes committed within organizational settings involve networks of people working in a conspiratorial fashion, and organizational research indicates that even when women attain high-status positions in organizations, they are often excluded from male-dominated informal social networks (Gorman and Kmec, 2009). If the exclusion of women from informal networks extends to illegal networks, then this would explain lower rates of participation in white-collar crime for women even when they hold the same occupational positions as men.

To put it bluntly, while men may be willing to tolerate having women in leadership roles in the workplace, they still may not trust women and exclude them from "old boy" networks. Hence, women would be less likely to be invited to participate in criminal conspiracies than men. This is a variation on the "restricted access" interpretation of the low level of female involvement in corporate crimes in that it argues that it is women's access to informal networks that is restricted rather than their access to particular organizational roles.

Regardless of which form of "restricted access" is at work, we note that this interpretation implicitly assumes that women would behave as men do if they had access to similar positions or networks (Adler, 1975; Simon, 1975). However, it is also possible that even if they occupied the same positions and had the same opportunities, women would behave differently from men. Perhaps women are simply more law-abiding than men. Another possibility, reviewed further on, is that men and women offend at similar rates, but the criminal justice system and internal compliance programs are more chivalrous toward women offenders (Pollock, 1950).

Research suggests that though access to opportunities is important, it is not the only factor involved in the gender gap in white-collar crime. Men and women share some of the same pathways into crime and contact with the criminal justice system, but it is also clear that some routes into crime are gendered. Motivations for white-collar offending appear to differ by gender (Daly, 1989; Zietz, 1981). In their analysis of the post-Enron frauds, the researchers found that one of the main pathways into white-collar crime for women arose out of their close personal or romantic ties to a male co-offender. This relational pathway was characteristic for many of the women involved in the post-Enron era of corporate frauds, and it suggests that women's motivations for their involvement in high-level corporate frauds may be substantially different from men's (Steffensmeier et al., 2013).

Another possible explanation for the paucity of women in white-collar crime is that women are treated differently than men by investigators and prosecutors. According to this line of reasoning, investigators and prosecutors do not think of women as potential criminal predators and hence treat them in a chivalrous manner. While the evidence on women's different motivations and pathways into white-collar crime is fairly consistent, the evidence regarding the so-called chivalry effect is more mixed. What appears to be chivalry toward women offenders may actually reflect stereotypical ideas on the part of criminal justice agents about "typical" offenders being male (Silberman, 1978), judicial concerns about family responsibilities (Daly, 1994), or differences in criminal history records that favor women in sentencing. Some studies have found that women offenders are actually treated more harshly than males when the crimes they commit are non-stereotypical (Chesney-Lind, 1989; Sealock and Simpson, 1998).

Taken together, these studies suggest that it is more than mere opportunity that creates the gender differences in white-collar offending. Numerous books have been written about this very topic, and there are many different points of view. We suggest that there are gender differences in how men and women view opportunities for white-collar crime. These perceptual differences may arise from a number of sources. For instance, women who move into top management positions—by virtue of their uniqueness—are more visible to others. They are probably watched more carefully than males in these positions, are less "trusted" by others to go along with illicit activity, and thus are more apt to blow the whistle when illegality occurs than their male counterparts. Indeed, it could be argued that women may be better suited for positions of trust and security than men because they are better socialized, have more self-control, and score better on measures of integrity and ethicality. Do women have a different conception of morality than males, that is, a "different voice" (Gilligan, 1993)? If so, this would affect many facets of crime, including women's willingness to engage in illegal behavior, their motivations for doing so, and how they respond when they learn about criminal activity by others.

In their gendered theory of focal concerns, Steffensmeier and Allan (2000) contend that women are socialized to accept nurturant role obligations that emphasize the importance of social relationships and communalistic orientations toward others. Through the assimilation of these obligations, women develop identities as caregivers. In addition, women's concern with beauty and virtue contrasts with the sordidness of stereotypical images of criminals, making the role of criminal or lawbreaker inconsistent with the taken-for-granted female identity (Steffensmeier et al., 2013). According to the theory of gendered focal concerns, women's adoption of identities based on beauty, virtue, and caregiving also affects their risk preferences, making them less willing to take risks than men. Hence, excluding only certain sex-related crimes such as prostitution, women are expected to be less involved in all forms of crime than men. Finally, the management literature also highlights risk aversion and ethicality to explain lower levels of fraud in firms that have greater female representation on the board of directors while adding the argument that gender diversity facilitates more effective monitoring through expanding board expertise, experience, interests, perspectives, and creativity (Cumming, Leung, and Rui, 2015).

There are no studies that directly test some of these contentions, but statistics and results from other research on crime are informative. We know, for instance, that female participation in white-collar offending has been on the rise for over 30 years (Simon, 1975), and that this risk is concurrent with the entry of more women into positions of trust, primarily in lower-level service positions. If women are becoming the norm rather than just tokens in lower-level positions (say, as tellers in banks), they should stand out less and socialize more with others in similar positions that may increase their knowledge of and exposure to white-collar crime opportunities and neutralizations about this type of illegality. Recall that our review of Brickey's (2008) data showed that Health-South had the most female co-defendants. The health care industry is not as gender stratified as other industries. Yet these may not be the best data to address how industry structure affects offending opportunities because most of the companies in the database are service industry providers (telecommunications, financial services, retail). The absence of women as co-defendants for most corporate defendants may suggest a relatively high level of vertical stratification in the service industry such that women are unwilling to participate in or have been left out of the illegal "loop".

Indeed, the data collected by Brickey (2008) and Steffensmeier et al. (2013) may even over-represent women's involvement in corporate crime. If their data included cases involving environmental illegality or health and safety violations, which are typically associated with basic manufacturing industries that are much more stratified by gender, they might have found an even smaller number of female co-defendants. Though the Brickey data and the CFTF data are intriguing, they do not tell us whether women and men in similar positions are equally likely to take advantage of illicit opportunities or whether gender diversity is likely to increase female white-collar offending or decrease offending overall. Work by Michelle Howe (2003) gives us some clues about these questions. She looked at whether a group of 77 survey respondents (including students and managers) were willing to engage in three types of corporate crime: price fixing, bribery, and environmental offending (Howe, 2003). Offending conditions were experimentally varied across the offense types. Her research revealed that gender *per se* did not affect the overall offending decision (i.e., females and males appeared to be equally willing to offend). However, the decision to offend was influenced by different factors for males and females (e.g., religiosity was more important for females), and the magnitude of the effects of different factors varied by gender.

The Gender Gap in White-Collar Crime: Victimization

We have argued and presented evidence to suggest that white-collar offending opportunities are structured by gender. What we have not yet discussed is how white-collar victimization can also vary by gender. Gerber and Weeks (1992, p. 325) first called attention to the lack of research on this subject by noting their inability "to locate even a single study that focuses specifically on women as victims of corporate crime". Shortly thereafter, Szockyj and Fox (1996) collected a group of original essays from scholars in the field who drew on case studies focusing on how differences in gender roles (e.g., employment, consumption), male and female socialization, and legal protections, exclusions, and access to redress (such as union membership) affect contemporary patterns of corporate victimization. The historical record in Great Britain has been examined and found to show that rigid stereotypes and institutional sexism in the Victorian era increased the risk of fraud victimization for middle-class white women. Robb (2006, p. 1062) suggests that these women were almost certainly targeted for victimization because they were inexperienced (and therefore "easily duped") and because women shareholders were excluded from any board of director oversight:

> Considerable evidence exists that women were sought out as victims by frauds and embezzlers who well understood their vulnerability. During the 1860s, for example, the shady company promoter Albert Grant compiled lists of widows, unmarried women and other small investors to whom he sent circulars advertising his dubious speculations. ... Not only were these women lacking in business experience and acumen, but they were ill-placed to fight him in court should it come to that.

Women's vulnerability was emphasized in Victorian society—and women were warned away from the unregulated capital markets at the same time their investments were highly sought.

Just as women's risk of fraud victimization in the Victorian era was exacerbated by gender stereotypes and institutional sexism, these same factors continue to play a role in gendered patterns of white-collar victimization in the modern era. Obviously, both men and women can be victims of white-collar crime, but the types of white-collar harms that they experience are not entirely the same. Rather, differential exposure to types of white-collar victimizations is influenced by cultural norms and gender-based stereotypes. For example, pharmaceutical and consumer products and services related to birth control, health, and beauty, such as cosmetics, diet products, and cosmetic surgery, are marketed much more heavily toward women than men. Certainly, this happens in part because marketers recognize and wish to take advantage of the culturally conditioned sensitivity that women have toward physical appearance. To the extent that these products and services are dangerous or advertised in misleading ways, women are correspondingly more likely to be harmed than men (Croall, 2009). Unfortunately, and despite the protestations of pharmaceutical and cosmetic manufacturers concerning the safety of their products, there are many examples of misleading advertising and dangerous products (Lister, 2005). Dow Corning was found in civil proceedings to have acted with "fraud, malice and oppression" in regard to the way that it marketed silicone breast implants that harmed many women (Croall, 2009, p. 134). Likewise, the Dalkon shield, an intrauterine device for birth control manufactured by A. H. Robins, "exposed millions of women to serious infection, sterility, and even death" (Mintz, 1995, p. 191). A 2011 survey conducted by the U.S. Federal Trade Commission (2013) revealed that women were almost 20 percent more likely to be consumer fraud victims compared with men, a difference mostly due to fraudulent weight loss products (2.6 percent of women were victims of this type of fraud compared with 1.6 percent of men). Men, of course, also consume weight loss and "grooming products" and elective plastic surgery, but not at the same rate as women. Their susceptibility to these types of white-collar victimizations is correspondingly lower. In contrast, compared with women, men are more likely to be employed in high-risk occupations, such as construction and mining, where their exposure to work-place safety violations is elevated.

In summary, the gendered nature of white-collar victimization patterns mirrors the gendered nature of white-collar offending. Women's differential access to particular types of occupations, professions, and organizational positions is shaped by culturally based focal concerns and institutional sex segregation, which in turn influences women's exposure to white-collar offending opportunities. These same focal concerns and institutional practices influence the types of products and services that women consume and the types of interactions that they experience in the marketplace. These patterns of consumption and interaction, in turn, make them differentially susceptible to some forms of white-collar victimization more so than others. And the same is true for men. Their patterns of consumption and the types of economic activities that they engage in differentially expose them to some forms of white-collar victimization more so than others.

Race, Ethnicity and White-Collar Crime: Offending

Race and ethnicity are characteristics that are highly correlated with traditional offending regardless of how the data are collected (e.g., self-reports, victimization reports, official statistics). The strength of the association between race and crime varies by offense type, crime seriousness, and whether participation or frequency of offending is considered. Generally, compared with whites, members of racial minority groups have higher rates of crime, are more likely to engage in more serious types of crime, and are more apt to be chronic offenders (Harris and Shaw, 2000). Yet, when the lens is shifted from traditional street crime to white-collar crime, the relationship between race and crime changes dramatically as we showed in Chapter 2.

The typical gestalt of crime in the United States is one of a minority offender in the foreground framed against a sea of conforming white faces (Harris and Shaw, 2000). However, as the Yale study demonstrated, the higher one moves toward Sutherland's "elite" offenders, the more that image changes and permutates. This is not to say that white-collar crime is an exclusively "white" form of crime. As we showed in Chapter 2, for certain types of lower-level white-collar offenses, such as false claims, mail fraud, and credit fraud, significant proportions of offenders are non-white, and there is some evidence that non-whites are becoming more involved in middle- and upper-level white-collar offenses such as antitrust violations and securities fraud (see Chapter 2). However, it is still the case that a substantial majority of those involved in antitrust violations and securities frauds are white males. Indeed, when it comes to the high-level corporate frauds of the post-Enron era, the number of non-white offenders is almost zero. Of the 436 defendants studied by Steffensmeier and colleagues (2013), only six were African-American, that is, just a little more than 1 percent (Steffensmeier, personal communication). No doubt, this is primarily because corporate CEOs, presidents, and other top managers are overwhelmingly white and male.

Harris and Shaw (2000) found that blacks were overrepresented among lower-level offenders in the Yale data by a factor of about 2.5 to 1 at the same time that whites were overrepresented among middle-level offenders by a factor of about 2.7 to 1. The middle-level offenders were also much more likely to have a college education than the lower-level offenders. Figure 9.1 (taken from Harris and Shaw, 2000, p. 156) demonstrates the hypothetical race ratios as one compares traditional street crime with white-collar crime.

Again, one might wonder whether opportunity alone accounts for these racial disparities in crime patterns. Harris's earlier work on gender, race, and typescripts suggests that there is more than mere opportunity at play here (Harris, 1976, 1977; Harris and Hill, 1982). Societal stereotypes about who commits crime are likely to affect the perceptions of potential offenders about criminal opportunities and whether they should take advantage of them. Stereotypes also influence how people respond to the illegal behavior of others when it

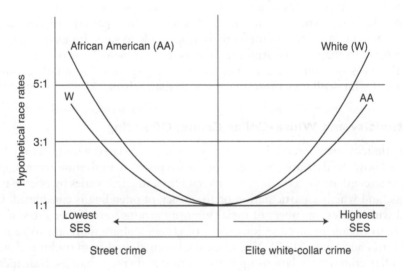

Figure 9.1 Possible relationships among crime, race, and socioeconomic status (SES)

occurs (as a leader, a business peer or associate, or justice agent). The parabolic relationship depicted in Figure 9.1 demonstrates, according to Harris and Shaw (2000, p. 156), that:

> [R]ace or caste differences net of class have the greatest impact at the extreme edges of the class spectrum. Ironically, upper class whites and underclass blacks may well have something rare but theoretically very important in common: a pronounced, and perhaps highly rational, lack of fear when it comes to committing crime. On the one hand, elite whites are likely to believe that their chances of being caught or severely punished for committing crimes are very low. On the other hand, if, as an underclass black, one feels that 'the joint is like the projects, except they feed you free,' then one is likely to believe that, in getting caught for crime, you do not have very much left to lose.

An important question regarding the connection between race and white-collar crime is whether it can be reduced to social class. Perhaps African-Americans are so under-represented among elite white-collar offenders simply because there are so relatively few African-Americans in the middle and upper social classes. In other words, can the association between race and white-collar crime be reduced to the association between social class and white-collar crime? Although this is still an open question, some believe that it will eventually be answered in the negative (Harris and Shaw, 2000). Class-advantaged whites have greater opportunities to commit certain types of white-collar crime than do class-advantaged African-Americans.

There are a couple of possible reasons why class-advantaged whites may have more opportunities. First, like women, African-Americans who make it to the top of the corporate hierarchy are exceptional. Similar to women, they may feel that because of their uniqueness, they are subject to additional scrutiny and supervision: someone is watching every move they make. Hence, for them, the possibility of detection and exposure must be weighted more heavily in their calculations of the costs and benefits of potential white-collar crime opportunities. White managers and executives, on the other hand, do not have to worry as much about being watched because they do not stand out from the crowd. Second, for reasons of race, African-American managers may not have access to as much social capital as white managers. Like women, they may not be as embedded in informal occupational and organizational networks as whites. Research on occupational mobility in organizations certainly supports this interpretation. Compared with white males, African-American males do not have access to the same networking and sponsorship opportunities that people use to advance into managerial positions. Rather, they have to rely on more formal mechanisms for advancement, such as accumulating human capital through education and workforce experience, in order to advance (Smith, 2005; Wilson, 2012). Since African-Americans lack access to informal networks for organizational advancement, it seems likely that they also are denied access to the informal networks of high-level white-collar crime. Access to these networks is a source of freedom and power, power to commit large-scale white-collar crimes (Hagan, 1994, p. 101).

Although discussions of the relationship between race and crime typically focus on black/white differences, it is important to recognize that a large and growing segment of the American population is comprised of non-white ethnic minorities, specifically people of Hispanic and Asian background. Recent research has found that since 2000, Hispanics and Asians have accounted for an increasing proportion of people convicted of low-level white-collar crimes, such as mail theft and false statements (Benson, Feldmeyer, Gabbidon, and

Chio, 2020). Indeed, considered together, blacks, Hispanics and Asians now constitute a majority of the people convicted of these sorts of white-collar crimes. We may be witnessing the democratization of white-collar crimes.

Race and White-Collar Crime: Victimization

The link between social class and race also has implications for white-collar victimization. Because African-Americans are disproportionately represented among the lower social classes, they are also disproportionately subject to the types of white-collar crime that target the poor and disadvantaged. Regrettably, some of these are among the most serious forms of white-collar crime, including environmental offenses and workplace safety violations as well as the more mundane forms of consumer fraud.

Not all communities are created equal. In the United States, garbage dumps, hazardous waste collection facilities, incinerators, chemical plants, paper mills, and other polluting industries are almost never located in upper-class communities. Rather, for decades, they have been situated in economically disadvantaged and politically powerless minority communities (Bullard, 1990). The residents of these communities face elevated risks of exposure to environmental toxins and hazardous wastes.

The term that has been coined to describe this situation is *environmental racism*, and it is clear that race and social class play a key role in environmental planning and decision making (Bullard, 2000). The most polluted urban environments are, not surprisingly, those that are poorest and largely inhabited by minorities. For example, in the Los Angeles area, more than 70 percent of African-Americans and 50 percent of Latinos live in areas of heavy air pollution compared with only a third of whites (Bullard, 2000, p. 224). This pattern is not unique to Los Angeles or even California, but rather is found nationwide. Air pollution is not the only environmental risk facing minority communities. The U.S. General Accounting Office found a strong relationship between the siting of hazardous waste facilities and the race and socioeconomic status of an area (Bullard, 2000, p. 32). The siting of a hazardous waste facility or any potentially polluting industry near a minority community does not necessarily mean that the residents of that particular community have been victimized by environmental crime. However, as environmental crimes are found more often in some industries than others (Epstein and Hammett, 1995; Hammett and Epstein, 1993), the people who live nearby necessarily face elevated risks of victimization. More often than not, those people are minorities.

Similarly, minorities are more likely to work in occupations and industries that expose them to elevated risks of work-related disease, injury, and death (Leeth and Ruser, 2006). Using data from the Bureau of Labor Statistics, Leeth and Ruser recently found that the rate of work-related fatalities for African-American and Hispanic men was 35 percent higher than it was for white men. To put it another way, for every three white men killed at work, four African-American and Hispanic workers die. This gap in fatality rates is largely, but not entirely, accounted for by occupational differences between minorities and whites (Leeth and Ruser, 2006). Even within dangerous occupations, African-Americans and Hispanics suffer proportionately more fatalities than whites. As we noted in Chapter 7, not all work-related injuries and fatalities are the result of occupational safety violations. Most result from accidents. However, to the extent that work-related fatalities are caused by safety violations, minority workers are more likely to be the victims of those violations than white workers. As Leeth and Ruser put it, safety is segregated.

What accounts for the elevated risk of environmental and occupational victimization for minorities? Our opportunity perspective suggests two important factors: proximity and lack of access to guardianship. As implied earlier, minorities suffer proportionately more than whites from environmental and occupational violations simply because they often are in closer proximity to the places or settings in which these violations occur. For reasons of class and race, they are more likely than whites to live in the communities or work in the industries where these violations are concentrated. By lack of access to guardianship, we mean the relatively low capacity of minority group members and minority communities to call upon the state to exert control and oversight over potential offenders. Minority communities often lack economic and political power. Because of this lack of power, they are ill-equipped to resist the siting of polluting industries nearby, and potential offenders take this into account when making decisions. A particularly bald example of such thinking is provided by Bullard (2000). He quotes from a report prepared by a company called Cerrell Associates for the California Waste Management Board. This report, which focused on the siting of hazardous waste incinerators, presented a detailed profile of the types of communities most likely to organize effective resistance against incinerators. According to the report by Cerrell Associates:

> All socioeconomic groupings tend to resent the nearby siting of major facilities, but middle and upper socioeconomic strata possess better resources to effectuate their opposition. Middle and higher socioeconomic strata neighborhoods should not fall within the one-mile and five-mile radius of the proposed site.
>
> (quoted in Bullard, 2000, p. 225)

As Bullard notes, if incinerators aren't sited near middle and upper socioeconomic neighborhoods, the only place left for them to go is low socioeconomic communities. And these are disproportionately minority communities. And, as we noted in Chapter 7, firms operating across national borders transfer "social and environmental risks" from wealthy developed countries to less developed (and protected) parts of the world (van Wingerde, 2015, p. 260).

Summary

This chapter has addressed how the distribution of white-collar crime opportunities is influenced by social class, gender, and race. That these demographic characteristics are strongly related to white-collar offending and victimization should not come as a big surprise. All three have obvious connections to the occupational structure, and occupations determine access to white-collar crime opportunities. Separating out the unique effects of class, race, and gender is difficult because both gender and race are closely related to class position. As a result, it is often hard to establish what is a race or gender effect independent of social class (Harris and Shaw, 2000). It seems likely that the importance of race and gender on white-collar offending depends on the circumstances. For example, within organizations, gender may have an indirect effect on white-collar offending via its effects on access to class-linked occupational positions. Because of the glass ceiling, not many women or minorities hold top management positions, and hence they do not have access to the criminal opportunities available to top managers; and even when they advance to senior management positions, women and minorities may still be excluded from the informal networks that carry out high-level corporate frauds. However, outside of organizations, gender may have a direct influence on offending. Women are excluded from certain types of crime groups precisely because they are women, not because of their class position (Steffensmeier, 1983; Steffensmeier et al., 2013). Members of racial minorities may face similar obstacles. The effects of class, race, and gender on criminal offending, then, are complex and variable.

Social class has long been recognized as an important influence on individual involvement in crime. Prior to Sutherland, it was commonplace for criminologists to think that crime was concentrated in the lower social classes. However, as Sutherland and those who followed him have shown, the traditional view is mistaken. Crime is spread throughout the class structure, but different classes engage in different forms of crime.

Although research on the connection between class and crime is complicated by many methodological difficulties, insofar as can be determined, traditional forms of serious predatory street crime do appear to be more common in the lower social classes (Braithwaite, 1981; Harris and Shaw, 2000). However, the connection between class and crime is reversed for serious white-collar crimes, wherein people from the upper class clearly predominate.

Social status and social class are related, but they are not exactly the same thing. Social status is a relative concept in the sense that one can have more or less of it based on certain criteria, such as education, income, and occupational prestige. Social class, on the other hand, at least as used here, is a relational concept. It refers to whether one has or does not have control over organizational assets and resources. The most serious and complex white-collar crimes tend to be committed by those who have control over organizational assets and resources, that is, by owners, managers, and supervisors (Wheeler and Rothman, 1980). Thus, what really matters in white-collar crime is organizational position rather than social status per se. Attending a prestigious university and getting a business or law degree does not necessarily put one in position to commit a big-time white-collar crime, but on the other hand, it may provide access to an occupation or organizational position that does.

As the data reviewed in this chapter and previously in Chapter 2 show, women are now and have been for some time severely underrepresented in big-time white-collar crime. By "big-time", we mean crimes that are organizationally complex and have serious and widespread consequences for victims. Antitrust violations, securities fraud, and, in more recent times, accounting fraud are classic examples of big-time white-collar crime. According to the Yale data, in the 1970s, women accounted for less than 1 percent of antitrust offenders, and according to the data collected by Kathleen Brickey and Darrell Steffensmeier, they make up a similarly small percentage of the individuals charged in the spate of accounting frauds that have come to light since the year 2000. Women make a better showing in low-level unsophisticated white-collar offenses, such as bank embezzlement.

Although a good deal of the gender gap in white-collar offending can be explained by the relative paucity of women in high-level corporate positions, this may not account for all of the disparity. Other differences between men and women may be involved besides their relative levels of access to leadership positions. Even when men and women do commit the same type of white-collar crime, research has found that they do so for different reasons (Daly, 1989; Zietz, 1981). That is, at times men and women appear to follow different motivational routes to white-collar crime. Women may be less likely to take advantage of white-collar offending opportunities for several other reasons, such as greater self-control, a lower taste for risk, a perception that they are under greater scrutiny, or greater empathy with potential victims. At this point, it is not clear how much of the gender gap in offending is accounted for by occupational discrimination and how much by other social or psychological differences between men and women.

A similar situation confronts us with respect to race and white-collar crime. Whites are significantly overrepresented among serious white-collar offenders. As with the gender gap in white-collar offending, the racial gap is certainly largely due to disparities in access to the appropriate types of occupational positions. However, other differences may also be involved. It remains an open question whether African-Americans who attain leadership positions in large organizations engage in white-collar crime at the same rate as whites or at a rate that is lower.

Finally, we add one caveat in regard to our discussion of victimization. It is important to keep in mind that for some forms of white-collar crime, it may be misleading to think of victimization in individual terms. As Sutherland (1983) noted long ago, a distinguishing characteristic of white-collar crime is diffuse victimization. For example, the price-fixing case involving automobile parts discussed in Chapter 6 affected in one way or another virtually everyone who bought or used an automobile. It does not really make sense to think of this as a crime that affects one gender, race, or ethnic group more than another, except perhaps in the trivial sense that it affects automobile users more than those who rely on public transportation. The same is often true of some types of securities offenses, such as insider trading, stock manipulation, and accounting fraud. These offenses affect the general operation of the economy. Since everyone is affected to some degree by the ups and downs of the economy, everyone (even those who do not own stocks themselves) can be affected by these forms of white-collar crime.

In addition, for some types of white-collar crime, the real victim is a government program or another organization. Frauds committed against the Medicare and Medicaid programs, as well as other health insurers, are good examples of white-collar crimes that directly victimize organizations more so than individuals. Likewise, in the mortgage fraud scandal of 2008, fraudulent mortgage-backed securities were not bought by individual investors, but rather by banks, insurance companies, and pension funds. That the victims of white-collar crime can be organizations, corporations, and the government itself has important implications for the control of these offenses. For one thing, unlike most individual crime victims, organizational victims have significant political and economic power that they can employ against their victimizers. Organizations have the economic and political wherewithal to file civil lawsuits, press for vigorous investigations, or even lobby for new laws and regulations. All of these activities can affect opportunity structures for white-collar crime.

Notes

1 The formula for the Executive Parity Index (EPI) is EPI = Percentage of Executives/Percentage of Professionals.

2 Slightly different patterns are revealed in the Dutch study (van Onna et al., 2014). While women are clearly less involved in offending overall compared with men, they constitute a larger share of the stereotypical white-collar offender group (18.6 percent) than of the other trajectory groups: Adult Onset (15.8 percent), Adult Persisters (7.4 percent), and stereotypical criminals (4 percent).

Part V

Control, Prevention, and the Future of White-Collar Crime

It should no longer be necessary to argue that white-collar crime represents a grave threat to individuals and nations, indeed to the world. The devastating effects of what Sutherland (1940, p. 1) called "crime in relation to business" have been repeatedly and publicly demonstrated in financial scandals that result in billion-dollar losses, in environmental disasters that cost billions to clean up, and in workplace catastrophes whose emotional and physical costs are so heartbreaking that it would be tactless to put a price on them. That white-collar crime is a serious social problem should be obvious to anyone who pays attention to the news. Given the size and gravity of the problem, one might assume that controlling white-collar crime would be a top priority at all levels of government, but that assumption would be wrong. Certainly, more political attention and criminal justice resources are devoted to controlling crime on the streets as opposed to crime in the suites.

Nevertheless, even though official responses to white-collar crime are perhaps best described as "limp" (Shover and Hochstetler, 2006), they are not entirely absent and are not entirely ineffective. In this final section of the book, we describe the divergent approaches that are taken toward controlling and preventing white-collar crime. That there are divergent approaches is significant, because it represents yet another way in which white-collar crime differs from other forms of crime. The control of street crime is largely, though not entirely, relegated to the criminal justice system. We expect the police to uncover and arrest those who perpetrate street crimes, courts to convict them, and the correctional system to incapacitate or rehabilitate them. All of these measures we hope will make us and our streets safer.

The criminal justice system is also involved in the control of white-collar crime, but for a variety of reasons discussed in Chapter 10, this system of justice is not, and probably never will be, exceedingly effective as a response to the perpetrators of white-collar offenses. There are, however, other approaches to white-collar crime control and prevention that hold more promise. These other approaches include regulation, the civil justice system, a variety of extralegal measures, and situational crime prevention strategies. Taken individually, none of these approaches is a panacea, but collectively they have made a difference in some areas. Following other commentators, we advocate here for a pluralistic approach to white-collar crime control and prevention.

DOI: 10.4324/9781003175322-14

Part V

Control, Prevention and the Future of White-Collar Crime

Legal Controls

The Criminal Justice, Regulatory, and Civil Justice Systems

Legal Remedies

Traditional street crimes are controlled almost exclusively by criminal law, but in the case of white-collar crime, two other kinds of legal systems—regulatory and civil—can also come into play. These three systems operate in distinct ways, with different philosophical approaches, legal standards, policing, and sanctioning methods. In this section, we focus on these different legal systems and how each of them intersects with opportunity structures. We distinguish among the legal interventions as they operate in the United States and between different sanction targets (individuals versus organizations). We then discuss some of the failures and limits of law (see also Van Rooij and Fine, 2021), especially the danger of over-criminalization (i.e., unnecessarily broadening the scope of the criminal law), the emergence of non-prosecution and deferred prosecution agreements, the politics of white-collar crime enforcement expressly under the Trump administration (Barak, 2022), and what some have called creative compliance (McBarnet, 2005) or cultures of resistance (Bardach and Kagan, 1982). If law is perceived as illegitimate, unnecessarily restrictive, or overly punitive, firms may "fight back" through noncompliance and challenges to the legal system. On the other hand, because much of the regulatory arena is not black and white but shades of gray, companies may seek out legal gaps to exploit in their favor. Finally, we highlight and assess responsive regulation as an approach and tool to build trust and enhance compliance. We conclude this chapter with suggestions for how the legal systems could be changed to become more effective in the fight against white-collar and corporate crime.

The Criminal Justice System

It goes without saying that the prevention and control of crime are two of the primary objectives and functions of the criminal justice system. Like other types of offenders, white-collar criminals can be pursued through the process of criminal prosecution. The criminal law is used to punish violators and to convey the message that the behavior in question is harmful, morally repugnant, and not to be tolerated. Legal philosophers long have argued that law and punishment are part of the social contract in which individuals surrender a degree of freedom in exchange for protection against harm and the enjoyment of peace and safety (Beccaria, 1983). From this perspective, when individuals violate the law, they are acting against the common good, and therefore, society has a need, responsibility and right to punish them for their violations and deter them from future acts that would be harmful to others.

DOI: 10.4324/9781003175322-15

Punishment for legal transgressions is necessary to preserve and protect society, but it will operate effectively only within the context of a "reasoned" system of justice, that is, a system that is fair and not subject to abuse (Bentham, 1948). Because there is always the potential for abuse and corruption by law enforcers, society has put in place a number of safeguards to protect individual rights and freedoms. For example, the criminal law has high evidentiary standards. To be convicted of a crime, a defendant's guilt must be proved beyond reasonable doubt by evidence that has been gathered and handled in accordance with strict procedural rules. In addition, defendants have a number of legal rights to protect them against the misuse of authority by law enforcers. These rights include such fundamental principles as the right to be free from unreasonable searches and seizures, to an attorney, to trial by jury, to confront witnesses, and to not be compelled to incriminate oneself. Criminal law requires proof that an offender meant to commit the illegal act and did so with a guilty mind (*mens rea*).

While these legal safeguards protect everyone from abuse by criminal justice functionaries, they can be especially helpful to those who are accused of white-collar crimes. Defendants in white-collar cases benefit in particular from the requirement that prosecutors must prove beyond a reasonable doubt that the accused acted with criminal intent (Benson and Kerley, 2000). In other words, the prosecutor must show that the defendant knew that what he or she was doing was illegal and intentionally went ahead and did it anyway. Of course, this legal standard applies to ordinary street criminals, but it is often much easier to meet in their cases because the crimes that street criminals commit, such as robbery, burglary, assault, and theft, involve physical actions that are obviously illegal. But this is not true in many white-collar cases. As we noted, for example, in our discussion of health care fraud, when a physician submits a fraudulent claim to Medicaid, the fact that it is fraudulent is not readily apparent because on the surface fraudulent claims look just like legitimate claims. The difficulty of detecting illegal acts that is created by the superficial appearance of legitimacy in white-collar cases is a major constraint on the effectiveness of the criminal justice system in this area and is exacerbated by the use of *ex post facto* "pay and chase" crime detection techniques. This detection model assumes that health care claims are submitted in good faith by legitimate actors, and therefore they should be paid as quickly as possible by government and major insurers. Unfortunately, this means that when fraud is suspected the money has to be recovered after funds have already been disbursed. This process is much more labor-intensive and time-consuming than preventing and deterring improper payments in the first place (Simpson, Agarwal, and Gao, 2023).

Even if a fraudulent claim by a physician is discovered, the physician can always say that he or she just made a mistake or that this was just a onetime accident made by office staff. While this assertion of innocence can be defeated in court, it is not necessarily easy to do so. Rather, it requires that prosecutors and investigators gather additional evidence that relates to the defendant's state of mind. This additional work takes time, effort, and resources. The inherent ambiguity in the state of mind of defendants in white-collar cases is exploited by defense attorneys who try to construct a favorable interpretation of the facts to present to a jury. A favorable interpretation is one in which the defendant's state of mind appears ambiguous, and the requirement of proof beyond a reasonable doubt cannot be met. Almost without exception, the defendant's state of mind is a critical and contested issue when white-collar cases are adjudicated in court (Benson, 1985; Benson and Kerley, 2000; Katz, 1979; Mann, 1985).

Even though white-collar cases raise special problems for investigators and prosecutors, successful prosecutions do happen, and when they do, they can send a powerful message of deterrence to others. In a closely followed case, Massey Energy CEO Don Blankenship was prosecuted, found guilty, and sentenced to a year in prison for his involvement in the deadliest U.S. mine explosion in four decades where 29 miners perished. Although his prosecution and conviction were not directly tied to the miners' deaths (i.e., he was not indicted for murder), Blankenship was charged with one misdemeanor count of conspiring willfully to violate mandatory federal mine safety and health standards at the Upper Big Branch mine and two felony counts of lying to the SEC and investors. On April 6, 2016, Blankenship was sentenced to a year in prison and ordered to pay a $250,000 fine for knowingly conspiring to violate mine safety. He was convicted on the misdemeanor charge, but acquitted on the two felony counts.

Prosecutions of top executives are extremely rare, but in this particular case prosecutors described a CEO who was fully aware of the day-to-day risks confronting miners and flouted mine safety laws while personally benefitting financially from the profits of his mining operation:

> How does one take the measure of such a crime? Defendant was the chief executive of one of America's largest coal companies—a multibillion-dollar behemoth with its shares traded on the New York Stock Exchange, a fleet of private aircraft, luxurious board meetings at posh resorts around the country, and vast resources to support its mining operations. He had every opportunity to run UBB [Upper Big Branch] safely and legally. Instead, he actively conspired to break the laws that protect coal miners' lives. Although already fabulously wealthy by the time of the criminal conspiracy of which he stands convicted, Defendant's greed was such that he would willfully imperil his workers' survival to further fatten his bank account. What punishment can suffice for wrongdoing so monstrous? The United States knows of no other case in which a major company's CEO has been convicted of a crime against worker protection laws, so direct reference points are difficult to come by. But compare this crime to others seen more regularly. Which is worse: a poor, uneducated young man who sells drugs because he sees no other opportunity, or a multimillionaire executive, at the pinnacle of his power, who decides to subject his workers to a daily game of Russian roulette? Which is worse: that young man carrying a gun during a single drug deal—a crime that will earn him a five-year mandatory minimum prison sentence—or a CEO jeopardizing the lives of hundreds, day after day? Which is worse: stealing money or trampling on laws that protect human life? In each case, to ask the question is to answer it. Under any fair assessment, only a sentence of many years in prison could truly reflect the seriousness of Defendant's crime and provide just punishment, which the law requires the court to do. Other statutory provisions, of course, make such a sentence impossible here. The law says that willfully violating mine safety and health standards is worth at most a year in prison.
>
> (United States Sentencing Memorandum, 2016, pp. 2–5)

Although the criminal law was used successfully in the Blankenship case (but not without controversy[1]), criminal prosecutions can be very challenging in a corporate context (Stone, 1975). Not only is it difficult to show that someone acted with criminal intent, it is often just as difficult to tell precisely who should be held responsible for decision making within large organizational or corporate entities. Decision making is often fragmented and not in the hands of any one single person. And decision makers can practice concerted ignorance to shield themselves from criminal liability (Katz, 1979). Consequently, "individual accountability is frequently displaced by corporate liability, which now serves as a rough-and-ready catch-all device" (Fisse and Braithwaite, 1993, p. 1). When the defendant is an organization instead of an individual, it is frequently difficult to utilize the criminal law against the violator. As Celia Wells (1993, p. 15) observes, the language of the law "assumes that state coercion is to be exercised against an individual and that the harm which that individual might bring about will injure other specific individuals. Corporate activities do not fit that paradigm". Hence, criminal law is most often used successfully against individual white-collar offenders—those who commit frauds, forgeries, embezzlement, and other offenses by their own hand and in their own self-interest or against entities where the management structure is flatter and easier to identify responsible parties (Braithwaite and Makkai, 1991) such as the recent collapse of crypto-currency firm FTX and the arrest of its founder Sam Bankman-Fried on charges of fraud, money laundering and campaign finance offenses (Helsel, 2022).

Although the criminal law has adopted the notion of corporate personhood to substitute for natural persons and has broadened the reach of the law through corporate liability, it is still difficult for prosecutors to challenge corporations in criminal court (Benson et al., 1998). It is not surprising then that criminal prosecutions of corporations are relatively rare. In recent years, the federal government has redirected its focus on the prosecution of responsible officers and managers with the goal of "enhanced deterrence". The U.S. Sentencing Commission has developed new and tougher guidelines for organizational sentencing, and the U.S. Department of Justice has established new guidelines for corporate prosecutions (Cullen et al., 2006). As we discussed in Chapter 9, the Corporate Fraud Task Force did investigate and prosecute a number of individuals involved in the corporate accounting frauds of the early 2000s. Yet, even with this renewed attention on corporate decision makers, criminal prosecution of individuals within corporations is uncommon, expensive, and often unsuccessful. As Clinard and Yeager observe in the updated introduction to their classic book, *Corporate Crime*, criminal actions against those responsible for company oversight (i.e., board members) are highly unusual (Clinard and Yeager, 2006, pp. xxxvi–xxxvii).

Oftentimes, a successful conviction against a major corporate crime figure is appealed (Martha Stewart is a notable exception, as she chose not to appeal and served her sentence) and sometimes reversed at the higher court. Indeed, many legal scholars believed that Enron's Jeffrey Skilling had a "reasonable" chance of overturning his 2006 conviction on some of the charges against him because the government failed to hand over evidence that would have aided his defense and because of other serious legal flaws in Skilling's conviction (Hawn, 2008). Skilling did appeal his case repeatedly, and the government finally agreed to reduce his sentence from 24 to 14 years. In return for the sentence reduction, Skilling agreed to no longer challenge his conviction (Wilbanks, 2013).

When the government sets its sights on the company as a criminal offender, most successful prosecutions do not land the big fish but instead capture smaller and relatively newer companies (Cullen et al., 2006, p. 360; U.S. Sentencing Commission, 1993–2004). This may be due, in part, to the self-reporting provisions of the Sentencing Guidelines. As per the Guidelines, firms will qualify for mitigation of punishment when they self-report, cooperate with the authorities, or accept responsibility. Thus, mitigation of punishment might be attractive to some firms who could benefit from this provision. But if the crime committed is substantial—falling within a hefty fine range even with mitigation—there is a disincentive for firms to self-report. In her critique of the Guidelines, Arlen (2012, p. 349) suggests that the self-reporting provision perversely rewards unsophisticated offenders who would be the easiest to discover by authorities (newer and smaller firms). These firms also are, from the viewpoint of the state authority, the least troublesome offenders because the scope and consequence of their offenses tend to be of a lesser magnitude than those of companies such as Enron and General Motors.

As a means of controlling white-collar and corporate crime, the criminal justice system is difficult to use and has not been exceedingly successful. The very legal safeguards that protect our individual freedom from government abuse and oppression ironically also make us more vulnerable to victimization by white-collar criminals. Despite these problems, however, the criminal justice system still can play an important role in the fight against white-collar crime. Much more so than the civil and regulatory systems that we will discuss below, the criminal justice system can impose sanctions that are very stigmatizing—especially against offenders who see themselves as upstanding and law-abiding citizens. The criminal law thus has the potential for great deterrent effects, but there is relatively little empirical evidence to determine if that potential actually translates into deterrence. A recent meta-analysis attempted to answer this question—specifically, whether formal legal interventions "deter" corporate offending (Simpson et al., 2014; Schell-Busey et al., 2016). The study examined a wide array of interventions, including law, punitive sanctions, non-punitive actions by regulatory agencies, and regulatory policy, and assessed whether the intervention was directed against individual managers/employees, or companies. The results, however, were far from conclusive. Punitive sanctions (that is, those associated with criminal justice punishment) tilted toward deterrence but effects rarely were statistically significant for either individuals or the firms themselves. Similarly, results for the impact of "law" (specific legal element, new law, changed law) on deterrence showed a general tendency toward deterrence. However, in cases where significant findings were observed, several were iatrogenic (that is, contrary to expectations). In other words, adding a new law or changing an old one was associated with more offending, not less.

Because the meta-analysis did not solely focus on criminal law and criminal justice interventions as a source of crime control and prevention, in the next sections we also highlight results that relate to civil and regulatory justice processes. But before we move to these other formal legal mechanisms, it is worthwhile discussing non-prosecution and deferred prosecution agreements (N/DPAs) as relatively new and increasingly utilized tools at the disposal of Federal prosecutors. These agreements incrementally expand the prosecutor's traditional role "from an ex-post focus on punishment to an ex-ante emphasis on compliance" (Kaal and Lacine, 2014, p. 2). An N/DPA is an agreement between the prosecution and corporate offender in which the Department of Justice or the Securities and Exchange Commission agrees either not to prosecute a criminal case (NPA) or to defer prosecution (DPA) under a specific set of conditions agreed upon by both parties. If a company complies with the conditions of the agreement (which usually involves such things as governance changes, the firm's acknowledgment of criminal conduct and acceptance of wrongdoing, as well as additional reporting and monitoring duties during the term of the agreement), the firm can avoid criminal indictment.

N/DPAs are controversial for a number of legal and policy reasons. While some actors on both sides of the ledger see benefits, critics suggest that there are three major problems with this practice: (1) most of the agreements fail to achieve meaningful structural or ethical reform within the company (Garrett, 2014), (2) the emergence of N/DPAs in some arenas (such as Foreign Corrupt Practices Act enforcement) has led to lower quality of enforcement compared with quantity (Koehler, 2015), and (3) the agreements undermine the separation of powers by turning the prosecutor into judge and jury (Epstein, 2006).

On the benefits side, N/DPAs are seen as a means to gain leverage and control over a company to ensure better overall compliance in exchange for avoiding the pernicious collateral consequences of a corporate criminal indictment, including the corporate death penalty, which is exemplified in the bankruptcy of Arthur Andersen (Kaal and Lacine, 2014, p. 10). Thus, supporters see N/DPAs as, in effect, a win-win. The instruments are versatile and flexible and, because the agreements offer greater guarantee of certainty and finality over other legal options, firms may actually prefer them to a plea agreement or civil litigation (Noked, 2012).

Others are highly suspicious of the agreements, suggesting that they lack transparency, undermine general deterrence, and mitigate the potential for adverse publicity (stigma) associated with prosecution and conviction (Noked, 2012; Mokhiber, 2005 cited in Alexander and Cohen, 2015). Brandon Garrett (2014) has also observed that the agreements, which are between prosecutors and the firm, shield those within the company who are personally responsible for the crimes. But even a critic like Garrett, who has conducted extensive empirical analyses of the agreements, does not advocate eliminating N/DPAs. He believes that the content of the agreements can be made more comprehensive and stricter in order to force structural changes in firms. Another empirical analysis compared 486 N/DPAs versus plea agreements between public companies and the Department of Justice (Alexander and Cohen, 2015). The researchers concluded that while the two sets of agreements are structurally similar, there are some notable differences. First, the emergence and growth of N/DPAs is not a substitute for plea agreements. The authors observe that the popularity of N/DPAs is not associated with a decline in the use of plea agreements. Moreover, the kinds of offenses and offenders in which the agreements are utilized appear to be different. Offense seriousness (as measured by the Sentencing Guidelines offense score) is higher for N/DPAs compared with plea agreements, but culpability is higher for plea agreements. Finally, Alexander and Cohen (2015) show that N/DPAs tend to require more non-monetary sanctions than do plea agreements. These results are consistent with analyses conducted by Kaal and Lacine (2014) that uncover significant governance changes associated with the execution of N/DPAs. That said, the authors are unsure whether the observed changes will continue over the long term.

In sum, the overall impact of N/DPAs is hard to assess. The increased utilization of these agreements and their spread across offense types and federal agencies suggest that they are an increasingly common feature in the fight against corporate crime. However, the lack of evidence-based research on key outcomes of interest, such as corporate recidivism and long-term effects, suggests that the jury is still out on the relative success of N/DPAs vis-à-vis other interventions and controls.

Civil Law Enforcement

For the criminal law to work, people must believe that illegal behavior will be discovered and punished. In addition, the system must operate in an efficient and fair manner. Yet, as we have pointed out, one of the distinguishing features of white-collar crime is that it is hard to detect, and even when wrongdoing is detected, it is often difficult to successfully prosecute the wrongdoer in white-collar cases—particularly when the wrongdoer is a powerful corporation. Because of these obstacles, legal redress is often sought through means other than criminal law. Civil law, for instance, is easier to use. It requires a lower standard of evidence to prove responsibility (i.e., a preponderance of evidence rather than proof beyond a reasonable doubt). Moreover, the punishments, although they can be economically costly to the defendant, do not involve deprivation of freedom. Consequently, defendants have fewer legal and due process protections. As we know from one of the most infamous cases of the late twentieth century, former football player and actor O. J. Simpson was found not guilty in a criminal trial but was found responsible (and culpable) in a civil trial for the death of his ex-wife, Nicole Brown Simpson, and her companion, Ronald Goldman.

Although the Simpson murder tragedy differs substantially from the more common forms of white-collar crime, the process in civil court is similar. The government (as the moving agent) will elect to bring a civil case instead of a criminal one against a corporate offender. U.S. antitrust laws, for instance, have both criminal and civil provisions, giving the government greater leeway to select the most appropriate justice process for the crime after taking into consideration the quality of the evidence and the perceived seriousness of the case. Civil law lacks the punitive and stigmatic capacity of criminal prosecution because it has a different goal. Rather than incapacitation, deterrence, and retribution, which are the main objectives of the criminal justice system, the goal of civil justice is to compensate and repair the damage to victims. This is achieved primarily through the use of fines.

Relative to criminal prosecution, corporate civil cases are sought more often by the state (not to mention individuals who seek tort actions against corporate offenders), and although the empirical evidence is sketchy, these cases may be more successful (see Simpson, 2002). The government needs to meet a much lower standard of evidence, and legal reforms make it easier to demand documents and compel information from offenders. Punitive sanctions (double and treble damages), when added to the civil remedies (such as fines and court injunctions), increase pressure on defendants to settle cases. Moreover, responsible individuals, whether they are operating outside of the organizational context (such as a credit card fraudster) or within it (such as an owner who fails to protect workers from exposure to dangerous substances), can be sued and sanctioned. Both the government and victims can bring a civil case, although it is much more difficult for individual claimants to challenge corporate defendants than it is for the government to do so on their behalf. Unfortunately, civil litigation may be unduly costly for individual plaintiffs, especially if they must also pay the court costs for the defendant if the case is lost.

In spite of the availability and appropriateness of civil actions, their use depends on victims recognizing their own victimization and being able to identify those responsible for it. As we discussed earlier, this link is easier to make when the relationship between offender and victim is more direct. For example, a mechanic takes money to fix a problem that is not repaired. An embezzler steals money from her employer. A physician overcharges the Medicare program. A financial consultant fails to invest his client's money and pockets it instead. In these types of cases, it may take the victim some time to determine that she or he has been victimized, but once the offense comes to light, it is relatively easy to determine the perpetrator in each instance. This is one of the reasons that criminal prosecution is more common in white-collar cases that involve a direct interaction between an individual offender and a victim. When the perpetrator is a company, however, it is often more difficult to determine exactly who the victims are and exactly who is responsible for the harm.

But what do we know empirically about civil law and corporate deterrence? In the meta-analysis discussed earlier, fines were included in the category of punitive sanctions, as they are an important source of redress in civil law. Similarly, new laws or changes in laws of a civil nature were also captured in the "law" intervention category. Thus, the study results described above are relevant here as well. Law and sanctions appear to move the needle toward deterrence, but only modestly so at best. As Paternoster (2016, p. 383; see also Yeager, 2016a) argues, this shouldn't surprise us:

> The risk of formal legal penalties for corporations or individuals within corporations is small (as are the perceived risks), with deferred and non-prosecution agreements the costs of punishment are low, corporate cultures that stress profit maximization reward noncompliance, and the rewards for corporate crime in all likelihood vastly exceed the costs.

Although there are specific instances of policies and interventions that change managerial or firm behavior, such as the Sarbanes-Oxley (SOX) Act—Yeager (2016a) cites as evidence the large number of company "restatements" post SOX—it is unclear what it is about a specific law, policy, or practice that works for most offenders in most circumstances. Indeed, the meta-analysis revealed some differences by offense type and by unit of analysis in the effects of specific interventions and treatments (Simpson et al., 2014).

The Regulatory Justice System

The regulatory justice system evolved in the United States to monitor and control the behavior of economic institutions. In the regulatory system, control tends to be more persuasive and less punitive (e.g., consent agreements not to violate the law again, recalls of products, monetary penalties, or warnings) (Clinard and Yeager, 2006, p. xiii). The goal is to bring the offender into compliance with the law. Administrative law is the most common means of legal redress in the United States for corporate offenses, but it is far from a monolithic system. Many regulatory agencies have the authority to investigate criminal cases and pursue civil judicial sanctions against corporate offenders. Agencies typically refer criminal cases to U.S. attorneys for prosecution. Frank and Lombness (1988) suggest that there are four ways to view the regulatory justice system—each view has its own assumptions about how the system works. These different views include the justice model, the rational-legal model, the economic model, and the conflict model.

Adherents to the justice model assume that the primary goal of the regulatory justice system is the social control of economic institutions. Criminologists, in particular, draw from Sutherland (1983), whose research on corporate offenders revealed that corporations generally operate outside the purview of criminal law. Instead, violators are subject to civil and regulatory statutes. Sutherland suggested that this difference was not due to any moral ambiguity about the harmfulness of white-collar crime compared with traditional street crime, nor confusion over the culpability of white-collar offenders (1983, pp. 52–53). Rather, Sutherland believed that corporate crime cases were "administratively segregated" and processed differently because the offenders, who are rich and powerful, demand and receive preferential treatment (1983, p. 6). Sutherland's pioneering work led criminologists to study civil and regulatory law from a criminal justice point of view. "Studies within the justice model describe the processes of investigation, adjudication, and punishment, focusing on issues of discretion, due process, and effectiveness" (Frank and Lombness, 1988, p. 5). However, because the regulatory justice system differs in significant ways from the criminal justice system (inspectors versus police; administrative courts versus criminal courts; an emphasis on compliance versus punishment), the comparison is superficial at best (Garner, 2007; Scott, 1989).

The rational-legal model of regulation assumes that regulatory law is a response to a set of social problems, recognized and acted upon by legislators. Somewhat similar to how problem-oriented policing works, a particular problem is brought to the attention of lawmakers, who then create policies and laws to "solve" the problem. Obviously, some problems are much easier to "legislate" than others (consider, for example, product safety laws versus global warming), and a critical challenge for lawmakers is to find the right balance between law and other societal strategies to problem-solve (such as public awareness campaigns). The rational-legal approach is liberal in the sense that it assumes that government-imposed controls in the form of laws can improve social conditions.

Another model of regulation suggested by Frank and Lombness (1988) is the conflict model. Based on conflict theory, this approach assumes that society is composed of groups with competing and contradictory interests. The regulatory arena (agencies, laws, policies, processes, and outcomes) is just one of many sites wherein the power struggle among group interests is contested. In the competitive struggle among groups, the powerful typically win. Regulatory law, which may initially appear to be responsive to the interests of the less powerful in society (e.g., worker health and safety) is eventually usurped, perverted, and manipulated to protect the interests, rights, and privileges of business owners.

Last, for the past three decades, the most prominent model of regulation has been the economic model. This approach adopts a utilitarian "cost-benefit" strategy to assess whether, on balance, the benefits of regulation exceed its costs. Regulatory agencies are required to conduct cost-benefit analyses when major initiatives are proposed. However, it is far from clear whether it is possible to assess accurately the assorted costs and benefits of regulation (especially social costs that are not easily quantifiable). Recent attempts to quantify the costs of crime demonstrate both the utility and weaknesses of this approach (Cohen, 2000). Much of the contemporary regulatory debate has centered on whether regulation is "efficient". Anti-regulatory critics claim that business regulation (particularly in its "social" forms) is inefficient and generally costly to a free-market system (Shover, Clelland, and Lynxwiler, 1986). An unfettered system—or at least one that has as few fetters as possible—will produce greater social good with fewer costs than a system that is stifled with legal restrictions. Critics on the other side of the debate assert that left to their own devices, corporations naturally pursue their own self-interest (profit seeking) with little regard for the common societal good. For the critics of the economic perspective, regulation of business is necessary to force corporations to behave properly and "do the right thing".

Whether regulation can be said to "work" as a means of controlling white-collar crime depends a great deal on one's perspective or model of the regulatory system. For example, from a justice model point of view, the regulatory system is supposed to catch and punish violators. From this perspective, regulatory control could reasonably be seen as a stark failure. On the one hand, there are far too few inspectors to "police" corporations and too much discretion in the application of the law; the sanctions levied are neither certain nor severe enough to deter corporate offenders (see, Hunter's 2023 study of the UK's Environmental Agency in England), and cases are rarely nominated for more severe legal consequences (such as criminal enforcement referrals), although this may vary by type of offense (Simpson, Garner, and Gibbs, 2007). On the other hand, when they are challenged by charges that regulatory processes are unfair and biased, some regulators adopt a strict "legalistic" enforcement style. This style decreases discretion and the perception of unfairness, but it carries with it a lack of flexibility. All violators, regardless of circumstance, are treated in a similar manner (Bardach and Kagan, 1982). The end result is the meaningless enforcement of rules, not the control of serious white-collar violations.

Viewed from a rational-legal perspective, however, regulation can be said to have had some degree of success in that many socially costly corporate behaviors have been redefined as social problems with attached legal remedies that appear to have had a positive impact on the extent of the problem in question (e.g., accounting and stock fraud, health and worker safety, environmental pollution, consumer product safety). For example, even though the Occupational Safety and Health Administration is often criticized as being a weak and ineffectual agency, occupational safety regulations undoubtedly have had a positive effect on the lives and safety of workers. Fifty years ago, workers were injured at a rate that is estimated to have been three times higher than the injury rate now (Cullen et al., 2006, p. 298). However, redefining harmful corporate behavior as a social problem is a difficult undertaking, one that can have unintended negative consequences. If the government unilaterally redefines some formerly legal activity as now illegal, and if it does so without the support and concurrence of the regulated entities, this action can increase the likelihood of deception, concealment, and conspiracy by companies. Subterranean resistance such as this is especially likely to happen if regulators adopt a legalistic approach to enforcement (Makkai and Braithwaite, 1994). Oppositional and criminogenic business subcultures develop, and these subcultures "supply rationalizations for non-compliance and disseminate knowledge about methods of legal resistance and counterattack" (Braithwaite, 1989, p. 343).

This problem is not unique to regulatory justice and can be a problem for criminal law as well (see Simpson, 2002). Similarly, the economic approach also may facilitate defiance and resistance if companies and their supporters believe that regulations are overly restrictive and inefficient. Corporations learn to "game" regulators, taking advantage of the shades of gray in regulations while appearing to be socially responsible (McBarnet, 2005).

According to the conflict approach, regulation is a contested terrain. Powerful corporations utilize political supporters to push their own legislative agenda. Pro- and anti-regulation forces engage in a battle of scientific wits, both utilizing their own cost-benefit assessments and scientific experts to demonstrate the "truth" of their positions. For example, one anti–climate-change bureaucrat was quoted as saying, "You've got your science, I've got mine" (Simpson, 2006, p. 68). When there is a lack of agreement among businesses, regulators, corporations, and the general public regarding normative standards and the moral wrongfulness of behaviors, then regulation as a means of control is likely to be ineffectual.

Like the criminal justice system, the regulatory system has both strengths and weaknesses as a means of controlling white-collar and corporate crime. Compared with the criminal justice system, three aspects of the regulatory system are particularly important: its proactive nature, specialized expertise, and fewer legal constraints.

In our legal tradition, the criminal justice system is conceived to be primarily a reactive force of control. When someone breaks the law, then the police can spring into action to find and bring the lawbreaker to justice. With only a few exceptions, such as vice crimes, the police generally do not enforce the law by actively seeking out offenses. Rather, they wait until someone files a complaint and then they react. Regulatory agencies, however, are expected to prevent harms from happening in the first place, not just to react to them after they have occurred. OSHA inspectors, for example, can require business owners to remedy dangerous work conditions even though no one may actually have been harmed. As we explain in more detail in the next chapter, the proactive nature of the regulatory system makes it at times more suitable for situational crime prevention than the criminal justice system.

A second advantage of the regulatory system is that regulatory agencies and their agents typically have specialized expertise in a particular area of business activity. For example, the EPA focuses on the potential harmful effects of manufacturing processes on the environment, while OSHA concentrates on workplace safety, and the SEC applies itself to securities. Specialized expertise enables regulatory agents to detect and understand complex corporate offenses better than can most criminal justice personnel.

A final advantage that regulatory agents have over the police is that they are not subject to the same legal constraints regarding their interactions with regulated entities. For example, before the police can conduct a search of a business, they must obtain a search warrant based upon a demonstration of probable cause that a crime has been committed there. Regulatory agents, on the other hand, have the authority to enter business premises and conduct inspections within their area of expertise to look for violations. Because they can enter and inspect businesses without having to get a search warrant, regulatory agents can act to prevent harm before it actually occurs rather than having to wait until something bad happens. Depending on the agency involved, the ability of regulatory agents to inspect is not limited to physical searches of premises. Rather, their powers often extend to searches of records, files, and other types of documentary evidence.

Unfortunately, regulatory agencies are often unable to make much use of the investigatory and preventive advantages that they have over criminal justice agencies because they are understaffed and underfunded compared with the size of the regulated community. The failure of governments to allocate sufficient resources to regulatory agencies has been and remains a fundamental weakness of regulation as a means of controlling white-collar and corporate crime. It is one thing to establish an agency to protect, for instance, worker safety, but it is quite another to give it enough resources to provide the credible oversight needed to actually achieve that goal.

Another fundamental weakness of regulation is inadequate sanctioning power. The sanctions that regulatory agencies can impose simply do not have the same deterrent power as criminal sanctions. Depending on the circumstances, agencies can impose large fines, issue cease and desist orders, or force expensive recalls. However, in the eyes of businessmen and women, the threat imposed by these sanctions is trivial compared with the threat of conviction for a crime and incarceration. Simply put, for a multibillion-dollar company, a multimillion-dollar fine most of the time is nothing to really be concerned about.

Based on these significant limitations, we might dismiss regulatory justice as a relatively toothless and inefficient mechanism to prevent and control corporate crime. This is especially likely during periods of regulatory retrenchment (such as the one that occurred in the United States under the Trump administration). Certainly, compared to other justice systems, administrative justice appears more susceptible to the vicissitudes of politics but other legal processes are not immune to these pressures. According to Syracuse University's Transactional Records Access Clearinghouse (TRAC), enforcement of white-collar crime declined significantly during Trump's first 20 months in office compared with Obama's last 20 months due, in part, to changes in DOJ practices (Hurtado, Dolmetsch, Roth, and Voreacos, 2020). Critics suggest that the Trump administration sent a signal that white-collar crime prosecutions should not be a DOJ priority (Coffee, 2020) and that Trump's own corrupt behavior and that of many others associated with his administration was effectively "neutralized" by condemning the condemners (Pontell, Tillman, and Ghazi-Tehrani, 2021).

Former President Trump is not unique in his abilities to "shape" opinions. Because of their position and status, U.S. Presidents can shape public opinion about many different things. However, in Trump's case, there is some evidence that the opinions of the Trump faithful about criminal law and white-collar crime reflect the rhetoric and justifications espoused by the former President. For instance, devotees are less supportive of punitive criminal sanctions (prison sentence) in the case of bank fraud (relative to the non-faithful)—perhaps reflecting Trump's precarious legal status vis-à-vis business fraud and dismissal of any criminal enforcement against him as a "witch hunt" (Reisig, Holtfreter, and Cullen 2022). However, non-punitiveness did not hold for everyone. When the perpetrator was depicted as a Chinese American man, Trump supporters expressed more punitive evaluations when compared to a white man (Reisig, et al., 2022: 22)—attitudes consistent with Trump's racial scapegoating, his zero-tolerance immigration policy and observations that linked immigration (of non-whites) to crime and drug trafficking.

The broader point here, as Sutherland noted more than 80 years ago, is that legal systems of all types can be politicized. But, what does the evidence say regarding successful enforcement? Is one system more effective at white-collar/corporate crime prevention and control than another? In the meta-analysis conducted by Simpson and associates (2014; Schell-Busey et al., 2016), regulatory policy reveals a significant deterrent effect, albeit modest and only at the company level. In the meta-analysis, regulatory policy is measured broadly, including such things as the impact of inspections, agency resources, and shifts in regulatory policy (such as deregulation) on firm offending. The deterrent effect of regulatory policy is not replicated at the individual manager or geographical level, so it is unwise to suggest that the regulatory bucket alone is where we should focus prevention and control resources. However, there are conceptual and empirical justifications for enhancing and strengthening all of the legal remedies—not as separate and distinct mechanisms of control, but rather as part of a hybridized and coordinated regulatory strategy. This approach is called responsive regulation.

Responsive Regulation

Offered as an answer to the conundrum facing state authorities of what strategy to adopt with violators (punishment or persuasion), Ayres and Braithwaite (1992) drew on game theory and economic regulation theory coupled with a number of empirical studies to formulate the strategy of responsive regulation. The idea behind responsive regulation is that a one-size-fits-all approach will not work for all offenders and all conditions, nor should regulation be a binary either/or strategy. Instead, regulation must be flexible, dynamic, cooperative (until it makes no sense to be cooperative), and respectful. The regulated community and regulators are tied together in a shared goal to achieve compliance.

At the center of responsive regulation is an enforcement pyramid that highlights the pivotal roles of ethics and self-regulation along with graduated levels (moving up the pyramid) of formal legal oversight and punishment. As Braithwaite (2008) explains, at the wide bottom of the pyramid are the most inclusive, collaborative, and cooperative approaches to ensure compliance with law. However, at each successive level up the pyramid, more resolute and punitive interventions are imposed. These sanctions are ostensibly reserved for the more egregious and uncooperative offenders.

While the ideas of responsive regulation and the enforcement pyramid have been tested, modified, challenged, and expanded (see, e.g., Kolieb, 2015; Grabosky, 2012; Neilsen and

Parker, 2009), the basic components and principles remain intact. Responsive regulation has been widely adopted globally, but not without concerns and challenges to do more with the pyramid than responsive regulation per se (Mascini, 2013; Parker, 2013). If we return to the meta-analysis discussed throughout this chapter, it would be difficult to prescribe any policy recommendations from what we have reported thus far (Paternoster, 2016). And yet, one set of treatments, those that encompassed a variety of different interventions that could not be unpacked from one another, showed consistent deterrent effects at both the individual and company levels. Importantly, these results also were the least subject to publication bias and poor methodological design (Schell-Busey, 2009). So while it is impossible to disaggregate the unique role of each treatment strategy, or to ascertain whether deterrence was achieved via the layered multi-prong approach of the enforcement pyramid or some specific tool or lever associated with criminal, civil, or regulatory justice measured as part of the multiple interventions category, we can conclude that—consistent with the enforcement pyramid—a combination of treatment appears to work better than any single treatment method for preventing corporate crime.

Summary

The criminal justice, civil justice, and regulatory systems represent different approaches to controlling harmful conduct by businesses and professionals. None of these approaches can serve as a panacea to the problem of white-collar crime. Each approach has its strengths and weaknesses, but taken together they represent the traditional lines of defense against white-collar and corporate crime, and collectively they comprise a critical component of a responsive regulation strategy. The traditional justice systems have had some success. As we noted above, while injuries and deaths have not been entirely eliminated from the workplace, they have been significantly reduced in number, at least in the United States and other developed nations. This is progress that should be built on in the future and extended to developing countries.

Although we have presented the three systems of legal control separately, we know that they can work together in practice. However, while recognizing that progress has been made in some areas, there is still a long way to go in others. Particularly in regard to evolving and changing forms of financial fraud, legal controls often seem to be behind the curve, as the accounting frauds of 2001, the mortgage fraud scandals of 2008, and most recently the COVID-19 small business relief grants/loans frauds clearly revealed. The increased use of computer technology to facilitate white-collar crime is also on the rise. So, new approaches need to be considered. In the next chapter, we attempt to do that through an examination of the potential effectiveness of extra-legal controls on corporate wrongdoing and the applicability of situational crime prevention theory to white-collar and corporate crime.

Note

1 While in jail, Blankenship publicly released a manifesto declaring himself a "political prisoner" (Mattise, Associated Press, 2016).

Chapter 11

Opportunities and Situational Prevention of White-Collar Crime

Using Legal and Extralegal Controls

Opportunities, Criminal Laws, and Regulations

From an opportunity perspective, laws and regulations are best viewed as tools that can be used to shape and control white-collar crime opportunities. Recall that white-collar crimes have certain characteristics (the offender has legitimate access to the victim, a physical separation from the victim, and the superficial appearance of legitimacy). These characteristics make possible the use of particular criminal techniques (e.g., deception, abuse of trust, concealment, and conspiracy). In addition, these distinctive characteristics and techniques influence how laws and regulations can be used to disrupt white-collar crime opportunities.

One way in which regulatory law affects white-collar crime opportunities is by setting the parameters of "legitimate" access. For instance, many professions require a degree or certification for an individual to offer services. Businesses often must be registered with a state or local authority before they can open their doors. There are age restrictions regarding who can enter into a contract, and so forth. The effect of these regulations is to limit who can have legitimate access to particular types of victims or criminal opportunities. Though such regulations do not stop those who have legitimate access from abusing their positions, they at least make it more difficult for the criminally motivated to get legitimate access in the first place.

Regulations can also be used to make it more difficult or riskier for potential offenders to deceive potential victims. For example, regulations that require contractors to provide written estimates for proposed work make it more difficult (but certainly not impossible) for them to promise one thing and do another. The passage of the Sarbanes-Oxley (SOX) Act in the wake of the Enron scandal provides another example. One part of the SOX Act requires chief executive officers and chief financial officers to certify their company's financial records (Cullen et al., 2006, p. 323). Failure to do so or certifying false financial statements can expose the executives to criminal penalties. In effect, this new requirement makes it more difficult for corporate executives to feign ignorance as a way of avoiding being held responsible for fraudulent accounting. There are other examples, such as the labeling that is required on appliances regarding energy efficiency or the nutritional labels on food products. Manufacturers and retailers can try to lie and cheat, of course, on these labels—as, for example, Volkswagen did about the emissions efficiency of its "green cars"—but if the lies are exposed, then consequences follow. In addition, it seems likely that they face a greater risk that their deception will be exposed than they would face if there were no legally required labels. In general, one of the best ways that regulations can help reduce white-collar crime is by increasing transparency, making it harder for potential offenders to deceive consumers and other victims.

DOI: 10.4324/9781003175322-16

The Limits of the Law and Legal Controls

Christopher Stone (1975), one of the first critics to call attention to the multiple ways in which law fails to control corporate misconduct, acknowledged the burdens of applying traditional legal forms to corporations. However, Stone's observation is also relevant for other (non-corporate) kinds of white-collar offenses. Some white-collar crimes emerge as new technologies develop. For instance, there was no such thing as Internet fraud until the Internet was developed. For this reason, law needs to be flexible and adaptable when new opportunities emerge. The common law is impressively adjustable to changing social conditions, but when developments (like the Internet) are truly innovative, the common law cannot adapt rapidly enough to the potential risks posed by such a new and expansive global phenomenon.

> [T]he rapidity with which changes occur in the digital age … makes the conventional processes of law reform cumbersome. Introducing a legislative change to accommodate the latest development in computer user authentication technologies, for example, may take years, by which time the technological development in question may be outmoded and the reform no longer applicable.
>
> (Grabosky, Smith, and Dempsey, 2001, p. 185)

Referencing the Enron case, Malcolm S. Salter (as quoted in Hawn, 2008, p. 3) suggests that many of the acts were innovative "new ideas and new financial instruments for which there is not established accounting, or that don't conform with old principles". More recently, confusion about whether and how to regulate cryptocurrencies demonstrates the problem on a global scale. In their attempt to crack down on fraud and cybercrime, China has banned all transactions of virtual currencies. In contrast, the United States has dithered and disagreed on how best to respond.

> …[T]he U.S. government finds itself caught between two extremes: unwilling to actively block cryptocurrency transactions for fear of restricting a growing and potentially lucrative industry but also determined not to give up completely on policing illegal cryptocurrency payments and going after their role in the cybercrime ecosystem.
>
> (Wolff, 2022)

Confirming what we noted in the preceding chapter that the law often seems to trail behind technological developments, these criticisms suggest that law, in its many forms, is—at best—marginal in its ability to restrict white-collar crime opportunities and may, on occasion, increase offending opportunities either through its limitations (gray areas) or through how it affects perceptions. In the next section, we discuss some alternative remedies for the control of white-collar crime that rely on extralegal strategies.

Extralegal Remedies

Strategies to prevent white-collar crime that are not centered in legal controls focus mainly on reducing criminal opportunity. Routine activity theory suggests that crime results from three interrelated events that intersect at the same time, in the same place: a motivated offender, a suitable target, and the lack of capable guardianship (Cohen and Felson, 1979).

From this point of view, crime can be prevented by somehow decreasing the suitability of the target, increasing the level of guardianship, or reducing the offender's motivation. The suitability of a target can be reduced by target hardening (i.e., making it harder to get at the target). Guardianship can be increased by providing more, or more effective, surveillance. Prevention efforts can also focus on the motivated offender such as when companies develop internal programs that include ethics training, whistle-blowing hotlines, and random audits to ensure compliance with legal and regulatory rules (Van Rooij and Rorie, 2022). However, for a myriad of reasons, these may be more difficult to accomplish and less successful than increasing guardianship and hardening the crime target. From a practical point of view, however, situational crime prevention theory predicts that any intervention that disrupts the crime triad will reduce crime.

The risk of many traditional forms of white-collar crime can be mitigated by increasing public awareness about particular forms of crime and enhancing victim protection. For instance, after the dangers posed by the COVID-19 virus were officially recognized, the U.S. Department of Justice and many other federal agencies quickly began issuing warnings about frauds related to COVID-19 cures and protection products (Kennedy, Rorie, and Benson, 2021). Credit card companies now require card recipients to call and "activate" their cards before use and, when using the card remotely, to report the security code on the back of the card. Consumers are encouraged not to use debit cards to purchase items remotely over the telephone or Internet, because it is easier for fraudsters to gain unwarranted access to bank account information. Anyone who has an e-mail account is familiar with the common warnings about e-mail scams, and we are warned not to respond to or give out any personal information (such as bank account information or social security numbers) in response to "phishing" expeditions. With respect to white-collar crime control, consumer education is a form of target hardening.

To guard against employee (and consumer) theft, department stores at the turn of the twentieth century implemented a number of new ways to display merchandise (locked in glass cabinets) that provided better control (Abelson, 1989). Today, businesses utilize cameras, alarms, security codes, and guards; they limit access to sensitive information and products; potential employees are interviewed, psychologically tested, and assessed before employment to determine crime risks (among other things). Employees are watched by their colleagues, and suspect behavior can be anonymously reported to "hotlines". Randomized audits of accounts, expense statements, legally sanctioned policies and procedures, coupled with other types of surveillance, affect both objective and perceptual opportunities for crime. None of these tactics are foolproof, but they do change the calculus of potential offenders, and it seems safe to assume that some of the time they reduce offending.

There are many creative strategies to prevent white-collar crime, ranging from the simple (computer passwords) to the sophisticated (tracking data to pick up unusual activity). For example, the Securities and Exchange Commission (SEC) now uses sophisticated data analytics to track the buying and selling of stocks, looking for unusual patterns that may indicate some form of insider trading or other form of stock fraud (Robinson, 2013). At the Federal Trade Commission (FTC), the Bureau of Consumer Protection maintains a website where consumers can file complaints about deceptive or fraudulent businesses practices. These complaints are shared with law enforcement and, at the end of the year, the FTC issues a report to consumers that documents the kinds and number of complaints received. These kinds of prevention programs are flexible and timely, capable of responding quickly to new forms of white-collar crime. They also extend beyond the reach of our justice systems and, as such, are a broader and more comprehensive way to reduce white-collar crime opportunities. However, they tend to neglect the motivated offender.

In *Crime, Shame, and Reintegration*, John Braithwaite (1989) argues that the key to crime control rests in a society's capacity and ability to communicate the wrongfulness of behaviors to citizens and respond to wrongful acts in ways that shame but also reintegrate offenders. Although his argument focuses more on recidivism than on the initial decision to offend, his main point (which he shares with Bentham) is that there are alternatives to formal justice that carry tremendous potential for controlling all types of crime. These alternatives build around the notion that individuals are generally embedded in some kind of social network (religious organizations, families, neighborhoods, corporations, professional associations) that can impose shame and punishment outside of (or in conjunction with) the legal process. The effectiveness of these controls, like the legal process, will affect the attractiveness of white-collar crime opportunities.

Extralegal social controls can take many different forms. The most basic form is socialization (by parents, peers, schools, churches, and businesses) that emphasize the right norms and values. Ethical standards are the backbone of any social control system that promotes pro-social behavior in children and adults, and it is the foundation on which the enforcement pyramid (discussed in Chapter 10) is based, but even under the best of circumstances, socialization can fail. And in the case of white-collar crime, the standards of right and wrong can be unclear in ways that do not exist for traditional crime because the offenses are often new and their legal status may be ambiguous for a while. For example, at what point should the predatory lending of subprime loans be considered morally unacceptable as opposed to just an aggressive business practice? The *mala prohibita* nature of many corporate offenses complicates efforts to communicate the seriousness and consequences of these types of crime. However, a national survey conducted by the National White Collar Crime Center in 2010 suggests that the public does recognize the seriousness of white-collar crime (Huff, Desilets, and Kane, 2010). Respondents viewed white-collar crime as slightly more serious than traditional crime types; organizational crimes were viewed more harshly than those committed by individuals; and crimes involving high-status individuals (i.e., those in a position of trust) were viewed as more serious than those committed by low-status persons. Another study has also discovered similar patterns using national survey data from 2015 (Simpson et al., 2017). In this study, most types of identity theft, financial fraud, and unfair and deceptive practices targeting consumers are ranked equal to or more serious than burglary. In addition, offenses involving organizational offenders are regarded as more serious than those with individual offenders.

Criminologists know that the greatest risk of crime is likely to be found in those offenses around which there is little moral consensus. After the stock market scandals of the 1980s (often perpetrated by highly credentialed MBAs), several well-regarded and influential graduate programs adopted ethics-training modules within traditional classes or added specific classes in business ethics as a way to introduce future managers to the kinds of ethical (and legal) dilemmas they were apt to face in the workplace. Similarly, many companies incorporated ethics codes and ethics training as integral parts of their internal compliance programs. Although the jury is still out on whether training programs have had any impact on offending (Schell-Busey, 2009)—in part because it is debatable whether those who implement the programs are "serious" about ethics—it is clear that this type of intervention has grown in popularity and legitimacy. But we must also acknowledge that some respected scholars regard the whole business ethics movement as a failure (Clinard and Yeager, 1980).

Because a lot of white-collar crime occurs within organizations, it is important to consider how social control systems within organizations can affect white-collar crime opportunities. Braithwaite (1989, p. 143) suggests that the organizational environment can effectively shame offenders when punishment for white-collar crime "maximizes the sense of shame [and] ... communicates the message that white-collar crime is as abhorrent to the community as crime in the streets". Of course, having the potential to shame is not the same as actually shaming the offender. So, what kinds of practices are effective for corporate shaming? One way to sanction individual and corporate offenders is through negative publicity (Fisse and Braithwaite, 1983), and one way to tell that publicity is an effective tool is to observe how corporate public relations departments go on the offensive after a negative incident. Consider, for example, how Wells Fargo Bank started running television advertisements touting their renewed commitment to integrity and customer satisfaction after their scandal with fraudulent accounts. In 2023, the company announced plans to shift completely away from the home-lending mortgage market. As one senior executive VP for the company stated, "We are acutely aware of Wells Fargo's history since 2016 and *the work we need to do to restore public confidence*". Managers also fear discovery of their illicit activities by significant others, such as family, friends, and business associates. In fact, Simpson's research shows that intentions to engage in illegal corporate activity by managers was significantly inhibited by the potential informal sanctions brought by significant others—and this effect is equal to or actually greater than the threat of formal legal sanctions (Simpson, 2002; Simpson, Garner, and Gibbs, 2007). In a vignette study of cybercrime, formal sanction threats were unrelated to offending intentions among college students, but shame and embarrassment were likely to reduce all forms of cyberattacks under study (Bossler, 2019).

Smith, Simpson, and Huang (2007) suggest that informal sanctions and formal sanctions interact to lower corporate crime offending risk. Managers' perceptions of negative informal consequences (outcome expectancies) affect their perceptions of formal sanction threats, which in turn lower their willingness to engage in three types of corporate offenses (price fixing, environmental offenses, and bribery). Thus, as Ayres and Braithwaite (1992) argue, prevention and control of white-collar crime will be accomplished best through a pyramid of enforcement. Informal controls and sanctions operate at the base of the pyramid as the first (and most important set of controls), followed by more punitive and "formal" kinds of interventions. In addition, complementary combinations of policy instruments from third parties can buttress and expand control mechanisms beyond the state (Gunningham, Grabosky, and Sinclair, 1998).

Situational Crime Prevention Theory

Situational crime prevention theory (SCPT) focuses on ways to make criminal opportunities less attractive to potential offenders. It takes a pluralistic approach toward this objective. By pluralistic, we mean SCPT holds that when it comes to crime control, we should not put all our eggs in one basket, regardless of whether it is the criminal justice system, the regulatory system, the civil law, the market, professional associations, or any other legal or extralegal mechanism of control. Rather, we should recognize and take advantage of the usefulness of all of these mechanisms in different combinations, depending on the situation that confronts us.

To prevent any particular type of white-collar crime, we need to understand its opportunity structure and then figure out a way to intervene in and modify that specific structure.

From the perspective of potential offenders, criminal opportunities have five dimensions or characteristics (Cornish and Clarke, 1986):

1 The effort required to carry out the offense.
2 The risk of detection associated with committing the offense.
3 The rewards to be gained from the offense.
4 Situational conditions that may encourage criminal actions; and
5 Excuses offenders can use to justify their actions.

In short, from the offender's point of view, crimes, including white-collar crimes, are more attractive if they are easy to commit, have a low risk of detection, offer attractive rewards, are encouraged by the immediate environment, and are easy to justify (Benson, Madensen, and Eck, 2009). As we hope was made clear by our analysis of specific types of white-collar crime in Chapters 6 and 7, these conditions often are met for people who are contemplating committing a white-collar offense.

Before going on to discuss how SCPT may be applied to white-collar crime, we need to address one other important and distinctive aspect of opportunity structures for white-collar crimes. The term "opportunity structure" suggests something that is solid or fixed in place. For example, a house that is known to be unoccupied at night and that does not have an alarm system presents a fixed opportunity. From the perspective of a potential burglar, the target is sitting there waiting for him or her to take advantage of it. However, in regard to white-collar crime, opportunity structures are almost always not like this. That is, the opportunity is not present because a physical object has been left unguarded. Rather, the opportunity arises out of some sort of legitimate business activity or process. From our perspective, processes create opportunities. The procedure by which health care practitioners submit claims to health care insurers is a perfect example of a process that creates certain types of criminal opportunities.

Thus, white-collar crime opportunities almost always involve the intersection of two processes. The first is a legitimate process that is typically followed in the world of business or government, and the second is an illegitimate process that is parasitical on the first process (Benson, 2012). Recall, for instance, the Libor scandal in which unscrupulous traders took advantage of the system that was established to set interest rates for different types of financial transactions. Because the process for setting Libor rates was so haphazard and insecure, it was relatively easy for traders to pervert it to their advantage (Enrich, 2017). Likewise, the fraud and exploitation that once saturated the subprime mortgage market represented a subversion of the processes used in the legitimate mortgage market. From a broad strategic point of view, prevention requires making adjustments to the legitimate process that make it difficult for individuals to act parasitically in relation to the legitimate process. Thus, to prevent white-collar crimes, we need to develop legitimate processes that are difficult to copy or that raise the likelihood that an illegitimate use of the process will be detected. After the Libor scandal was exposed, this is exactly what the British Banking Association attempted to do when it promised to reform the process by which Libor rates were set (Kuchler and Masters, 2012). Unfortunately, it still remains to be seen whether the reforms that have been put in place will be effective in preventing further fraudulent manipulation of Libor in the future (Powell, 2014). To put this in the conceptual framework that we have used throughout this book, prevention involves making it hard or complicated for white-collar offenders either to maintain the superficial appearance of legitimacy or to appear to have an ambiguous state of mind or both (Benson et al., 2009; Benson and Madensen, 2007).

To accomplish these objectives, we can draw from and extend the basic principles of situational crime prevention theory (Clarke, 1983). SCPT recommends that to reduce any particular type of white-collar crime, we should try to modify its opportunity structure so that it:

1 Requires more effort to commit the offense.
2 Raises the risk of detection for committing the offense.
3 Reduces the rewards associated with the offense.
4 Reduces any situational provocations for the offense.
5 Makes it more difficult to justify or excuse the offense.

Depending on the type of crime under consideration, some of these objectives may be easier to meet than others, but it is not necessary to meet all of these objectives in every case. To pursue these objectives, it is important to recognize that white-collar crimes take a variety of different forms. Fraud in health care is not carried out in the same way as mortgage fraud. We need to be sensitive to these differences and focus on highly specific forms of crime (Benson and Madensen, 2007). What may work to reduce health care fraud may be useless in the case of mortgage fraud because the two offenses have different opportunity structures.

In the case of ordinary street crime, the effort required to commit the offense is usually increased by trying to block the offenders' access to the crime target. Because white-collar crimes are based on specialized access, simply blocking access is not an option for many types of white-collar crime, especially when the offense is based on the misuse of a legitimate occupational role. However, there are some instances in which variations on this strategy can be used to a degree. For example, laws and regulations that require practitioners to obtain licenses or certifications before they can practice a certain profession, in effect, block access to the target. Granted, those who have the license can misuse it, but licensing requirements, nevertheless, put limits on the number and type of people who can practice a particular line of work. A more sophisticated use of this tactic has already been put in place by the Center for Medicare and Medicaid Services (CMS), which is the government body charged with overseeing the operation of these two federal health care programs (King, 2014). The CMS has a system for classifying Medicare service providers into high-, medium-, and low-risk categories. For example, based on past experience, the CMS has learned that newly enrolling home health care services and newly enrolling suppliers of durable medical equipment (such as wheelchairs and oxygen equipment) are at high risk of engaging in fraud and abuse (King, 2014). So, these providers are subject to more scrutiny and oversight than low-risk providers, which include physician practitioners and ambulatory surgical centers, among others.

These sorts of programs and control mechanisms increase the effort for would-be offenders, and they also have the potential to change how offenders calculate the costs versus the benefits of a particular crime. White-collar offenders must consider not only the potential legal consequences (fines and jail time) but also the potential occupational consequences (loss of certification or license to practice) (Benson and Madensen, 2007). In both the Wells Fargo and Volkswagen cases, company leaders lost their jobs as a result of the scandals in their respective organizations. Similarly, one of the penalties that can be visited upon fraudulent health care providers is exclusion from access to the Medicare and Medicaid systems.

With regard to consumer-related frauds, the effort required to commit an offense can be increased through a form of target hardening. For consumer frauds to work, the offender must somehow fool the victim into thinking that he or she is legitimate. The victim must accept the offender's advantageous distortion of reality. This happened often during the early 2000s when predatory mortgage brokers and bankers talked eager home buyers into taking out loans with terms that were unfavorable to them (Nguyen and Pontell, 2010). However, to the extent that consumers can educate themselves so that they become harder to deceive, the offender's job becomes all that much more difficult. Individuals who can spot distortions of reality can avoid many forms of white-collar crime victimization. Simple things such as knowing who you are dealing with when you buy a product or service, getting recommendations from friends and neighbors, and checking references or the Better Business Bureau can help you avoid working with someone intent on defrauding you and can help you recognize when someone is trying to deceive you.

Raising the risk of detection is particularly important with respect to white-collar crime, because once the crime is exposed, it is usually relatively straightforward to identify the responsible persons or organizations (Braithwaite and Geis, 1982). Exposure is threatening to white-collar offenders. Having their names linked with anything that appears untoward or disreputable is troubling for white-collar offenders because of their public persona and self-image as upstanding, moral, and law-abiding citizens. In addition, corporate leaders have to be ever sensitive to the potential negative effects of bad publicity on corporate profitability and market share. Thus, even if corporate executives are insensitive to being pilloried in the press, their companies cannot avoid punishment by the market. The threat of potential negative publicity can act as a deterrent even in cases where formal sanctions are never actually administered (Fisse and Braithwaite, 1983).

In order to raise the risk of detection, however, we need to think beyond just hoping that the free press will uncover the wrongdoing. We need to think creatively and design strategies that are focused on particular opportunity structures. A good example of thinking creatively can be found in the enforcement of the Federal Crop Insurance Program (FCIP). The FCIP is supposed to insure farmers against risks such as floods and natural disasters. Significantly, it also insures farmers against crop failures. A simple scheme used by some farmers to take advantage of this program is to insure field A against failure. The farmer then takes the harvest from field A and records it as coming from field B, and then submits a claim to the FCIP to be indemnified for the "failure" of field A (Shover and Hochstetler, 2006). In effect, the farmer gets paid twice for the harvest of field A—once from the FCIP and once from the marketplace. White-collar crime in the FCIP program depends on the "failure" claim appearing normal, and on the inability or unwillingness of program managers to accurately ascertain the validity of those claims. The offenders attempt to create applications that look normal. They hope that their fraudulent applications will blend in with all of the legitimate applications. Because there may be only a few fraudulent applications scattered among the many legitimate applications, it is not cost-effective to examine each and every application to determine its credibility. To overcome this problem, the federal Risk Management Agency (RMA) figured out a clever and effective approach (Shover and Hochstetler, 2006, pp. 102–103). In 2001, the RMA developed a computer program to identify FCIP claims filed for crop failures that came from producers located in counties where most other farmers were successful. The producers with the suspicious claims were sent letters informing them that a federal fraud investigation was being initiated. A year later, indemnity pay outs to these farmers went down dramatically. The mere threat of exposure seemed to work as a deterrent.

Advances in computer hardware and software, coupled with the rise of data analytics and the use of machine learning algorithms, represent another way to raise the risk of detection. For example, the detection of certain types of securities cases, such as insider trading and market manipulation, often depends on uncovering hidden connections between people and identifying aberrant behavior patterns (Robinson, 2013). For the SEC, uncovering connections in insider trading cases almost always involves phone records. Less than a decade ago, it might have taken SEC investigators months to analyze phone records to determine whether two or more individuals were communicating, but now software is available that allows investigators to determine much more quickly if different phone numbers called the same phone line (Partnership for Public Service, 2013). Data analytics can also be used to identify "aberrational performance" such as, for example, if a hedge fund reports significantly better performance than its competitors during both good and bad markets (Robinson, 2013). Once the unusual pattern is identified, it can be investigated to see whether fraud or some other type of white-collar crime is involved. The general point here is that data analytics is a tool that can be used to help the SEC detect certain types of illegal activity more quickly and easily than in the past (Partnership for Public Service, 2013). Data analytics are also being used by the CMS to identify fraudulent fee-for-service claims (King, 2014). As part of the Affordable Care Act passed in 2010, the CMS set up a Fraud Prevention Service (FPS). The FPS uses "predictive analytic technologies" to examine claims and look for suspicious patterns before they are paid. It is not yet clear how well the FPS is working, but its existence is another illustration of the arms race between fraudsters and controllers (King, 2014). Of course, as with any enforcement tool, data analytics is not self-activating. Agency personnel must be empowered by institutional leaders to use it, and their results must be acted on to make the risk of detection palpable to potential offenders. This is often a weakness of control efforts in regard to all forms of white-collar crime. The enforcement tools are available, but the political will to use them vacillates over time and is sometimes not robust (Yeager, 2016b).

Other types of offenses will require other strategies. For example, some crimes, such as antitrust offenses, are based on conspiracies inside or between organizations. They can be very difficult to detect because they are hidden behind a corporate veil of secrecy. Only insiders have knowledge of them. Laws that promote and protect whistle-blowers, such as the U.S. Whistleblower Protection Act of 1989, can be potentially helpful in these cases. They raise the likelihood that someone inside an organization will break ranks and bring information about the illegal activity outside of the organization. Of course, how well such laws work is an empirical question, and they certainly do not work perfectly. Organizations retaliate against individual whistle-blowers, and sometimes these individuals pay a heavy price (Miethe and Rothschild, 1994; Rothschild and Miethe, 1999). Nevertheless, the important lesson here is that the threat of exposure is something to which white-collar offenders are sensitive. It's a tool that can be used to society's advantage.

Reducing the rewards of crime can be a very effective way of preventing ordinary street crimes. For example, so-called "smart objects" that require a code or password in order to be used can make a seemingly valuable object virtually worthless to a thief. It is pointless to steal a CD player from an automobile if it won't work after it has been taken out. Because most white-collar crimes do not involve objects, this strategy may not be applicable in many cases. However, in some situations, this strategy may work. For example, to prevent embezzlement or the misappropriation of property, organizations often require multiple signatures on checks or transactions that are valued above a certain amount. Though it might be possible for an individual employee or executive to use his or her position to steal a relatively small amount of money from his or her company, trying to take a big amount is made harder and riskier by the multiple-signature requirement. In effect, the potential reward for misappropriation has been reduced.

Television crime shows often portray criminal offenders as cold, calculating predators who stalk innocent victims. In reality, however, many crimes result from what is perceived by the offender as some sort of provocation by the victim (Felson, 2002). From the offender's point of view, the crime may represent a way to get even for a previous slight or transgression by the victim (Black, 1983). Crime control specialists have learned that to prevent ordinary street crimes, it is helpful to reduce the situational provocations that may encourage criminal activity (Benson and Madensen, 2007). For example, not allowing bars to serve drinks at two-for-one prices during happy hours may reduce the number of people who get drunk on Friday and end up in fights.

Unlike some street crimes, most white-collar crimes are not driven by spontaneous emotions. Because of their complexity, they require planning on the part of the perpetrator and are not the result of impulsive decision-making. Thus, the idea of reducing provocations may not work in regard to many types of white-collar crime. Nevertheless, there are some forms of white-collar crime that may result from perceived provocations by the victim. For example, embezzlers are sometimes motivated by the feeling that they have been mistreated by their employers and really deserve the money they take (Cressey, 1953). Similarly, doctors who cheat health insurers may feel justified in doing so because they think that insurers are not being fair to them or that inefficiency in the system makes the reimbursement procedures overly arduous (Vaughan, 1983). To counteract these feelings, both Medicare and Medicaid have tried to design claims-processing systems that are simple, easy, and fast for physicians. By making it easy to file legitimate claims, the programs hope to reduce the number of illegitimate claims filed out of frustration and stress.

The lesson to be learned from the experience of Medicare and Medicaid is that whenever large corporate entities interact with individuals in a way that is perceived as unfair, they open themselves up to the possibility of retaliation. Individuals may try to cheat or otherwise offend against large organizations because they feel frustrated and because offending against an organization as opposed to another individual is more excusable (Coleman, 1982). Organizations that fail to treat people fairly should not be surprised to find themselves victimized by the white-collar crimes of their employees, clients, and customers.

Finally, removing excuses should be another area of focus. Because white-collar offenders think of themselves as moral and upstanding citizens, they cannot easily engage in activities that are obviously illegal. White-collar offenders are loath to think of themselves or their behavior as criminal (Benson, 1985). They simply do not want to see that what they are doing is wrong. In their eyes, whatever they do is justified, and they are very creative at finding justifications for their misconduct (Box, 1983; Geis, 1977; Shover, 2007; White, Bandura, and Bero, 2009). They have to be, because the excuses and justifications are necessary conditions in the causal chain leading to the offense. Thus, white-collar offenders must not only perceive a criminal opportunity, they must be able to define the opportunity in morally acceptable terms.

This feature of the psychological makeup of white-collar offenders presents both an opportunity and an obstacle for control via the criminal law. To the extent that the criminal law can be used to convey to potential white-collar offenders that a particular form of behavior is morally wrong, it may reduce that particular type of white-collar crime. If white-collar offenders cannot define their behavior in morally acceptable terms, then they are less likely to engage in that behavior. We need to foster cultures of compliance rather than subcultures of resistance to the law (Braithwaite, 1989). Unfortunately, as we showed in Chapter 8, white-collar offenders are very adept at avoiding or deflecting the moral strictures of the criminal law.

Also, it is important to recognize that white-collar crimes committed in organizational settings are rarely the work of lone actors. Rather, they result from groups of people working together to achieve some sort of organizational goal. The collective nature of these situations changes their psychological dimensions, because now we are not dealing with individual moral agents who are socially detached and thinking only about themselves. In groups, people interact, feed off of, and reinforce one another and, over time, a collective moral disengagement can emerge that permits the group to engage in harmful activities without any individual feeling personally responsible (White et al., 2009). As decades of research on collective behavior has shown, when people are in groups, they will often do things that they would never do on their own (Turner and Killian, 1987).

Finally, as Sutherland pointed out long ago, one of the reasons why white-collar crime flourishes is that American society suffers from a conflict of standards in regard to the control of business (Sutherland, 1983). The seemingly never-ending conflict between the business community and those who would regulate its harmful behavior prevents the development of a strong public consensus against white-collar crime. We need also to recognize that the values that lie at the heart of American culture, such as the pursuit of wealth and individualized success, provide a constant source of motivation for white-collar crime (Messner and Rosenfeld, 1997; Weisburd et al., 1991; Wheeler, 1992; Benson and Cullen, 2018). Thus, although it has potential, the strategy of removing excuses is one that is not likely to provide a quick fix.

Summary

In this chapter, we have explored how situational crime prevention theory can be used to analyze how legal and extralegal control mechanisms influence white-collar crime opportunities. We have reviewed how different legal systems (criminal, civil, and regulatory) can have different effects on white-collar crime opportunities. We also showed that extralegal factors, especially in conjunction with justice processes, can lower the risk of white-collar crime through their impact on opportunities. The key problems that must be confronted to prevent white-collar crimes are (1) the offender's legitimate access to the target, and (2) the superficial appearance of legitimacy of the offender's actions. These characteristics make it difficult for victims and law enforcers to see many white-collar crimes in the first place and to then take steps to prevent them.

In some situations, legitimate access to the target can be controlled via occupational licensing or regulations regarding access to certain government programs, such as, for example, the access of health care providers to the Medicare and Medicaid systems. In other cases, access can be reduced by hardening the target. Education programs and news reports that provide information to consumers on various forms of fraud and exploitation that they may encounter are examples of this form of situational prevention.

The superficial appearance of legitimacy can sometimes be undone through the use of strategies that look for unusual patterns in economic transactions. Both the SEC and the CMS now use sophisticated data analytics programs to uncover suspicious activity in their respective realms. It is difficult to tell how effective these programs are in uncovering offenses, and more importantly deterring potential offenders from even trying, but it seems not unreasonable to conclude that without these efforts, things would be worse.

Finally, although it should be abundantly clear that the control of white-collar crime is a difficult and never-ending task, we also note that it is not a hopeless one. Just as ordinary street crime will never be completely eliminated, neither will white-collar crime ever disappear, but specific forms and types can be reduced at some times and in some places. We believe the best way to pursue this goal is to think about white-collar crime opportunities and then to try to implement strategies and tactics to disrupt or modify those opportunities based on the principles of situational crime prevention.

Chapter 12

Opportunities and the Future of White-Collar Crime

The concept of white-collar crime has been ambiguous and problematic since its inception (Croall, 2001, pp. 143–144; Weisburd et al., 1991, p. 170). In some ways, the conceptual ambiguity surrounding white-collar crime has only gotten worse over time. When Sutherland first introduced the term, scholars primarily debated whether the concept should be restricted to activities that were encompassed by criminal legislation or more broadly construed to include activities that were illegal in the sense that they violated regulatory, but not necessarily criminal, codes (Sutherland, 1945; Tappan, 1947). It was a debate about what should count as crime and as the legitimate object of study for the criminologist. In the ensuing years, however, arguments have arisen regarding who the offender is or even *what* the offender is. Should the focus of study be limited to individuals, or does it make sense to conceive of organizations themselves as offenders (Braithwaite and Fisse, 1990; Cressey, 1989)? In regard to individuals, there is also disagreement over who should be included in the white-collar criminal category. Should it be restricted only to people of "respectability and high social status", or should we acknowledge, in light of recent research findings, that many people who do not have high social status commit offenses that for all intents and purposes seem to be white-collar crimes (Benson and Moore, 1992; Croall, 1989; Weisburd et al., 1991)? Thus, the debate over the concept of white-collar crime has broadened from a focus on what should count as crime to a consideration of who or what the offender is. In a way, it is a bit odd that criminologists have spent so much time debating the ontological status of white-collar crime, because "crime" itself is a socially constructed construct (Croall, 1989, p. 145).

In this book, we have tried not to get too bogged down in these debates and have opted for a more inclusive approach, one that recognizes offenders at all levels of the class structure and offenses of differing levels of illegality. This approach has the advantage of permitting more comparisons between different groups of offenders and offenses. It also enables us to analyze a very broad range of opportunities to engage in illegality and to explore how these opportunities are related to occupations, organizations, and the social structure of American society. But the main reason for adopting an inclusive approach to white-collar crime is that it permits us to focus on what we think is a more important issue: understanding opportunities to use deception, abuse of trust, concealment, and conspiracy as techniques in criminal offending.

Thus, instead of trying to decide who is or is not the white-collar offender or trying to figure out what should or should not count as white-collar crime, we have argued that it is more useful to focus on how occupations, organizations, industries, and government programs create situations in which some people can deceive or abuse the trust of other

DOI: 10.4324/9781003175322-17

people or organizations for their own advantage. Although we really cannot prove the point empirically here, we expect that the use of these techniques is more common among middle- and upper-class individuals than it is among individuals from less advantaged backgrounds. People of low socioeconomic status can use deception to cheat on taxes, welfare benefit applications, and in many other ways. On the other hand, people of middle and upper socioeconomic status do occasionally commit crimes of violence and force. But the relative proportion of offenses that involve deception, we think, rises as socioeconomic status rises. In other words, there is a strong link between social status and what we typically think of as white-collar crime, but the link between status and crime is better thought of as a continuum than as a dichotomy.

In this concluding chapter, we review the major themes that motivated this book, focusing primarily on the topic of opportunities and how these are shaped by the structure of occupational activities and organizations. However, it is important to recognize that opportunity structures for white-collar crime are not fixed in stone. Products, services, and forms of business constantly evolve or new ones are invented. In addition, technological change appears to be ceaseless. These developments and changes create new opportunities for deception and, to be fair, new opportunities for controlling deception. For example, since the last edition of this book was published, social media as a means and site for deception has exploded with so-called "influencers" hawking products deceptively. Thus, what we have to say here will eventually become dated as new forms of white-collar crime arise. Although it is always risky to speculate about the direction of future trends, we nevertheless take that risk and address what we think will be some of the future directions of white-collar crime. Finally, we conclude with some thoughts on the policy implications of our perspective.

Reconsidering Deception

Recall that deception is the advantageous distortion of perceived reality and that it can be achieved in different ways, including embellishment, mimicry, and concealing. The type or types of deception that are used in any particular white-collar crime depends in part on the relationship between the offender and the target. Offenders who are trying to sell a product or a service typically use embellishment to deceive their victims into doing something that is not in their best interests. Offenders attempt to make their products or services appear better than the competition and better than they really are by fraudulently embellishing their properties. For example, in the years before the 2008 collapse of the housing market, realtors and mortgage brokers would use embellishment to convince prospective home buyers that subprime loans were in their best interests when really such loans were likely to turn into financial traps. In contrast, offenders who are trying to secure some benefit from a governmental program are more likely to use mimicry rather than embellishment. For example, health care fraud offenders submit claims to Medicare or Medicaid that they hope will look just like all the other legitimate claims that are received every day. Finally, there is concealment. As a form of deception, concealment is used when offenders do not want others, especially the government, media, or general public, to know about the true nature of their activities. For example, the illegal disposal of e-waste is accomplished by brokers and traders in e-waste who conspire together to create invoices that hide information about the nature of the waste in shipping containers. Then, in violation of national and international laws and regulations, the e-waste can be shipped to third world countries, such as Ghana, where it is handled in ways that harm the environment and human health (Bisschop, 2015).

Bid rigging and price fixing are other forms of white-collar crime that rely on the offenders' abilities to conceal the activities from law enforcers and the public. In a typical bid-rigging scenario, companies submit their contract bids ostensibly in competition with other firms, but the firms have colluded beforehand to allocate low bids amongst themselves. From the outside, the bidding process appears to be legitimate.

The Characteristics of White-Collar Crime

Regardless of the form it takes—embellishment, mimicry, or concealment—the point of deception is to help the offender maintain the superficial appearance of legitimacy. This is one of the distinguishing features of white-collar crime and one that makes white-collar crime so difficult to control. Unlike most so-called traditional street crimes, such as robbery, burglary, auto theft, and assault, white-collar crimes are not obvious. They often do not leave visible traces of their occurrence. Even the victims may not be aware that a crime has taken place, let alone law enforcers. Efforts to control white-collar crime, therefore, must start with the problem of detection, finding the offense.

A second important feature of white-collar crime is that the offender has legitimate access to the target or victim of the offense. In all of the white-collar crimes discussed here, the offenders do not have to worry about gaining access to the targets of their offenses. They have a legitimate right to be there and to be involved in the kinds of activities out of which their offenses arise. Physicians, for example, are supposed to treat patients and submit claims to health insurers. Mortgage brokers are supposed to help home buyers apply for loans, and bankers are supposed to make loans. Manufacturers and retail stores are supposed to advertise and promote their products. These are all normal and expected economic activities, and they provide the basis for white-collar crime opportunities. White-collar offenders use their occupational positions to take advantage of these legitimate activities in illegal ways.

As with the superficial appearance of legitimacy, specialized access complicates the control of white-collar crime in a couple of ways. For one, it makes it difficult to use a standard crime-prevention tool—blocking the offender's access to the target. Many conventional crimes can be prevented or reduced simply by making it difficult for offenders to gain access to the crime target. This general strategy has to be modified to prevent white-collar crimes, because there are actually two ways to approach it. First, we can try to block access to the occupational or organizational position that is needed to get access to the target. One way to accomplish this is through occupational licensing standards. Second, procedures can be put in place to block the opportunity to illicitly use the position and resources that are associated with it. This form of blockage is conceptually different than the first type, but both can contribute to reductions in certain types of offending.

Specialized access also complicates control in another way. Whatever mechanisms are put in place to control the illegal activity of white-collar offenders will necessarily affect the legal activities of their law-abiding counterparts. To use health care fraud as an example, one way to try to control it better would be for the Medicare and Medicaid programs to take more time reviewing claims before paying. Doing so would probably help the programs identify fraudulent claims more effectively, but it would also slow down the speed with which honest physicians get reimbursed. Honest physicians, of course, will not be happy with that state of affairs and, as Sparrow (1996, 1998) notes, companies that handle claims are under pressure to process them quickly. Thus, because white-collar crimes are embedded in legitimate activities, the benefits of using any particular control measure always have to be balanced against the costs that its use would impose on the aspirations and creativity of those who are law-abiding (Weisburd et al., 1991, pp. 191–192).

Although offenders have legitimate access to the location or target of their offenses, they are often spatially separated from the actual victims. The company owner who decides not to invest in required safety equipment may never even visit the plant in which workers are injured. The executives who conspire to fix prices never actually deal with the people who have to pay extra. Physicians who cheat Medicaid do so via computer networks and are located hundreds if not thousands of miles away from the program's main office. Spatial separation facilitates the invisibility of white-collar crime and white-collar offenders. It makes it difficult to see the crime, because the crime does not happen at a particular time and place, nor does it involve a visible interaction between an offender and a victim. The separation of offender and victim is yet another feature of white-collar crime that distinguishes it from the stereotypical image of crime.

Problems and Possibilities for Control

In some ways, it is surprising that white-collar crime is such a problem, because the people who commit white-collar offenses are assumed to be law abiding, highly rational, and sensitive to the stigma of criminal sanctions. They are certainly much more afraid of being caught and sent to prison than ordinary street offenders (Braithwaite and Geis, 1982). The possibility of being publicly stigmatized as a criminal should act as a strong deterrent for people who have a stake in conformity and care about their public personae (Geerken and Gove, 1975; Zimring and Hawkins, 1973). Thus, the threat of punishment ought to deter the types of people who commit white-collar crimes. Yet, white-collar crime seems to be ubiquitous. Why is it so hard to control?

Certainly, a major problem is what Shover and Hochstetler (2006) call a lack of "credible oversight". Many of those who commit white-collar crimes simply do not think they will be caught and punished. There are several reasons why this is often a safe assumption on their part. To begin with, the crimes themselves are difficult to detect. Done correctly, many white-collar crimes blend into the ongoing flow of economic transactions. They do not stand out as being unusual or a cause for concern. Hence, the whole criminal justice process may never get started. There are other factors as well that work against the establishment of credible oversight.

One very important factor is the influence that white-collar offenders have over the law itself. Unlike ordinary street criminals, the people and organizations that commit white-collar crimes play an active role in shaping the laws that govern their behavior. Businesses fight whenever state or federal governments attempt to impose stricter controls or harsher penalties on their misconduct. They hire lobbyists and call legislators to do whatever they can to weaken the imposition of controls. For example, the General Motors case of a few years ago exposed a culture of secrecy at the company in which cars with defective ignition switches knowingly were sold to consumers. As the case unfolded, it was unclear how many employees knew about the defect. The CEO, Mary Barra, in her report to Congress, has claimed that only one engineer knew about the problem (Vlasic and Ivory, 2014). Yet, in the face of numerous consumer injuries and death, GM chose not to recall the affected automobiles. Unfortunately, as so often happens in large-scale corporate scandals, GM was never adjudicated in a criminal court. Rather, GM entered into a deferred prosecution agreement with Federal prosecutors in which the company agreed to a settlement and to pay fines in order to avoid going to court (Blau, 2016). This case parallels one in the late 1980s and early 1990s, where the Firestone Tire Company manufactured a defective tire that was used on Ford Explorers. The tire had a disturbing tendency to shred at high speeds, causing rollovers that killed hundreds of people and injured many others (Cullen et al., 2006). When it came to light that both Ford and Firestone knew about the problems with the tire but did not recall them or notify owners of the dangers they faced, the public was outraged. Members of the U.S. Congress were also outraged. Hearings were held, executives were publicly castigated, and a law was proposed that would have made it a crime to manufacture and sell a vehicle with a serious safety defect. However, that law was never enacted because of strenuous lobbying by the U.S. Chamber of Commerce, the tire industry, the auto industry, and other manufacturers (Cullen et al., 2006). This story, unfortunately, is a familiar one. Sutherland, himself, noted that business corporations almost always resist the imposition of criminal law as a control (Sutherland, 1983).

Corporations, of course, are not always successful in their attempts to avoid the criminalization of their conduct. There are many laws against white-collar crimes, but the enforcement of these laws is not as strong as it could be. Because of their hidden nature and complexity, white-collar crimes are difficult to investigate and prosecute (Benson, 2001a; Benson and Cullen, 1998; Braithwaite and Geis, 1982). The cases are expensive and time-consuming to bring to court. Prosecutors must be selective in deciding which cases are worth the effort and which are not (Benson, 2001b; Benson, Cullen, and Maakestad, 1990; Maakestad et al., 1987). Hence, the criminal law is not activated against white-collar crime as often as or as effectively as it could be.

Besides the criminal law, there are other forms of legal control, including regulatory codes and the civil law. As a means of control, regulation has both strengths and weaknesses. Perhaps the most important strength of regulation, and a major difference between it and the criminal law, is that regulations are proactive. They seek primarily to prevent harms from happening in the first place rather than reacting to offenders after they have broken the law, as the criminal justice system is constrained to do. On the downside, regulatory sanctions do not carry the bite and deterrent power of criminal justice sanctions, and the whole regulatory system is subject to even greater influence by corporations than is the criminal justice system. Corporations can influence both the way in which regulations are written and the way in which they are enforced. Nevertheless, because of their proactive nature, regulatory controls accord better with our opportunity perspective than the criminal law. From an opportunity perspective, the most effective way to control any type of crime, including white-collar crime, is not to catch and punish offenders severely. Rather, it is more effective and less costly to modify opportunity structures so as to make the crimes themselves less attractive to potential offenders. Regulations can help do this by making it more difficult for white-collar offenders to conceal their activities or to engage in deception.

The Future of White-Collar Crime

We began this book by noting that what we today call "white-collar crime" is really nothing new. Evidence of it or something very much like it can be found throughout the historical record, dating back to biblical times and probably long before that. Although it would be impossible to prove, we suspect that the use of fraud and deception in transactions arose simultaneously with the invention of trade itself. Indeed, it probably arose even earlier, with the evolution of social interaction among humans, considering that our ancestor primate species engage in deception on a regular basis (Mitchell and Thompson, 1986). Indeed, evolutionary theory would suggest that deception as a technique of both survival and predation must go back nearly to the origin of life itself (Dawkins, 2004), and if the historical record is accurate, it has been recognized as a problem in human groups for a long time. Recall that the crime of embezzlement was well known in ancient Greece, and corrupt politicians and the counsellors of fraud were excoriated in Dante's *Inferno* (Chevigny, 2001).

Although crimes that are based on deception have not been a central focus of research in American criminology, their dangers appear to be recognized by the general public. A surprisingly large body of research shows that the public regards some forms of white-collar crime as equal in seriousness to traditional street crimes and has felt this way for some time (Cullen, Chouhy, and Jonson, 2020; Cullen, Hartman, and Jonson, 2009). We think that the general public is correct about the threat posed by white-collar crime and that it is likely to remain a significant social problem for the future. There are several reasons for our pessimism.

First, because of changes in the nature of work, more people than ever before have access to the "white-collar world of paper fraud" (Weisburd et al., 1991, p. 183). The explosive growth in the use of computers, fax machines, scanners, copiers, the Internet, smart phones, and all sorts of other electronic information-processing technologies in industries and occupations has given more and more people access to the basic tools of white-collar crime. These are the tools that can be used to deceive others and to create an advantageous distortion of reality. Further, even three years after Covid 19 restrictions began to lift, many workers continue to telework. They are thus less subjected to surveillance and guardianship than if they were spending 40 hours a week in the workplace.

Second, another condition that fosters white-collar crime has been the tremendous growth in state largesse that has come in the wake of the welfare state (Shover and Hochstetler, 2006; Weisburd et al., 1991). In Chapter 6, we concentrated on fraud against the Medicare and Medicaid programs because they are the largest and probably most important sites for fraud in government programs. However, it would be naive to think that fraud is limited to federal health care programs. There are hundreds, if not thousands, of other government programs that distribute financial and other types of benefits to millions of people and organizations. For example, millions of college students apply for government-backed educational loans, and as we noted in Chapter 11 some American farmers, those traditional icons of the American way, are not above trying to cheat the government in the Federal Crop Insurance Program. Finally, virtually every time there is a disaster of any kind, a state or the federal government or both step in to provide assistance to the victims. All of these programs depend on paper or electronic applications, and all of them can be targets of fraud and exploitation by individuals and organizations.

The rise in agent–client relationships also has contributed to the expansion of white-collar crime opportunities. Increasingly, we must hire or depend on experts to help us navigate the world. Specialization is the order of the day. We cannot do it all ourselves. We find ourselves having to trust doctors, financial advisors, mechanics, insurance agents, pension fund managers, mortgage brokers, and a host of other professionals (Shapiro, 1990). All of these agent–client relationships carry with them the possibility of the abuse of trust. As more people enter into more agent–client relationships, an increase in abuses of trust is almost guaranteed.

A buzz word of the modern world is globalization. It represents a political, economic, and social reality that increasingly influences our lives in myriad ways. For our purposes, the aspect of globalization that is most important involves the development of a global system of production and exchange. As we are sure you know, the label "Made in America" applies to only a small percentage of the goods—and increasingly even the services—that we use in our daily lives. From automobiles to banking to pharmaceuticals to toys to wrapping paper to technical support for our electronic devices, much of what we buy comes from other countries. From the perspective of our opportunity theory of white-collar crime, this development makes oversight and control more difficult (Grabosky, 2009; Shover and Hochstetler, 2006). All of the laws and regulations that have been developed to control how goods are designed, tested, manufactured, and distributed, and that govern how workers are treated, lose much of their force when companies locate outside our borders. For transnational corporations, opportunities to exploit workers, to pollute the environment, and to manufacture faulty and dangerous products are always available somewhere. Some developing nation is always willing to trade safety for jobs and capital investments. Indeed, as Shover and Hochstetler (2006, p. 105) nicely put it, "lax oversight is a developmental tool for some nations". However, developed countries also suffer from the insidious economic and physical consequences of white-collar crime (for an insightful overview of white-collar crime in Europe, see Lord, Inzelt, Huisman, and Faria, 2022).

However, as Grabosky (2009) points out, globalization is not all bad when it comes to white-collar crime control. International agreements between nation-states on shared regulatory frameworks are now common in many areas of economic and productive activity. Thus, the possibility of "transnational" corporate control in response to transnational corporate crime is no longer just a fantasy, but rather increasingly it is becoming a reality (Braithwaite and Drahos, 2000). This is a positive development.

One of the most disturbing aspects of the Enron case and the others like it in the most recent round of corporate frauds in accounting and the mortgage industry was that the frauds took new forms. The complex accounting schemes created by Enron's executives represented new and creative ways of hiding information (McLean and Elkind, 2004; Swartz, 2003). These new forms of fraud allowed Enron's leaders to avoid detection and the frauds to persist for several years. More recently, the mortgage industry has been the site of new forms of mortgage fraud (Gibeaut, 2007; Vickers and Burke, 2006). In the 1980s, many of the offenses that were committed in the savings and loan debacle represented new forms of bank fraud (Calavita and Pontell, 1990). All of these cases should remind us of an important point regarding white-collar crime: it evolves and changes with the times (Sparrow, 1996).

White-collar crime, of course, is not unique in this regard. Ordinary street criminals change with the times as well (Felson, 2002). Train robbery, safe cracking, and pickpocketing have all but disappeared as crimes, while credit card theft and now identity theft have risen in popularity. Nevertheless, we suspect that white-collar crime techniques evolve more continuously and with greater rapidity than the techniques used for ordinary street crimes. Mainly this happens because white-collar crimes are always based on some type of legitimate economic activity, and the legitimate economic world is constantly changing and evolving. Hence, white-collar offenders always have new material to work with.

Because white-collar crime continuously changes and evolves, we should not be overly optimistic regarding our ability to control or reduce it. Besides its ever-changing nature, there are other reasons why the development of white-collar crime control policies should be approached cautiously. We need to recognize that policy changes always carry risks. They can have unintended consequences and negative side effects (McGarrell and Gibbs,

2014; Weisburd et al., 1991, p. 190). This can be especially true with respect to white-collar crime control, because white-collar offenses are always based in some sort of legitimate economic activity. The policies that we institute to control illegal or harmful activities in an industry may inadvertently make it more difficult and costly to conduct legal activities. So, to put it simply, the problem of white-collar crime control is complex. But we do not wish to leave the reader with the impression that it is, therefore, hopeless and that nothing can be done. By focusing on specific crimes or specific forms of harm, improvements can be and have been made. Being realistic about the limits to our ability to prevent white-collar crime is not the same as being fatalistic. The important thing is to continue to study the problem of white-collar crime and to continually search for new ways to respond to it.

Summary

White-collar crimes are based on deception, and deception can be achieved in a variety of different ways. Deception is facilitated by the special characteristics of white-collar crimes. These characteristics include specialized access to the victim or target of the crime, the superficial appearance of legitimacy, and a spatial separation from the victim or target. These characteristics make the control of white-collar crime different in a number of ways from the control of ordinary street crime. The main difference is that for white-collar crime, the problem is to find the offense rather than the offender. Just because we do not see a crime, we cannot assume therefore that there is no crime (Sparrow, 1998). The problem, as Malcom Sparrow astutely notes, is always larger than you think it is. The key to white-collar crime control depends first on understanding how legitimate economic activities create opportunities to deceive, abuse trust, and conspire against others and then, second, on developing the ability and political will to marshal multiple tools in an arsenal of control.

Because the world of legitimate economic activities evolves continuously, we need to accept the fact that white-collar crime will also continue to evolve. As technology, markets, and industries change and develop, new forms of white-collar crime will arise. Technological and economic change always create new opportunities. This means that our strategies and mechanisms of control must also change in order to keep pace, and we need to view white-collar crime control as an ongoing arms race between offenders and society.

References

Abelson, E. S. (1989). *When Ladies Go a-Thieving: Middle-Class Shoplifters in the Victorian Department Store*. New York: Oxford University Press.

Abidin, C., Lee, J., Barbetta, T., and Miao, W. S. (2021). "Influencers and COVID-19: Reviewing Key Issues in Press Coverage Across Australia, China, Japan, and South Korea." *Media International Australia* 178(1): 114–135.

Acuff, S. F., Tucker, J. A., and Murphy, J. G. (2020). "Behavioral Economics of Substance Use: Understanding and Reducing Harmful Use During the COVID-19 Pandemic." *Experimental and Clinical Psychopharmacology*. Advance online publication. https://doi.org/10.1037/pha0000431.

Adler, F. (1975). *Sisters in Crime: The Rise of the New Female Criminal*. New York: McGraw-Hill.

Akpinar, T. (2010). "The Seaman's Manslaughter Statute." Retrieved July 2, 2014 (www.workboat.com/newsdetail.aspx?id=4294987724).

Albanese, J. S. (1995). *White-Collar Crime in America*. Englewood Cliffs, NJ: Prentice Hall.

Albanese, J. S. (1999). "The Mafia Mystique: Organized Crime." Pp. 265–285 in *Criminology: A Contemporary Handbook* (3rd ed.), edited by J. F. Sheley. Belmont, CA: Wadsworth.

Alexander, C. R., Arlen, J., and Cohen, M. A. (2001). "Evaluating Data on Corporate Sentencing: How Reliable Are the U.S. Sentencing Commission's Data?" *Federal Sentencing Reporter* 13: 108. Available at SSRN (http://ssrn.com/abstract=269356 or http://dx.doi.org/10.2139/ssrn.269356). Revised, April 2001.

Alexander, C. R., and Cohen, M. A. (2015). "The Evolution of Corporate Criminal Settlements: An Empirical Perspective on Non-Prosecution, Deferred Prosecution, and Plea Agreements." *American Criminal Law Review* 52: 537–593.

Anderson, J., and Fingerhut, H. (2021, August 20). COVID anxiety rising amid delta surge, AP-NORC poll finds. *Associated Press*. https://apnews.com/article/lifestyle-business-health-travel-coronavirus-pandemic-27bf20514cd3da917c54bf71a41f2e8e

Anonymous. (2007). "Medicare Fraud Strike Force Convicts Owner of Miami Durable Medical Equipment Company of Defrauding Medicare." Retrieved September 10, 2008 (https://www.justice.gov/archive/opa/pr/2007/June/07_crm_472.html).

Arlen, J. (2012). "The Failure of the Organizational Sentencing Guidelines." *U. Miami L. Rev* 66: 321. Retrieved (http://repository.law.miami.edu/umlr/vol66/iss2/2).

Arlen, J. (2015). "Ex-BP Exec David Rainey Not Guilty of Lying in Oil Spill." *CBS News.com*, June 5. Retrieved April 4, 2017 (www.cbsnews.com/news/ex-bp-exec-david-rainey-not-guilty-of-lying-in-oil-spill/).

Arlen, J. (2016). "Appeals Court to Review Ex Coal CEO Blankenship's Case." *IEN*, October 26. Retrieved July 14, 2017 (www.ien.com/safety/news/20838521/appeals-court-to-review-excoal-ceo-blankenships-case).

Associated Press. (2014). "Turkey Mine Disaster: 2 More Arrested after 301 Killed." Retrieved July 2, 2014 (www.cbc.ca/news/turkey-mine-disaster-2-more-arrests-after-301-killed-1.2647141).

Ayres, I., and Braithwaite, J. (1992). *Responsive Regulation*. Oxford: Oxford University Press.

Babiak, P., and Hare, R. (2006). *Snakes in Suits: When Psychopaths Go to Work*. New York: Regan Books.

Babiak, P., Newmann, C., and Hare, R. (2010). "Corporate Psychopathy: Talking the Walk." *Behavioral Sciences and the Law 28*: 174–193.

Baker, W. E., and Faulkner, R. R. (2003). "Diffusion of Fraud: Intermediate Economic Crime and Investor Dynamics." *Criminology 41*, no. 4: 1173–1206.

Bandura, A. (1999). "Moral Disengagement in the Perpetration of Inhumanities." *Personality and Social Psychology Review 3*: 193–209.

Bandura, A. (2004). "The Role of Selective Moral Disengagement in Terrorism and Counterterrorism." Pp. 121–150 in *Understanding Terrorism: Psychosocial Roots, Consequences, and Interventions*, edited by F. M. Mogahaddam and A. J. Marsella. Washington, DC: American Psychological Association Press.

Barak, G. (2012). *Theft of a Nation*. Lanham, MD: Rowman & Littlefield.

Barak, G. (2022). *Criminology on Trump*. New York: Routledge.

Bardach, E., and Kagan. R. A. (1982). *Going by the Book*. Philadelphia: Temple University Press.

Barlow, H. D. (1993). "From Fiddle Factors to Networks of Collusion: Charting the Waters of Small Business Crime." *Crime, Law and Social Change 20*: 319–337.

Barnett, H. C. (2013). "And Some with a Fountain Pen: Mortgage Fraud, Securitization, and the Sub-prime Bubble." Pp. 104–129 in *How They Got Away with It: White-Collar Criminals and the Financial Meltdown*, edited by S. Will, S. Handelman, and D. C. Brotherton. New York: Columbia University Press.

Barrett, P. M. (2014). "Who Runs Freedom Industries? West Virginia's Chemical Spill Mystery." *Bloomberg Business Week*, February 3. Retrieved September 10, 2014 (www.businessweek.com/articles/2014-01-30/west-virginia-chemical-spill-mystery-who-runs-freedom-industries).

Barstow, D., and Bergman, L. (2003). "At a Texas Foundry, an Indifference to Life." *New York Times*, January 8, 2003, p. A1.

Beccaria, C. (1983). *An Essay on Crimes and Punishment*. Boston: Branden Books.

Benson, M. L. (1984). "The Fall from Grace: Loss of Occupational Status among Convicted White-Collar Offenders." *Criminology 22*: 573–593.

Benson, M. L. (1985). "Denying the Guilty Mind: Accounting for Involvement in a White-Collar Crime." *Criminology 23*: 583–608.

Benson, M. L. (2001a). "Investigating Corporate Crime: Local Responses to Fraud and Environmental Offenses." *Western State University Law Review 28*: 87–116.

Benson, M. L. (2001b). "Prosecuting Corporate Crime: Problems and Constraints." Pp. 381–391 in *Crimes of Privilege: Readings in White-Collar Crime*, edited by N. Shover and J. P. Wright. New York: Oxford University Press.

Benson, M. L. (2012). "Evolutionary Ecology, Fraud, and the Global Financial Crisis." Pp. 299–306 in *Contemporary Issues in Criminological Theory and Research: The Role of Social Institutions*, edited by Richard Rosenfeld, Karen Quinet, and Crystal Garcia. Belmont, CA: Wadsworth.

Benson, M. L. (2016). "Developmental Perspectives on White-Collar Crime." Pp. 253–271 in *The Oxford Handbook of White-Collar Crime*, edited by S. V. Slyke, M. L. Benson, and F. T. Cullen. New York: Oxford University Press.

Benson, M. L. (2021). "Theoretical and Empirical Advances in the Study and Control of White-Collar Offenders." *Journal of Justice Evaluation 4 (1)*: 1–20.

Benson, M. L., and Cullen, F. T. (1988). "The Special Sensitivity of White-Collar Offenders to Prison: A Critique and a Research Agenda." *Journal of Criminal Justice 16*: 207–215.

Benson, M. L., and Cullen, F. T. (1998). *Combating Corporate Crime: Local Prosecutors at Work*. Boston: Northeastern University Press.

Benson, M. L., and Cullen, F. T. (2018). "Subterranean Values, Deception, and White-Collar Crime." Pp. 99–124 in *Delinquency and Drift Revisited: The Criminology of David Matza and Beyond: Advances in Criminological Theory*, edited by T. G. Blomberg, F. T. Cullen, C. Carlsson, and C. L. Jonson.

Benson, M. L., Cullen, F. T., and Maakestad, W. J. (1990). "Local Prosecutors and Corporate Crime." *Crime & Delinquency 36*: 356–372.

Benson, M. L. and Kennedy, J. P. (2018). "Forgotten Offenders: Race, White-Collar Crime and the Black Church." Chapter 10 in *Building a Black Criminology, Volume 24: Race, Theory and Crime*, edited by J. D. Unnever, S. L. Gabbidon, and C. Chouhy

Benson, M. L., Feldmeyer, B., Gabbidon, S., and Chio, H. L. (2020). "Race, Ethnicity, and Social Change: The Democratization of Middle-Class Crime." *Criminology 59*: 10–41.

Benson, M. L., Kennedy, J., and Logan, M. (2016). "White-Collar and Corporate Crime." Pp. 92–110 in *The Handbook of Measurement Issues in Criminology and Criminal Justice*, edited by B. M. Huebner and T. S. Bynum. Hoboken, NJ: John Wiley & Sons.

Benson, M. L., and Kerley, K. R. (2000). "Life Course Theory and White-Collar Crime." Pp. 121–136 in *Contemporary Issues in Crime and Criminal Justice: Essays in Honor of Gilbert Geis*, edited by H. N. Pontell and D. Shichor. Upper Saddle River, NJ: Prentice Hall.

Benson, M. L., Maakestad, W. J., Cullen, F. T., and Geis, G. (1998). "District Attorneys and Corporate Crime: Surveying the Prosecutorial Gatekeepers." *Criminology 26*: 505–518.

Benson, M. L., and Madensen, T. D. (2007). "Situational Crime Prevention and White-Collar Crime." Pp. 609–626 in *International Handbook of White-Collar and Corporate Crime*, edited by H. N. Pontell and G. Geis. New York: Springer.

Benson, M. L., Madensen, T. D., and Eck, J. E. (2009). "White-Collar Crime from an Opportunity Perspective." Pp. 175–194 in *The Criminology of White-Collar Crime*, edited by S. S. Simpson and D. Weisburd. New York: Springer.

Benson, M. L., and Manchak, S. L. (2014). "The Psychology of White-Collar Crime," in *Oxford Handbooks Online in Criminology and Criminal Justice*. New York: Oxford University Press. Retrieved October 10, 2017 (http://www.oxfordhandbooks.com/view/10.1093/oxfordhb/9780199935383.001.0001/oxfordhb-9780199935383-e-008).

Benson, M. L., and Moore, E. (1992). "Are White-Collar and Common Offenders the Same? An Empirical and Theoretical Critique of a Recently Proposed General Theory of Crime." *Journal of Research in Crime and Delinquency 29*: 251–272.

Benson, M. L., Van Slyke, S., and Cullen, F. T. (2016). "Core Themes in the Study of White-Collar Crime." Pp. 1–21 in *The Oxford Handbook of White-Collar Crime*, edited by S. Van Slyke, M. L. Benson, and F. T. Cullen. New York: Oxford University Press.

Benson, M. L., and Walker, E. (1988). "Sentencing the White-Collar Offender." *American Sociological Review 53*: 294–302.

Bentham, J. (1948). *An Introduction to the Principles of Morals and Legislation*. New York: Macmillan.

Berman, J. (2015). "Soon Not Even 1 Percent of Fortune 500 Companies Will Have Black CEOs." *Huffington Post*, February 2. Retrieved June 20, 2017 (www.huffingtonpost.com/2015/01/29/black-ceos-fortune-500_n_6572074.html).

Bero, L. A. (2005). "Tobacco Industry Manipulation of Scientific Research." *Public Health Reports 120*: 200–208.

Bertrams, A., Englert, C., and Dickhäuser, O. (2010). "Self-control Strength in the Relation Between Trait Test Anxiety and State Anxiety." *Journal of Research in Personality 44*(6): 738–741.

Bidgood, J., and Tavernise, S. (2014). "Pharmacy Executives Face Murder Charges in Meningitis Deaths." *New York Times*, December 17, 2014. Retrieved May 4, 2017 (www.nytimes.com/2014/12/18/us/new-england-compounding-center-steroid-meningitis-arrests.html).

Birnbaum, S. E., and Savitz, J. (2014). "The Deepwater Horizon Threat." *New York Times*. Retrieved July 2, 2014 (www.nytimes.com/2014/04/17/opinion/the-deepwater-horizon-threat.html).

Bisschop, L. (2015). "Facilitators of Environmental Crime: Corporations and Governments in the Port of Antwerp." Pp. 246–259 in *The Routledge Handbook of White-Collar and Corporate Crime in Europe*, edited by J. van Erp, W. Huisman, and G. Vande Walle. New York: Routledge.

Black, D. (1983). "Crime as Social Control." *American Sociological Review 48*: 34.

Black, W. (2010). "Echo Epidemics: Control Frauds Generate 'White-Collar Street Crime' waves." *Criminology & Public Policy 9 (3)*: 613–618.

Blau, M. (2016). "No Accident: Inside GM's Deadly Ignition Switch Scandal." *Atlanta Magazine*, January. Retrieved July 10, 2017 (www.atlantamagazine.com/great-reads/no-accident-inside-gms-deadly-ignition-switch-scandal/).

Blokland, A., Kluin, M., and Huisman, W. (2021). "Life-Course Criminology and Corporate Offending." Pp. 684–704 in *The Cambridge Handbook of Compliance,* edited by B. Van Rooij and D. D. Sokol. Cambridge: Cambridge University Press.

Blumstein, A., Cohen, J., Roth, J. A., and Visher, C. A. (eds). (1986). *Criminal Careers and Career Criminals*, Vol. 1. Washington, DC: National Academy Press.

Board, B. J., and Fritzon, K. (2005). "Disordered Personalities at Work." *Psychology, Crime & Law 11*: 17–32.

Boddy, C. R. (2011). "The Corporate Psychopaths Theory of the Global Financial Crisis." *Journal of Business Ethics 102*: 255–259.

Bonta, J., and Andrews, D. A. (2023). *The Psychology of Criminal Conduct* (7th ed.) New York: Routledge.

Bossler, A. M. (2019). "Perceived Formal and Informal Sanctions on the Willingness to Commit Cyber Attacks against Domestic and Foreign Targets." *Journal of Crime and Justice 42*(5): 599–615.

Boudette, N. E., and Fuller, A. (2014). "General Motors Recall: A Burden of Proof." *Wall Street Journal*. Retrieved July 2, 2014 (http://online.wsj.com/articles/general-motors-recall-a-burden-of-proof-1403478781).

Bowyer, J. B. (1982). *Cheating: Deception in War & Magic, Games & Sports, Sex & Religion, Business & Con Games, Politics & Espionage, Art & Science*. New York: St. Martin's Press.

Box, S. (1983). *Power, Crime, and Mystification*. London: Tavistock Publications.

Braithwaite, J. (1981). "The Myth of Social Class and Criminality Reconsidered." *American Sociological Review 46*: 36–57.

Braithwaite, J. (1984). *Corporate Crime in the Pharmaceutical Industry*. London: Routledge & Kegan Paul.

Braithwaite, J. (1985). "White Collar Crime." *Annual Review of Sociology 11*: 1–25.

Braithwaite, J. (1989). *Crime, Shame, and Reintegration*. Cambridge: Cambridge University Press.

Braithwaite, J. (1989). "Criminological Theory and Organizational Crime." *Justice Quarterly 6*: 333–358.

Braithwaite, J. (2008). *Regulatory capitalism: How it works, ideas for making it work better*. Cheltenham: Edward Elgar Publishing.

Braithwaite, J. (2016). "In Search of Donald Campbell: Mix and Multimethods." *Criminology & Public Policy 15*: 417–437.

Braithwaite, J., and Drahos, P. (2000). *Global Business Regulation*. Cambridge: Cambridge University Press.

Braithwaite, J., and Fisse, B. (1990). "On the Plausibility of Corporate Crime Control." *Advances in Criminological Theory 2*: 15–37.

Braithwaite, J., and Geis, G. (1982). "On Theory and Action for Corporate Crime Control." *Crime & Delinquency 28*: 292–314.

Braithwaite, J., and Makkai, T. (1991). "Testing an Expected Utility Model of Corporate Deterrence." *Law & Society Review 25*(1): 7–40. https://doi.org/10.2307/3053888

Branham, V. C., and Kutash, S. B. (1949). *Encyclopedia of Criminology*. New York: Philosophical Library.

Brickey, K. (2008). Major Corporate Fraud Prosecutions, March 2002–July 2007. Private data used with permission.

Brodeur, P. (1985). *Outrageous Misconduct*. New York: Pantheon.

Brook, Y., and Epstein, A. (2002). "Paralyzing America's Producers: The Government's Crackdown on American Businessmen Is Devastating Our Economy." *Capitalism Magazine*. Retrieved December 20, 2007 (https://www.capitalismmagazine.com/2002/10/paralyzing-americas-producers-the-governments-crackdown-on-american-businessmen-is-devastating-our-economy/).

Brooks, C., Parr, L., Smith, J. M., Buchanan, D., Snioch, D., and Hebishy, E. (2021). A Review of Food Fraud and Food Authenticity across the Food Supply Chain, with an Examination of the Impact of the COVID-19 Pandemic and Brexit on Food Industry. *Food Control 130*, 108171.

Brown, P., and Mikkelsen E. J. (1990). *No Safe Place: Toxic Waste, Leukemia, and Community Action*. Berkeley, CA: University of California Press.

Buil-Gil, D., and Zeng, Y. (2022). "Meeting You Was a Fake: Investigating the Increase in Romance Fraud during COVID-19". *Journal of Financial Crime* 29(2): 460–475.

Bukh, A. (2012). "Justice Department Defends the Role of Deferred-Prosecution Agreements in Corporate Crime Enforcement". *NY Criminal Defense*. Retrieved November 8th, 2023 (https://nyccriminallawyer.com/justice-department-defends-the-role-of-deferred-prosecution-agreements-in-corporate-crime-enforcement/)

Bullard, R. (1990). *Dumping in Dixie: Race, Class, and Environmental Quality*. Boulder, CO: Westview Press.

Bullard, R. (2000). "Anatomy of Environmental Racism." Pp. 223–231 in *Environmental Discourse and Practice: A Reader*, edited by L. M. Benton and J. R. Short. Oxford: Blackwell Publishers.

Burns, R. G., and Lynch, M. J. (2004). *Environmental Crime: A Sourcebook*. New York: LFB Scholarly Publishers.

Calavita, K. (1983). "The Demise of the Occupational Safety and Health Administration: A Case Study in Symbolic Interaction." *Social Problems* 30: 437–448.

Calavita, K., and Pontell, H. N. (1990). "'Heads I Win, Tails You Lose': Deregulation, Crime, and Crisis in the Savings and Loan Industry." *Crime & Delinquency* 36: 309–341.

Calem, P. S., Herschaff, J. E., and Wachter, S. M. (2004). "Neighborhood Patterns of Subprime Lending: Evidence from Disparate Cities." *Housing Policy Debate* 15(3): 603–622.

Calhoun, C., and Hiller, H. (1992). "Insidious Injuries: The Case of Johns-Manville and Asbestos Exposure." Pp. 259–284 in *Corporate and Governmental Deviance: Problems of Organizational Behavior in Contemporary Society* (4th ed.), edited by M. D. Ermann and R. J. Lundman. New York: Oxford University Press.

Carson, R. (1962). *Silent Spring*. Boston: Houghton Mifflin.

Catalyst (2006). "2005 Catalyst Census of Women Corporate Officers and Top Earners of the Fortune 500." Retrieved September 5, 2014 (https://www.catalyst.org/research/2005-catalyst-census-of-women-corporate-officers-and-top-earners-of-the-fortune-500/).

Catalyst (2020). *Women in Management (Quick Take)* (August 11). Retrieved October 27, 2021. (https://www.catalyst.org/research/women-in-management/).

Catalyst (2021). *Historical List of Women CEOs of the Fortune Lists: 1972–2021* (June 2021). Retrieved October 27, 2021. (https://www.catalyst.org/research/historical-list-of-women-ceos-of-the-fortune-lists-1972-2021/).

Catan, T., Trachtenberg, J. A., and Bray, C. (2012). "U.S. Alleges E-Book Scheme." *Wall Street Journal*. Retrieved May 16, 2014 (http://online.wsj.com/news/articles/SB10001424052702304444604577337573054615152).

CBS. (2014, December 5). Fake UGG boots, North Face jackets seized in dollar store raid. Retrieved from: https://www.cbsnews.com/detroit/news/fake-ugg-boots-northface-jackets-seized-in-dollar-store-raid/

Center for Global Development. (2016). "CGD Europe Seminar: Unearthing Toxic Waste Dumping in the Horn of Africa, June 21." Retrieved April 4, 2017 (www.cgdev.org/event/cgd-europe-seminar-unearthing-toxic-waste-dumping-horn-africa).

Centers for Medicare & Medicaid Services. (2021). "CMS Releases Latest Enrollment Figures for Medicare, Medicaid, and Children's Health Insurance Program (CHIP)." https://www.cms.gov/newsroom/news-alert/cms-releases-latest-enrollment-figures-medicare-medicaid-and-childrens-health-insurance-program-chip

Centers for Medicare & Medicaid Services. (2023). "National Health Care Expenditure Data." https://www.cms.gov/data-research/statistics-trends-and-reports/national-health-expenditure-data/historical. Retrieved March 14, 2022.

Chan, F., and Gibbs, C. (2022). "When Guardians Become Offenders: Understanding Guardian Capability through the Lens of Corporate Crime." *Criminology* 60: 321–341.

Chavda, V. P., Sonak, S. S., Munshi, N. K., and Dhamade, P. N. (2022). "Pseudoscience and Fraudulent Products for COVID-19 Management." *Environmental Science and Pollution Research. Online first* – DOI: 10.1007/s11356-022-21967-4.

Checker, M. (2005). *Polluted Promises: Environmental Racism and the Search for Justice in a Southern Town.* New York: New York University Press.

Chesney-Lind, M. (1989). "Girls' Crime and Woman's Place: Toward a Feminist Model of Female Delinquency." *Crime & Delinquency 35*: 10–27.

Chevigny, P. G. (2001). "From Betrayal to Violence: Dante's Inferno and the Social Construction of Crime." *Law & Social Inquiry 26*: 787–818.

Chibnall, S., and Saunders, P. (1977). "Worlds Apart: Notes on the Social Reality of Corruption." *British Journal of Sociology 28*: 138–154.

Christensen, R. (1967). *Projected Percentage of U.S. Population with Criminal Arrest and Conviction Records.* Washington, DC: U.S. Government Printing Office.

Clarke, R. V. (1983). "Situational Crime Prevention: Its Theoretical Basis and Practical Scope." Pp. 225–256 in *Crime and Justice: An Annual Review*, edited by Michael Tonry and Norval Morris. Chicago: University of Chicago Press.

Cleckley, H. M. (1982). *The Mask of Sanity.* New York: New American Library.

Cleveland, C. J. (2013). "Deepwater Horizon Oil Spill." Retrieved July 2, 2014 (www.eoearth.org/view/article/161185/).

Click On Detroit. (2014). "GM CEO Mary Barra Testifies Again on Capitol Hill about Ignition Recall." Retrieved July 2, 2014 (www.clickondetroit.com/news/gm-ceo-mary-barra-to-testify-again-on-capitol-hill-about-ignition-recall/26532480).

Clinard, M. B., and Yeager, P. C. (1980). *Corporate Crime.* New York: Free Press.

Clinard, M. B., and Yeager, P. C. (2006). *Corporate Crime.* New Brunswick, NJ: Transaction.

Coffee, J. C., Jr. (2002). "Understanding Enron: It's about the Gatekeepers, Stupid." *The Business Lawyer 57*: 1–2.

Coffee, J. C., Jr. (2020). *Corporate Crime and Punishment: The Crisis of Underenforcement.* Oakland, CA: Berrett-Koehler.

Cohen, L. E., and Felson, M. (1979). "Social Change and Crime Rate Trends: A Routine Activity Approach." *American Sociological Review 44*: 588–608.

Cohen, M. A. (1998). "Sentencing the Environmental Criminal." Pp. 229–252 in *Environmental Crime: Enforcement, Policy, and Social Responsibility*, edited by M. Cliffords and T. E. Edwards. Gaithersburg, MD: Aspen.

Cohen, M. A. (2000). "Measuring the Costs and Benefits of Crime and Justice." Pp. 263–316 in *Measurement and Analysis of Crime and Justice*, Volume 4. Washington, DC: National Institute of Justice.

Coleman, J. S. (1982). *The Asymmetric Society.* Syracuse, NY: Syracuse University Press.

Coleman, J. W. (1987). "Toward an Integrated Theory of White-Collar Crime." *American Journal of Sociology 93*: 406–439.

Coleman, J. W. (1989). *The Criminal Elite.* New York: St. Martin's Press.

Collins, R. (1979). *The Credential Society: An Historical Sociology of Education and Stratification.* New York: Academic Press.

Collins, S.M. (1997). *Black Corporate Executives: The Making and Breaking of a Black Middle Class.* Philadelphia, PA: Temple University Press.

Comerton-Forde, C., and Putnins, T. J. (2014). "Stock Price Manipulation: Prevalence and Determinants." *Review of Finance 18*: 23–66.

Commoner, B. (1971). *The Closing Circle: Nature, Man, and Technology.* New York: Knopf.

Congressional Research Service. (2014). "Deepwater Horizon Oil Spill: Recent Activities and Ongoing Developments." Retrieved September 12, 2014 (http://fas.org/sgp/crs/misc/R42942.pdf).

Conklin, J. E. (1977). *Illegal but Not Criminal: Business Crime in America.* Englewood Cliffs, NJ: Prentice Hall.

Corkery, M. (2016). "Trump Expected to Seek Deep Cuts in Business Regulations." *New York Times*. Retrieved January 18, 2017 (www.nytimes.com/2016/11/10/business/dealbook/trump-expected-to-seek-deep-cuts-in-business-regulations.html).

Cornish, D. B., and Clarke, R. V. (1986). "Opportunities, Precipitators, and Criminal Decisions: A Reply to Wortley's Critique of Situational Crime Prevention." *Crime Prevention Studies 16*: 41–96.

Cressey, D. (1953). *Other People's Money*. New York: The Free Press.

Cressey, D. (1989). "The Poverty of Theory in Corporate Crime Research." Pp. 31–55 in *Advances in Criminological Theory*, edited by W. S. Laufer and F. Adler. New Brunswick, NJ: Transaction.

Croall, H. (1989). "Who Is the White-Collar Criminal?" *British Journal of Criminology 29*: 157–174.

Croall, H. (2001). *Understanding White Collar Crime*. Buckingham, UK: Open University Press.

Croall, H. (2009). "White-Collar Crime, Consumers, and Victimization." *Crime, Law and Social Change 51*: 127–146.

Cross, C. (2022). "Theorising the Impact of COVID-19 on the Fraud Victimisation of Older Persons." *The Journal of Adult Protection 23*(2): 98–110.

Cullen, F. T., Agnew, R., and Wilcox, P. (2014). "Critical Criminology: Power Peace and Crime." Pp. 284–294 in *Criminological Theory: Past to Present* (5th ed.), edited by F. T. Cullen, R. Agnew, and P. Wilcox. New York: Oxford University Press.

Cullen, F. T., Cavender, G., Maakestad, W. J., and Benson, M. L. (2006). *Corporate Crime under Attack: The Fight to Criminalize Business Violence* (2nd ed.). New York: Routledge.

Cullen, F. T., Chouhy, C., and Jonson, C. L. (2020). "Public Opinion about White-Collar Crime." Pp. 211–228 in *The Handbook of White-Collar Crime*, edited by M. L. Rorie. Hoboken, NJ: John Wiley & Sons.

Cullen, F. T., Hartman, J. L., and Jonson, C. L. (2009). "Bad Guys: Why the Public Supports Punishing White-Collar Offenders." *Crime, Law, and Social Change 51*: 31–44.

Cumming, D., Leung, T. Y., and Rui, O. (2015). "Gender Diversity and Securities Fraud." *Academy of Management Journal 58*(5): 1572–1593.

Daly, K. (1989). "Gender and Varieties of White-Collar Crime." *Criminology 27*: 769–794.

Daly, K. (1994). *Gender, Crime, and Punishment*. New Haven, CT: Yale University Press.

Davidoff, S. M. (2013). "Why So Few Women Reach the Executive Rank." *NY Times.com*. Retrieved July 2, 2014 (http://dealbook.nytimes.com/2013/04/02/why-so-few-women-reach-the-executive-rank/).

Davila, M. A. (2005). *After the Flood: Fraud Among the Elderly after Natural Disasters*. Huntsville, TX: Sam Houston State University.

Davila, M. A., Marquart, J. W., and Mullings, J. L. (2005). "Beyond Mother Nature: Contractor Fraud in the Wake of Natural Disasters." *Deviant Behavior, 26*(3), 271–293.

Dawkins, R. (2004). *The Ancestor's Tale: A Pilgrimage to the Dawn of Evolution*. Boston: Houghton Mifflin.

Dilanian, K., Ramgopal, K., and Atkins, C. (2021, August 15). "Easy Money": How International Scam Artists Pulled Off an Epic Theft of COVID Benefits. *NBC News*. https://www.nbcnews.com/news/us-news/easy-money-how-international-scam-artists-pulled-epic-theft-covid-n1276789

Dowie, M. (1987). "Pinto Madness." Pp. 13–29 in *Corporate Violence*, edited by Stuart L. Hills. Totowa, NJ: Rowman & Littlefield.

Downes, J., and Goodman, J. E. (2006). *Dictionary of Finance and Investment Terms* (7th ed.). Hauppauge, NY: Barron's.

Durkheim, E. (1951). *Suicide, a Study in Sociology*. New York: Free Press.

Dutton, K. (2012). *The Wisdom of Psychopaths: What Saints, Spies, and Serial Killers Can Teach Us about Success*. New York: Scientific American/Farrar, Straus, and Giroux.

Dyck, A., Morse, A., and Zingales, L. (2013). "How Pervasive is Corporate Fraud?" *Rotman School of Management Working Paper No. 2222608*. Retrieved July 2, 2014 (http://papers.ssrn.com/sol3/papers.cfm?abstract_id=2222608).

Dye, J. (2016). "GM Not Protected from Ignition Switch Claims: US Appeals Court." *Reuters*, July 13. Retrieved May 2, 2017 (www.reuters.com/article/us-gm-ruling-idUSKCN0ZT1RR).

Edelhertz, H. (1970). *The Nature, Impact and Prosecution of White-Collar Crime*. Washington, DC: U.S. Department of Justice.

Eichenwald, K. (2015). "Killer Pharmacy: Inside a Medical Mass Murder Case." *Newsweek*, April 16. Retrieved May 4 (www.newsweek.com/2015/04/24/inside-one-most-murderous-corporate-crimes-us-history-322665.html).

Eilperin, J., Mooney, C., and Mufson, S. (2017). "New EPA Documents Reveal Even Deeper Proposed Cuts to Staff and Programs." *Washington Post*, March 31. Retrieved April 5, 2017 (www.wash-ingtonpost.com/news/energy-environment/wp/2017/03/31/new-epa-documents-reveal-even-deeper-proposed-cuts-to-staff-and-programs/?utm_term=.773186db7cdc).

Elder, G. H. (1996). "Human Lives in Changing Societies: Life-Course and Developmental Insights." Pp. 31–62 in *Developmental Science*, edited by R. B. Cairns, G. H. Elder, and E.J. Costello. New York: Cambridge University Press.

Engdahl, O. (2011). "White Collar Crime and Informal Social Control: The Case of 'Crisis Responders' in the Swedish Banking and Finance Sector." *Sociology Mind* 1: 81–89.

Enrich, D. (2017). *The Spider Network: The Wild Story of a Math Genius, a Gang of Backstabbing Bankers, and One of the Greatest Scams in Financial History*. New York: Custom House.

Epstein, J., and Hammett, T. M. (1995). *Law Enforcement Responses to Environmental Crime*. Washington, DC: National Institute of Justice.

Epstein, R. A. (2006). "The Deferred Prosecution Racket." *Wall Street Journal*, November 28. Retrieved July 21, 2017 (www.wsj.com/articles/SB116468395737834160).

Ermann, M. D., and Lundman, R. J. (eds). (1978). *Corporate and Governmental Deviance: Problems of Organizational Behavior in Contemporary Society*. New York: Oxford University Press.

Eurostat (2022, June 27). *EU Small and Medium-sized Enterprises: An Overview*. Retrieved from: https://ec.europa.eu/eurostat/web/products-eurostat-news/-/edn-20220627-1

Faber, J. (2013). "Racial Dynamics of Subprime Mortgage Lending at the Peak." *Housing Policy Debate* 23(2): 328–349.

Farrall, S., and Karstedt, S. (2020). *Respectable Citizens – Shady Practices: The Economic Morality of the Middle Classes*. Oxford: Oxford University Press.

Felson, M. (2002). *Crime and Everyday Life*. Thousand Oaks, CA: Sage.

Felson, R. B. (1996). "Big People Hit Little People: Sex Differences in Physical Power and Interpersonal Violence." *Criminology* 34: 433–452.

Financial Crimes Enforcement Network. (2006). "Mortgage Loan Fraud: An Industry Assessment Based upon Suspicious Activity Report Analysis." November 2006. Retrieved September 12, 2014 (file:///C:/Users/bensonm/Documents/Current%20Projects/WCC%202nd%20Edition/2nd%20Edition/Articles/FINCEN%20mortgage_fraud112006.pdf).

Fishman, S. (2010). "Bernie Madoff, Free at Last." *New York Magazine*. Retrieved January 11, 2017 (http://nymag.com/news/crimelaw/66468/).

Fisk, M. C., Brubaker Calkins, L., and Feeley, J. (2014). "BP Found Grossly Negligent in 2010 Gulf of Mexico Spill" *Bloomberg*. Retrieved November 8, 2023 (https://www.bloomberg.com/news/articles/2014-09-04/bp-found-grossly-negligent-in-2010-gulf-of-mexico-spill#xj4y7vzkg)

Fisse, B., and Braithwaite, J. (1983). *The Impact of Publicity on Corporate Offenders*. Albany: State University of New York Press.

Fisse, B., and Braithwaite, J. (1993). *Corporations, Crime, and Accountability*. Cambridge: Cambridge University Press.

Fontaine, D. C. (1993). *Examining the corporate environment towards women managers: A comparative study of perceptions between black and white women* (Order No. 9414722). Available from ProQuest Dissertations & Theses Global. (304098563). Retrieved from https://www.proquest.com/dissertations-theses/examining-corporate-environment-towards-women/docview/304098563/se-2

Forst, B., and Rhodes, W. (1987). *Sentencing in Eight United States District Courts, 1973–1978*. Washington, D.C.: U.S. Department of Justice

Frank, N. (1985). *Crimes against Health and Safety*. New York: Harrow and Heston.

Frank, N. (1993). "Maiming and Killing: Occupational Health Crimes." *Annals 525*: 107–118.

Frank, N., and Lombness, M. (1988). *Controlling Corporate Illegality: The Regulatory Justice System*. Cincinnati: Anderson.

Frenkel, S. (2021, July 24). "The Most Influential Spreader of Coronavirus Misinformation Online." *The New York Times*. https://www.nytimes.com/2021/07/24/technology/joseph-mercola-coronavirus-misinformation-online.html

Friedman, H. H. (1980). "Talmudic Business Ethics: An Historical Perspective." *Akron Business and Economic Review 11*: 45–49.

Friedrichs, D. O. (2002). "Occupational Crime, Occupational Deviance, and Workplace Crime: Sorting Out the Difference." *Criminal Justice 2*: 243–256.

Friedrichs, D. O. (2009). "White-Collar Crime and Critical Criminology: Convergence and Divergence." Pp. 27–39 in *Cutting the Edge: Current Perspectives in Radical/Critical Criminology and Criminal Justice*, edited by J. I. Ross. New Brunswick, NJ: Transaction.

Friedrichs, D. O. (2010). *Trusted Criminals: White Collar Crime in Contemporary Society* (4th ed). Belmont, CA: Thomson Wadsworth.

Gallup. (2022). *Coronavirus Pandemic*. https://news.gallup.com/poll/308222/coronavirus-pandemic.aspx

Gao, Y., and Raine, A. (2010). "Successful and Unsuccessful Psychopaths: A Neurobiological Model." *Behavioral Sciences and Law 28*: 194–210.

Garner, J. (2007). "Understanding the Nature and Context of Local Environmental Enforcement: What We Learned from Interviews with Inspectors." Pp. 9–24 in *Why Do Corporations Obey Environmental Law?* edited by S. S. Simpson, J. Garner, and C. Gibbs. Washington, DC: National Institute of Justice, U.S. Department of Justice.

Garrett, B. (2014). *Too Big to Jail: How Prosecutors Compromise with Corporations*. Cambridge, MA: The Belknap Press of Harvard University Press.

Gassman-Pines, A. (2015). "Effects of Mexican immigrant parents' daily workplace discrimination on child behavior and family functioning". *Child Development, 86(4)*: 1175–1190.

Geerken, M. R., and Gove, W. R. (1975). "Deterrence: Some Theoretical Considerations." *Law & Society Review 9*: 497–514.

Geis, G. (1977). "The Heavy Electrical Equipment Antitrust Cases of 1961." Pp. 117–132 in *White-Collar Crime: Offenses in Business, Politics, and the Professions*, edited by G. Geis and R. F. Meier. New York: The Free Press.

Geis, G. (1988). "From Deuteronomy to Deniability: A Historical Perlustration on White-Collar Crime." *Justice Quarterly 5*: 7–32.

Geis, G. (1996). "Definition in White-Collar Crime Scholarship: Sometimes It Can Matter." Pp. 159–211 in *Definitional Dilemma: Can and Should There be a Universal Definition of White-Collar Crime? Proceedings of the Academic Workshop*, edited by J. Helmkamp, R. Ball, and K. Townsend. Morgantown, WV: National White-Collar Crime Center.

Geis, G. (2000). "On the Absence of Self-Control as the Basis for a General Theory of Crime: A Critique." *Theoretical Criminology 4*: 35–53.

Geis, G. (2016). "The Roots and Variant Definitions of the Concept of 'White-Collar Crime'." Pp. 25–38 in *The Oxford Handbook of White-Collar Crime*, edited by S. Van Slyke, M. L. Benson, and F. T. Cullen. New York: Oxford University Press.

Geis, G., and Goff, C. (1983). "Introduction" to *White-Collar Crime: The Uncut Version*, Pp. ix–xxxiii, edited by E. H. Sutherland. New Haven, CT: Yale University Press.

Gerber, J., and Weeks, S. L. (1992). "Women as Victims of Corporate Crime: A Call for Research on a Neglected Topic." *Deviant Behavior 13*: 325–347.

Gibbs, C., Gore, M. L., McGarrell, E. F., and Rivers, L., III. (2010). "Introducing Conservation Criminology: Towards Interdisciplinary Scholarship on Environmental Crimes and Risks." *British Journal of Criminology 50*: 124–144.

Gibeaut, J. (2007). "Mortgage Fraud Mess." *ABA Journal 93*: 50–56.

Gilligan, C. (1993). *In a Different Voice: Psychological Theory and Women's Development*. Cambridge, MA: Harvard University Press.

Gioia, D. A. (1992). "Pinto Fires and Personal Ethics: A Script Analysis of Missed Opportunities." *Journal of Business Ethics 11*: 379–389.

Glass Ceiling Commission. (1995). *Good for Business: Making Full Use of the Nation's Human Capital: A Fact-Finding Report of the Federal Glass Ceiling Commission.* Washington, DC: U.S. Government Printing Office.

Gold, S. (1989). "Occidental Petroleum: Politics, Pollution, and Profit." *Multinational Monitor.* Retrieved September 11, 2008 (http://multinationalmonitor.org/hyper/issues/1989/07/gold.html).

Gorman, E. H., and Kmec, J. A. (2009). "Hierarchical Rank and Women's Organizational Mobility: Glass Ceilings in Corporate Law Firms." *American Journal of Sociology 114*: 1428–1474.

Gottfredson, M. R., and Hirschi, T. (1990). *A General Theory of Crime.* Stanford, CA: Stanford University Press.

Grabosky, P. N. (2009). "Globalization and White-Collar Crime." Pp. 129–151 in *The Criminology of White-Collar Crime*, edited by S. S. Simpson and D. Weisburd. New York: Springer.

Grabosky, P. N. (2012). "Beyond Responsive Regulation: The Expanding Role of Non-State Actors in the Regulatory Process." *Regulation & Governance 7*: 114–123.

Grabosky, P. N., Smith, R. G., and Dempsey, G. (2001). *Electronic Theft: Unlawful Acquisition in Cyberspace.* Cambridge: Cambridge University Press.

Gross, E. (1978). "Organizational Crime: A Theoretical Perspective." Pp. 55–85 in *Studies in Symbolic Interaction*, edited by N. Denzin. Greenwich, CT: JAI Press.

Gross, E. (1980). "Organization Structure and Organizational Crime." Pp. 52–76 in *White-Collar Crime: Theory and Research*, edited by G. Geis and E. Stotland. Beverly Hills, CA: Sage.

Gunningham, N., Grabosky, P., and Sinclair, D. (1998). *Smart Regulation: Designing Environmental Policy.* Oxford: Clarendon Press.

Hagan, J. L. (1994). *Crime and Disrepute.* Thousand Oaks, CA: Pine Forge Press.

Hagan, J. L., and Nagel, I. H. (1982). "White-Collar Crime, White-Collar Time: The Sentencing of White-Collar Offenders in the Southern District of New York." *American Criminal Law Review 20*: 259–289.

Hagan, J. L., Nagel (Bernstein), I. H., and Albonetti, C. (1980). "The Differential Sentencing of White-Collar Offenders in Ten Federal District Courts." *American Sociological Review 45*: 802–820.

Hamama, R., Ronen, T., and Feigin, R. (2000). "Self-control, Anxiety, and Loneliness in Siblings of Children with Cancer." *Social Work in Health Care*, 31(1): 63–83.

Hammett, T. M., and Epstein, J. (1993). *Local Prosecution of Environmental Crime.* Washington, DC: U.S. National Institute of Justice.

Harbinson, E., and Benson, M. L. (2020). "Gender and Criminal Thinking among Individuals Convicted of White-collar Crimes." *Criminal Justice Studies 33*(1): 46–60.

Hare, R. (1993). *Without Conscience: The Disturbing World of the Psychopaths among Us.* New York: Pocket Books.

Harris, A. R. (1976). "Race, Commitment to Deviance, and Spoiled Identity." *American Sociological Review 41*: 432–442.

Harris, A. R. (1977). "Sex and Theories of Deviance: Toward a Functional Theory of Deviant Typescripts." *American Sociological Review 42*: 3–16.

Harris, A. R. (1991). "Race, Class, and Crime." Pp. 95–120 in *Criminology: A Contemporary Handbook*, edited by J. F. Sheley. Belmont, CA: Wadsworth.

Harris, A. R., and Hill, G. D. (1982). "The Social Psychology of Deviance: Toward a Reconciliation with Social Structure." *Annual Review of Sociology 8*: 161–186.

Harris, A. R., and Shaw, J. A. W. (2000). "Looking for Patterns: Race, Class, and Crime." Pp. 129–164 in *Criminology: A Contemporary Handbook*, edited by J. F. Sheley. Belmont, CA: Wadsworth/ Thompson Learning.

Hast, R. H. (2000). "Health Care Fraud: Schemes to Defraud Medicare, Medicaid and Private Health Care Insurers: Statement of Robert H. Hast, Associate Comptroller, General for Special Investigations, Office of Special Investigations, before the Subcommittee on Government Management, Information and Technology, Committee on Government Reform, House of Representatives." GAO/T-OSI-00–15:10. Retrieved October 10, 2017 (https://www.gao.gov/assets/t-osi-00-15.pdf).

Hawkins, K. (2002). *Law as Last Resort: Prosecution Decision-Making in a Regulatory Agency*. New York: Oxford University Press.

Hawn, C. (2008). "Enron's Skilling Sprung? It Could Happen This Week." *Financial Week*, June 9, 2008. Retrieved September 10, 2014 (https://infoweb-newsbank-com.uc.idm.oclc.org/apps/news/document-view?p=AWNB&t=pubname%3AFWN9%21Financial%2BWeek%2B%2528USA%2529/year%3A2008%212008/mody%3A0609%21June%2B09&action=browse&format=text&docref=news/1214BAFB4FE3B7F0).

Headworth, S., and Hagan, J. L. (2016). "White-Collar Crimes of the Financial Crisis." Pp. 275–293 in *The Oxford Handbook of White-Collar Crime*, edited by S. Van Slyke, M. L. Benson, and F. T. Cullen. New York: Oxford University Press.

Heimer, K. (2000). "Changes in the Gender Gap in Crime and Women's Economic Marginalization," in *Criminal Justice 2000: The Changing Nature of Crime*, Vol. 1, edited by G. LaFree, R. J. Bursik, Jr., J. F. Short, Jr., R. B. Taylor, and R. J. Sampson. Washington, DC: National Institute of Justice. Retrieved (www.ojp.usdoj.gov/nij/criminal_justice2000/vol1_2000.html).

Helsel, P. (2022). "FTX Co-founder Sam Bankman-Fried Agrees to Extradition in Crypto Fraud Case." *NBC News*. December 20, 2022.

Henriques, D. B. (2011). *The Wizard of Lies: Bernie Madoff and the Death of Trust*. New York: Times Books.

Herbig, F. J. W., and Joubert, S. J. (2006). "Criminological Semantics: Conservation Criminology—Vision or Vagary?" *Acta Criminologica* 19: 88–103.

Hills, S., (1987). *Corporate Violence: Injury and Death for Profit*. Totowa, N.J.: Roman and Littlefield.

Hirschi, T., (1969). *Causes of Delinquency*. Berkeley: University of California Press.

Hirschi, T., and Gottfredson, M. (1987a). "Causes of White-Collar Crime." *Criminology* 25: 949–974.

Hirschi, T., and Gottfredson, M. (1987b). "Toward a General Theory of Crime." Pp. 8–26 in *Crime & Capitalism*, edited by W. Buikhuisen and S. Mednick. Leiden: Brill.

Hochstetler, A., and Copes, H. (2001). "Organizational Culture and Organizational Crime." Pp. 210–221 in *Crimes of Privilege: Readings in White-Collar Crime*, edited by N. Shover and J. P. Wright. New York: Oxford University Press.

Holtfreter, K. (2005). "Is Occupational Fraud 'Typical' White-Collar Crime? A Comparison of Individual and Organizational Characteristics." *Journal of Criminal Justice* 33: 353–365.

Holtfreter, K., Resig, M. D., and Pratt, T. C. (2008). "Low Self-Control, Routine Activities, and Fraud Victimization." *Criminology* 46(1): 189–220.

Howe, M. (2003). *"Gender, Morality, and Corporate Crime."* Unpublished Master's thesis, University of Maryland, Department of Criminology and Criminal Justice, College Park.

Huff, R., Desilets, C., and Kane, J. (2010). *The 2010 National Public Survey on White Collar Crime*. Fairmont, WV: National White Collar Crime Center.

Huffington Post. (2014). "David Rainey, Former BP Executive, Given More Time for Gulf Oil Spill Trial." Retrieved July 2, 2014 (www.huffingtonpost.com/2013/07/04/david-rainey-bp-gulf-oil-spill_n_3543426.html).

Hugh, S. (January 11, 2023). "Wells Fargo, Once the No, 1 Player in Mortgages, is Stepping Back from the Housing Market." CNBC News Report.

Huisman, W., Karstedt, S., and van Baar, A. (2022). "The Involvement of Corporations in Atrocity Crimes." In B. Hola, N. B. Hollie, and M. Weerdesteijn (eds). *The Oxford Handbook of Atrocity Crimes* (pp. 393–422). Oxford University Press. https://doi.org/10.1093/oxfordhb/9780190915629.013.17

Hunter, B. (2021). "Corporate criminal careers: Thinking about organizational offending." *Journal of Theoretical and Philosophical Criminology, 13*.

Hunter, B. (2023). "Pinpointing Persistent Polluters: Environmental Offending and Recidivist Companies in England", *Deviant Behavior, 44:9*: 1287–1302, DOI: 10.1080/01639625.2023.2179902

Hurtado, P., Dolmetsch, C., Roth, C., and Voreacos, D. (August 10, 2020). "Trump Oversees All-Time Low in White Collar Crime Enforcement." Bloomberg News.

Iglehart, J. K. (2010). "The ACA's New Weapons against Health Care Fraud." *New England Journal of Medicine 363*: 304–306.

Ingels, S. J., Glennie, E., Lauff, E., and Wirt, J. G. (2012). "Trends among Young Adults over Three Decades, 1974–2006 (NCES 2012–345)," in *U.S. Department of Education, National Center for Education Statistics.* Washington, DC. Retrieved July 2, 2014 (http://nces.ed.gov/pubs2012/2012345.pdf).

Isidore, C. (2017). "Fiat Chrysler Cheated on Diesel Emissions, EPA Says." *CNN Money.* Retrieved June 23, 2017 (http://money.cnn.com/2017/01/12/news/companies/epa-emissions-cheating-fiat-chrysler/index.html).

Ivory, D. (2014). "GMs Faulty Ignition Switch: Who Knew What When." *New York Times.* Retrieved January 18, 2017 (www.nytimes.com/interactive/2014/05/18/business/gms-ignition-problem-who-knew-what-when.html).

Javaras, K. N., Schaefer, S. M., van Reekum, C. M., Lapate, R. C., Greischar, L. L., Bachhuber, D. R., Love, G. D., Ryff, C. D., and Davidson, R. J. (2012). "Conscientiousness Predicts Greater Recovery from Negative Emotion." *Emotion, 12(5)*: 875–881. https://doi.org/10.1037/a0028105

Jesilow, P., Geis, G., and Pontell, H. (1991). "Fraud by Physicians Against Medicaid." *Journal of the American Medical Association 266*: 3318–3324.

Jodhka, S. S., and Shah, G. (2010). "Comparative Contexts of Discrimination: Caste and Untouchability in South Asia". *Economic and Political Weekly, 45(48)*: 99–106. http://www.jstor.org/stable/25764189

Jordanoska, A. (2018). "The Social Ecology of White-Collar Crime: Applying Situational Action Theory to White-Collar Offending." *Deviant Behavior: an interdisciplinary journal, 39(11)*: 1427–1449.

Jordanoska, A., and Lord, N. (2019). "Scripting the Mechanics of the Benchmark Manipulation Corporate Scandals: The 'Guardian' Paradox." *European Journal of Criminology 17(1)*: 9–30.

Kaal, W. A., and Lacine, T. A. (2014). "The Effect of Deferred and Non-Prosecution Agreements on Corporate Governance: Evidence from 1993–2013." *The Business Lawyer 70*: 1–59.

Kalev, A. (2009). "Cracking the Glass Cages: Restructuring and Ascriptive Inequality at Work." *American Journal of Sociology 114(6)*: 1591–1643.

Karstedt, S., and Farrall, S. (2006). "The Moral Economy of Everyday Crime: Markets, Consumers, and Citizens." *British Journal of Criminology 46 (6)*: 1011–1036.

Katz, J. (1979). "Concerted Ignorance: The Social Construction of Cover-Up." *Urban Life 8*: 295–316.

Katz, J. (1980). "The Social Movement Against White-Collar Crime." *Criminology Review Yearbook 2*: 161–184.

Kazemian, L., and Farrington, D. P. (2005). "Comparing the validity of prospective, retrospective, and official onset for different offending categories." *Journal of Quantitative Criminology, 21*: 127–147.

Kemp, S., Buil-Gil, D., Moneva, A., Miró-Llinares, F., and Díaz-Castaño, N. (2021). "Empty Streets, Busy Internet: A Time-series Analysis of Cybercrime and Fraud Trends during COVID-19." *Journal of Contemporary Criminal Justice 37(4)*: 480–501.

Kena, G., Musu-Gillette, L., Robinson, J., Wang, X., Rathbun, A., Zhang, J., Wilkinson-Flicker, S., Barmer, A., and Dunlop Velez, E. (2015). "The Condition of Education 2015 (NCES 2015–144)." *U.S. Department of Education, National Center for Education Statistics.* Washington, DC. Retrieved from http://nces.ed.gov/pubsearch

Kennedy, J. P. (2019). "A-CAPP Center Product Counterfeiting Database: Insights into Converging Crimes." Retrieved from: https://a-capp.msu.edu/article/a-capp-center-product-counterfeiting-database-insights-into-converging-crimes/

Kennedy, J. P., Rorie, M., and Benson, M. L. (2021). "COVID-19 Frauds: An Exploratory Study of Victimization during a Global Crisis." *Criminology & Public Policy 20(3)*: 493–543.

Kim, T., Peck, D., and Gee, B. (2020). "Race, Gender & the Double Glass Ceiling: An Analysis of EEOC National Workforce Data." https://www.ascendleadershipfoundation.org/research/race-gender-double-glass-ceiling (accessed on January 31, 2023).

King, K. M. (2014). "Medicare Fraud: Further Actions Needed to Address Fraud, Waste, and Abuse." *Testimony before the Subcommittee on Oversight and Investigations, Committee on Energy and Commerce,* House of Representatives June 25, 2014. Washington, DC: U.S. Government Accountability Office.

Klenowski, P. M., Copes, H., and Mullins, C. W. (2011). "Gender, Identity, and Accounts: How White-Collar Offenders Do Gender When Making Sense of Their Crimes." *Justice Quarterly 28*(1): 46–69.

Klein, J. R. (2014) "Corporate Violence", in *The Encyclopedia of Theoretical Criminology,* edited by J. M. Miller. Hoboken: Wiley.

Kmietowicz, Z. (2013). "Johnson & Johnson to Pay $2.2bn to Settle Charges of False Marketing on Three Drugs." *British Medical Journal 347*: f6696. Retrieved July 2, 2014 (www.bmj.com/content/347/bmj.f6696?tab=citation).

Koehler, M. (2015). "Measuring the Impact of Non-Prosecution and Deferred Prosecution Agreements on Foreign Corrupt Practices Act Enforcement." *UC Davis Law Review 49*: 497–565.

Kolieb, J. (2015). "When to punish, when to persuade, and when to reward: Strengthening responsive regulation with the regulatory diamond". *Monash University Law Review 41(1)*: 136–162

Kramer, R. C., and Michalowski, R. J. (1990). "State-Corporate Crime," prepared for the American Society of Criminology Meeting, Baltimore, MD, 7–12 November.

Krantz, M. (2016). "Wells Fargo Scam Latest in a String of Infractions." *USA Today*. Retrieved January 18, 2017 (www.usatoday.com/story/money/markets/2016/09/11/wells-fargo-scam-latest-string-infractions/90139724/).

Kravets, D. (2015). "Manslaughter Charges Dropped in BP Case—Nobody Will Go to Prison." *Ars Technica*, December 3. Retrieved April 4, 2017 (https://arstechnica.com/tech-policy/2015/12/manslaughter-charges-dropped-in-bp-spill-case-nobody-from-bp-will-go-to-prison/).

Kuchler, H., and Masters, B. (2012). "UK Promises to Reform Libor." *Financial Times*. Retrieved June 28, 2017 (www.ft.com/content/a6807516-0947-11e2-a5a9-00144feabdc0).

Lasley, J. R. (1988). "Toward a Control Theory of White-Collar Offending." *Journal of Quantitative Criminology 4*: 347–362.

Lee, B. Y. (2021, March 12). *One Year After Coronavirus Pandemic Declared, How Many Deaths from Covid-19?* Forbes.com. Retrieved from https://www.forbes.com/sites/brucelee/2021/03/13/one-year-after-coronavirus-pandemic-declared-how-many-deaths-from-covid-19/?sh=7d58fbce6900

Lee, M. T., and Ermann, M. D. (1999). "Pinto 'Madness' as a Flawed Landmark Narrative: An Organizational and Network Analysis." *Social Problems 46*: 30–47.

Leeth, J. D., and Ruser, J. (2006). "Safety Segregation: The Importance of Gender, Race, and Ethnicity on Workplace Risk." *Journal of Economic Inequality 4*: 123–152.

Lev, B. (2003). "Corporate Earnings: Facts and Fiction." *Journal of Economic Perspectives 17*(2): 27–50.

Levi, M. (2010). "Individual Differences and White-Collar Crime." in *Encyclopedia of Criminological Theory,* edited by F. Cullen, and P. Wilcox. Thousand Oaks, CA: SAGE Publications.

Lister, S. (2005). "Secrets and Lies of Beauty Industry Laid Bare by Advertising Watchdog." *The Times* [of London], January 28, p. 11.

Lord, N., Inzelt, E., Huisman, W., and Faria, R. (eds). (2022). *European White-Collar Crime: Exploring the Nature of European Realities.* Bristol: Bristol University Press.

Lord, N., and Levi, M. (2017). "Organising the Finances for and the Finances from Transnational Bribery." *European Journal of Criminology 14*: 365–389.

Ma, K. W. F., and McKinnon, T. (2022). "COVID-19 and Cyber Fraud: Emerging Threats during the Pandemic." *Journal of Financial Crime 29*(2): 433–446. https://www.emerald.com/insight/content/doi/10.1108/JFC-01-2021-0016/full/html?casa_token=x22EPj5sgpQAAAAA:hGkuQArBxWs5FEQny6fVO6kE9dQSLA_p3L2wxniMgvDaVLFy_QZAsH5k67wbxTSDJ8UhWpP5ZG1lv8Ye-BIuLFAWw5AfdbzcXKN5sVj6BSq8mReBZDk

Maakestad, W. J., Benson, M. L., Cullen, F. T., and Geis, G. (1987). "Prosecuting Corporate Crime in California." Unpublished manuscript, presented at Symposium '87: White-Collar and Institutional Crime, Berkeley, CA.

MacLaury, J. (2008). "The Occupational Safety and Health Administration: A History of the First Thirteen Years, 1971–1984." Retrieved March 26, 2008 (https://www.dol.gov/general/aboutdol/history/mono-osha13introtoc).

Maher, L. (1997). *Sexed Work: Gender, Race, and Resistance in a Brooklyn Drug Market*. New York: Clarendon Press.

Makkai, T., and Braithwaite, J. (1994). "The Dialectics of Corporate Deterrence." *Journal of Research in Crime and Delinquency 31*: 347–373.

Maloney, J., and Chaudhuri, S. (2017). "Against All Odds, the U. S. Tobacco Industry Is Rolling in Money." *Wall Street Journal*, April 23, 2017. Retrieved June 16, 2017 (www.wsj.com/articles/u-s-tobacco-industry-rebounds-from-its-near-death-experience-1492968698).

Mann, K. (1985). *Defending White-Collar Crime: A Portrait of Attorneys at Work*. New Haven, CT: Yale University Press.

Martin, A. B., Hartman, M., Washington, B., Catlin, A., and National Expenditure Accounts Team. (2017). "National Health Care Spending: Faster Growth in 2015 as Coverage Expands and Utilization Increases." *Health Affairs 36*: 1–11.

Maruna, S., and Copes, H. (2005). "What Have We Learned from Five Decades of Neutralization Research?" *Crime and Justice 32*: 221–320.

Mascini, P. (2013). "Why Was the Enforcement Pyramid So Influential? And What Price Was Paid?" *Regulation & Governance 7*: 48–60.

Mattise, J. (2016). In jail, ex-coal CEO says he's 'American political prisoner.' *Associated Press.* https://apnews.com/article/338d4c77472b4c8eaa1311edd67f96bb

Mayer, R. N. (2012). "The U.S. Consumer Movement: A New Era amid Old Challenges." *Journal of Consumer Affairs 46*: 171–189.

McBarnet, D. (2005). "After Enron: Corporate Governance, Creative Compliance and the Uses of Corporate Social Responsibility." Pp. 205–222 in *Governing the Corporation*, edited by J. O'Brien. New York: John Wiley.

McBride, J. (2016). "Understanding the Libor Scandal." Retrieved (https://www.cfr.org/backgrounder/understanding-libor-scandal).

McCormick, A., and Eberle, W. (2013). "Discovering Fraud in Online Classified Ads." In C. Boonthum-Denecke and G. Michael Youngblood (eds). *Proceedings of the Twenty-Sixth International Florida Artificial Intelligence Research Society Conference*. Available online: https://www.aaai.org/ocs/index.php/FLAIRS/FLAIRS13/paper/view/5928

McGarrell, E. F., and Gibbs, C. (2014). "Conservation Criminology, Environmental Crime and Risk: An Application to Climate Change." *Oxford Handbooks Online—Criminology and Criminal Justice.* http://www.oxfordhandbooks.com/view/10.1093/oxfordhb/9780199935383.001.0001/oxfordhb-9780199935383-e-54

McGovern, B. (2015). "Settlement Reached in NECC Victim Case." *Boston Herald*, May 20. Retrieved May 4, 2017 (www.bostonherald.com/business/healthcare/2015/05/settlement_reached_in_necc_victims_case).

McLean, B., and Elkind, P. (2004). *The Smartest Guys in the Room: The Amazing Rise and Scandalous Fall of Enron*. New York: Penguin Group.

McMullen, T. (2010). "Dannon to Pay $45 Billion to Settle Yogurt Lawsuit." *ABC News.* Retrieved July 2, 2014 (http://abcnews.go.com/Business/dannon-settles-lawsuit/story?id=9950269).

Meier, R. F., and Geis, G. (1982). "The Psychology of the White-Collar Offender." Pp. 85–102 in *On White-Collar Crime*, edited by G. Geis. Lexington, MA: Lexington Books.

Merton, R. K. (1938). "Social Structure and Anomie." *American Sociological Review 3*: 672–682.

Merton, R. K. (1964). "Anomie, Anomia, and Social Interaction: Contexts of Deviant Behavior." Pp. 213–242 in *Anomie and Deviant Behavior: A Discussion and Critique*, edited by M. B. Clinard. New York: The Free Press.

Messner, S., and Rosenfeld, R. (1997). *Crime and the American Dream*. Belmont, CA: Wadsworth.

Messner, S., and Rosenfeld, R. (2013). *Crime and the American Dream* (5th ed.). Belmont, CA: Wadsworth.

Miethe, T. D., and Rothschild, J. (1994). "Whistleblowing and the Control of Organizational Misconduct." *Sociological Inquiry 64*: 322–347.

Miller, G. A. (1987). "Meta-Analysis and the Culture Free Hypothesis." *Organization Studies 8*(4): 309–326.

Miller, J. (2001). *One of the Guys: Girls, Gangs, and Gender*. New York: Oxford University Press.

Miller, M. (2006). "A Visual Essay: Post-Recessionary Employment Growth Related to the Housing Market." *Monthly Labor Review*, October, pp. 23–34.

Mintz, M. (1995). "Corporate Greed, Women, and the Dalkon Shield." Pp. 191–199 in *White-Collar Crime: Classic and Contemporary View* (3rd ed.), edited by G. Geis, R. F. Meier, and L. M. Salinger. New York: The Free Press.

Mitchell, R. W., and Thompson, N. S. (eds). (1986). *Deception, Perspectives on Human and Non-Human Deceit*. Albany, NY: State University of New York Press.

Moffat, S. (1993). "Brothers Enter Guilty Pleas in Massive Insurance Fraud." *Los Angeles Times*, March 17, p. 12.

Moffitt, T. E. (1993). "Adolescent-Limited and Life-Course Persistent Antisocial Behavior: A Developmental Taxonomy." *Psychological Review 100*: 674–701

Moffitt, T. E., Caspi, A., Harrington, H., and Milne, B. J. (2002). "Males on the Life-course-persistent and Adolescence-limited Antisocial Pathways: Follow-up at Age 26 Years." *Development and Psychopathology 14*(1): 179–207.

Mokhiber, R. (2005). Speech Delivered at the National Press Club: Crime without Conviction: The Rise of Deferred and Non-Prosecution Agreements (December 28). Reprinted in *Corporate Crime Reporter*, Reports and Speeches, 8:04 pm, December 28, 2005.

Mullins, C., and Wright, R. (2003). "Gender, Social Networks, and Residential Burglary." *Criminology 42*: 911–940.

Murrar, F. (2022). "Fraud Schemes during COVID-19: A Comparison from FATF Countries." *Journal of Financial Crime 29*(2): 533–540.

Nagin, D. S. (2010). "Group-based Trajectory Modeling: An Overview." In the *Handbook of Quantitative Criminology*, edited by Alex R. Piqeuro and David Weisburd, pp. 53–67. New York: Springer.

Nash, R., Bouchard, M., and Malm, A. (2013). "Investing in People: The Role of Social Networks in the Diffusion of a Large-scale Fraud." *Social Networks 35*(4): 686–698.

National Academy of Engineering. (2011). *Macondo Well Deepwater Horizon Blowout: Lessons for Improving Offshore Drilling Safety: National Research Council*. Washington, DC: National Academies of Science.

National White Collar Crime Center. (2009). "Disaster Fraud." Retrieved September 10, 2014 (file:///C:/Users/bensonm/Documents/Current%20Projects/WCC%202nd%20Edition/Articles/NW3C-%20disaster_fraud.pdf).

New York Times. (2006). "The Sago Mine Disaster." January 5. Retrieved July 2, 2014 (http://query.nytimes.com/gst/fullpage.html?res=9E0CEFD71130F936A35752C0A9609C8B63&module=Search&mabReward=relbias%3Aw%2C[%22RI%3A6%22%2C%22RI%3A17%22]).

Nguyen, T. H., and Pontell, H. N. (2010). "Mortgage Origination Fraud and the Global Economic Crisis: A Criminological Analysis." *Criminology and Public Policy 9*(3): 591–612.

Nielsen, V. L., and Parker, C. (2009). "Testing Responsive Regulation in Regulatory Enforcement." *Regulation & Governance 3*: 376–399.

Noked, N. (2012). *Update on Corporate Deferred Prosecution and Non-Prosecution Agreements*. Harvard Law School Forum on Corporate Governance and Financial Regulation. Retrieved July 21, 2017 (https://corpgov.law.harvard.edu/2012/07/26/update-on-corporate-deferred-prosecution-and-non-prosecution-agreements/).

Nolte, J., Hanoch, Y., Wood, S., and Hengerer, D. (2021). "Susceptibility to COVID-19 Scams: The Roles of Age, Individual Difference Measures, and Scam-Related Perceptions." *Frontiers in Psychology 12*: 789883–789883.

OECD. (2019, April 24). *Latin America and the Caribbean 2019: Policies for Competitive SMEs in the Pacific Alliance and Participating South American Countries*. DOI: 10.1787/d9e1e5f0-en. Retrieved from:https://www.oecd-ilibrary.org/development/latin-america-and-the-caribbean-2019_d9e1e5f0-en

OECD. (2020, June 15). *Safeguarding COVID-19 Social Benefit Programs from Fraud and Error*. https://read.oecd-ilibrary.org/view/?ref=134_134461-lvckm8fbba&title=Safeguarding-COVID-19-Social-Benefit-Programmes-from-Fraud-and-Error

OSHA. (2022). "Industry Profile for OSHA Citations Issued." Retrieved from:https://www.osha.gov/ords/imis/industryprofile.stand?p_esize=&p_state=FEFederal&p_type=2&p_stand=All

Paoli, L. (2014). *The Oxford Handbook of Organized Crime.* Oxford: Oxford University Press.

Parker, C. (2013). "Twenty Years of Responsive Regulation: An Appreciation and Appraisal." *Regulation & Governance* 7: 2–13.

Partnership for Public Service. (2013). "Helping the SEC Crack Securities Fraud Cases Using Cutting-Edge Technology and Data Analysis." *The Washington Post.* Retrieved June 25, 2014 (https://www.washingtonpost.com/politics/federal_government/helping-the-sec-crack-securities-fraud-cases-using-c-utting-edge-technology-and-data-analysis/2014/05/13/9c99de8a-daa5-11e3-b745-87d39690c5c0_story.html).

Partnoy, F. (2003). *Infectious Greed: How Deceit and Risk Corrupted the Financial Markets.* New York: Times Books.

Passas, N. (1990). "Anomie and Corporate Deviance." *Contemporary Crises* 14: 157–178.

Paternoster, R. (2016). "Deterring Corporate Crime: Evidence and Outlook." *Criminology & Public Policy* 15: 383–386.

Paternoster, R., and Simpson, S. (1993). "A Rational Choice Theory of Corporate Crime." Pp. 37–58 in *Routine Activity and Rational Choice,* edited by R. V. Clarke and M. Felson. New Brunswick, NJ: Transaction.

Patterson, P. D., Huang, D. T., Fairbanks, R. J., Simeone, S., Weaver, M., and Wang, H. E. (2010). "Variation in Emergency Medical Services Workplace Safety Culture", *Prehospital Emergency Care,* 14:4: 448–460, DOI: 10.3109/10903127.2010.497900

Payne, B. K. (2017). *White-Collar Crime: The Essentials* (2nd ed.). Los Angeles: Sage.

Perez, Z., Cochran, E., and Sousa, C. (2008). "Securities Fraud." *American Criminal Law Review* 45: 923–994.

Pike, L. O. (1873). *A History of Crime in England: Illustrating the Changes of the Laws in the Progress of Civilisation.* London: Smith, Elder & Co.

Piquero, A. R. (2008). "Taking Stock of Developmental Trajectories over the Life Course." Pp. 23–78 in *The Long View of Crime: A Synthesis of Longitudinal Research,* edited by A. Liberman. New York: Springer.

Piquero, N. L. (2012). "The Only Thing We Have to Fear Is Fear Itself: Investigating the Relationship Between Fear of Falling and White-Collar Crime." *Crime and Delinquency* 58: 362–379

Piquero, N. L., and Piquero, A. (2016). "White-Collar Criminal Participation and the Life Course." Pp. 238–252 in *Oxford Handbook of White-Collar Crime,* edited S. Van Slyke, M. L. Benson, and F. T. Cullen. New York: Oxford University Press.

Piquero, N. L., and Weisburd, D. (2009). "Developmental Trajectories in White-Collar Crime." Pp. 153–174 in *The Criminology of White-Collar Crime,* edited by S. S. Simpson and D. Weisburd. New York: Springer.

Podgor, E. S. (1999). "Criminal Fraud." *American Law Review* 48: 730–770.

Pollock, O. (1950). *The Criminality of Women.* Philadelphia: University of Pennsylvania Press.

Pontell, H. N. (2016). "Theoretical, Empirical, and Policy Implications of Alternative Definitions of 'White-Collar Crime': 'Trivializing the Lunatic Crime Rate'." Pp. 39–56 in *The Oxford Handbook of White-Collar Crime,* edited by S. Van Slyke, M. L. Benson, and F. T. Cullen. New York: Oxford University Press.

Pontell, H. N., and Geis, G. (2014). "The Trajectory of White-Collar Crime Following the Great Economic Meltdown." *Journal of Contemporary Criminal Justice* 30(1): 70–82.

Pontell, H. N., Tillman, R., and Ghazi-Tehrani, A. K. (2021). "In-your-face Watergate: Neutralizing Government Lawbreaking and the War against White-collar Crime." *Crime, Law and Social Change,* 75: 201–219.

Portney, P. R. (2000). "EPA and the Evolution of Federal Regulation." Pp. 11–30 in *Public Policies for Environmental Protection,* edited by P. R. Portney and R. N. Stavins. Washington, DC: Resources for the Future.

Powell, J. H. (2014). "Reforming the U. S. Dollar LIBOR: The Path Forward." *Presentation at the Money Marketeers of New York University.* Retrieved June 28, 2017 (www.federalreserve.gov/newsevents/speech/powell20140904a.htm).

Powers, J. P., Moshontz, H., Hoyle, R. H., and Donnellan, M. B. (2020). "Self-control and Affect Regulation Styles Predict Anxiety Longitudinally in University Students." *Collabra: Psychology* 6(1).

Prechel, H., and Morris, T. (2010). "The Effects of Organizational and Political Embeddedness on Financial Malfeasance in the Largest U.S. Corporations: Dependence, Incentives, and Opportunities." *American Sociological Review* 75: 331–352.

Punch, M. (1996). *Dirty business: Exploring corporate misconduct analysis and cases.* London: SAGE Publications Ltd, DOI: https://doi.org/10.4135/9781446250440

Ragatz, L. L., Fremous, W., and Baker, E. (2012). "The Psychological Profile of White-collar Offenders." *Criminal Justice and Behavior* 39(7): 978–997.

Reasons, C. E., Ross, L. L., and Paterson, C. (1981). *Assault on the Worker: Occupational Health and Safety in Canada.* Toronto: Butterworths.

Rebovich, D. J. (1992). *Dangerous Ground: The World of Hazardous Waste Crime.* New Brunswick, NJ: Transaction.

Reed, G. E., and Yeager, P. C. (1996). "Organizational Offending and Neoclassical Criminology: Challenging the Reach of a General Theory of Crime." *Criminology* 34: 357–382.

Reichman, N. (1993). "Insider Trading." *Crime and Justice* 18: 55–96.

Reiman, J. H. (1979). *The Rich Get Richer and the Poor Get Prison: Ideology, Class, and Criminal Justice.* New York: Wiley.

Reiman, J., and Leighton, P. (2023). *The Rich Get Richer and the Poor Get Prison* (13th ed.). New York: Routledge.

Reisig, M. D., Holtfreter, K., and Cullen, F. T. (2022). "Faith in Trump and the Willingness to Punish White-collar Crime: Chinese Americans as an Out-group." *Journal of Experimental Criminology.* https://doi.org/10.1007/s11292-022-09528-8

Reiss, A. J., and Biderman, A. D. (1981). *Data Sources on White-Collar Law-Breaking.* Washington, DC: U.S. Department of Justice, National Institute of Justice.

Reuter, P. (1993). "The Cartage Industry in New York." *Crime and Justice* 18: 149–201.

Robb, G. (2006). "Women and White-Collar Crime: Debates on Gender, Fraud and the Corporate Economy in England and America, 1850–1930." *British Journal of Criminology* 46: 1058–1072.

Roberts, J. (2004). "Enron Traders Caught on Tape." *CBS News.* Retrieved October 9, 2017 (https://www.cbsnews.com/news/enron-traders-caught-on-tape/).

Robinson, K. (2013). "The Role of Data Analytics in SEC Fraud Investigations." Retrieved June 25, 2014 (http://blogs.cfainstitute.org/marketintegrity/2013/10/23/the-role-of-data-analytics-in-sec-fraud-investigations).

Rorie, M., and Simpson, S. S. (2012). "The 'American Dream' Gone Wrong: Applying a Criminogenic Tiers Approach to Explain American's Mortgage Fraud Epidemic." Annual Meeting of Law & Society Association, Honolulu, Hawaii, June 2012.

Rorie, M., Sohoni, T., and Reed, S. (2020). "The Role of "Whiteness" in White-Collar Crime: A Test of the Theory of Racial Privilege and Offending". Presentation at the 2020 EuroCrim Conference

Rosoff, S., Pontell, H. N., and Tillman, R. (2013). *Profit without Honor: White-Collar Crime and the Looting of America.* Upper Saddle River, NJ: Prentice Hall.

Ross, E. A. (1907). *Sin and Society; An Analysis of Latter-Day Iniquity.* Boston and New York: Houghton, Mifflin and Company.

Ross, E. A. (1977). "The Criminaloid." Pp. 29–37 in *White-Collar Crime,* revised ed., edited by G. Geis and R. F. Meier. New York: Macmillan.

Rothman, M. L., and Gandossy, R. P. (1982). "Sad Tales: The Accounts of White-Collar Defendants and the Decision to Sanction." *Pacific Sociological Review* 25: 449–473.

Rothschild, J., and Miethe, T. D. (1999). "Whistle-Blower Disclosures and Management Retaliation: The Battle to Control Information about Organizational Corruption." *Work and Organizations* 26: 107–128.

Rowland, C. (2005). "US Fraud Inquiry Targets Fresenius: Probe Comes 5 Years after Dialysis Chain Settled Medicare Case." *Boston Globe*, April 7, 2005. Retrieved September 10, 2014 (www.highbeam.com/doc/1P2-7895826.html).

Rue, L. (1994). *By the Grace of Guile: The Role of Deception in Natural History and Human Affairs.* New York: Oxford University Press.

Ruggiero, V. (2009). "Corporate Crime: A Panacea for Critical Criminology." Pp. 41–54 in *Cutting the Edge: Current Perspectives in Radical/Critical Criminology and Criminal Justice* (2nd ed.), edited by J. I. Ross. New Brunswick, NJ: Transaction.

Rushe, D. (2013). "Deepwater Trial: U.S. Lawyers Say BP Ignored Warnings on 'Well from Hell'." *The Guardian.* Retrieved July 1, 2014 (www.theguardian.com/environment/2013/feb/25/deepwater-trial-justice-bp-warnings).

Sampson, R. J., and Bean, L. (2006) "Cultural Mechanisms and Killing Fields: A Revised Theory of Community-Level Racial Inequality." Pp. 8–37 in *The Many Colors of Crime: Inequalities of Race, Ethnicity, and Crime in America,* edited by R. Peterson, L. Krivo, and J. Hagan. New York: New York University Press.

Sampson, R. J., and Laub, J. (1990). "Crime and Deviance over the Life Course." *American Sociological Review 55:* 609–627.

Sampson, R. J., and Laub, J. (1993). *Crime in the Making: Pathways and Turning Points through Life.* Cambridge, MA: Harvard University Press.

Sampson, R. J., and Wilson, J. W. (1995). "Toward a Theory of Race, Crime, and Urban Inequality." Pp. 37–56 in *Crime and Inequality,* edited by J. Hagan and R. D. Peteerson. Stanford, CA: Stanford University Press.

Sampson, R. J., Wilson, J. W. and Katz, H. (2018). "Reassessing 'Toward a Theory of Race, Crime and Urban Inequality': Enduring and New Challenges in 21st Century America." *Du Bois Review: Social Science Research on Race, 15 (1):* 13–35.

Scalia, J. (1999). "Federal Enforcement of Environmental Laws, 1997." *Bureau of Justice Statistics Special Report. Federal Justice Statistics Program. NCJ 175686.*

Schell-Busey, N. (2009). "The Deterrent Effects of Ethics Codes for Corporate Crime: A Meta-Analysis." Dissertation. Digital Repository at the University of Maryland, College Park. Retrieved July 2, 2014 (http://hdl.handle.net/1903/9289).

Schell-Busey, N., Simpson, S. S., Rorie, M., and Alper, M. (2016). "What Works? A Systematic Review of Corporate Crime Deterrence." *Criminology & Public Policy 15:* 387–416.

Schlanger, Z. (2015). "How BP's 18.7 Billion Gulf Spill Fine Could be One Giant Tax Deduction." Retrieved April 4, 2017 (www.newsweek.com/how-bps-187-billion-gulf-spill-fine-could-be-one-giant-tax-deduction-349637).

Scott, D. (1989). "Policing Corporate Collusion." *Criminology 27:* 559–587.

Scott, M. B., and Lyman, S. M. (1968). "Accounts." *American Sociological Review 33:* 46–62.

Sealock, M. D., and Simpson, S. S. (1998). "Unraveling Bias in Arrest Decisions: The Role of Juvenile Typescripts." *Justice Quarterly 15:* 427–457.

Senerdem, E. (2014). "Turkey's Mining Safety: Bleak Track Record." *BBC Turkish Service.* Retrieved July 2, 2014 (www.bbc.com/news/world-europe-27414972).

Shapiro, S. P. (1984). *Wayward Capitalists: Target of the Securities and Exchange Commission.* New Haven, CT: Yale University Press.

Shapiro, S. P. (1985). "The Road Not Taken: The Elusive Path to Criminal Prosecution for White-Collar Offenders." *Law and Society Review 19:* 179–217.

Shapiro, S. P. (1990). "Collaring the Crime, Not the Criminal: Reconsidering the Concept of White-Collar Crime." *American Sociological Review 55:* 346–365.

Sharp, K. (2011). "To Save on Health Care, First Crack Down on Fraud." *New York Times.* Retrieved March 6, 2014 (www.nytimes.com/2011/09/27/opinion/to-save-on-health-care-first-crack-down-on-fraud.html?_r=0).

Shover, N. (2007). "Generative Worlds of White-Collar Crime." Pp. 81–97 in *International Handbook of White-Collar and Corporate Crime*, edited by H. N. Pontell and G. Geis. New York: Springer.

Shover, N., Clelland, D. A., and Lynxwiler, J. (1986). *Enforcement or Negotiation*. Albany, NY: State University of New York Press.

Shover, N., and Cullen, F. T. (2011). "White-Collar Crime: Interpretative Disagreement and Prospects for Change." Pp. 47–62 in *Reflecting on White-Collar and Corporate Crime: Discerning Readings*, edited by D. Shichor, L. Gaines, and A. Schoepfer. Long Grove, IL: Waveland.

Shover, N., and Hochstetler, A. (2006). *Choosing White-Collar Crime*. New York: Cambridge University Press.

Silberman, C. E. (1978). *Criminal Violence, Criminal Justice*. New York: Random House.

Silver, L., and Connaughton, A. (2022). "Partisanship Colors Views of COVID-19 Handling Across Advanced Economies." *Pew Research Center*

Simon, D. R., and Etizen, S. D. (1990). *Elite Deviance*. Boston: Allyn & Bacon.

Simon, R. J. (1975). *Women and Crime*. Lexington, MA: Lexington Books.

Simpson, S. S. (1986). "The Decomposition of Antitrust: Testing a Multilevel, Longitudinal Model of Profit-Squeeze." *American Sociological Review* 51: 859–975.

Simpson, S. S. (2002). *Corporate Crime, Law, and Social Control*. Cambridge: Cambridge University Press.

Simpson, S. S. (2006). "Corporate Crime and Regulation." Pp. 63–90 in *Managing and Maintaining Compliance*, edited by H. Elffers, P. Verboon, and W. Huisman. The Hague: Boom Legal.

Simpson, S. S. (2012). "Making Sense of White-Collar Crime: Theory and Research." *Ohio State Journal of Criminal Law* 8: 481–502.

Simpson, S. S. (2013a). "Illuminating the Dark Figure of White-Collar Crime." *Invited Keynote Lecture*, Griffith University, Brisbane Australia, June.

Simpson, S. S. (2013b). "White-Collar Crime." *Annual Review of Sociology* 39: 309–331.

Simpson, S. S. (2019). "Reimaging Sutherland 80 Years after White-Collar Crime." *Criminology, 57 (2):* 189–207.

Simpson, S. S., Agarwal, R., and Gao, G. (2023). "Using Physician Behavioral Big Data for High Precision Fraud Prediction and Detection." Final summary report for NIJ-funded grant project # 2019 R2 CX 0016. Office of Justice Programs. Washington, DC.

Simpson, S. S., Alper, M., and Benson, M. L. (2012). "Gender, Organizational Crime, and Opportunity." Paper presented at the Annual Meeting of the American Society of Criminology, Chicago, IL, 14–17 November.

Simpson, S. S., Galvin, M. A., Loughran, T. A., and Cohen, M. A. (2022). "Perceptions of White-Collar Crime Seriousness: Unpacking and Translating Attitudes into Policy Preferences." *Journal of Research in Crime and Delinquency,* https://doi.org/10.1177%2F00224278221092094, first published online, May 6.

Simpson, S. S., Garner, J., and Gibbs, C. (2007). *Why Do Corporations Obey Environmental Law?* Washington, DC: National Institute of Justice.

Simpson, S. S., Layana, M. C., and Galvin, M. A. (forthcoming, 2023). "Patterns of Corporate Life-Course Offending." In *Advances in Criminological Theory: Corporate Crime: The Firm as Victim and Offender*, edited by M. A. Galvin and W. S. Laufer. New York, NY: Routledge.

Simpson, S. S., and Piquero, N. L. (2002). "Low Self-Control, Organizational Theory, and Corporate Crime." *Law & Society Review* 36: 509–548.

Simpson, S. S., Rorie, M., Alper, M., Schell-Busey, N., Laufer, W., and Smith, N. C. (2014). "Corporate Crime Deterrence: A Systematic Review." *Campbell Systematic Reviews* 4: 1–105, January 2014. DOI: 10.4073/csr.2014.4.

Simpson, S.S., and Schell, N. (2009). "Persistent Heterogeneity or State Dependence: An exploration of corporate deterrence." In *The Criminology of White-Collar Crime,* edited by S. S. Simpson and D. Weisburd. New York, Springer.

Simpson, S. S., and Yeager, P. C. (2015). "Building a Comprehensive White-Collar Violations Database." *Final Technical Report submitted to the US DOJ and published by NCJRS*. Retrieved from www.ncjrs.gov/pdffiles1/bjs/grants/248667.pdf

Sinclair, U. (1906). *The Jungle*. New York: Doubleday.

Singh, B. K., and Adams, L. D. (1979). "Variations in Self-Reported Arrests: An Epidemiological Perspective." *Criminal Justice Review 4*: 73–83.

Smith, D. A., and Visher, C. A. (1980). "Sex and Involvement in Deviance/Crime: A Quantitative Review of the Empirical Literature." *American Sociological Review 45*: 691–701.

Smith, G., and Parloff, R. (2016). "Hoaxwagen." *Fortune*. Retrieved January 11, 2017 (http://fortune.com/inside-volkswagen-emissions-scandal/).

Smith, N. C., Simpson, S. S., and Huang, C. (2007). "Why Managers Fail to Do the Right Thing: An Empirical Study of Unethical and Illegal Conduct." *Business Ethics Quarterly 17*: 633–667.

Smith, R. (2005). "Do the Determinants of Promotion Differ for White Men versus Women and Minorities?" *American Behavioral Scientist 48*: 1182–1199.

Sohoni, T., and Rorie, M. (2019). "The Whiteness of White-Collar Crime in the United States: Examining the Role of Race in a Culture of Elite White-Collar Offending." *Theoretical Criminology 25 (1)*: 66–87.

Sorokonish, R. (2017). "U. S. EPA Accuses Fiat Chrysler of Using Diesel Emission Cheating Software." Retrieved (www.roadandtrack.com/new-cars/car-technology/news/a32267/us-epa-accuses-fiat-chrysler-of-using-diesel-emission-cheating-software/).

Sparrow, M. K. (1996). *License to Steal: Why Fraud Plagues America's HealthCare System*. Boulder, CO: Westview.

Sparrow, M. K. (1998). "Fraud Control in the Health Care Industry: Assessing the State of the Art," *Research in Brief*. Washington, DC: National Institute of Justice.

Stafford, K. (2015). "Cancer Doctor was Really Just 'A Monster'." *Detroit Free Press*, July 6. Retrieved March 21, 2022. https://www.freep.com/story/news/local/michigan/oakland/2015/07/06/farid-fata-court-sentencing/29762499/

Steffensmeier, D. J. (1983). "Organization Properties and Sex Segregation in the Underworld: Building a Sociological Theory of Sex Differences in Crime." *Social Forces 61*: 1010–1032.

Steffensmeier, D. J. (1989). "On the Causes of 'White-Collar' Crime: An Assessment of Hirschi and Gottfredson's Claims." *Criminology 27*: 345–358.

Steffensmeier, D. J., and Allan, E. (2000). "Looking for Patterns: Gender, Age, and Crime." Pp. 83–113 in *Criminology: A Contemporary Handbook*, edited by J. F. Sheley. Stamford, CT: Wadsworth/Thompson Learning.

Steffensmeier, D. J., Schwartz, J., and Roche, M. (2013). "Gender and Twenty-First-Century Corporate Crime: Female Involvement and the Gender Gap in Enron-Era Corporate Frauds." *American Sociological Review 78(3)*: 448–476.

Stempel, J. (2014). "Ex-BP Well Managers Must Face Gulf Spill Criminal Charges." *Reuters*, January 28. Retrieved September 11, 2014 (https://www.reuters.com/article/us-bp-usa/u-s-says-bp-to-pay-20-billion-in-fines-for-2010-oil-spill-idUSKCN0RZ14A20151005).

Stewart, J. B. (2011). *Tangled Webs: How False Statements Are Undermining America: From Martha Stewart to Bernie Madoff*. New York: Penguin Press.

Stone, C. D. (1975). *Where the Law Ends: The Social Control of Corporate Behavior*. New York: Harper & Row.

Stotland, E. (1977). "White Collar Criminals." *Journal of Social Issues 33*: 179–196.

Stretesky, P. B., Long, M. A., and Lynch, M. J. (2013). "Does Environmental Enforcement Slow the Treadmill of Production? The Relationship between Large Monetary Penalties, Ecological Disorganization and Toxic Releases within Offending Organizations." *Journal of Crime and Justice 36*: 233–237.

Sutherland, E. H. (1940). "White-Collar Criminality." *American Sociological Review 5*: 1–12.

Sutherland, E. H. (1941). "Crime and Business." *Annals of the American Academy of Political and Social Science 217*: 112–118.

Sutherland, E. H. (1945). "Is 'White-Collar Crime' Crime?" *American Sociological Review 10*: 132–139.

Sutherland, E. H. (1949). *White-Collar Crime*. New York: Holt, Rinehart, and Winston.

Sutherland, E. H. (1983). *White-Collar Crime: The Uncut Version*. New Haven, CT: Yale University Press.

Swartz, M. (2003). *Power Failure: The Inside Story of the Collapse of Enron*. New York: Doubleday.

Swigert, V. L., and Farrell, R. A. (1981). "Corporate Homicide—Definitional Processes in the Creation of Deviance." *Law & Society Review 15(1)*: 161–182.

Sykes, G. M., and Matza, D. (1957). "Techniques of Neutralization: A Theory of Delinquency." *American Sociological Review 22*: 664–670.

Szasz, A. (1984). "Industrial Resistance to Occupational Safety and Health Legislation, 1971–1981." *Social Problems 32*: 103–116.

Szockyj, E. (1993). "Insider Trading: The SEC Meets Carl Karcher." *Annals of the American Academy of Political and Social Science 525*: 46–58.

Szockyj, E., and Fox, J. G. (1996). *Corporate Victimization of Women*. Boston: Northeastern University Press.

Tabuchi, H. (2017). "E.P.A. Accuses Fiat Chrysler of Secretly Violating Emissions Standards." *New York Times*. Retrieved June 23, 2017 (www.nytimes.com/2017/01/12/business/epa-emissions-cheating-diesel-fiat-chrysler-jeep-dodge.html).

Tabuchi, H., Ewing, J., and Apuzzo, M. (2017). "6 Volkswagen Executives Charged as Company Pleads Guilty in Emissions Case." *New York Times*. Retrieved January 13, 2017 (www.nytimes.com/2017/01/11/business/volkswagen-diesel-vw-settlement-charges-criminal.html?_r=0).

Takasaki, Y. (2013). *Do Natural Disasters Beget Fraud Victimization?: Unrealized Coping through Labor Migration among the Poor* (No. 2013-002). Faculty of Humanities and Social Sciences, University of Tsukuba.

Tallmer, M. (1987). "Chemical Dumping as a Corporate Way of Life." Pp. 111–120 in *Corporate Violence*, edited by S. L. Hills. Totowa, NJ: Rowman & Littlefield.

Tang, Z., Miller, A. S., Zhou, Z., and Warkentin, M. (2021). "Does Government Social Media Promote Users' Information Security Behavior Towards COVID-19 Scams? Cultivation Effects and Protective Motivations." *Government Information Quarterly 38(2)*: 101572. https://doi.org/10.1016/j.giq.2021.101572

Taodang, D., and Gundur, R. V. (2022). "How Frauds in Times of Crisis Target People." *Victims & Offenders*. DOI: https://www.tandfonline.com/doi/full/10.1080/15564886.2022.2043968

Tappan, P. W. (1947). "Who Is the Criminal." *American Sociological Review 12*: 96–102.

Thompson, R., and Galofaro, C. (2013). "Defendants in BP Oil Spill Say Justice Department Scapegoating Them." *The Advocate*, December 5. Retrieved September 11, 2014 (http://theadvocate.com/news/7715100-123/defendants-in-bp-oil-spill).

Thurber, K. A., Colonna, E., Jones, R., Gee, G. C., Priest, N., Cohen, R., ... and Mayi Kuwayu Study Team. (2021). "Prevalence of everyday discrimination and relation with wellbeing among Aboriginal and Torres Strait Islander adults in Australia". *International Journal of Environmental Research and Public Health, 18(12)*: 6577.

Tillman, R. (1987). "The Size of the 'Criminal Population': The Prevalence and Incidence of Adult Arrest." *Criminology 25*: 561–579.

Tillman, R., and Indergaard, M. H. (2005). *Pump and Dump: The Rancid Rules of the New Economy*. New Brunswick, NJ: Rutgers University Press.

Tillman, R., Pontell, H. N., and Black, W. K. (2018). *Financial Crime and Crises in the Era of False Profits*. New York: Oxford University Press.

Tittle, C. R. (1991). "Review of *A General Theory of Crime*." *American Journal of Sociology 96*: 1609–1613.

Tracy, P., Wolfgang, M., and Figlio, R. (1990). *Delinquency Careers in Two Birth Cohorts*. New York: Plenum.

Trefis Team. (2014). *BP's Oil Settlement Could Cost Over $15 Billion as the Court Upholds the Original Agreement*. Retrieved July 2, 2014 (www.trefis.com/stock/bp/articles/222367/bps-oil-spill-settlement-could-cost-over-15-billion-as-the-court-upholds-the-original-agreement/2014-01-14).

Trop, J. (2013). "Companies Admit They Fixed Prices of Car Parts." *New York Times*. Retrieved June 3, 2014 (www.nytimes.com/2013/09/27/business/9-auto-parts-makers-plead-guilty-to-fixing-prices.html?pagewanted=all&_r=0).

Trost, C. (1981). *Good Neighbor Policy*. Retrieved April 2, 2008 (https://aliciapatterson.org/cathy-trost/good-neighbor-policy/).

Turner, R. H., and Killian, L. M. (1987). *Collective Behavior*. Englewood Cliffs, NJ: Prentice Hall.

United States Attorney's Office, District of Massachusetts. (2021, July 28). *Miami Woman Indicted for Wire Fraud and Identity Theft Related to COVID-19 Pandemic*. https://www.justice.gov/usao-ma/pr/miami-woman-indicted-wire-fraud-and-identity-theft-related-covid-19-pandemic

United States Sentencing Memorandum, Case 5:14-cr-00244. Document 571, filed 03/28/16. *In the United States District Court for the Southern District of West Virginia. United States of America V. Donald L. Blankenship*. Criminal NO. 5:14–00244.

Unnever, J. D., Barnes, J. C., and Cullen, F. T. (2016). "The Racial Invariance Thesis Revisted: Testing an African American Theory of Offending." *Journal of Contemporary Criminal Justice 32 (1)*: 7–26.

Unnever, J. D., Benson, M. L., and Cullen, F. T. (2008). "Public Support for Getting Tough on Corporate Crime: Racial and Political Divides." *Journal of Research in Crime and Delinquency 45 (2)*: 163–190.

USA Today. (2014). "Halliburton Settles Deepwater Horizon Claims for $1.1B." Retrieved September 15, 2014 (www.usatoday.com/story/money/business/2014/09/02/halliburton-settles-gulf-explosion-claims/14958979/).

U.S. Bureau of Labor Statistics. (2017). "BLS Reports: Report 1065: Women in the Labor Force: A Databook." Retrieved October 6, 2017 (https://www.bls.gov/opub/reports/womens-databook/2016/home.htm).

U.S. Bureau of Labor Statistics. (2019). "BLS Reports: Report 1084: Women in the Labor Force: A Databook." Retrieved November 19, 2021 (https://www.bls.gov/opub/reports/womens-databook/2019/home.htm).

U.S. Census. (2018, December). "2016 Statistics of U.S. Businesses (SUBS) Annual Data Tables by Establishment Industry." Retrieved from: https://www.census.gov/data/tables/2016/econ/susb/2016-susb-annual.html

U.S. Department of Health and Human Services and Department of Justice. (2021). "Health Care Fraud and Abuse Program Control Program FY 2020." Retrieved March 17, 2022. https://oig.hhs.gov/publications/docs/hcfac/FY2020-hcfac.pdf

U.S. Department of Health and Human Services. (2022, February 2). *Fraud Alert: COVID-19 Scams*. https://oig.hhs.gov/fraud/consumer-alerts/fraud-alert-covid-19-scams/

U.S. Department of Justice. (2014). *Deepwater Horizon (BP) Oil Spill Fraud*. Retrieved July 2, 2014 (www.justice.gov/criminal/oilspill/).

U.S. Department of Justice. (2019, February 21). "Nine Real Estate Investors Sentenced for Rigging Bids at Mississippi Public Foreclosure Auctions." Retrieved on March 4, 2022. https://www.justice.gov/usao-sdms/pr/nine-real-estate-investors-sentenced-rigging-bids-mississippi-public-foreclosure

U.S. Department of Justice. (2021, March 26). *Justice Department Takes Action Against COVID-19 Fraud*. https://www.justice.gov/opa/pr/justice-department-takes-action-against-covid-19-fraud

U.S. Environmental Protection Agency. (2001). *Pulping and Bleaching System NESHAP for the Pulp and Paper Industry: A Plain English Description*. Retrieved July 2, 2014 (www.epa.gov/ttn/atw/pulp/guidance.pdf).

U.S. Environmental Protection Agency. (2013). *Enforcement Annual Results Numbers at a Glance for Fiscal Year (FY) 2013a*. Retrieved July 2, 2014 (https://archive.epa.gov/enforcement/annual-results/web/pdf/eoy2013.pdf).

U.S. Environmental Protection Agency. (2014). *Enforcement and Compliance History Online*. Retrieved July 2, 2014 (https://echo.epa.gov/trends/comparative-maps-dashboards/state-air-dashboard).

U.S. Environmental Protection Agency. (2016). *EPA Enforcement and Compliance Annual Results.* Office of Enforcement and Compliance Assurance, December 19. Retrieved from the EPA website; link is no longer active.

U.S. Environmental Protection Agency. (2022). *EPA Enforcement and Compliance Annual Results.* Office of Enforcement and Compliance Assurance. Retrieved from the EPA website.

U.S. Federal Bureau of Investigation. (2010). *Members of Organized Crime Enterprises Charged with Federal Health Care Fraud Offenses.* October 13, 2010. Retrieved September 12, 2014 (www.fbi.gov/albuquerque/press-releases/2010/aq101310-1.htm).

U.S. Federal Bureau of Investigation. (2011). *Financial Crimes Report to the Public.* Retrieved March 7, 2014 (https://www.fbi.gov/file-repository/stats-services-publications-financial-crimes-report-2010-2011-financial-crimes-report-2010-2011.pdf/view).

U.S. Federal Trade Commission. (2013). "Consumer Fraud in the United States, 2011: The Third FTC Survey." *Staff Report of the Bureau of Economics, Federal Trade Commission.* Retrieved July 2, 2014 (www.ftc.gov/sites/default/files/documents/reports/consumer-fraud-united-states-2011-third-ftc-survey/130419fraudsurvey_0.pdf).

U.S. Federal Trade Commission. (2020, March 6). "Tea Marketer Misled Consumers, Didn't Adequately Disclose Payments to Well-Known Social Influencers, FTC Alleges." Retrieved February 25, 2022 https://www.ftc.gov/news-events/press-releases/2020/03/tea-marketer-misled-consumers-didnt-adequately-disclose-payments

U.S. Federal Trade Commission. (2021, November 18). *FTC Analysis Shows COVID Fraud Thriving on Social Media Platforms.* United States Government. https://www.ftc.gov/business-guidance/blog/2021/11/ftc-analysis-shows-covid-fraud-thriving-social-media-platforms

U.S. Federal Trade Commission. (2022, January 19). "With Omicron Variant on the Rise, FTC Orders More Marketers to Stop Falsely Claiming Their Products Can Effectively Prevent or Treat COVID=19." Retrieved February 28, 2022. https://www.ftc.gov/news-events/press-releases/2022/01/omicron-variant-rise-ftc-orders-more-marketers-stop-falsely

U.S. Federal Trade Commission. (2022, February 22). *New Data Shows FTC Received 2.8 Million Fraud Reports from Consumers in 2021.* United States Government. https://www.ftc.gov/news-events/news/press-releases/2022/02/new-data-shows-ftc-received-28-million-fraud-reports-consumers-2021-0

U.S. Federal Trade Commission Sentinel Network. (2022, November 3). *Number of Fraud, Identity Theft, and other Reports.* United States Government. https://public.tableau.com/app/profile/federal.trade.commission/viz/TheBigViewAllSentinelReports/TrendsOverTime

U.S. General Accounting Office. (2002). "Financial Statement Restatements: Trends, Market Impacts, Regulatory Responses, and Remaining Challenges." *Report to the Chairman, Committee on Banking, Housing, and Urban Affairs, U.S. Senate.* GAO-03–138. Retrieved October 11, 2017 (https://www.gao.gov/assets/240/236067.pdf).

U.S. National Center for Disaster Fraud. (2021). "About the Center." Retrieved November 29, 2021, (https://www.justice.gov/disaster-fraud).

U.S. Sentencing Commission. (1993–2004). *U.S. Federal Sentencing Guidelines.* Washington, DC: U.S. Sentencing Commission.

U.S. Sentencing Commission. (2016). *Interactive Sourcebook* (https://www.ussc.gov/research/sourcebook/archive/sourcebook-2016) Datafile, USSCFY2016.

U.S. Sentencing Commission. (2021). *2020 Sourcebook of Federal Sentencing Statistics.* Retrieved October 27, 2021.

U.S. Sentencing Commission. (2023). *2022 Annual Report and Sourcebook of Federal Sentencing Statistics.* Retrieved May 24, 2023. (https://www.ussc.gov/research/sourcebook-2022).

U.S. Small Business Administration. (2021, December). "Frequently Asked Questions." Retrieved from: https://advocacy.sba.gov/wp-content/uploads/2021/12/Small-Business-FAQ-Revised-December-2021.pdf

Valencia, M. J., and Lazar, K. (2017). "NECC Co-Owner Convicted in Meningitis Outbreak." *Boston Globe*, March 22. Retrieved May 4, 2017 (www.bostonglobe.com/metro/2017/03/22/jury-reaches-verdict-new-england-compounding-center-trial/AMxQoZBV3EIhGMf1q7gSbP/story.html).

Van Baar, A. (2019). "Corporate Involvement in International Crimes in Nazi Germany, Apartheid South Africa, and the Democratic Republic of the Congo." Doctoral Dissertation, Vrije University, The Netherlands.

Vandenbergh, M. P. (2001). "The Social Meaning of Environmental Command and Control." *Virginia Environmental Law Journal 20*: 191–219.

van Onna, J. H. R., van der Geest, V. R., Huisman, W., and Denkers, A. J. M. (2014). "Criminal Trajectories of White-Collar Offenders." *Journal of Research in Crime and Delinquency 51*: 759–784.

Van Rooij, B., and Fine, A. (2021). *The Behavioral Code: The Hidden Ways Law Makes Us Better.... Or Worse.* Boston: Beacon Press.

Van Rooij, B., and Rorie, M. (2022). *Measuring Compliance: Assessing Corporate Crime and Misconduct Prevention.* Cambridge: Cambridge University Press.

van Wingerde, K. (2015). "The Limits of Environmental Regulation in a Globalized Economy: Lessons from the Probo Koala Case." Pp. 260–275 in *The Routledge Handbook of White-Collar and Corporate Crime in Europe*, edited by J. van Erp, W. Huisman, G. Vande Walle, with the assistance of J. Beckers. New York: Routledge.

Vaughan, D. (1983). *Controlling Unlawful Organizational Behavior.* Chicago: University of Chicago Press.

Vaughan, D. (1990). "The Macro/Micro Connection in 'White-Collar Crime' Theory." Pp. 124–145 in *White-Collar Crime Reconsidered*, edited by K. Schlegel and D. Weisburd. Boston: Northeastern University Press.

Vaughan, D. (2005). "The Normalization of Deviance: Signals of Danger, Situated Action, and Risk." Pp. 255–276 in *How Professionals Make Decisions*, edited by H. Montgomery, R. Lipshitz, and B. Brehmer. Mahwah, NJ: Lawrence Erlbaum.

Vaughan, D. (2007). "Beyond Macro- and Micro-Levels of Analysis, Organizations, and the Cultural Fix." Pp. 3–24 in *International Handbook of White-Collar and Corporate Crime*, edited by H. N. Pontell and G. Geis. New York: Springer.

Vickers, M., and Burke, D. (2006). "The Bonnie and Clyde of Mortgage Fraud." *Fortune.* Retrieved April 18, 2008 (www.scopus.com/scopus/inward/record.url?eid=2-s2.0-35349031732&partnerID=40&rel=R7.0.0).

Vlasic, B., and Ivory, D. (2014). "Barra Faces Scrutiny in House over G. M. Recalls." *New York Times.* Retrieved July 2, 2014 (www.nytimes.com/2014/06/19/business/house-hearing-on-general-motors-recalls.html?_r=0).

von Fritz, K., and Kapp, E. (1950). *Aristotle's Constitution of Athens and Related Texts.* New York: Hafner.

Walters, G. (1995). "The Psychological Inventory of Criminal Thinking Styles. *Criminal Justice and Behavior 22*(3): 307–325.

Walters, G. (2002). "The Psychological Inventory of Criminal Thinking Styles (PICTS): A Review and Meta-analysis." *Assessment 9*: 283–296.

Walters, G. (2014). "An Item Response Theory Analysis of the Psychological Inventory of Criminal Thinking Styles: Comparing Male and Female Probationers and Prisoners." *Psychological Assessment, 26 (3)*: 1050–1055.

Walters, G., and Geyer, M. D. (2004). "Criminal Thinking and Identity in Male White-collar Offenders." *Criminal Justice and Behavior 31*(3): 263–281.

Warner, J. (2014). "Fact Sheet: The Women's Leadership Gap." *Center for American Progress.* Retrieved June 5, 2017 (www.americanprogress.org/issues/women/reports/2014/03/07/85457/fact-sheet-the-womens-leadership-gap/).

Weisburd, D., and Waring, E. J. (2001). *White-Collar Crime and Criminal Careers.* New York: Cambridge University Press.

Weisburd, D., Wheeler, S., Waring, E., and Bode, N. (1991). *Crimes of the Middle Classes: White-Collar Offenders in the Federal Courts.* New Haven, CT: Yale University Press.

Wells, C. (1993). *Corporations and Criminal Responsibility*. Oxford: Clarendon Press.

Wheeler, S. (1992). "The Problem of White-Collar Crime Motivation." Pp. 108–123 in *White-Collar Crime Reconsidered*, edited by Kip Schlegel and David Weisburd. Boston: Northeastern University Press.

Wheeler, S., Mann, K., and Sarat, A. (1988b). *Sitting in Judgment: The Sentencing of White-Collar Criminals*. New Haven, CT: Yale University Press.

Wheeler, S., and Rothman, M. L. (1980). "The Organization as Weapon in White-Collar Crime." *Michigan Law Review 80*: 1403–1426.

Wheeler, S., Weisburd, D., and Bode, N. (1982). "Sentencing the White-Collar Offender: Rhetoric and Reality." *American Sociological Review 47*: 641–659.

Wheeler, S., Weisburd, D., Waring, E., and Bode, N. (1988a). "White Collar Crimes and Criminals." *American Criminal Law Review 25*: 331–357.

White, J., Bandura, A., and Bero, L. A. (2009). "Moral Disengagement in the Corporate World." *Accountability in Research: Policies & Quality Assurance 16*: 41–74.

Wikström, P. O., Oberwittler, D., Treiber, K., and Hardie, B. (2017). "Situational Action Theory." Pp. 125–170 in *Developmental and Life Course Criminological Theories*, edited by T. R. McGee and P. Mazzerole. New York: Routledge.

Wilbanks, C. (2013). "Enron's Jeff Skilling May Get Early Release." *Money-Watch*, May 9, 2013. Retrieved September 12, 2014 (www.cbsnews.com/news/enrons-jeff-skilling-may-get-early-prison-release/).

Wilcox, P., and Cullen, F. T. (2018). "Situational Opportunity Theories of Crime." *Annual Review of Criminology, 1*:123–148.

Willott, S., Griffen, C., and Torrance, M. (2001). "Snakes and Ladders: Upper-Middle Class Male Offenders Talk about Economic Crime." *Criminology 39*(2): 441–466.

Wilson, G. (2012). "Starting the Same … Finishing the Same? Race, Occupational Origins, and Mobility into Managerial Positions." *American Behavioral Scientist 56*(5): 682–695.

Wolff, J. (2022, October 17). "The Competing Priorities Facing U.S. Crypto Regulations." *Tech Stream*, Washington, DC: Brookings Institution. Retrieved January 14, 2023. https://www.brookings.edu/techstream/the-competing-priorities-facing-u-s-crypto-regulations-bitcoin-ethereum/

Women Business Collaborative. (2021). *Women CEOs in America: Changing the Face of Business Leadership*. https://www.wbcollaborative.org/wp-content/uploads/2022/09/Women-CEOS-in-America_2022-0920221847.pdf

Woodyard, C. (2015). "GM Ignition Switch Deaths Hit 124." *USA Today*, July 13, 2015. Retrieved May 3, 2017 (www.usatoday.com/story/money/cars/2015/07/13/gm-ignition-switch-death-toll/30092693/).

World Bank. (2022). *Small and Medium enterprises (SMEs) Finance*. https://www.worldbank.org/en/topic/smefinance

World Health Organization. (2022, December 8). *WHO Coronavirus (COVID-19) Dashboard*. https://covid19.who.int/

Wright, E. O. (1997). *Class Counts: Comparative Studies in Class Analysis*. New York: Cambridge University Press.

Yang, F., Jin, S., Xu, Y., and Lu, Y. (2011). "Comparisons of IL-8, ROS and p53 Responses in Human Lung Epithelial Cells Exposed to Two Extracts of PM2.5 Collected from an e-Waste Recycling Area, China." *Environmental Research Letters 6*: 1–6.

Yeager, P. C. (2016a). "The Elusive Deterrence of Corporate Crime." *Criminology & Public Policy 15*: 439–451.

Yeager, P. C. (2016b). "The Practical Challenges of Responding to Corporate Crime." Pp. 643–661 in *The Oxford Handbook of White-Collar Crime*, edited by S. Van Slyke, M. L. Benson, and F. T. Cullen. New York: Oxford University Press.

Yeager, P. C., and Reed, G. E. (1998). "Of Corporate Persons and Straw Men: A Reply to Herbert, Green, and Larragoite." *Criminology 36*: 885–897.

Zick, A., Pettigrew, T. F., and Wagner, U. (2008). "Ethnic prejudice and discrimination in Europe." *Journal of Social Issues, 64(2):* 233–251.

Zietz, D. (1981). *Women Who Embezzle or Defraud: A Study of Convicted Felons.* New York: Praeger.

Zimring, F. E., and Hawkins, G. (1973). *Deterrence: The Legal Threat in Crime Control.* Chicago: University of Chicago Press.

Index

References to tables are in **bold**
References to illustrations are in *italics*.

abuse of trust 9, 78–79; and agency
    relationships 78–79
accountancy: differential association theory 41
accounting fraud 45–46, 155
Affordable Care Act (2010) 95, 196
African-Americans: CEOs 156; and street crime
    166
agency relationships: and abuse of trust 78–79;
    ambivalence 79
air pollution 168
American Dream 42, 43, 50–51; and home
    ownership 101
American Therapeutic Corporation (ATC):
    health care fraud 93
ancient world: white-collar crime 4–5
anomie: definition 42; *see also* market anomie
anomie/strain theory 42–44
anti-fraud measures: health care fraud 95, 194;
    RMA 195–196
antitrust fraud 105–108; conspiracies 196;
    opportunities 108–109
antitrust violators: age 22, **22, 26**; college
    graduates **22, 26**; convictions (2009-
    2015) **26**; homeowners **22**; median assets
    22; median liabilities **22**; prior arrests **27**
Aristotle 4, 5
ARMs (adjustable rate mortgages) 96; subprime
    97, 99, 114n1
arrogance: white-collar criminals 64
Association of Certified Fraud Examiners 160

Bandura, Albert 144
bank embezzlement 21, **24**
bank embezzlers: average age **22**; college
    graduates **22**; female 22, 159;
    homeowners **22**; median assets **22**;
    median liabilities **22**; prior arrests **27**
Bankman-Fried, Sam 178
Benson, Michael L. & Kerley, Kent R. 54

bid rigging 106, 107, 202
Blankenship, Don 177
Braithwaite, John 11, 49–50; *Corporate Crime
    in the Pharmaceutical Industry* 130;
    Crime, Shame, and Reintegration 191
Braithwaite, John & Fisse, Brent 35
bribery offenders **24**; college graduates **22,
    26**; convictions (2009-2015) **26**;
    homeowners **22**; median assets **22**;
    median liabilities **22**; and opportunity
    51; prior arrests **27, 28**
Brickey, Kathleen 160, 164
Bureau of Consumer Protection 190
business culture: and law-breaking 62; *see also*
    cognitive landscape concept

careers: white-collar criminals 28–29
Catalyst organization 8
CEOs: African-Americans 156
CFTF (Corporate Fraud Task Force: Dept of
    Justice) 160–161
Challenger tragedy 153; causes 147; information
    context 147–148; organizational
    culture 148; political environment 148;
    structural secrecy 148–149; warnings
    ignored 147
Chapter 8 offenses: corporate offenders 32
civil law enforcement 180–182
clean diesel scandal: Volkswagen 30
Clinard, Marshall B. & Yeager, Peter C.:
    Corporate Crime 178
CMOs (collateralized mortgage obligations):
    definition 97; failure 101; and housing
    market collapse 97; and risk ratings 100
CMS (Center for Medicare and Medicaid
    Services) 194
cognitive landscape concept 62; and market
    anomie 63
Coleman, JamesW. 50, 51, 52

college graduates: antitrust violators 22, 26; bank embezzlers 22; bribery offenders 22; credit fraudsters 22; false claimants 22; mail fraudsters 22; securities fraudsters 22; tax violators 22, 26; white-collar criminals 20, 22, 24, 26

common criminals: bank robbery, prior arrests 28; forgery, prior arrests 28; narcotics, prior arrests 28; prior arrests 27, 28; white-collar criminals, comparison 20, 20, 21, 24–25, 28, 54, 56, 74–75

common law: adaptability 189

Commoner, Barry: *The Closing Circle: Nature, Men, and Technology* 116

competition: culture of 50–51

concealment and conspiracy: deception 201; examples 80; role coordination 81–82; stock manipulation 81; white-collar crime 82, 84

concerted ignorance: corporate crime 177; Ford Pinto 151–152; white-collar criminals 140–141

condemning the condemners 142, 153

conservation criminology 120; perspective, Deepwater Horizon disaster 122

conspiracies: antitrust fraud 196; *see also* concealment and conspiracy

control theory 50

conviction records: limitations 18

corporate crime 14; African-Americans/whites views on 63; competing narratives 152; complexity 157–158; concerted ignorance 177; convictions 14; corporate liability 178; and developmental and life-course theories 56–57; and environmental contingencies 43–44; gender gap 160–161; and goal displacement 44; and performance measures 43; responsibility issues 177; and shaming 50; sources 43–44; structural ambiguity 152–153; *see also* white-collar crime

corporate deterrence: and civil law enforcement 181–182

Corporate Fraud Task Force 160–161, 178

corporate liability: corporate crime 178

corporate offenders 30–31; Chapter 8 offenses 32; environmental offenses 32; fraud 32; money laundering 32; moral flexibility 65; number of employees 31; self-reporting 32, 36n3, 178–179

corporate violence: definition 115

corporations: as offenders 35

costs and benefits: rational choice theory 47

counterfeit goods: Dollar Castle 34

COVID-19 pandemic: deaths 109; fraud opportunities 48, 78, 110, 190

credit fraud 16

credit fraudsters: average age 22; college graduates 22; homeowners 22; median assets 22; median liabilities 22; prior arrests 27

Cressey, Donald 35

crime: and company loyalty 142–143; and networks 161; and neutralizations 143; and poverty 39; as social construct 58, 200; and socioeconomic status 166; as viable option 62; *see also* environmental crime; manufacturing crimes; street crime; war crimes; workplace crime

criminal justice system: purpose 175–176; and street crime 173; and white-collar crime 179; *see also* regulatory justice system

criminal law: defendant' rights 176; and deterrence 179

criminal opportunities: antitrust fraud 108–109; bank vs liquor store 71; and blocking access 73; and bribery 51; COVID-19 pandemic, fraud 48, 78, 110, 190; and deregulation 58, 63; dimensions 193; elements 72; and Ford Pinto development 151; fraud victimization 111; and fungibility 72; gender gap 163; and guardianship 73; health care fraud 91, 92, 92, 94, 137; and industry structure 51; insider trading 105; and occupation types 51; preventive modification 194; restrictive trade agreements 108; and risk 73; securities fraud 23, 105; stock manipulation 105; structures 87; and surveillance 73; techniques 74; toxic waste dumping 119; white-collar crime 49, 51, 70, 135, 152, 188, 193, 205, 206; workplace crime 125, 127, 128

criminal thinking: PICTS scale 67; proactive thinking 68; reactive thinking 67–68

criminality: definition 37

"criminaloid" 5, 6; description 60

criminogenic exposure 62–63

criminological theory: Sutherland 39, 60–61; and white-collar crime 37

crisis situations: fraud in 109–112

criterion offenses 16

critical and postmodern perspectives 57–58

cryptocurrency: regulation 189

data analytics: fraud detection 196; use by SEC 190, 199

DBCP pesticide 127–128

deception 205, 207; concealment and conspiracy 201; definition 77, 85, 113, 201; and embellishment 83–84, 201; examples 77–78; and mimicry 84, 201; purpose 202; relational nature of 77; varieties of 78, 82–84; *see also* abuse of trust; concealment and conspiracy

Deepwater Horizon disaster: causes 121–122; class action claims 121; conservation criminology perspective 122; criminal charges 121; equipment shortcomings 122; explosion 120; and MMS Guidelines 121–122; oil spill 120–121
deregulation: and opportunity 58, 63
detection problems: white-collar crime 18
deterrence: and the criminal law 179
Detroit: pill mill operation 92, 95
developmental and life-course theories 53–57; and corporate crime 56–57
deviance: neutralized 146–147; normalized 146, 149–153, 153–154
differential association theory: accountancy 41; shoe business 40; Sutherland 40–42, 62; and white-collar crime 39, 40–42
disaster relief programs: and lure concept 48
Dollar Castle: counterfeit goods 34

Earth Day (1970) 116
Ebbers, Bernard 19
Edelhertz, Herbert: types of white-collar crime 9, 10
electronic waste dumping 119
elites: influence of 58
Elk River spillage 12
embellishment: and deception 83–84
embezzlers: college graduates 26; convictions (2009-2015) 26; Middle Ages 5; prior arrests 28; see also bank embezzlers; postal embezzlement
employment status: white-collar criminals 21
Encyclopedia of Criminology 6
engrossing crime 5
Enron scandal 64, 65; accounting fraud 81, 206; gender gap 160
environmental contingencies: and corporate crime 43–44
environmental crime 116–124; consequences 124; corporate offenders 32; criminal prosecutions 117–118; enforcement actions 116, 117, 123; examples 116; exposure means 123; whistle-blowing 123
environmental injustice 124
EPA (Environmental Protection Agency) 12, 30; budget decrease 123
EPI (Executive Parity Index) 156
ethical standards: and social controls 191
ethics: and profit 143
ethics training: and white-collar crime 191
extralegal remedies: white-collar crime 189–192

false claimants 22, 24; average age 22; college graduates 22; homeowners 22; median

assets 22; median liabilities 22; prior arrests 27, 28
"Fanny Mae" mortgage association 96
Fastow, Andrew 19
FCIP (Federal Crop Insurance Program) 195
Felson, Marcus 112
financial crime 11–12, 16, 19; high-profile offenders 19
Firestone Tire Company: defective tires 204
Ford Pinto 150–153, 153
Forst, Brian & Rhodes, William: study on white-collar criminals 23–25, 24, 54
FPS (Fraud Prevention Service) 196
fraud: by contractors 109; college graduates 26; convictions (2009-2015) 26; corporate offenders 32; COVID-19 pandemic 48, 78, 110, 190; credit 16, 22; in crisis situations 109–112; and Dante's Inferno 5, 205; detection methods 196; disaster-related 109; health care industry 4; home mortgage industry 3–4; Libor 107–108, 141, 193; mail and wire 16, 22; preventive measures 112–113, 196; scale of 109; and social media 78, 111–112; see also accounting fraud; antitrust fraud; credit fraud; health care fraud; Libor fraud; mail fraud; mortgage fraud; securities fraud; tax violators
fraud conspiracies: women 161
fraud victimization 109; opportunities 111, 190
"Freddie Mac" mortgage association 96
fungibility: and opportunity 72; property 72

Garrett, Brandon 180
Geis, Gilbert 80
gender: and the glass ceiling 155–156; and white collar-victimization 164–165; and white-collar crime 67–69, 143
gender gap: corporate crime 160–161; criminal networks 161; Enron scandal 160; male/female stereotypes 163; opportunities 163; white-collar crime 159–165
gendered focal concerns: theory 163
General Motors Corporation: defective autos 129, 203–204
glass ceiling: and gender 155–156
Glass Ceiling Commission (1995) 156
globalization 205–206
goal displacement: and corporate crime 44
Grant, Albert 164
Gross, Edward 43, 65
guardian-offender overlap 73–74
guardianship: and opportunity 73; white-collar crime 190

Hayes, Tom 141, 142
hazardous waste: illegal disposal of 12
health care fraud 4, 89–95, 155, 176; American
    Therapeutic Corporation 93; anti-fraud
    measures 95, 194; claim checking issues
    94; harm to patients 94; Medicare and
    Medicaid programs 91, 92, 93, 95, 142,
    171, 201, 202; opportunities 91, 92, 92,
    94, 137; prevention measures 202; "rent-
    a-patient," health care fraud 92, 93
health care industry: size 89, 94; structure 90,
    90; see also Medicare and Medicaid
    programs
Hirschi, Travis & Gottfredson, Michael 44, 52
Holmes, Elizabeth 157
Holtfrteter, Kristy 160
home ownership: and the American Dream 101
homeowners: antitrust violators 22; bank
    embezzlers 22; bribery offenders 22;
    false claimants 22; mail fraudsters 22;
    securities fraudsters 22; tax violators 22;
    white-collar criminals 24
Hooker Chemical Corporation: Love Canal
    tragedy 12–13
house buyers: fraud 98
house buying: process 97–98; see also mortgage
    fraud
Howe, Michelle 164

ICC (International Criminal Court) 131
immigration: and lure concept 48
industry structure: and opportunity 51
information context 154; and new products 150
insider trading 7, 75, 76, 103–104; detection by
    SEC 196; opportunities 105; securities
    fraud 103
integrated theory 49–51
intentionality: and neutralizations 146
IPOs (initial public offerings) 103

Johns-Manville Corporation: asbestosis
    126–127
Jordanoska, Aleksandra 62–63

Kardashian, Kim 78
Kozlowski, Dennis 19

law-breaking: and business culture 62
law-making: as political process 57
Lay, Ken 19
Libor (London Interbank Offered Rate) fraud
    107–108, 141, 193
life-course theories see developmental and life-
    course theories
longitudinal data: white-collar criminals 54–55

Love Canal tragedy: Hooker Chemical
    Corporation 12–13
lure concept: and disaster relief programs 48;
    and federal health care programs 48; and
    illegal immigration 48; and oversight
    48–49; rational choice theory 48

Madoff, Bernard 19; Ponzi scheme 64, 76,
    104–105, 105
mail fraud 16, 24; see also postal embezzlement
mail fraudsters: average age 22; college
    graduates 22; homeowners 22; median
    assets 22; median liabilities 22; prior
    arrests 27, 28
manufacturing crimes 128–131; definition 129;
    examples 129; motor industry 129;
    pharmaceutical industry 129–131
market allocation 106
market anomie: and cognitive landscape
    concept 63
Master Settlement Agreement: tobacco industry 145
McWane Inc.: workplace safety violations
    125–126
medical insurance 90, 90–91, 91
Medicare and Medicaid programs 48, 83;
    annual number of claims 91; health care
    fraud 91, 92, 93, 95, 142, 171, 201,
    202; numbers enrolled 94; simplification
    of claims-processing 197
Merton, Robert: anomie/strain theory 42
mimicry: and deception 84, 201
mining industry: safety violations 127, 177
MMS (Minerals Management Service)
    Guidelines: and Deepwater Horizon rig
    disaster 121–122
money laundering: corporate offenders 32
moral disengagement: collective 144; definition
    144; justification 145; theory of 144;
    tobacco industry 145; ways of 144; see
    also neutralizations
moral flexibility: corporate offenders 65
mortgage brokers: fraud 98, 99
mortgage fraud 3–4, 95–101, 195; examples
    96–97, 98–99; home buyers 98; subprime
    loans 96, 99
mortgage industry: risk ratings 100; secondary
    mortgage market 96; structure 95–97, 99
mortgage market: secondary 96–97
motor industry: manufacturing crimes 129
MSHA (Mine Safety and Health
    Administration) 124, 127

N/DPAs (non-prosecution and deferred
    prosecution agreements) 179–180
National White Collar Crime Center 191

Netherlands: white-collar criminals 158–159, 171n2
networks *see* criminal networks
neutralizations: and crime 143; and intentionality 146; white-collar criminals 140, 153; *see also* moral disengagement
NOx emissions 30
Nuclear Regulatory Commission 124
nuclear waste contamination: Rocky Flats (Colorado) 13

occupation types: and opportunity 51
Occupational Safety and Health Act (1970) 124–125
opportunities *see* criminal opportunities
organizational crime *see* corporate crime
OSHA (Occupational Safety and Health Administration) 124–125, 184
oversight: and lure concept 48–49

paper making: and risk 120
Paternoster, Raymond & Simpson, Sally 47–48
peoples of color: and white-collar crime 8
performance measures: and corporate crime 43
personality characteristics: white-collar criminals 69
pharmaceutical industry: manufacturing crimes 129–131
PICTS (Psychological Inventory of Criminal Thinking Styles) 67; gender differences 67–69
Piquero, Alex & Weisburd, David 54
pollution: cost 124
Ponzi schemes: Madoff 64, 76, 104–105
postal embezzlement **24**, 36n1; *see also* mail fraud
poverty: and crime 39
price fixing 80–81, 83, 114, 202; examples 106; justification 142
profit: and ethics 143
property: fungibility 72; portability 72; value 72
property crimes: females 159; nonphysical 15
PSI (presentence investigation report): content 16–17
psychology: white-collar criminals 60–62, 138, 197–198
psychopaths: corporate 66; successful 66
psychopathy: measurement 66; and white-collar crime 65–67
Pure Food and Drug Act (1906) 129
pyramid schemes *see* Ponzi schemes

race: and socioeconomic status *166*; and white-collar crime **22**, 53, 165, 167, 168–169
race-based theories 52–53
racial exceptionalism perspective 52, 53
racial invariance 52

racism: environmental 168
rational choice theory 47–49; costs and benefits 47; *see also* lure concept
regulatory justice system 182–186; agencies 182, 185; conflict model 183, 184; criticism of 183–184, 185, 204; economic model 183, 184; efficacy 186; enforcement powers 185; justice model 182–183; politicization 185–186; purpose 182; rational-legal model 183; as reactive system 184; success factors 184; viability 183; *see also* responsive regulation
Reiss, Albert J. & Biderman, Albert D. 8
"rent-a-patient": health care fraud 92, *93*
responsibility denial: white-collar criminals 140, 153
responsive regulation 186–187
restrictive trade agreements 106–107; examples 108; opportunities 108; *see also* bid rigging; price fixing
risk: and opportunity 73; and paper making 120
risk ratings: and CMOs 100; measurement 100; mortgage industry 100
RMA (Risk Management Agency): anti-fraud measures 195–196
Rocky Flats (Colorado): nuclear waste contamination 13
Ross, E.A. 5, 6, 60, 69
Routine Activity Theory 110, 189

safety violations: mining industry 127, 177; workplace crime 125–127
Sarbanes-Oxley (SOX) Act (2002) 182, 188
SCPT (situational crime prevention theory) 192–198
SEC (Securities and Exchange Commission) 65, 74, 105, 177; insider trading, detection 196; use of data analytics 190, 199
securities: definition 101
securities fraud **22**, **22**, 102–105; insider trading 103; investment schemes 104; misappropriation 102; opportunities 23, 105; stock manipulation 102–103; types 102–103; *see also* insider trading
securities fraudsters: average age **22**; college graduates **22**; homeowners **22**; median assets **22**; median liabilities **22**; prior arrests **27**
securitization: and subprime loans 99
self-control theory 44–47; limitations 45–46; and white-collar crime 45, 137
self-reporting: corporate offenders 32, 36n3, 178, 178–179
shaming: and corporate crime 50; reintegrative 50; stigmatizing 50; and white-collar crime 192, 203
Shapiro, Susan 9

shoe business: differential association theory 40
Shover, Neal & Hochstetler, Andrew 48, 49, 73, 206
Simpson, O.J. 181
Sinclair, Upton: *The Jungle* 129
situational crime prevention theory *see* SCPT
small businesses: as offenders 33–34; United States 33
social class: typology 157; and Yale studies 158
social controls: and ethical standards 191; forms of 191
social and demographic status: white-collar criminals 19–23, **22**, 137
social media: and fraud 78, 111–112
social status: and white-collar crime 7, 7–8, 11
socioeconomic status: and crime *166*; and race *166*
SPEs (special purpose entities) 81, 97
Spitzer, Elliot 18
Steffensmeier, Darrell. J. & Allan, Emilie. 163, 164
Stewart, Martha 19, 103, 157, 178
stock manipulation 81; opportunities 105
Stone, Christopher 189
strain theory 49
street crime: and African-Americans *166*; and criminal justice system 173; prevention 194
subprime loans: mortgage fraud 96, 99; and securitization 99
surveillance: and opportunity 73
Sutherland, Edwin H. 1, 3, 11, 14, 15, 69, 142; achievements 84; controversy 6–8; criminological theory 39, 60–61; differential association theory 40–42, 62; *White-Collar Crime* 6, 157; on white-collar crime 156–157

tax violators 16, 24, **24**; average age **22**, **26**; college graduates **22**, **26**; convictions (2009-2015) **26**; homeowners **22**; median assets **22**; median liabilities **22**; prior arrests **27**, **28**
theft: and fungibility 72
TIRC (Tobacco Industry Research Committee) 145–146
tobacco industry: Master Settlement Agreement 145; moral disengagement 145
toxic waste dumping: lack of oversight 120; opportunities 119; transnational 118; W.R. Grace Corporation 118–119, 120, 123
trust *see* abuse of trust

United States: small businesses 33; social and demographic changes 25
upper classes: white-collar crime 14

US National Center for Disaster Fraud 48
USSC (U.S. Sentencing Commission) 14, 159; white-collar crime statistics 25–26, **26**, 32

Vaughan, Diane 148
victim denial: white-collar criminals 141–142, 153
victims: white-collar crime 83, 168–169
Volkswagen: clean diesel scandal 30

war crimes: corporate involvement 131
Wells, Celia 178
Wells Fargo Bank: fraud 45, 192
Wheeler, Stanton & Rothman, Mitchell L. 158
whistle-blowing: environmental crime 123; retaliation against 196
Whistleblower Protection Act (1989) 19, 196
white-collar crime 1; abuse of trust 9; agencies monitoring 13; ambiguity 200; and American values 198; ancient world 4–5; business 9; causes 205; characteristics 202–203; complexity 3; con games 9; concealment and conspiracy 82, 84; control problems 203; corporate dimension 35, 36; and criminal justice system 179; and criminological theory 37; definitions 3, 6, 8–11, 13, 14, 129, 157; detection problems 18; differential association theory 39, 40–42; and ethics training 191; examples 45; extralegal remedies 189–192; facilitators 158; future 204–207; and gender 67–69, 143; gender gap 159–165; guardianship 190; measurement 13–14; motivation for 47, 50; offender-based 8, 9, 12, 13, 14; offense-based 8–11, 12; official responses 173; opportunities 49, 51, 70, 135, 152, 188, 193, 205, 206; as organized crime 82; and peoples of color 8; personal crimes 9; properties 75–76, 118; psychopathy 65–67; public view of 191; and race **22**, 53, 165, 167, 168–169; scope 6–7; and self-control theory 45, 137; and shame 192, 203; and social status 7–8, 11; statistics 25–26, **26**, 32; superficial appearance of legitimacy 75–76; Sutherland on 156–157; theories 39–57; types of 9, 10, 11, 16; underestimation of 46; and upper classes 14; victims 83, 168–169; and women 8, 160, 162, 163; *see also* corporate crime; financial crime; fraud
white-collar criminals 1; ages 20, **20**, **22**; antitrust violators *see* antitrust violators; arrogance 64; assets **22**, 23; careers 28–29; college graduates 20, **22**, **24**, **26**;

common criminals, comparison 20, 20, 21, 24–25, 28, 54, 56, 74–75; concerted ignorance 140–141; constraints on 56; demographics 24, 26, 56; education 20–21, 20, 21, 22; employment status 20, 21; financial standing 22; Forst & Rhodes study 23–25, 24; high school graduates 20; homeowners 22, 24; justification for actions 61–62, 138–139; legitimate access to targets 75, 202; liabilities 22; longitudinal data 54–55; male 19, 20, 21, 22, 24; middle class 157, 201; motivations 69–70, 87; Netherlands 158–159, 171n2; neutralizations 140, 153; offending patterns 29; personality characteristics 69; prior arrests 27; psychological factors 64, 138; psychology of 60–62, 138, 197–198; repeat offenders 28; responsibility denial 140, 153; self-identity 138–139; social and demographic data 20; social and demographic status 19–23, 22, 137; spatial separation from victims 75;

statutory offenses 22; stereotypical 159; techniques 76–82, 85; triggers 56; ubiquity 3; unemployed 20, 21; victim denial 141–142, 153; white 19, 20, 22, 22, 24; and workplace culture 62; Yale studies 16–19, 158, 166
white-collar victimization: and gender 164–165
Winterkorn, Martin 30
women: bank embezzlers 22, 159; in corporate leadership positions 8; fraud conspiracies 161; in the labor force 25; and white-collar crime 8, 160, 162, 163
workplace crime 124–127; criminal prosecutions 125; examples 125–126; opportunities 125, 127, 128; safety violations 125–127
workplace culture: and white-collar criminals 62
W.R. Grace Corporation: toxic waste dumping 118–119, 120, 123
Wright, Erik Olin 157

Yale studies: shortcomings 17–19; and social class 158; white-collar criminals 16–19, 158, 166